THE SHORT STORY OF QUEER ART

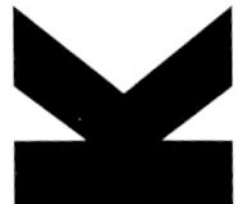

First published in Great Britain in 2025 by Laurence King, an imprint of The Orion Publishing Group Ltd, Carmelite House, 50 Victoria Embankment, London EC4Y 0DZ

An Hachette UK Company

10 9 8 7 6 5 4 3 2 1

A CIP catalogue record for this book is available from the British Library.

ISBN (Flexiback) 978 1 399618748
ISBN (eBook) 978 1 399622301

Origination by f1 colour
Printed in Hong Kong, China

The authorised representative in the EEA is Hachette Ireland, 8 Castlecourt Centre, Dublin 15, D15 XTP3, Ireland (email: info@hbgi.ie)

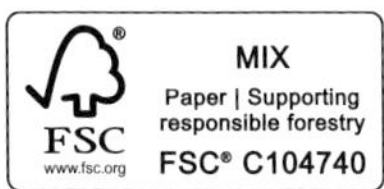

www.laurenceking.com
www.orionbooks.co.uk

THE SHORT STORY OF QUEER ART

A Pocket Guide to Movements, Works, Themes & Breakthroughs

Dawn Hoskin

Laurence King

Contents

6 Introduction
9 How to use this book

MOVEMENTS

12 Renaissance
13 Baroque
14 Rococo
15 Neoclassicism
16 Realism
17 Pre-Raphaelites
18 Impressionism
19 Aestheticism
20 Art Nouveau
21 Dada
22 Harlem Renaissance
23 Surrealism
24 Art Deco
25 Constructivism
26 Abstract Expressionism
27 Pop Art
28 Film and Video Art
29 Performance Art
30 Feminist Art
31 Digital Art
32 Conceptual Art
33 Postmodernism
34 Afrofuturism
35 Postminimalism
36 Street Art
37 Internet Art

THE WORKS

40 *David*, Michelangelo Buonarroti
42 *A Punch Party*, Thomas Patch
46 *Bacchus*, Simeon Solomon
48 *Polychrome Bowl*, We'wha
50 *The Peacock Skirt*, Aubrey Beardsley
52 *Pegasus Drinking from the Fountain of Hippocrene*, Charles de Sousy Ricketts
56 *La vie pensive* (*Pensive Life*), Louise Catherine Breslau
58 *Loge de Théâtre*, Erté
60 *Handsome Drinks*, Marsden Hartley
62 *Da-Dandy*, Hannah Höch
64 *Asbury Park South*, Florine Stettheimer
68 *Les Amazones*, Marie Laurencin
70 *Semi-Nude in Front of Prickly Pear Cactus*, Anita Rée
72 *La Bague Symbolique*, George Barbier
74 *The Critics*, Henry Scott Tuke
76 *I.O.U. (Self-Pride)*, Claude Cahun
78 *Stephen Tennant in Costume as Prince Charming*, Cecil Beaton
80 *A Summer Day*, Gerda Wegener
84 *Autoportrait (Tamara in a Green Bugatti)*, Tamara de Lempicka
86 *The Fleet's In!*, Paul Cadmus
90 *Feral Benga*, James Richmond Barthé
92 *Dancing Figures*, Richard Bruce Nugent
94 *Medallion (YouWe)*, Gluck
96 *Objet (Le Déjeuner en Fourrure)*, Méret Oppenheim
98 *Self Portrait with Cropped Hair*, Frida Kahlo
100 *Untitled*, Tom of Finland (Touko Laaksonen)
102 *Ladies and Gentlemen (Marsha P. Johnson)*, Andy Warhol
104 *Cunt Coloring Book*, Tee A. Corinne
108 *Ranchodbhai Relaxing in the Winter*, Bhupen Khakhar
110 *Hunkertime*, Harmony Hammond
114 *The Wrestlers after Muybridge*, Francis Bacon
116 *Freedom and Change*, Lubaina Himid
120 *Jama Masjid*, Sunil Gupta
122 *Every Moment Counts (Ecstatic Antibodies)*, Rotimi Fani-Kayode
124 *Once Upon a Time*, Keith Haring

126 *Untitled*, from Dream Girls, Deborah Bright
128 *Notes on the Margin of the Black Book*, Glenn Ligon
132 *Gate* 门, Xiyadie
134 *Blue*, Derek Jarman
136 *Memorial to a Marriage*, Patricia Cronin
138 *Passing / Posing, from Coronation of the Virgin*, Kehinde Wiley
140 *Becoming an Image*, Cassils
142 *Night of the Long Knives I*, Athi-Patra Ruga
144 *Vanishing Point*, Anna Campbell
146 *Qusuquzah Lounging with Pink + Black Flower*, Mickalene Thomas
150 *Phila I, Parktown*, Zanele Muholi
152 *Resurgence of the People*, Kent Monkman
156 *The Latecomer*, Salman Toor
158 *Sous le ciel de Shiraz (PaykanArtCar)*, Alireza Shojaian

THEMES

162 A Documented History
163 Glimpses of Utopia
164 Personal Realization
165 Intimacies
166 Textual Power
167 Presenting the Artist
168 Queer Coding
169 Powerful Protest
170 Chosen Family
171 Assembling
172 Space of the Body
173 In the Studio
174 Masks
175 Crafting Threads
176 Summoning Sappho
177 Queer Ecologies
178 Divine Connection
179 Call of the Sea
180 Rising Camp
181 Theatrical Types
182 Queer Eye
183 Erotic Exchanges
184 Queer Icons
185 Straight Expectations
186 To Be Seen
187 On Screen
188 Dance
189 Places to Be
190 Transforming
191 Reworking Art History

BREAKTHROUGHS

194 Desire for Antiquity
195 Ruling Relationships
196 Picturing a Chevalier
197 Public Presence
198 Exposing Desires
199 The Ballets Russes
200 Commercial Allure
201 Weimar Berlin
202 Bloomsbury Shapes
203 *FIRE!!* Magazine
204 Gay Paris
205 Making Rainbows
206 Fashioning Style
207 On the Cover
208 Facing AIDS
209 Collective Response
210 Queer Crip
211 Out in the Gallery
212 Institutional Critique
213 Life Online
214 In Memorial
215 Indigenous Queer Love

216 Index
222 Museums
223 Picture Credits

Introduction

BELL HOOKS: 'QUEER NOT AS BEING ABOUT WHO YOU'RE HAVING SEX WITH (THAT CAN BE A DIMENSION OF IT); BUT QUEER AS BEING ABOUT THE SELF THAT IS AT ODDS WITH EVERYTHING AROUND IT AND HAS TO INVENT AND CREATE AND FIND A PLACE TO SPEAK AND THRIVE AND TO LIVE.'

This book focuses a queer eye upon art history to find queer resonances, disrupt heteronormative interpretations and explore shared points of connection, expression and experience. 'Queer' is a distinctly slippery and subjective term, with a varied history – from self-adopted description to pejorative insult, to a reclaimed word of liberation. It has been used to convey personal identity, political stance and an active process. Two core facets of contemporary use are: queer as 'otherness' – disrupting, challenging or contradicting established expectations; and queer as related to genders and sexualities that diverge from 'normative' conceptions.

Consideration of 'queerness' in art is often entwined with, but not solely reliant upon, biography. This book embraces queer as inclusive of the rainbow of current LGBTQ+ identities and those whose self-conception may not easily map onto modern terms. It recognizes some artists may identify solely with specific identities (e.g. lesbian, not queer) and that globally many cultures view gender and sexuality differently to essentialist, binary views that 'queer' usually exists against.

Film historian Vito Russo (1946–1990) often gleefully quoted the writer Jeff Weinstein (1947–), who declared, 'No, there is no such thing as a gay sensibility and yes, it has an enormous impact on our culture'. The same may be applied to notions of queer art. Influenced by varying social and political contexts, artists have individual varying palettes of references, materials and perspectives to draw upon.

Many artists featured here are known to have identified with terms encompassed by the queer umbrella. However, rather than pin down identities, or suggest that knowledge of an artist's gender or sexual identity determines a singular frame or explanation for an artwork, our aim is to encourage expansive interpretation. To quote Judith Butler (1956–): 'if the term "queer" is to be a site of collective contestation, the point of departure for a set of historical reflections and futural imaginings, it will have to remain that which is, in the present, never fully owned …'

Movements

ERTÉ: 'I BELONG TO NO SCHOOL OF ART … I AM INDIVIDUALISTIC IN ART.'

Art movements are the names given to the styles or approaches developed during certain periods by artists who shared similar philosophies and aesthetics. An endeavour to map distinct moments and shifts in expression and production, the arrangement of art into movements appears mainly in Western art. Some were named as they developed, their artists publishing accompanying manifestos as with Dada and Surrealism. Others, like Afrofuturism, have gained recognition and names retrospectively as historians and cultural theorists connect similarities.

Movements can vary in scale and evolve as they cross geographic and sociopolitical boundaries, absorbing and reflecting nuances of different contexts. Artists' connections with art movements vary too. Anton Prinner (1902–1983) was initially unaware he was creating 'constructivist art' and, although synonymous with Art Deco, Erté (1892–1990) didn't welcome association with a particular style. Some movements were formed from loose associations, others governed by strict rules. Movements were sometimes a point of temporary convergence, with artists grouping in early activity before evolving separately.

Frequently bound up in changing sociopolitical circumstances, emerging movements offered new potential to express experiences and challenge the status quo. This held obvious appeal for artists looking to explore gender and sexuality beyond existing social constructs – be it through sensuous Surrealism, clear Constructionism or amorphous Abstract Expressionism. More recently artists have increasingly selected appealing aspects of previous movements without adhering to their 'rules'. In this chapter, queer-relevant individuals and works have predominantly been foregrounded, but others are included to provide broader context.

Works

CASSILS: 'I WANT MY ART TO MOVE PEOPLE. I LIKE THE IDEA THAT VISUAL ART CAN SPUR SOCIAL CHANGE.'

This section focuses on notable works of art from the sixteenth century to the 2020s which reflect concerns associated with LGBTQ+ experiences, histories and representations. The artists encompass a variety of intersecting identities, and their works present aspects of queer significance with varying intensity. Some are well-known within the established Western art canon, others less so. Recognition and reputations have varied over time, with a number undergoing revivals or being considered anew in relation to the expanding field of 'queer history'.

Covert, overt and at times ambiguous in their queerness, they run across eras and cultures that would not have recognized current terminologies used to express a veritable rainbow of sexual and gender identities and where directly addressing these subjects could (and still can) be an endeavour laden with risk. However, from coded expressions to artists who publicly centre queerness in their work, shared threads can be found, which collectively form a rich tapestry of queer creativity.

Breakthroughs

HAL FOSTER: 'MARGINALITY IS NOT ALWAYS DISEMPOWERMENT. IT CAN BE A PRIVILEGED SPACE OF AESTHETIC TRANSGRESSION, OF POLITICAL TRANSFORMATION.'

LGBTQ+ people have often had to navigate landscapes of social and legal persecution when expressing and representing ourselves, our identities, intimacies, passions and fantasies. Many of the widespread laws criminalizing homosexual acts were repealed only in the second half of the twentieth century and homosexuality no longer deemed a psychiatric pathology in the late twentieth century. Throughout circumstances of oppression and suppression artists have covertly and overtly conveyed issues around non-heteronormativity – developing visual languages, increasing visibility and advocating for social change – with 'queer' increasingly meaning taking a political stand. Breakthroughs have occurred over varying lengths of time. Pushes for legal, medical and social recognition, respect and acceptance continue across the LGBTQ+ spectrum.

This section explores some of those breakthroughs, including: key moments of social and creative convergence that allowed bolder queer expression to flourish; the influence of queer creatives on wider culture; and specific works that broke boundaries in the artworld and beyond.

Themes

KATE MILLETT: 'IF IT SUCCEEDS ... THEN THE OBJECT MADE ITS OWN MEANING, STRONGER AND BETTER THAN WORDS COULD SAY.'

Themes are the underlying topics or presence in artworks, often connected to broad concerns about life or human nature. They may reflect specific interests of the artist or philosophical approaches to expression and creativity. Their presence may be a deliberate intention of the artist or have evolved organically. Embedded themes can bring deeper resonance beyond the surface level subject. They may be implicitly or subtly inherent or directly evoked by the subject depicted. For example, in 'Presenting the Artist' portrait subjects can arouse wider philosophical themes of giving visual form to personal identity. This section of the book considers themes of varying visibility that have featured in works by LGBTQ+ artists, or been identified by LGBTQ+ viewers, and fashioned anew through the ages.

How to use this book

The book is divided into four sections: Movements, The Works, Themes and Breakthroughs. It can be read as a whole, or you can read sections freely in any order. At the bottom of each page, you'll find useful cross-references to other parts of the book. These give an insight to how elements of art histories interconnect, and how aesthetics, intentions, ideas and identities have developed in varying ways. Feature boxes discuss crucial developments and artists' backgrounds.

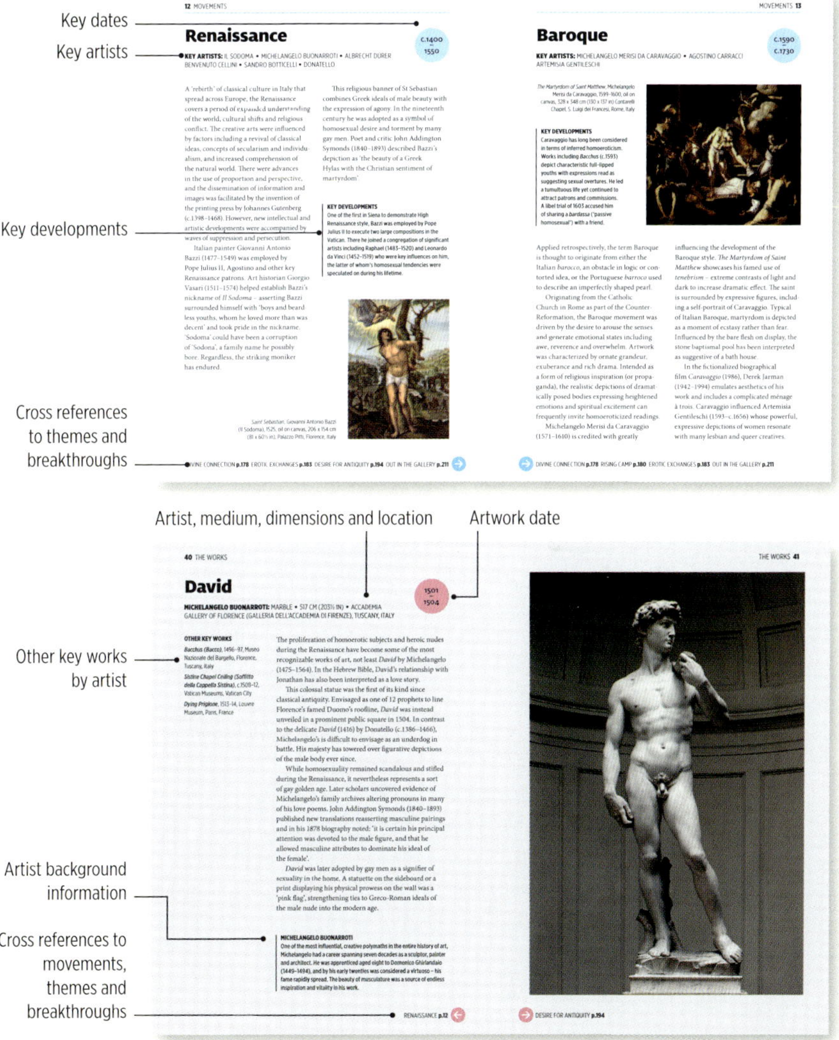

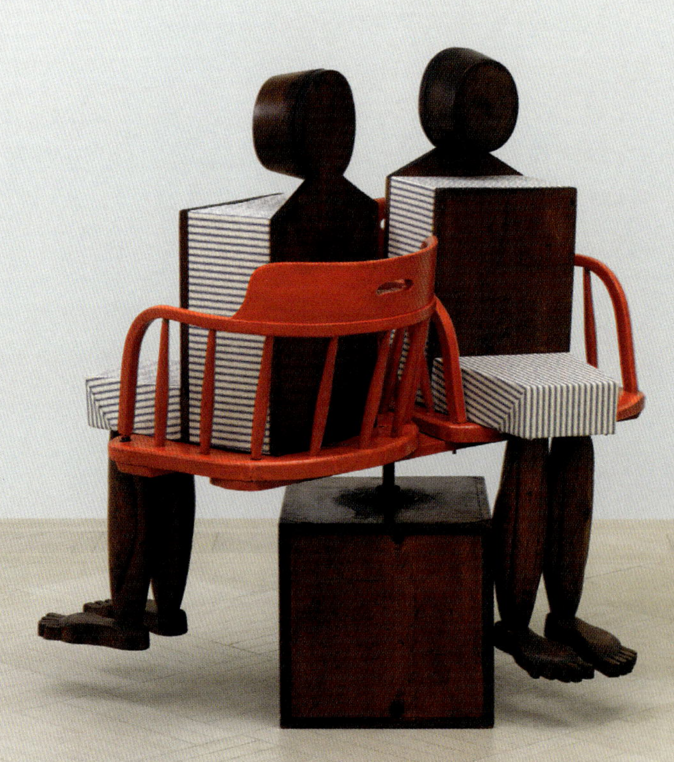

Movements

RENAISSANCE 12 • **BAROQUE** 13 • **ROCOCO** 14 • **NEOCLASSICISM** 15 • **REALISM** 16 **PRE-RAPHAELITES** 17 • **IMPRESSIONISM** 18 • **AESTHETICISM** 19 • **ART NOUVEAU** 20 • **DADA** 21 • **HARLEM RENAISSANCE** 22 • **SURREALISM** 23 • **ART DECO** 24 • **CONSTRUCTIVISM** 25 **ABSTRACT EXPRESSIONISM** 26 • **POP ART** 27 • **FILM AND VIDEO ART** 28 • **PERFORMANCE ART** 29 • **FEMINIST ART** 30 • **DIGITAL ART** 31 • **CONCEPTUAL ART** 32 • **POSTMODERNISM** 33 **AFROFUTURISM** 34 **POSTMINIMALISM** 35 • **STREET ART** 36 • **INTERNET ART** 37

Renaissance

c.1400 – 1550

KEY ARTISTS: IL SODOMA • MICHELANGELO BUONARROTI • ALBRECHT DÜRER BENVENUTO CELLINI • SANDRO BOTTICELLI • DONATELLO

A 'rebirth' of classical culture in Italy that spread across Europe, the Renaissance covers a period of expanded understanding of the world, cultural shifts and religious conflict. The creative arts were influenced by factors including a revival of classical ideas, concepts of secularism and individualism, and increased comprehension of the natural world. There were advances in the use of proportion and perspective, and the dissemination of information and images was facilitated by the invention of the printing press by Johannes Gutenberg (c.1398–1468). However, new intellectual and artistic developments were accompanied by waves of suppression and persecution.

Italian painter Giovanni Antonio Bazzi (1477–1549) was employed by Pope Julius II, Agostino and other key Renaissance patrons. Art historian Giorgio Vasari (1511–1574) helped establish Bazzi's nickname of *Il Sodoma* – asserting Bazzi surrounded himself with 'boys and beardless youths, whom he loved more than was decent' and took pride in the nickname. 'Sodoma' could have been a corruption of 'Sodona', a family name he possibly bore. Regardless, the striking moniker has endured.

This religious banner of St Sebastian combines Greek ideals of male beauty with the expression of agony. In the nineteenth century he was adopted as a symbol of homosexual desire and torment by many gay men. Poet and critic John Addington Symonds (1840–1893) described Bazzi's depiction as 'the beauty of a Greek Hylas with the Christian sentiment of martyrdom'.

KEY DEVELOPMENTS

One of the first in Siena to demonstrate High Renaissance style, Bazzi was employed by Pope Julius II to execute two large compositions in the Vatican. There he joined a congregation of significant artists including Raphael (1483–1520) and Leonardo da Vinci (1452–1519) who were key influences on him, the latter of whom's homosexual tendencies were speculated on during his lifetime.

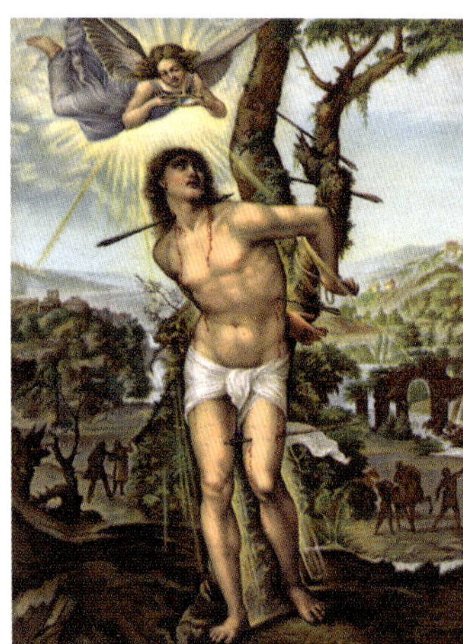

Saint Sebastian, Giovanni Antonio Bazzi (Il Sodoma), 1525, oil on canvas, 206 x 154 cm (81 x 60½ in), Palazzo Pitti, Florence, Italy

DIVINE CONNECTION **p.178** EROTIC EXCHANGES **p.183** DESIRE FOR ANTIQUITY **p.194** OUT IN THE GALLERY **p.211**

Baroque

c.1590 – c.1730

KEY ARTISTS: MICHELANGELO MERISI DA CARAVAGGIO • AGOSTINO CARRACCI
ARTEMISIA GENTILESCHI

The Martyrdom of Saint Matthew, Michelangelo Merisi da Caravaggio, 1599–1600, oil on canvas, 328 x 348 cm (130 x 137 in) Contarelli Chapel, S. Luigi dei Francesi, Rome, Italy

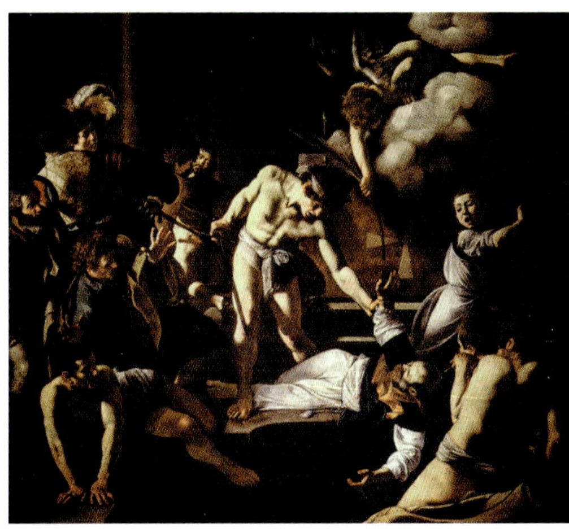

KEY DEVELOPMENTS
Caravaggio has long been considered in terms of inferred homoeroticism. Works including *Bacchus* (c.1593) depict characteristic full-lipped youths with expressions read as suggesting sexual overtures. He led a tumultuous life yet continued to attract patrons and commissions. A libel trial of 1603 accused him of sharing a *bardassa* ('passive homosexual') with a friend.

Applied retrospectively, the term Baroque is thought to originate from either the Italian *barocco*, an obstacle in logic or contorted idea, or the Portuguese *barroco* used to describe an imperfectly shaped pearl.

Originating from the Catholic Church in Rome as part of the Counter-Reformation, the Baroque movement was driven by the desire to arouse the senses and generate emotional states including awe, reverence and overwhelm. Artwork was characterized by ornate grandeur, exuberance and rich drama. Intended as a form of religious inspiration (or propaganda), the realistic depictions of dramatically posed bodies expressing heightened emotions and spiritual excitement can frequently invite homoeroticized readings.

Michelangelo Merisi da Caravaggio (1571–1610) is credited with greatly influencing the development of the Baroque style. *The Martyrdom of Saint Matthew* showcases his famed use of *tenebrism* – extreme contrasts of light and dark to increase dramatic effect. The saint is surrounded by expressive figures, including a self-portrait of Caravaggio. Typical of Italian Baroque, martyrdom is depicted as a moment of ecstasy rather than fear. Influenced by the bare flesh on display, the stone baptismal pool has been interpreted as suggestive of a bath house.

In the fictionalized biographical film *Caravaggio* (1986), Derek Jarman (1942–1994) emulates aesthetics of his work and includes a complicated ménage à trois. Caravaggio influenced Artemisia Gentileschi (1593–c.1656) whose powerful, expressive depictions of women resonate with many lesbian and queer creatives.

DIVINE CONNECTION **p.178** RISING CAMP **p.180** EROTIC EXCHANGES **p.183** OUT IN THE GALLERY **p.211**

Rococo

c.1720 – 1780

KEY ARTISTS: FRANÇOIS BOUCHER • JEAN-HONORÉ FRAGONARD ÉLISABETH LOUISE VIGÉE LE BRUN • JEAN-ANTOINE WATTEAU • ROSALBA CARRIERA

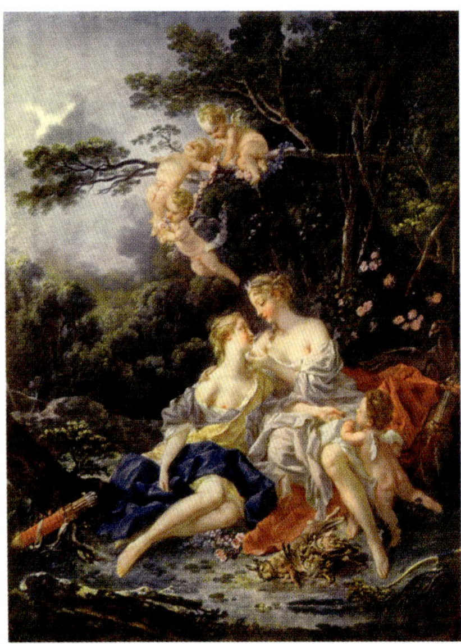

Jupiter and Callisto, François Boucher, 1744, oil on canvas, 98 x 72 cm (39 x 28 in), Pushkin Museum, Moscow, Russia

Characterized by elaborate ornamentation, intricate detailing and floral abundance, depicted with ardent pastel colours and glistening gilding, Rococo offered a lightness in contrast to the intensity of Baroque. Rococo aesthetics developed in early eighteenth-century France before spreading across continental Europe with geographic variations. The term derived from the French *rocaille*, meaning decorative 'pebble or shellwork' and was first used in the early nineteenth century to describe a then out-of-date 'rocaille style' of the previous century.

Celebrating a joyous lust for life, works often presented the natural world as a stage setting for pleasure and entertainment, with scenes of whimsical recreation in idealized Arcadian landscapes. Luxurious, light-hearted frivolity frequently created a flirtation between innocence and amorosity.

Popular subjects included classical myths as described by Ovid (43 BCE–17/18 CE) in *Metamorphoses* (8 CE), particularly that of Jupiter taking on the appearance of Diana to seduce her favourite nymph, Callisto. The scenario allows depiction of a seemingly sapphic seduction that is 'justified' or made acceptable by its classical source. This could both titillate and pacify moral sensibilities. François Boucher (1703–1770) depicted this scene of suggestive intimacy multiple times.

Queer artists in subsequent centuries have revisited Rococo aesthetics and Arcadian notions as a playground of spirited pleasure and flamboyance that rouses camp and 'queer maximalism'.

KEY DEVELOPMENTS

Boucher transformed the Rococo period with sensual depictions of notable individuals and seductive rural and mythological scenes. Influenced by Rubens (1577–1640) and Watteau (1684–1721), he was noted for combining aristocratic elegance with erotic nudes and famed for his patronage by Madame de Pompadour (1721–1764). He frequently portrayed scenes of female intimacy and myths that allowed depictions of sapphic scenarios.

GLIMPSES OF UTOPIA **p.163** DIVINE CONNECTION **p.178** RISING CAMP **p.180** EROTIC EXCHANGES **p.183** TRANSFORMING **p.190** OUT IN THE GALLERY **p.211**

Neoclassicism

c.1750 – 1850

KEY ARTISTS: ANNE SEYMOUR DAMER • ANTONIO CANOVA • JACQUES-LOUIS DAVID JOHN FLAXMAN

'There is but one way for the moderns to become great, and perhaps unequalled; I mean by imitating the ancient … especially the Greek arts' – so wrote Johann Joachim Winckelmann (1717–1768), whose texts on ancient Greek art were instrumental in establishing the aesthetic and theory of Neoclassicism. His descriptions of superior Greek taste and celebration of their 'noble simplicity and sedate grandeur in Gesture and Expression' chimed with a wider revisiting of Classical philosophical and political thought across Europe in the Enlightenment.

Neoclassicism was stimulated by discoveries of ancient Greek and Roman archaeological sites, and its rise was supported by the popularity of 'The Grand Tour', undertaken by artists and aristocrats to experience cultures, art, antiquity and architecture across Europe.

Neoclassical art frequently depicted Classical subjects, with an emphasis on strong lines and smooth contours, and architecture adopted principles of simplicity and symmetry. This contrasted with preceding Rococo and Baroque styles that revelled in exaggerated decoration and were criticized as encouraging a frivolous culture of vanity. Neoclassicism aspired to emulate ideas of order, restraint and reason. A central principle was that art could improve and civilize society, so should express virtuous ideals and moral messages. However, a focus on heroic, idealized bodies and Winckelmann's sensual descriptions of male sculptures allowed a rich seam of male homoeroticism.

Mary Berry, Anne Seymour Damer, cast from a work dated 1793, bronze, 45.5 x 20 cm (17⅞ x 7⅞ in) overall, National Portrait Gallery, London, UK

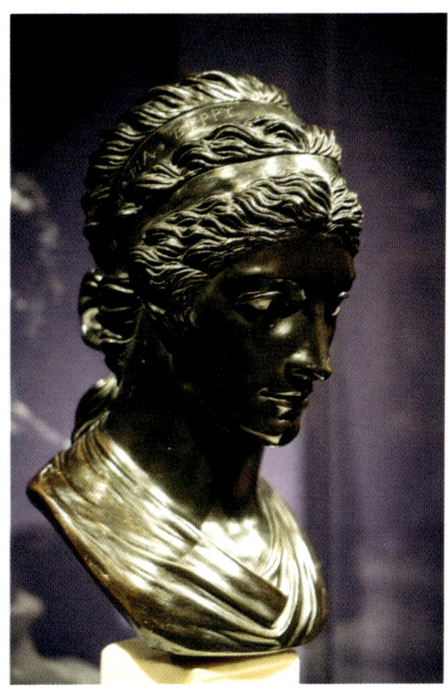

KEY DEVELOPMENTS

Horace Walpole (1717–1797) praised the work of 'female genius' Anne Seymour Damer (1748–1828) as 'not inferior to the antique'. A celebrated society sculptor, Damer exhibited at the Royal Academy repeatedly. The few women with artistic careers rarely worked in sculpture. Damer's 'masculine' pursuits and female friendships were scrutinized and satirized, including in *A Sapphick Epistle* (1782) which remarked on her relationship with writer Mary Berry (1762–1852).

DIVINE CONNECTION **p.178** EROTIC EXCHANGES **p.183** DESIRE FOR ANTIQUITY **p.194** PUBLIC PRESENCE **p.197** OUT IN THE GALLERY **p.211**

Realism

1840s – c.1890

KEY ARTISTS: GUSTAVE CAILLEBOTTE • ROSA BONHEUR • THOMAS EAKINS LOTTE LASERSTEIN • GRANT WOOD

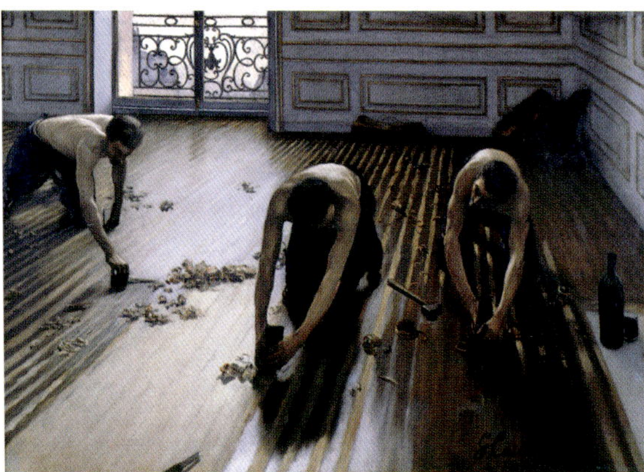

Les raboteurs de parquet (The Floor Scrapers), Gustave Caillebotte, 1875, oil on canvas, 102 x 146.5 cm (40⅛ x 57⅝ in), Musee D'Orsay, Paris, France

Realism has a broad meaning across many art forms and time periods. In the visual arts, it typically means the movement innovated by Gustave Courbet (1819–1877) in France in the late 1840s. Concerned with a naturalistic portrayal of life, its hallmark was documenting workers without romanticizing the harsh precarities of their daily grind yet evolved into the wider definition of simply presenting the world as seen.

A notable exponent was Gustave Caillebotte (1848–1894). He was a man of privilege, whose crisp depictions of Belle Epoque street-life tended to focus on *flaneurs*, bourgeois men cruising the city and cultivating their gazes. One of his earliest works, *The Floor Scrapers*, was both praised and ridiculed upon its first outing in 1876. The humble act of three men scraping the artist's new studio floor is presented on a heroic scale; the city heat palpable through their shirtless exertions. His frequent depictions of burly oarsmen, their muscular backs bathed in dappled light on the river, are equally infused with this homoerotic atmosphere. Caillebotte walked to the beat of his own drum, unfazed by the delineations and dramas of the late-nineteenth-century artworld. He was recognized for his unusual vantage points, and these too can be 'queered' for literally taking another view, one which throws us off the conventional perspective.

KEY DEVELOPMENTS

Caillebotte's cinematic style is deeply of its time and yet streets ahead. Included in the second Impressionist exhibition of 1877, *The Floor Scrapers* was described by contemporary critics 'as crude but more witty than Courbet and as violent but more precise than Manet'. With his naturalistic approach and choices of subject matter, his works straddled Impressionism and Realism, and were also likened to what colour photography might one day look like.

QUEER EYE **p.182** EROTIC EXCHANGES **p.183** GAY PARIS **p.204**

Pre-Raphaelites

1848 – c.1890

KEY ARTISTS: SIMEON SOLOMON • EVELYN DE MORGAN • FREDERIC LEIGHTON WILLIAM HOLMAN HUNT • JOHN EVERETT MILLAIS • DANTE GABRIEL ROSSETTI

The rubric of Pre-Raphaelitism originated with the Pre-Raphaelite Brotherhood in 1848, a small group of English painters, poets and art critics, founded by three Royal Academy students – William Holman Hunt (1827–1910), John Everett Millais (1829–1896) and Dante Gabriel Rossetti (1828–1882). Disillusioned with the Academy's narrow approach to art (drawn from Italian Renaissance and Classical art), they shared reformist intentions. Inspired by earlier periods – before Raphael (1483–1520) – they believed medieval and early Renaissance cultures to be creatively and spiritually superior.

They advocated for artists to have honesty, sincerity, truth to nature and 'genuine ideas to express'. Their work was characterized by luminous colours, clear imagery and minute details. They attempted to disseminate ideas through their periodical *The Germ* (1850). The Brotherhood later dispersed, but the term 'Pre-Raphaelite' persisted in association with other artists, and their principals influenced the development of the Arts and Crafts movement, forged by William Morris (1834–1896), and Aestheticism.

Recurrence of androgynous figures in works by Evelyn de Morgan (1855–1919), Simeon Solomon (1840–1905) and others have been increasingly recognized as defying conventions of binary gender and attraction. De Morgan's early career was associated with the Pre-Raphaelites, but her depictions of women with agency pushed against the Brotherhood's male-centric perspectives. It has been suggested that she later employed Pre-Raphaelite styles with satiric intent.

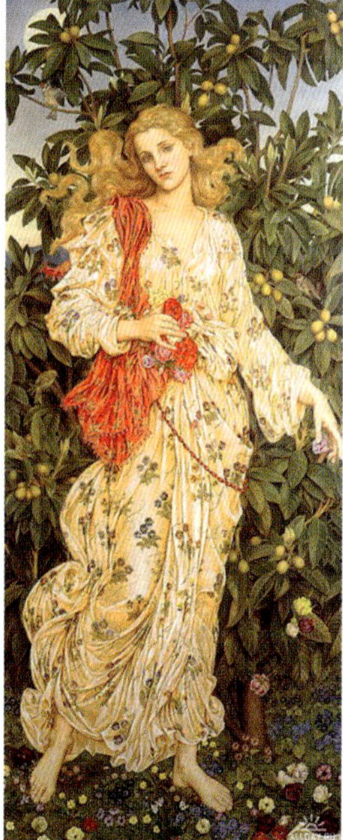

Flora, Evelyn de Morgan, 1894, oil on canvas, 198.12 x 86.4 cm (78 x 34 in), De Morgan Collection, UK

KEY DEVELOPMENTS

Flora is an amalgam of inspiration from *Primavera* (1482) and *The Birth of Venus* (1485) by Botticelli (c.1445–1510), whose work experienced a renaissance through the Pre-Raphaelites. De Morgan shunned conventional femininity and adopted her gender-neutral middle name, Evelyn. Her mother reportedly remarked that she wanted a 'daughter, not an artist'. While in a supportive marriage with William De Morgan (1839–1917), she had a close relationship with Jane Hales (1851–1926), a favoured muse among the Pre-Raphaelites.

CRAFTING THREADS **p.175** DIVINE CONNECTION **p.178** DESIRE FOR ANTIQUITY **p.194**

Impressionism

1860s – 1900s

KEY ARTISTS: HENRY SCOTT TUKE • CLAUDE MONET • MARIE BRACQUEMOND FRÉDÉRIC BAZILLE • CAMILLE PISSARRO

Often painting *en plein air* with loose, spontaneous brushstrokes, the Impressionists reflected ephemeral effects of light and visual perceptions in caught moments of daily hustle and bustle. They shunned historical conventions of style and inclusion of subjects, their progressive approaches having roots in Realism and Naturalism, similarly challenging conventional notions of aesthetic beauty and formal art appreciation. Women in the movement like Berthe Morisot (1841–1895) and Mary Cassatt (1844–1926) notably applied impressionist approaches to domestic depictions of women and girls.

At its height in 1870s Paris, many artists further afield adopted their motivations and techniques. Inspired by a stint in Paris, Henry Scott Tuke (1858–1929) eschewed mythological contexts of his earlier nudes to paint outdoors from life. This freer and more naturalistic approach to painting young men and boys bathing, fishing and sunning themselves on Cornish beaches nevertheless retains a Hellenistic celebration of homoeroticism.

Gustave Caillebotte (1848–1894) was a member and patron of the Impressionists, although he adopted a more realistic manner than most [see *Realism*]. His scenes of newly built boulevards share similarities with photographic framing, imbuing them with an uncanny modernity. Funding several of their exhibitions and purchasing many paintings, Caillebotte bequeathed his unrivalled collection of Impressionist works to the Musée d'Orsay.

The Critics, Henry Scott Tuke, 1923, oil on board, 41.2 x 51.4 cm (16¼ x 20¼ in), Leamington Spa Art Gallery and Museum, UK (see Works p.74)

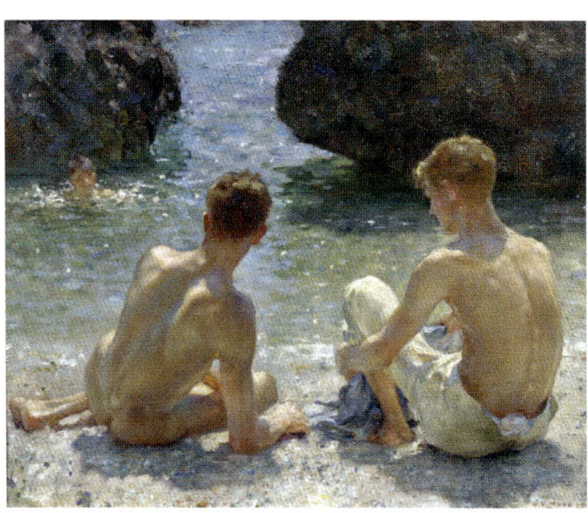

KEY DEVELOPMENTS

The term 'Impressionism' arose from a review by critic Louis Leroy (1812–1885) after the inaugural 1874 exhibition of the 'Cooperative and Anonymous Association of Painters, Sculptors and Engravers' in Paris. Appropriating the title of *Impression, Sunrise* (1872) by Claude Monet (1840–1926), Leroy ridiculed the artists for creating nothing but unrefined impressions. They daringly embraced the name and challenged the stronghold of the exclusionary Salon system.

Aestheticism

1860s – 1900

KEY ARTISTS: AUBREY BEARDSLEY • FREDERICK LEIGHTON • KONSTANTIN SOMOV JAMES MCNEILL WHISTLER

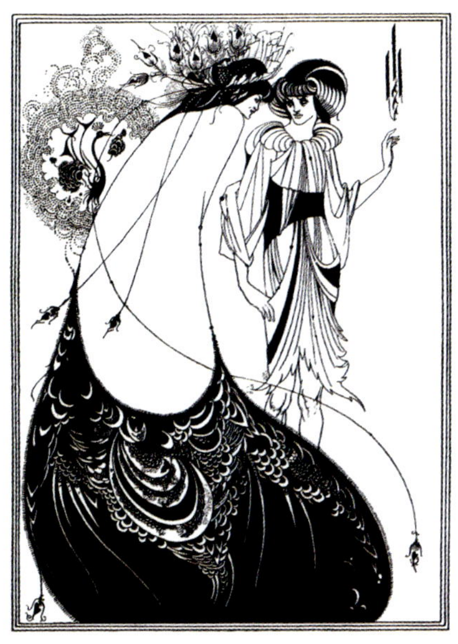

The Peacock Skirt, Aubrey Beardsley, 1893, ink drawing, 23 x 16.8 cm (9 x 6½ in), Private Collection (see Works p.50)

KEY DEVELOPMENTS

Beardsley's *The Peacock Skirt* was one of 16 plates drawn to illustrate Oscar Wilde's *Salome* (1893/1894). While universally symbolic of beauty, in the *fin de siècle*, a peacock feather was often seen as a proclamation of queerness and as confirmation that all male Aesthetes were of a 'flamboyant persuasion'.

The Aesthetic movement aimed to break away from the heavy-handed moralizing of Victorian art. Valuing appearance over ethics, its devotees were described as belonging to the 'cult of beauty', collapsing into sheer Decadence by the century's end. In his influential essays of the 1860s, Walter Pater (1839–1894) evoked this intoxicating new way of being: 'we may well grasp at any exquisite passion, or any contribution to knowledge … to set the spirit free for a moment, or any stirring of the sense, strange dyes, strange colours, and curious odours …'.

Aubrey Beardsley (1872–1898) ties together several strands of Aestheticism. He was deeply impressed by a visit to the Gesamtkunstwerk known as *Harmony in Blue and Gold: The Peacock Room* (1877) by James McNeill Whistler (1834–1903) and Thomas Jeckyll (1827–1881) and the collection of blue and white porcelain at the house of Frederick Leyland (1831–1892). Like many of his contemporaries, he was influenced by the superior quality of Japanese prints, but Beardsley's superb sinewy linework demonstrates its inspiration more than most, and he transforms it into something unique. As a teenager, Beardsley admired the androgyny and amorousness in the paintings of Edward Burne-Jones (1833–1898), seeking him out as a teacher. The Pre-Raphaelite Brotherhood had paved the way for Aestheticism with their particular style of bohemianism and probing of sexual morality, class and gender.

TEXTUAL POWER **p.166** QUEER CODING **p.168** DIVINE CONNECTION **p.178** THEATRICAL TYPES **p.181** EROTIC EXCHANGES **p.183** EXPOSING DESIRES **p.198**

Art Nouveau

1890s – 1910s

KEY ARTISTS: CHARLES ROBERT ASHBEE • HENRI DE TOULOUSE-LAUTREC EUGÈNE SAMUEL GRASSET • ROBERTO MONTENEGRO NERVO • GERDA WEGENER

The Paris 1900 Exposition Universelle marked the high point of Art Nouveau. Robert de Montesquiou (1855–1921), the Proustian patron of the arts, was a driving force behind the style, commissioning designers to satisfy his desires for languid, luxurious aesthetics. Works emulated notions of natural elegance with flowing lines, asymmetry and frequently incorporating animal and plant motifs. Its appeal swept around Europe under many names: Style Moderne – France; Style Nouille (Noodle Style) – Belgium; Jugendstil (Youth Style) – Germany; Secessionism – Austrian Empire, where it flourished in rebellion against the exclusionary exhibition system; and Stile Liberty – Italy, referencing the London store (est. 1875).

Liberty commissioned work by the best Arts and Crafts and Art Nouveau designers of the day with C. R. Ashbee (1863–1942) straddling both camps. Inspired by William Morris (1834–1896) and the progressive thinking of gay socialist, philosopher and poet Edward Carpenter (1844–1929), he set up the Guild and School of Handicraft in the 1880s which trained working-class apprentices in metalwork and furniture making. He was affiliated with the Order of Chaeronea, a gay secret society founded in 1897 by George Cecil Ives (1867–1950), whose members probably included Oscar Wilde (1854–1900), Lord Alfred Douglas (1870–1945) and many of the controversial Uranian poets.

KEY DEVELOPMENTS

Ashbee was a leader in British Art Nouveau as a polymath designer of jewellery, metalwork, furniture and interiors. This cup was made to humorously commiserate the marriage of his friend James Headlam (1863–1929), inscribed 'To the ancient, from CRA, on the mournful occasion of his transition into matrimony'. Ashbee married in 1898, but admitted to his fiancé he was more interested in men and would continue to have 'many comrade friends'.

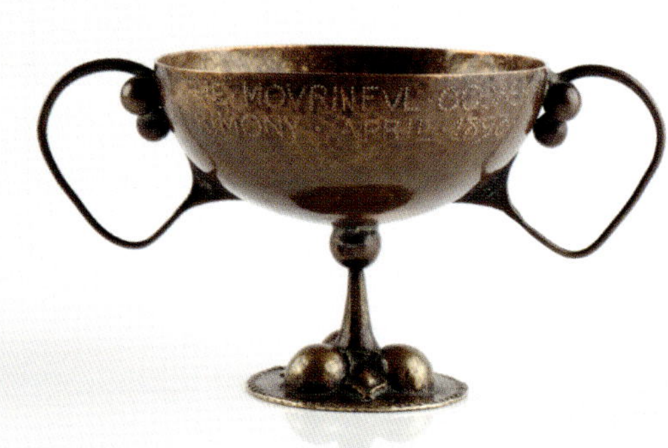

Twin-handled Cup, Charles Robert Ashbee, 1893, metal, 8.2 x 16.1 cm (3¼ x 6⅜ in), Private Collection

GLIMPSES OF UTOPIA **p.163** QUEER ECOLOGIES **p.177** QUEER EYE **p.182** GAY PARIS **p.204**

Dada

1916 – 1920s

KEY ARTISTS: HANNAH HÖCH • MARCEL DUCHAMP • FRANCIS PICABIA • MAN RAY

With roots in avant-garde art and cabaret, Dada emerged amid the First World War. Demonstrating a raucous, irreverent, anti-establishment attitude to art and society, Dadaists looked to provoke and subvert conventions and challenge bourgeois society whose apathy they believed had enabled war. Delighting in disruption and blurring boundaries, they blended critique with absurdity, rejecting reason and established 'good taste'.

Dada encompassed visual arts, theatre, graphic design, literature and poetry. With his '*manifeste dada 1918*', Tristan Tzara (1896–1963) articulated some principles merged with nonsensical statements and the paradox of 'in principle I am against manifestos, as I am against principles' – reflecting Dada's wilfully tangled contradictions and logic. The origin of the movement's name – a childish word meaning 'hobby-horse' in French – is debated. The exact birth of Dada is also disputed but closely associated with Zürich's artistic Cabaret Voltaire of 1916.

Artists embraced and critiqued the spreading technical advances of popular cinema, radio and the photo-illustrated press using strategies including collage, assemblage and performance.

Dada sowed conceptual and aesthetic seeds that later flourished in Abstract Art, Performance Art, Postmodernism and Pop Art. Its methods of disruption and challenging social norms lend themselves to queer re/presentation and methods of 'queering'. Chaotic performance interventions can be seen in 'radical drag' troupes of the 1970s and queer performers including Klaus Nomi (1944–1983) have revisited aspects of Dada aesthetics.

Da-Dandy, Hannah Höch, 1919, collage, 30 x 23 cm (11 13/16 x 9 1/16 in), Private Collection (see Works p.62)

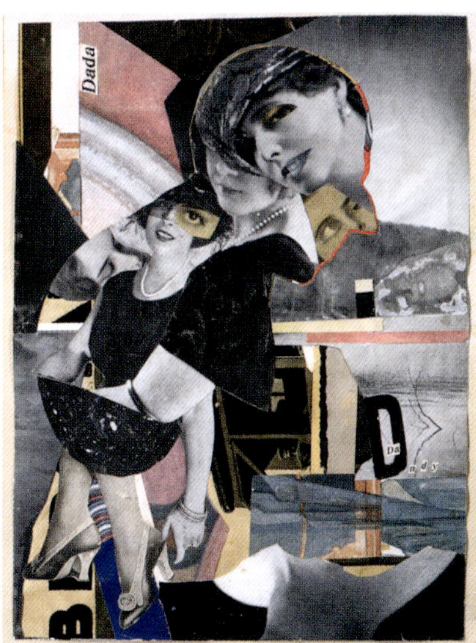

KEY DEVELOPMENTS

The Berlin Dadaists were more explicitly political than others but promptly targeted by the Third Reich. As one of the only women in the Berlin Dada scene, Hannah Höch (1889–1978) came up against misogyny and hypocrisy, observing: 'they all desired this "New Woman" and her ground-breaking will to freedom. But – they more or less brutally rejected the notion that they, too, had to adopt new attitudes."

ASSEMBLING **p.171** THEATRICAL TYPES **p.181** WEIMAR BERLIN **p.201** INSTITUTIONAL CRITIQUE **p.212**

Harlem Renaissance

1920 – 1940

KEY ARTISTS: AARON DOUGLAS • JAMES RICHMOND BARTHÉ BEAUFORD DELANEY • RICHARD BRUCE NUGENT • GWENDOLYN BENNETT

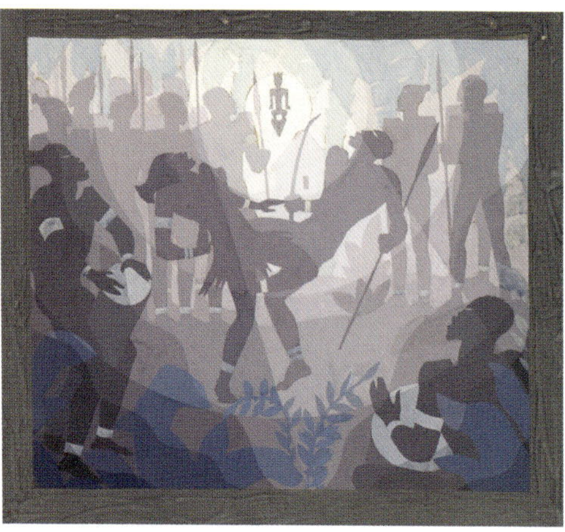

Study for Aspects of Negro Life: The Negro in an African Setting, Aaron Douglas, 1934, gouache and graphite on illustration board, 37.2 x 40.6 cm (14⅝ x 16 in), Art Institute of Chicago, USA

KEY DEVELOPMENTS

Douglas was a lynchpin of the Harlem Renaissance best known for his influential murals, and these large-scale public artworks had a galvanizing effect. This design was commissioned for the Countee Cullen branch of the New York Public Library, named in honour of the writer who had been inspired by Alain LeRoy Locke (1885–1954) and the work of Edward Carpenter (1844–1929) to explore queer desires.

Also dubbed 'The Jazz Age', the interwar years in Manhattan were a crucible of new music, literature, visual and dramatic art, philosophy and political thinking. In segregated America, Harlem was the epicentre of a Black cultural revolution which included many bisexual, gay and lesbian writers and artists, including James Richmond Barthé (1901–1989), Richard Bruce Nugent (1906–1987), Gwendolyn Bennett (1902–1981) and Langston Hughes (1901–1967). While they still faced widespread discrimination, it was a significant flourishing of tolerance and broadmindedness that would pave the way for the civil rights and gay rights movements.

Murals by Aaron Douglas (1899–1979), often assisted by Nugent, decorated many of the nightclubs popping up around Harlem at the time where many of the most popular performers were lesbian or bi women like Ma Rainey (1886–1939) and the tuxedo-sporting Gladys Bentley (1907–1960). The Hamilton Lodge Ball was the largest annual communal event of New York gay society, organized by the Black gay community. Nugent remembered 'be-ribboned and be-rouged "pansies" … "drag" balls were becoming more notorious and gender was becoming more and more conjectural'.

Looking for Langston (1989), a film by Isaac Julien (1960–), references literary legend Langston Hughes within a homage to luminaries of the Harlem scene and European writers of queer interest. The soundtrack includes excerpts from Nugent's *Smoke, Lilies, and Jade* (1926), considered the first prose poem by an African American to openly discuss homosexuality.

THEATRICAL TYPES **p.181** PLACES TO BE **p.189** PUBLIC PRESENCE **p.197** *FIRE!!* MAGAZINE **p.203**

Surrealism

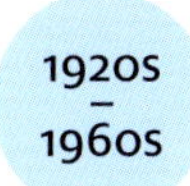

KEY ARTISTS: MÉRET OPPENHEIM • TOYEN • JEAN COCTEAU • FLORENCE HENRI
LEONOR FINI • ITHELL COLQUHOUN

Surrealism bloomed in Europe between the World Wars before disseminating internationally. Seeded by the Dadaists and their provocative defiance of reason, and interested in exploring the unconscious, dreams and psychology, Surrealism aspired to liberate the mind and artistic expression.

The term was first coined in 1917 by writer Guillaume Apollinaire (1880–1918). Poet and critic André Breton (1896–1966) later described it in *The Surrealist Manifesto* (1924) as a means to 'resolve the previously contradictory conditions of dream and reality into an absolute reality, a super-reality'.

Artists worked across mediums, including creating assemblages of familiar items in unfamiliar combinations. Many used automatic drawing or writing to access ideas and images from their subconscious. Paintings ranged from depictions of undefined, biomorphic forms to realistic scenes that distorted rational sense. Breton and others demanded strict adherence to doctrines and discouraged membership in other groups, so the movement witnessed various expulsions and disagreements.

Several queer artists were associated with Surrealism and connections can be made between 'queerness' and the 'uncanny' present in many works. Painter and illustrator Toyen (1902–1980) helped found the Czech Surrealist Group. With a gender-neutral mononym, their works often addressed gender and sexuality with erotic humour. Alexander Cañedo (1902–1978) worked with both surrealism and magic realism, depicting sensual, homoerotic, nude male figures in alien or abstracted landscapes with sci-fi elements.

KEY DEVELOPMENTS

This suggestively impractical fur-covered cup by Méret Oppenheim (1913–1985) became an icon of the movement. Interested in psycho-analysis, she often played with anthropomorphizing objects and drew inspiration from dreams and myths. Unlike many Surrealists, Oppenheim stressed the physicality of her creations, emphasizing them as 'not an illustration of an idea, but the thing itself'.

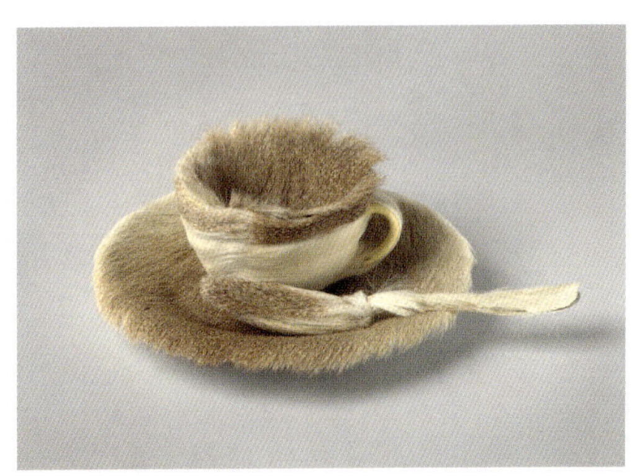

Object, known as *Le Déjeuner en Fourrure*, Méret Oppenheim, 1936, fur-covered cup, saucer and spoon, Cup 10.9 cm (4⅜ in) diameter; saucer 23.7 cm (9⅜ in) diameter; spoon 20.2 cm (8 in) length, overall height 7.3 cm (2⅞ in), Museum of Modern Art, New York, USA (see Works p.96)

QUEER CODING **p.168** ASSEMBLING **p.171** SPACE OF THE BODY **p.172** QUEER EYE **p.182** TRANSFORMING **p.190**

Art Deco

1920s – 1930s

KEY ARTISTS: TAMARA DE LEMPICKA • ERTÉ • GEORGE BARBIER J. C. LEYENDECKER • JEAN COCTEAU

Reflecting modernist ideas of progress and optimism, Art Deco presented an aesthetic, decadent, stylish and thoroughly modern mode of living. An amalgamation, rather than a fixed style, it embraced an array of influences. Aspects of Cubism, Expressionism, Futurism and Vorticism mingled with Ancient Egyptian and Mayan motifs, and the colourful thrill of the Ballets Russes. Its portrayal of a streamlined machine age – with technology applied to pursuing beauty rather than war – suggested liberation to luxurious lifestyles. A varying palette of bold angles, tonal contrasts and robust lines were employed to create sleek, strong designs. Both sensuous and illusive, their smooth stylized surfaces suggested cinematic illusion.

Art Deco took its name from the 1925 Exposition Internationale des Arts Décoratifs et Industriels Modernes in Paris which launched the style on a global scale. Exhibitors included Tamara de Lempicka (1898–1980) who became one of the style's most recognized painters. Her work demonstrates influences including Neo-Cubism and Futurism – infused with the dynamism of modern urban life populated with strong women.

Art Deco's embrace of progressive ideals became a style beacon for emerging queer identities. Many who shaped the style led LGBTQ+ lives, and designs became signifiers for emerging queer tastes. They include illustrator George Barbier (1882–1932) whose work drips with camp and same-sex activity – his men fawning and fey and female couplings loaded with lesbian longing.

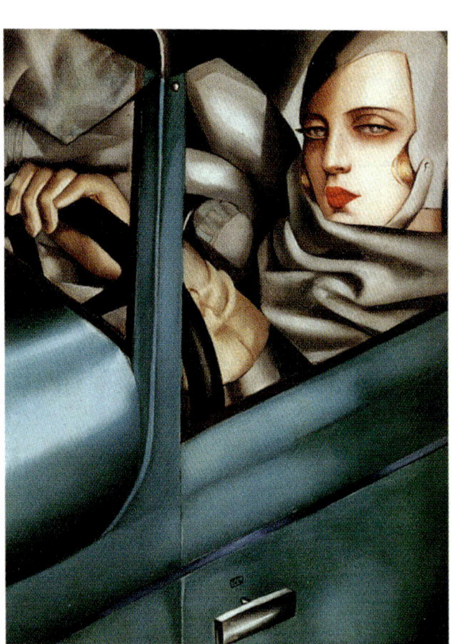

KEY DEVELOPMENTS

With its bold, bright and elegant sculptural angles, Lempicka's self-portrait is an iconic example of Art Deco portraiture. Commissioned for the cover of German fashion magazine *Die Dame*, she presents herself as a glamorous, independent woman driving into the future – her car a sleek, luxurious machine of emancipation. Sensuous surfaces and her direct yet cool eye contact make this a seductive proposition.

Autoportrait (Tamara in a Green Bugatti), Tamara de Lempicka, 1928, oil on panel, 35 x 27 cm (13¾ in x 10⅝ in), Private Collection (see Works p.84)

PRESENTING THE ARTIST **p.167** QUEER EYE **p.182** THE BALLETS RUSSES **p.199** COMMERCIAL ALLURE **p.200**

Constructivism

c.1915 – 1930s

KEY ARTISTS: MARLOW MOSS • ALEXANDER RODCHENKO • VLADIMIR TATLIN ANTON PRINNER

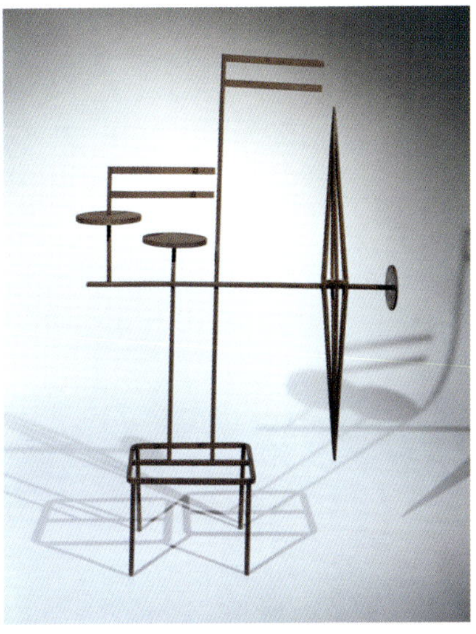

Spatial Construction in Steel, Marlow Moss, 1956–57, steel, 130 x 81.2 x 22.8 cm (51¼ x 32 x 9 in), Leeds Art Gallery, Leeds Museums and Galleries, UK

KEY DEVELOPMENTS

Described as the first British Constructivist, Marlow Moss (1889–1958) incorporated mathematical and geometric rules into works and in 1933 proposed that science and technology could enable 'a new reality: the reconstruction of human life by man himself'. Moss regarded identity as fluid, adopting their gender-neutral name in the 1920s, later describing 'I destroyed my old personality and created a new one.'

Constructivism was established in Russia c.1915 as an austere branch of abstract art. Influenced by the cubist constructions of Pablo Picasso (1881–1973), its founders Alexander Rodchenko (1891–1956) and Vladimir Tatlin (1885–1953) aspired to establish a new aesthetic language for a modern Soviet era.

A 1923 manifesto stated: 'Constructivism is a purely technical mastery and organisation of materials.' Constructivists believed art should reflect the modern world and be 'of no discernible "style" but simply a product of an industrial order'. They supported using art for sociopolitical purposes – considering it a tool for the Communist revolution. The movement was suppressed in the 1920s but spread beyond Russia, becoming a major influence on sculpture and graphic design with distinctive bold typography, shapes and colours.

Constructivism offered an artistic language detached from personality and biography, which was explored by several queer or gender-non-conforming artists. Hungarian-born Anton Prinner (1902–1983) adopted the name Anton and requested male pronouns when he moved to France in 1928. Initially unaware he was creating 'constructivist art', he was happy to discover that it 'actually had a name' but later tired of being 'named, grouped, and categorized like a grocer names his cheese'.

In 2021 artist Alex Rosborough Davis (1995–) proposed a *Queer Constructivism Manifesto*, asserting Queerness as 'an act of self-creation' and outlining 'the kind of art needed to bring about a Queer utopia'.

QUEER CODING **p.168** SPACE OF THE BODY **p.172**

Abstract Expressionism

1940s – 1950s

KEY ARTISTS: HILMA AF KLINT • SONJA SEKULA • CY TWOMBLY • ALFONSO ANGEL YANGCO OSSORIO • AGNES MARTIN

Abstract Expressionism took off in the USA in the aftermath of the Second World War. Quickly dominated by men whose reputations would tower over twentieth-century art, it is largely split into Action Painting and Colour Field Painting. However, its roots go much deeper.

Hilma af Klint (1862–1944) was a mystic visionary, credited with creating some of the first abstract paintings as early as 1906, including almost 200 works that form *The Paintings for the Temple* series. Such radical compositions predate many of her more famous male counterparts' experiments in abstraction including Wassily Kandinsky (1866–1944) and Piet Mondrian (1872–1944). Like them, she was heavily influenced by the emerging spiritualist movement.

Klint believed art was a vehicle for transcendental experience and that humanity would one day move beyond gender into a state of androgynous perfection. A lesbian identity has also been widely posited given her cohabitation with and affiliations to various women's groups like 'The Five'.

Abstraction freed many artists from constrictions around gender, race and class, offering pleasures beyond the earthly domain. Klint deliberately kept her abstract work under wraps until 20 years after death, believing the world was not ready for them. Now hailed as a major forerunner, she has been enthusiastically revisited in exhibitions eager to balance the scales against the stranglehold of a few male painters in the abstract canon.

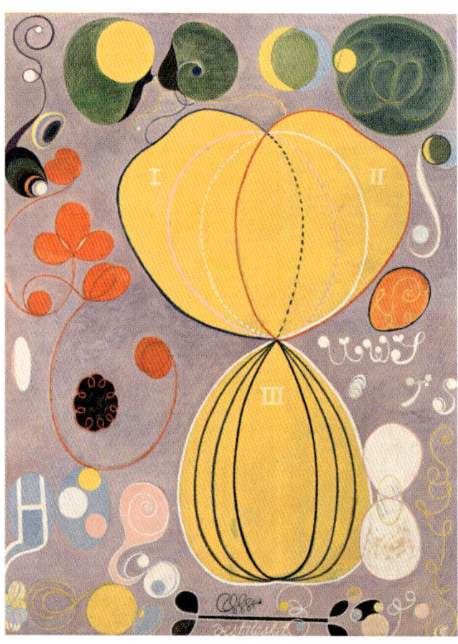

The Ten Largest, No. 7, Adulthood, Group IV, Hilma af Klint, 1907, tempera on paper, mounted on canvas, 315 x 235 cm (124 x 92½ in), Hilma af Klint Foundation, Stockholm, Sweden

KEY DEVELOPMENTS

A major pioneer in promoting the movement was influential gallerist and artist Betty Parsons (1900–1982). Champion of many LGBTQ+ abstract artists including Sonja Sekula (1918–1963), Agnes Martin (1912–2004), Ellsworth Kelly (1923–2015) and some who famously reacted against it like Robert Rauschenberg (1925–2008), Parsons opened her eponymous gallery in New York in 1946, giving many of the Abstract Expressionists their first exhibitions.

QUEER CODING **p.168** ASSEMBLING **p.171** SPACE OF THE BODY **p.172**

Pop Art

1950s – 1960s

KEY ARTISTS: ANDY WARHOL • MARISOL ESCOBAR • PAULINE BOTY ROBERT INDIANA • JASPER JOHNS • ROBERT RAUSCHENBERG

The seeds of Pop Art emerged in 1950s London as ideologies of consumerism and mass production increased following the Second World War. Artists contemplated how to engage with the growing dominance of television and the increasingly prevalent world of commercial graphic design. Combining commercial and fine art to create visually direct works, accessible to wider audiences, Pop took root in France, West Germany, the United States and beyond.

Within an apparent celebration of the 'superficial', artists frequently subverted visuals to add or suggest elements of depth. Kitsch and camp sensibilities, arch humour and postmodern irony were frequently employed, notably by Andy Warhol (1928–1987) who named his studio The Factory and declared 'Art is Business'.

Many queer artists engaged with Pop Art, using mainstream media imagery to explore 'life more on the margins'. Robert Indiana (1928–2018) had reservations about Pop's impersonal and consumerist nature and found the success of his iconic *Love* series problematic. The first *LOVE* sculpture was produced in 1970 after Indiana split with abstract artist Ellsworth Kelly (1923–2015), about whom he said: 'before [him] I was aesthetically at sea. With Ellsworth, my whole life perspective changed. All of a sudden, I was in the twentieth century.' In 1987, art collective General Idea provocatively substituted the word LOVE with AIDS in the same layout and colours as Indiana's original piece.

Allen Ginsberg, Ulrike Ottinger, 1966, puzzle, acrylic on pressboard, 81 x 115 cm (31⅞ x 45¼ in), Kunsthalle zu Kiel, Germany © Ulrike Ottinger

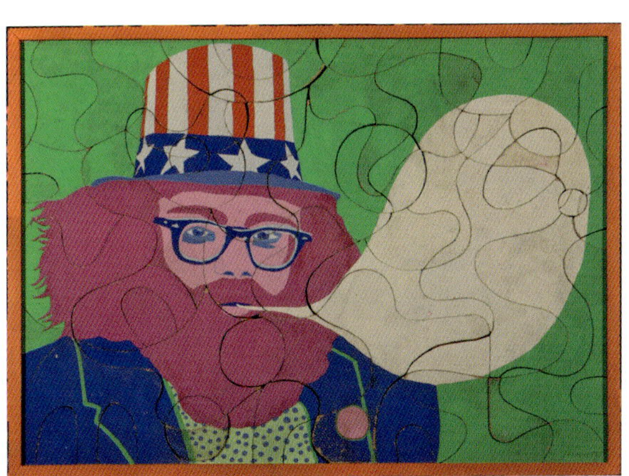

KEY DEVELOPMENTS

This painted jigsaw portrait of Allen Ginsberg (1926–1997), countercultural poet and icon of the Beat Generation, is inspired by comic book art, a hallmark of Pop Art. Working in 1960s Paris, Ulrike Ottinger (1942–) used the language of Pop alongside New or Nouvelle Figuration, a rejection of the impersonality of abstraction, reviving the figure in art. Ginsberg also appeared in Warhol's film *Couch* (1964).

ASSEMBLING **p.171** RISING CAMP **p.180** QUEER ICONS **p.184** COMMERCIAL ALLURE **p.200**

Film and Video Art

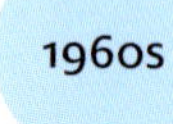

KEY ARTISTS: BARBARA HAMMER • ANDY WARHOL • JACK SMITH
DAVID WOJNAROWICZ • SADIE BENNING • ISAAC JULIEN • NAM JUNE PAIK

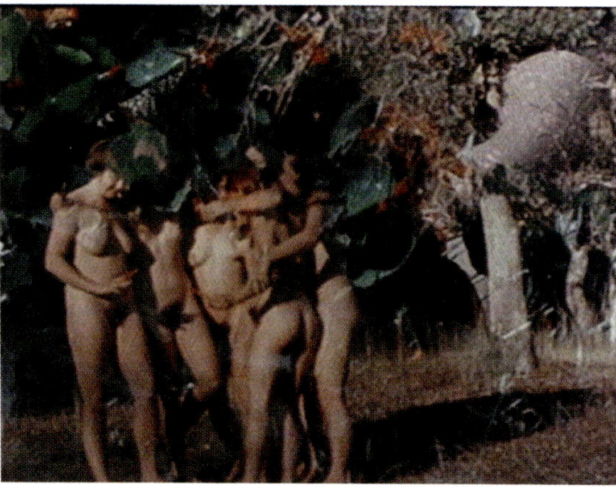

Dyketactics, Barbara Hammer, 1974, 16mm film, colour/sound, 4 mins

KEY DEVELOPMENTS
Introduction of the Sony Portapak in the 1960s was key in expanding video art. An early adopter was Nam June Paik (1932–2006), considered the founder of video art. Paik merged video, performance and installation. Also in New York, Jack Smith (1932–1989) and Andy Warhol (1928–1987) cast often caustic, queer and camp influences on video, film and performance.

Video art emerged alongside experimental film developments during the 1960s as increasingly affordable, streamlined equipment increased access and immediacy of production. Although it was more a technology toolkit than a specific movement, many artists shared focus in pushing the mediums to their limits, referencing their pervasive presence, and unpicking conventions. Film and video became incorporated with coinciding conceptual, performance and feminist art movements, and the increasingly prevalent creation of installation art.

Film and video allowed artists to play with time and sound as well as the visual plane. Brimming with opportunities to distort and subvert, or splice together fact and fiction, it had the added appeal for queer artists of making visible what had for so long been undocumented.

Barbara Hammer (1939–2019), the feminist filmmaker and pioneer of queer cinema, was inspired by Maya Deren (1917–1961) to make experimental films about her personal life. After coming out as a lesbian, she 'took off on a motorcycle with a super-8 camera'. *Dyketactics* (1974) is widely considered one of the first lesbian art films. Looking to create an aesthetic based on connecting sight and touch Hammer also blurred art, life and documentation, noting 'you could still say, "Okay, there's a group of women in nature, celebrating their bodies, touching each other, making love." But you could also say, "That's a documentary of the way we lived our lives in the 1970s."'

A DOCUMENTED HISTORY **p.162** INTIMACIES **p.165** THEATRICAL TYPES **p.181** TO BE SEEN **p.186** ON SCREEN **p.187**

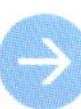

Performance Art

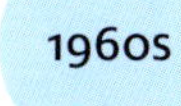

KEY ARTISTS: GINA PANE • STEPHEN VARBLE • RON ATHEY • THE COCKETTES BETSY DAMON • LAS YEGUAS DEL APOCALIPSIS

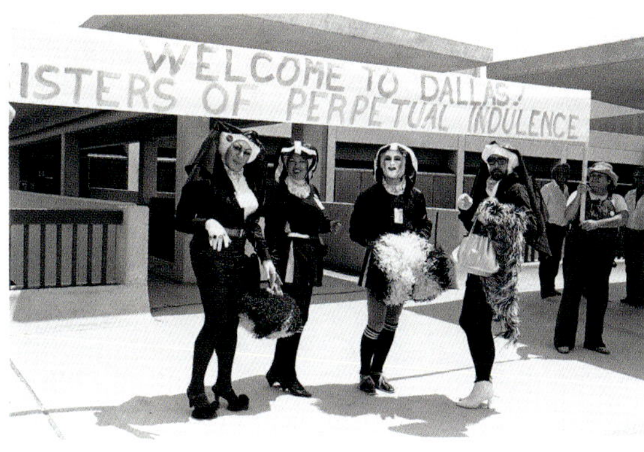

Members of The Sisters of Perpetual Indulgence at Dallas Airport, Texas, for the Republican National Convention, 1984, photograph, Associated Press

Modern performance in the visual arts thrived in Dada cabaret and Futurist public appearances (*serata*) of the 1910s. An often anarchic challenge to the confines of artworld hierarchies, the use of bodies in performances brought an invigorating 'life' and immediacy to the messages. Performance art could happen at any time in any location.

The 1970s saw increased use of the term 'performance art', encompassing work created by the artist(s) or other participants performing actions which may be scripted or spontaneous, live or recorded. For artists exploring gender and sexuality, the raw immediacy and intimate physicality of performance appealed. It could also be deployed in highly visible public interventions and as a tool of protest and dissent.

Artist and activist Miwako Itō (1951–2021) renamed herself Tāri, after Thalia, the Greek muse for comedy and bucolic poetry. She came to performance art via interests in mime, with works concerning bodily expression, femininity, sexuality and violence, expressing, 'What happens to a woman's body does not only concern her, but also the politics and society as a whole. This idea has been my backbone.' In *Jigazō (Self Portrait)* (1996), she wrapped her body with latex and blew certain areas into balloons and popped them. It was a consideration of internal and external aspects of womanhood and sexuality during which she declared herself a lesbian.

KEY DEVELOPMENTS

An indisputably queer example of performance art are the various avant-garde or 'radical drag theatre' groups such as The Cockettes, Bloolips, Blacklips Performance Cult, Hot Peaches and satiric street performance movement Sisters of Perpetual Indulgence. They blurred boundaries of the street, stage, amateurism and professionalism, while their spiritual ethos of connecting, and queer principles of creativity, were deliberately disruptive and chaotic.

PERSONAL REALIZATION **p.164** POWERFUL PROTEST **p.169** SPACE OF THE BODY **p.172** RISING CAMP **p.180** THEATRICAL TYPES **p.181**

Feminist Art

1960s

KEY ARTISTS: KATE MILLETT • HARMONY HAMMOND • ANA MENDIETA MARINA ABRAMOVIC • BETSY DAMON • MAUD SULTER

Female artists had previously produced work addressing aspects of women's experiences, but it wasn't until the 1960s that a recognized art movement, focused on supporting women and cultivating critical commentary on the conditions they faced, was formed. Feminist Art developed with 'second-wave feminism' (Women's Liberation Movement) emerging in the United States, Canada and Western Europe, fighting for women's rights.

Artists looked to challenge artworld hierarchies, often using crafts and materials traditionally dismissed as 'women's work'. The landmark essay *Why Have There Been No Great Women Artists?* (1971), by the art historian Linda Nochlin (1931–2017), interrogated factors that held back women artists, influencing ensuing art and art history.

Works by Kate Millett (1934–2017) reflect feminist themes. Her uncanny anthropomorphized assemblages offer a Surrealist-esque critique of social conformity and domestic trappings shared by couples. In *Love Seat*, two figures sit together without touching, stuck on a revolving (but decidedly un-thrilling) ride.

As different ideologies and priorities converged, schisms emerged within feminism and the art movement. New groups emerged in response to the lack of regard given to intersecting racial and sexual identities and pushed for increased inclusion across the movement. Subsequent generations have continued to address feminist concerns in new and frequently more inclusive and expansive ways.

Love Seat, Kate Millett, 1965, carved wood, milliner's form, ticking fabric, desk chairs, paint (1965) 91.4 x 121.9 x 121.9 cm (36 x 48 x 48 in), Private Collection

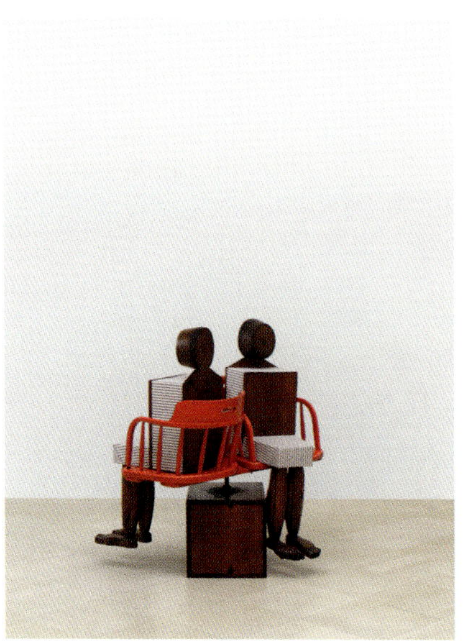

KEY DEVELOPMENTS

Millett's *Fantasy Furniture* (1965–67) preceded her influential feminist publication *Sexual Politics* (1970). Some viewed her art career as a distraction from academia and activism, but Millett believed that when sculpture 'succeeds' it makes 'its own meaning, stronger and better than words could say'. She used the book proceeds to establish the Woman's Art Colony Farm in LaGrange, New York, with her partner, photojournalist Sophie Keir.

POWERFUL PROTEST **p.169** SPACE OF THE BODY **p.172** CRAFTING THREADS **p.175**
STRAIGHT EXPECTATIONS **p.185** TO BE SEEN **p.186** OUT IN THE GALLERY **p.211**

Digital Art

1960s

KEY ARTISTS: LINDA DEMENT • SHU LEA CHEANG • RASHAAD NEWSOME JAKE ELWES • JAMIE FAYE FENTON • R E A • JACOLBY SATTERWHITE

Digital art refers to any artistic work or practice made or presented using digital technology. When the earliest computer-generated art was being produced in the 1960s (using mathematical processes), access to computers was largely restricted to universities and laboratories. As the size and cost of computers reduced, increasing numbers of artists were able to access and experiment with new technologies to transform the creation, distribution and consumption of art. Artists often encouraged reflection upon the potential social impact of the technologies they used.

Cyberflesh Girlmonster (1995) by Linda Dement (1960–) is a CD-ROM experience, which Dement described as 'a macabre comedy of monstrous femininity'. Users navigate a database of surreal 'girlmonsters' assembled from digitally manipulated scanned body parts donated by women. The fragmented and reformed bodies recall works of Hannah Höch (1889–1978). Dement declared: 'To use technologies which are really intended for a clean, slick commercial boy's world, to make personal, bodily, feminine work and to re-insert this work into mainstream culture, into art discourse and into society, is a political act.'

Digital tools and media now form such a pervasive part of life that an array of artwork is created without considered recognition of it being 'digital art' and the now seemingly infinite canopy of 'digital art' is not wholly considered an art movement in itself.

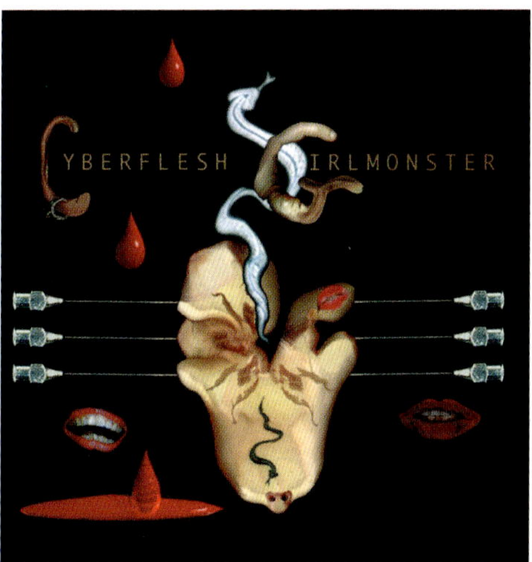

KEY DEVELOPMENTS

Cyber Feminism, a movement focused on restructuring power dynamics in the creation of digital media, emerged in the early 1990s. It was preceded by *A Cyborg Manifesto* (1983) by feminist theorist Donna Haraway (1944–), which imagined the future of feminism and proposed that, as part-human and part-machine, the cyborg challenged gendered and racial prejudices and therefore was 'the self feminists must code'.

Cyberflesh Girlmonster, Linda Dement, CD-ROM, 1995

GLIMPSES OF UTOPIA **p.163** QUEER CODING **p.168** ASSEMBLING **p.171** SPACE OF THE BODY **p.172** LIFE ONLINE **p.213**

Conceptual Art

1960s

KEY ARTISTS: FELIX GONZALEZ-TORRES • YEVGENIY FIKS • ORLAN • JENNY HOLZER

Conceptual Art prioritizes the thought or idea behind an artwork, over its aesthetics or craftsmanship. Its development gained traction in 1960s Europe and America, and it soon became an international movement incorporating various styles and methods, including performance, installation and readymades.

In rejecting traditional elements used to assess the value of art, Conceptual Art challenges the idea that art is a physical, marketable commodity. Influenced by Dada and the reduced simplicity of Minimalism, some artists minimized the physical presence of their works to emphasize their concept. There is often a reliance on the viewer to mentally or physically construct or complete the artwork, meaning that, like their predecessors, these works pushed boundaries of public acceptance.

Conceptual Art is often accused of being cold, theoretical and intellectually elitist. However, the intention, tone and points of reference vary – the use of metaphors and substitutions could enable works to address LGBTQ+ subjects and experiences that may otherwise be visually censured.

Expanded forms of Conceptual Art have developed through later generations of artists. Several adopted its (seemingly detached) techniques in attempts to comprehend the inconceivable impact of AIDS – to powerful effect. Felix Gonzalez-Torres (1957–1996) used mundane, everyday materials with poetic simplicity, wanting viewers to be 'intellectually challenged, moved and informed'. Anna Campbell (1979–) is among many queer artists who have noted his enduring influence.

KEY DEVELOPMENTS

Gonzalez-Torres' intended for his works to remain open to new interpretations and responses; however, some titles evoke specific emotive subjects. His famed *"Untitled" (Portrait of Ross in L.A.)* (1991) is a pile of wrapped candy weighing approx. 175 lb – the weight of his partner Ross before contracting HIV. Viewers can take candies, but this 'illicit' pleasure makes them complicit in the process of loss.

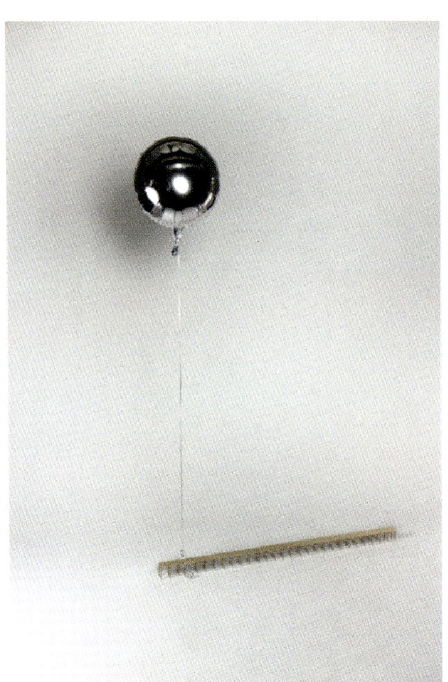

Vanishing Point, Anna Campbell, 2014, balsa wood, mylar helium balloon, ribbon, nylon hardware, 244 x 91 x 5 cm (96 x 36 x 2 in), artist's collection

QUEER CODING **p.168** ASSEMBLING **p.171** SPACE OF THE BODY **p.172** QUEER EYE **p.182** FACING AIDS **p.208**

Postmodernism

1960s

KEY ARTISTS: KLAUS NOMI • CINDY SHERMAN • BARBARA KRUGER CLAES OLDENBURG

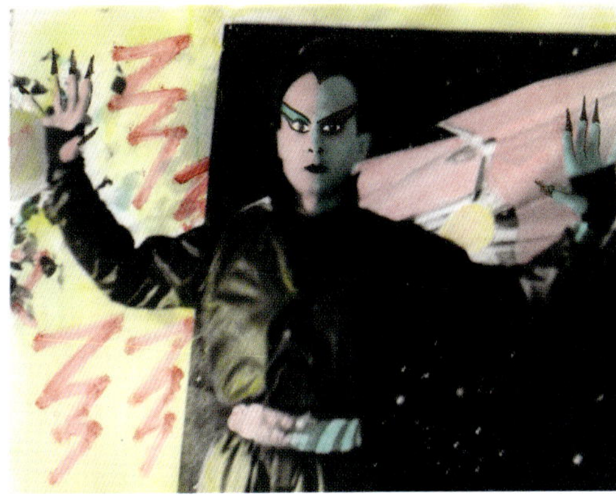

"Untitled" Klaus Nomi, Kenny Scharf, 1980, hand-coloured silver gelatin print, 21.59 x 27.94 cm (8½ x 11 in)

KEY DEVELOPMENTS

The term 'postmodern' was possibly first used in 1870 by artist John Watkins Chapman (1832–1903) when describing a departure from French Impressionism as 'a Postmodern style of painting'. Its twentieth century use was influenced by its introduction to philosophical vocabulary in *The Postmodern Condition* (1979) by Jean-François Lyotard (1924–1998) who gave a simplified definition of 'incredulity towards metanarratives'.

Postmodernism is wilfully elusive to define because it does not align with a particular style, theory or approach and incorporates numerous other movements. However, there is a somewhat shared stance of reaction against Modernism's idealism and reasoned visions for progress. Postmodernism countered Modernism's clarity of vision with contradiction and scepticism, questioning orthodoxies to a greater extreme.

Postmodern outlooks and artworks started to materialize following the Second World War but gained dominance in the 1980s. Interested in challenging and destabilizing distinctions between popular and high culture, it is influenced by Dada, Pop and Conceptual Art. Works are often irreverent or satirical, blending the theoretical and theatrical. With acute awareness of style and self-regard, artists could combine subversive statements with commercial appeal. Works often knowingly possess a cool archness or irony that can appear aloof or insincere.

Klaus Nomi, the persona of queer counter-tenor Klaus Sperber (1944–1983), criss-crossed the worlds of performance, music and fashion in 1970s and 1980s New York. He is captured here by 'pop-surrealist' Kenny Scharf (1958–), alongside Scharf's painting *KomicKaddy* '79. Nomi's other-worldly appearance – part elfin, kabuki, robot, alien – reflected alienation from mainstream society but also a freedom to build one's own identity. With a repertoire ranging from contemporary synth-pop to baroque opera, his confection of references provoked fascination and apprehension.

QUEER CODING **p.168** ASSEMBLING **p.171** RISING CAMP **p.180** QUEER EYE **p.182** COMMERCIAL ALLURE **p.200**

Afrofuturism

1970s

KEY ARTISTS: SUN-RA • JEAN-MICHEL BASQUIAT • NICK CAVE
LYLE ASHTON HARRIS • LAUREN HALSEY

Exploring intersections of African diaspora culture with science and technology, Afrofuturism draws on material from the past to reimagine histories of racism, empire and slavery and create alternative futures. Jazz musician Sun Ra's *Space Is the Place* (1973) is widely considered the definitive Afrofuturism album and its title became a mantra for many creatives. Afrofuturism's challenge to dominant ideas and cultural restrictions makes it an appealing space to explore Black queer identity and gender expression.

The striking portrait by Mark Amerika (1960–) of gay disco icon Sylvester (1947–1988) depicts him in a statuesque, yet languorous pose, with eye decoration and earpiece suggesting both historic Egyptian designs and cyborg components. This melding of Afrofuturist aesthetics and allusions to androgyny with polished poise can also be seen in the work of Grace Jones (1948–). Sylvester was part of avant-garde drag troupe The Cockettes but gained fame as a solo performer with a distinctive falsetto and presentation that challenged gender expectations. His single 'You Make Me Feel (Mighty Real)' (1978) is considered 'the cornerstone of gay disco'.

Artists including Lyle Ashton Harris (1965–), Amaryllis DeJesus Moleski (1985–) and Juliana Huxtable (1987–) continue to be inspired by Afrofuturistic ideas and aesthetics. For their visual album *Dirty Computer* (2018) Janelle Monáe (1985–) adopted the character Jane 57821 – a pansexual, polyamorous, Black femme android – to navigate the album's world.

KEY DEVELOPMENTS

Cultural critic Mark Dery introduced 'Afrofuturism' in his essay 'Black to the Future' in *Flame Wars: The Discourse of Cyberculture* (1994). Citing feminist science-fiction writer Octavia Butler (1947–2006) as an example, he described it as 'speculative fiction that treats African-American themes and addresses African-American concerns in the context of twentieth-century techno-culture, and, more generally, African-American significa-tion that appropriates images of technology and a prosthetically enhanced future'.

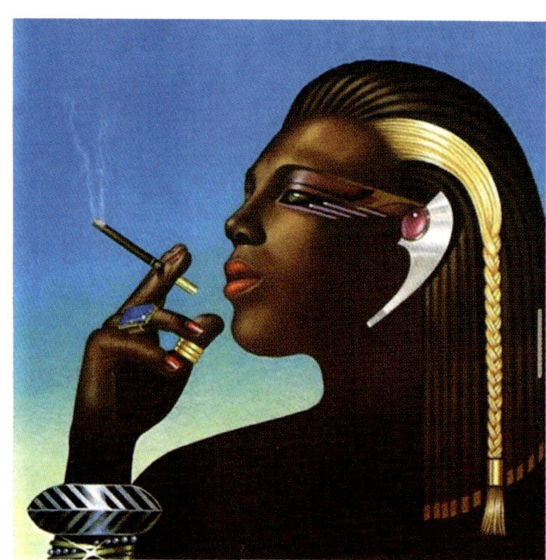

Cover artwork for Sylvester's 'Do Ya Wanna Funk', Mark Amerika, 1982

GLIMPSES OF UTOPIA **p.163** ASSEMBLING **p.171** *FIRE!!* MAGAZINE **p.203**

Postminimalism

1970s

KEY ARTISTS: SCOTT BURTON • FELIX GONZALEZ-TORRES • ZILIA SÁNCHEZ TONY FEHER • JIM HODGES • RONI HORN

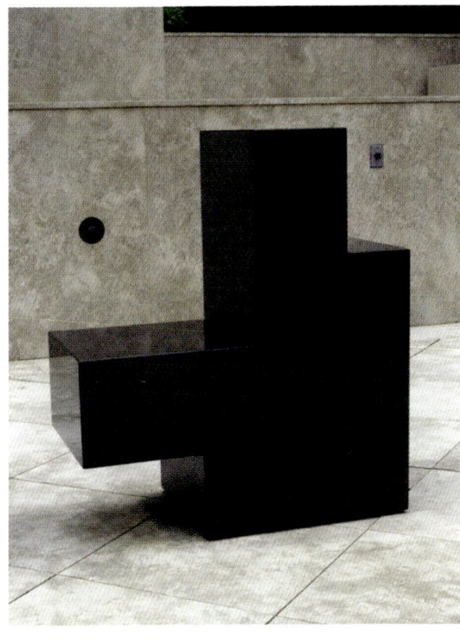

Two-Part Chair, Scott Burton, 1986 Lake Superior Green granite, 101.6 x 58.4 x 91.4 cm (40 x 23 x 36 in), installation view, Art Institute of Chicago, USA

KEY DEVELOPMENTS

Two-Part Chair (1986) by Scott Burton (1939–1989) embeds queer experiences within functional seating. Simultaneously bold and discrete, abstract and functional, minimal and figurative – the components allude to both anal sex and mutual support. Burton aimed to expand acceptance of difference and the unfamiliar – if viewers could become more open to what constitutes a chair, they could become more accepting of different people.

Postminimalism followed the Minimalism movement that first flourished in 1960s and 1970s America and was characterized by extremely restrained abstraction and a rejection of symbolism, emotion, subjectivity and signs of authorship.

Embracing various styles and interests, Postminimal artists employed aspects of Minimalism that appealed without adhering to its 'rules'. They crossed Minimalism's 'What you see is what you see' concept, creating works with additional purpose and intent. Artists varyingly introduced emotional expression to Minimalism's restrained, cold detachment, adding figurative elements to anonymous forms and looking beyond industrial materials.

Some artists explored the queer potential of Minimalism's formal tactics to expand thinking about gender and sexuality without explicitly depicting LGBTQ+ lives. Millie Wilson (1948–) viewed Minimalism as a target of irreverent subversion, describing its seeming 'blankness' as 'a convenient site of projection'. Artists including Jonah Groeneboer (1978–) and Math Bass (1981–) continue to craft forms of queer expression drawing on Minimalism in combination with other influences.

Historian and Curator David J. Getsy (1973-) highlighted increasing developments of trans and queer artists appropriating Minimalism and abstraction 'as resources for envisioning new ways to inhabit the body or to give an account of the self. [...] visualizing transformation and successive states in a way no figurative representation could'.

QUEER CODING **p.168** ASSEMBLING **p.171** SPACE OF THE BODY **p.172**

Street Art

1970s

KEY ARTISTS: KEITH HARING • DAVID WOJNAROWICZ • JEAN-MICHEL BASQUIAT
GUERILLA GIRLS • JILL POSENER • DYKE ACTION MACHINE! (DAM!)

KEY DEVELOPMENTS
Keith Haring (1958–1990) emerged from the 1980s New York graffiti subculture, creating chalk drawings in the streets and the subway, which he considered his 'laboratory'. He developed work across a range of contexts and was commissioned to produce many murals and public artworks. His designs possessed a kinetic energy and often featured his distinctive illuminated figures and sociopolitical messages around homosexuality and AIDS.

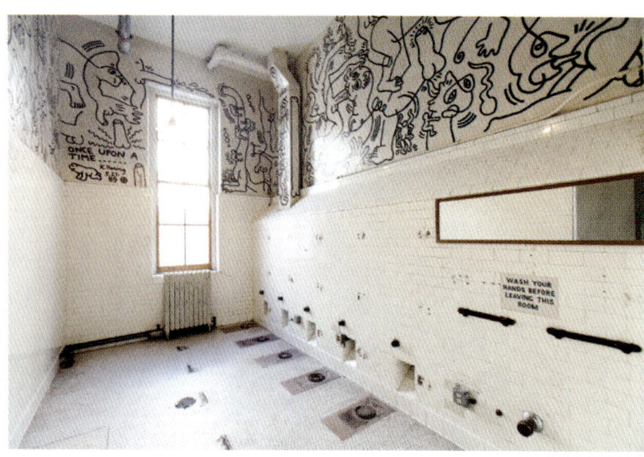

Once Upon A Time, Keith Haring, 1989, painted mural at The NYC LGBT Community Center, New York, USA (see Works p.124)

Street art encompasses a range of interventions in public spaces, including commissioned murals and unauthorized graffiti. 'Graffiti' comes from the Greek *graphein* (to scratch, draw or write). Contemporary styles are generally recognized as rising from 1970s New York City's Black and Latino neighbourhood street subcultures. Although associated with aerosol paint cans, it can be created using a range of methods including: fly-posting (aka wheat-pasting), stencilling, stickering, mosaicing, direct-drawing, cleaning (aka reverse-graffiti), lighting and projection.

Artists' motivations vary, with some focused on achieving notoriety and others on making sociopolitical statements. Graffiti has often been viewed as evidence of a lack of authoritarian order. However, artists counter that it is a proportionate response to the visual pollution of advertisers permitted in public places.

Due to its predominant illegality, artists usually keep anonymity, though a number have worked in both street and gallery spaces. This element has obvious appeal for queer artists for whom such urban spaces often mean risks or invisibility. Their work often challenges both a predominantly homophobic society and the street art scene itself.

Jill Posener (1953–) published two photography books recording political graffiti, *Spray It Loud* (1982) and *Louder than Words* (1986), which include lesbian graffiti interventions on commercial advertising. They align with her call for increased public lesbian visibility and confrontational representation: 'If we don't take public spaces, nobody will hear us.'

POWERFUL PROTEST **p.169** PUBLIC PRESENCE **p.197** INSTITUTIONAL CRITIQUE **p.212** →

Internet Art

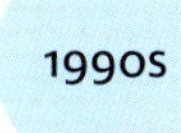

KEY ARTISTS: SHU LEA CHEANG • JAKE ELWES • RASHAAD NEWSOME JACOLBY SATTERWHITE

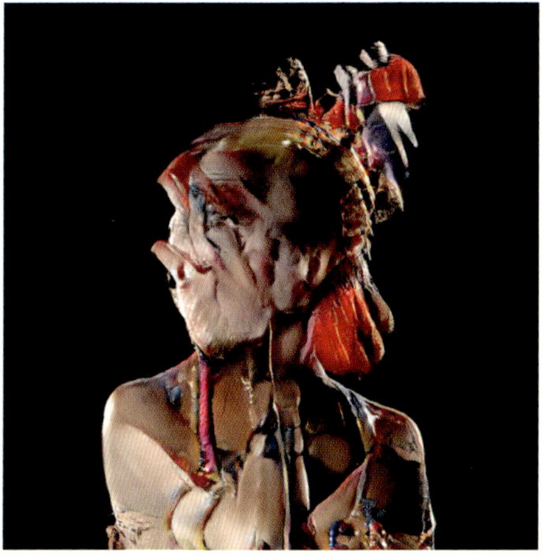

Still from *Zizi in Motion: A Deepfake Drag Utopia (Movement by Wet Mess)*, Jake Elwes, 2023

KEY DEVELOPMENTS
Elwes' *Zizi Project* explores intersections of Artificial Intelligence (A.I.) and drag performance, notably the biases computer systems have in responding to trans, non-binary and queer identities. *The Zizi Show* (2020) is a deepfake drag cabaret, experienced through a virtual, interactive online stage. Deepfake technology was used to create synthesized performers using datasets of films of a variety of drag artists.

The arrival of the World Wide Web in 1991 introduced the ability for users to connect with others through global digital networks. Online communities soon formed to discuss and exchange information and resources. Hackers and gamers quickly explored creative use of networked technology to make interventions and creations and artists started making works on and for the internet. A new online (art) world of possibilities opened.

The internet also introduced challenges for established artworld institutions and systems. Artworks incorporating online elements presented difficult questions around physical display and 'keeping them alive' as technology became obsolete. Artists were increasingly able to self-represent online, becoming less reliant on institutions for representation.

As with Digital Art, early adopters shared discernible traits, but rapid evolution of internet technology has spawned an array of artwork that sprawls beyond designation as a specific movement. Work addressing queer themes in the internet era, sometimes termed 'cyber-queer', have proliferated. Experiments in self-fashioning remains a recurring interest. However, feminist artist Faith Wilding (1943–) warned 'The Net is not a utopia of nongender.' In *The Digital Closet: How the Internet Became Straight* (2023) Alexander Monea (1986–) notes: 'Prejudices infect the training data, code, and coders behind automated content.' Heteronormative biases within technologies that enable, mediate and control online experiences have become the focus of artworks including *Zizi Project* (2019–) by Jake Elwes (1993–).

GLIMPSES OF UTOPIA **p.163** QUEER CODING **p.168** ASSEMBLING **p.171** SPACE OF THE BODY **p.172** LIFE ONLINE **p.213**

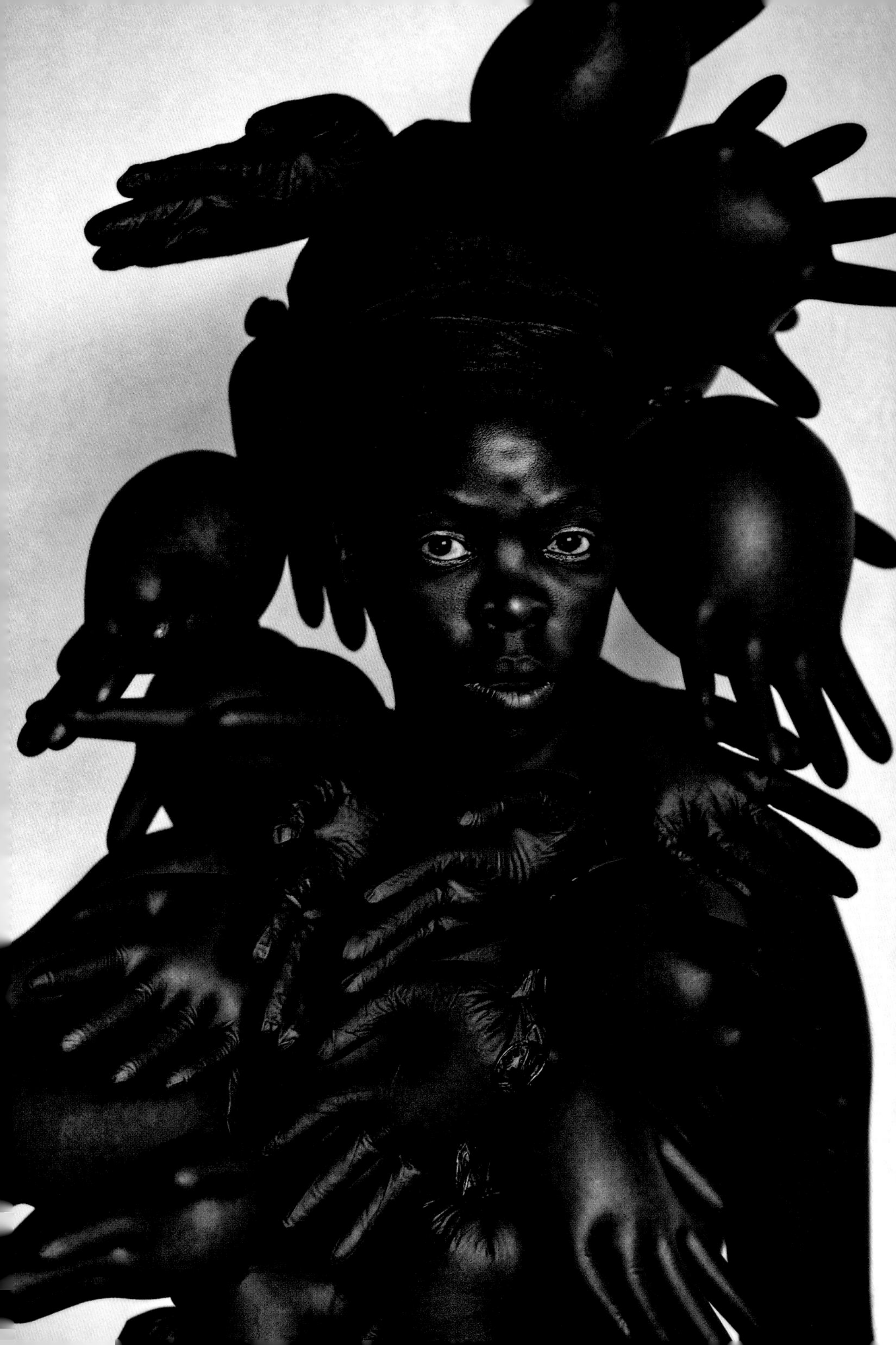

The Works

DAVID MICHELANGELO BUONARROTI 40 • **A PUNCH PARTY** THOMAS PATCH 42 • **BACCHUS** SIMEON SOLOMON 46 • **POLYCHROME BOWL** WE'WHA 48 • **THE PEACOCK SKIRT** AUBREY BEARDSLEY 50 • **PEGASUS DRINKING FROM THE FOUNTAIN OF THE HIPPOCRENE** CHARLES DE SOUSY RICKETTS 52 • **LA VIE PENSIVE (PENSIVE LIFE)** LOUISE CATHERINE BRESLAU 56 **LOGE DE THÉÂTRE** ERTÉ 58 • **HANDSOME DRINKS** MARSDEN HARTLEY 60 • **DA-DANDY** HANNAH HÖCH 62 • **ASBURY PARK SOUTH** FLORINE STETTHEIMER 64 • **LES AMAZONES** MARIE LAURENCIN 68 • **SEMI-NUDE IN FRONT OF PRICKLY PEAR CACTUS** ANITA RÉE 70 **LA BAGUE SYMBOLIQUE** GEORGE BARBIER 72 • **THE CRITICS** HENRY SCOTT TUKE 74 • **I.O.U. (SELF-PRIDE)** CLAUDE CAHUN 76 • **STEPHEN TENNANT IN COSTUME AS PRINCE CHARMING** CECIL BEATON 78 • **A SUMMER DAY** GERDA WEGENER 80 • **AUTOPORTRAIT (TAMARA IN A GREEN BUGATTI)** TAMARA DE LEMPICKA 84 • **THE FLEET'S IN!** PAUL CADMUS 86 • **FERAL BENGA** JAMES RICHMOND BARTHÉ 90 • **DANCING FIGURES** RICHARD BRUCE NUGENT 92 **MEDALLION (YOUWE)** GLUCK 94 • **OBJET (LE DÉJEUNER EN FOURRURE)** MÉRET OPPENHEIM 96 • **SELF PORTRAIT WITH CROPPED HAIR** FRIDA KAHLO 98 • **UNTITLED** TOM OF FINLAND (TOUKO LAAKSONEN) 100 • **LADIES AND GENTLEMEN (MARSHA P. JOHNSON)** ANDY WARHOL 102 • **CUNT COLORING BOOK** TEE A. CORINNE 104 • **RANCHODBHAI RELAXING IN THE WINTER** BHUPEN KHAKHAR 108 • **HUNKERTIME** HARMONY HAMMOND 110 • **THE WRESTLERS AFTER MUYBRIDGE** FRANCIS BACON 114 • **FREEDOM AND CHANGE** LUBAINA HIMID 116 **JAMA MASJID** SUNIL GUPTA 120 • **EVERY MOMENT COUNTS (ECSTATIC ANTIBODIES)** ROTIMI FANI-KAYODE 122 • **ONCE UPON A TIME** KEITH HARING 124 • **UNTITLED, FROM DREAM GIRLS** DEBORAH BRIGHT 126 • **NOTES ON THE MARGIN OF THE BLACK BOOK** GLENN LIGON 128 **GATE 门** XIYADIE 132 • **BLUE** DEREK JARMAN 134 • **MEMORIAL TO A MARRIAGE** PATRICIA CRONIN 136 • **PASSING / POSING, FROM CORONATION OF THE VIRGIN** KEHINDE WILEY 138 **BECOMING AN IMAGE** CASSILS 140 • **NIGHT OF THE LONG KNIVES I** ATHI-PATRA RUGA 142 **VANISHING POINT** ANNA CAMPBELL 144 • **QUSUQUZAH LOUNGING WITH PINK + BLACK FLOWER** MICKALENE THOMAS 146 • **PHILA I, PARKTOWN** ZANELE MUHOLI 150 • **RESURGENCE OF THE PEOPLE** KENT MONKMAN 152 • **THE LATECOMER** SALMAN TOOR 156 • **SOUS LE CIEL DE SHIRAZ (PAYKANARTCAR)** ALIREZA SHOJAIAN 158

David

1501 – 1504

MICHELANGELO BUONARROTI: MARBLE • 517 CM (203½ IN) • ACCADEMIA GALLERY OF FLORENCE (GALLERIA DELL'ACCADEMIA DI FIRENZE), TUSCANY, ITALY

OTHER KEY WORKS

Bacchus (Bacco), 1496–97, Museo Nazionale del Bargello, Florence, Tuscany, Italy

Sistine Chapel Ceiling (Soffitto della Cappella Sistina), c.1508–12, Vatican Museums, Vatican City

Dying Prigione, 1513–14, Louvre Museum, Paris, France

The proliferation of homoerotic subjects and heroic nudes during the Renaissance have become some of the most recognizable works of art, not least *David* by Michelangelo (1475–1564). In the Hebrew Bible, David's relationship with Jonathan has also been interpreted as a love story.

This colossal statue was the first of its kind since classical antiquity. Envisaged as one of 12 prophets to line Florence's famed Duomo's roofline, *David* was instead unveiled in a prominent public square in 1504. In contrast to the delicate *David* (1416) by Donatello (c.1386–1466), Michelangelo's is difficult to envisage as an underdog in battle. His majesty has towered over figurative depictions of the male body ever since.

While homosexuality remained scandalous and stifled during the Renaissance, it nevertheless represents a sort of gay golden age. Later scholars uncovered evidence of Michelangelo's family archives altering pronouns in many of his love poems. John Addington Symonds (1840–1893) published new translations reasserting masculine pairings and in his 1878 biography noted: 'it is certain his principal attention was devoted to the male figure, and that he allowed masculine attributes to dominate his ideal of the female'.

David was later adopted by gay men as a signifier of sexuality in the home. A statuette on the sideboard or a print displaying his physical prowess on the wall was a 'pink flag', strengthening ties to Greco-Roman ideals of the male nude into the modern age.

MICHELANGELO BUONARROTI

One of the most influential, creative polymaths in the entire history of art, Michelangelo had a career spanning seven decades as a sculptor, painter and architect. He was apprenticed aged eight to Domenico Ghirlandaio (1449–1494), and by his early twenties was considered a virtuoso – his fame rapidly spread. The beauty of musculature was a source of endless inspiration and vitality in his work.

RENAISSANCE **p.12**

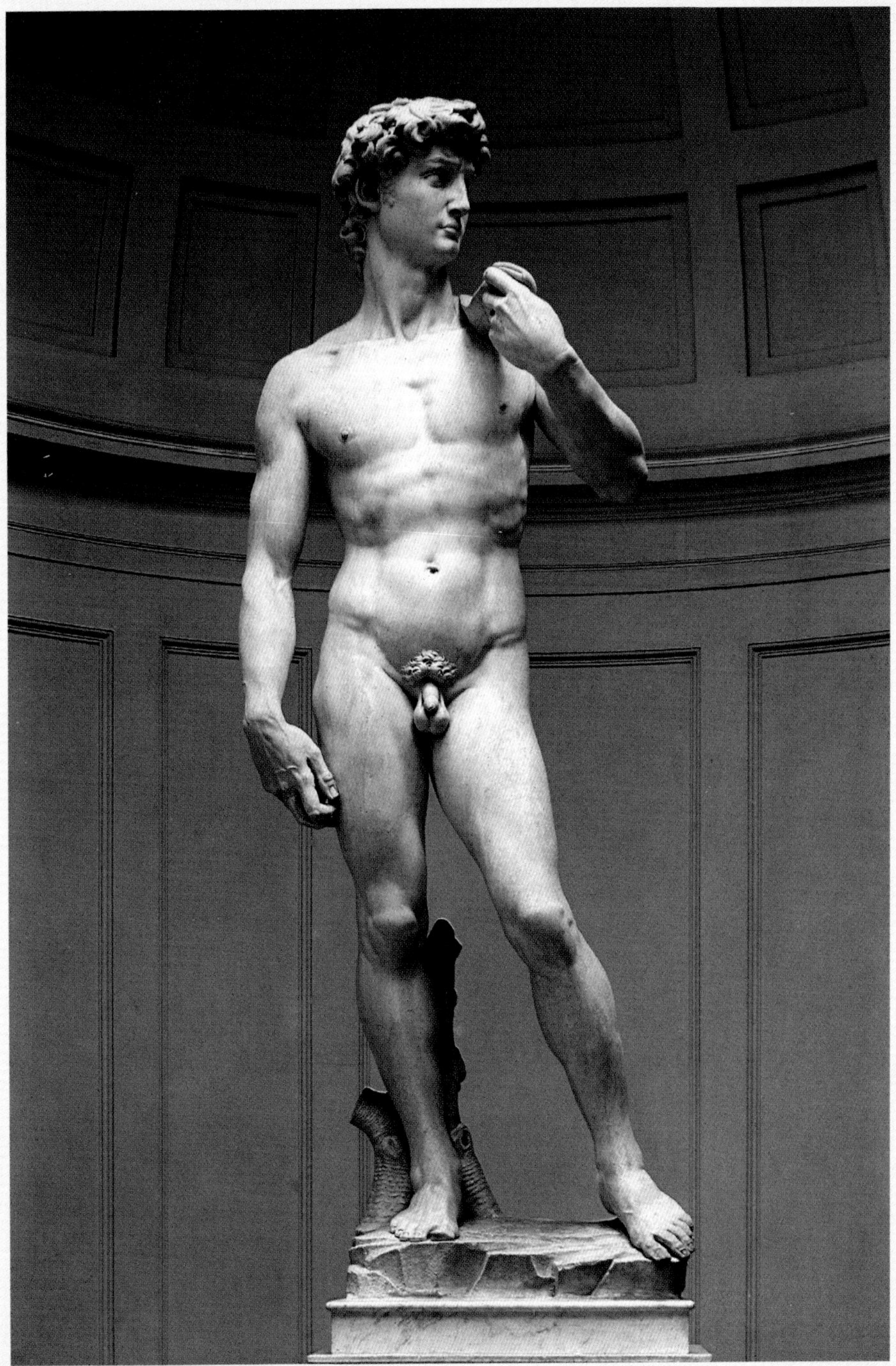

DESIRE FOR ANTIQUITY p.194

A Punch Party

THOMAS PATCH: OIL ON CANVAS • 114.3 X 171.5 CM (45 X 68 IN)

OTHER KEY WORKS

A Gathering of the Dilettanti around the Medici Venus, c.1760

British gentlemen at Sir Horace Mann's home in Florence, c.1763–65, Yale Center for British Art, Paul Mellon Collection, USA

Self-portrait as Bull, etching, late 1760s, National Portrait Gallery, London, UK

The Grand Tour was a way for men of means (and occasionally women) to immerse themselves in the art and antiquity of continental Europe. It opened access to more louche (and loose) worlds of gambling and sex, making hedonistic reasons for the voyage so commonplace they led to the creation of satirical prints, the 'macaroni' being particularly popular.

This painting depicts a lascivious gathering at Charles Hadfield's inn, Florence, a favoured haunt of English travellers. It is believed to have been commissioned by Lord Grey, later the 5th Earl of Stamford (on the far right), when he completed his Grand Tour. Patch brushes away the veneer of polite connoisseurship, instead revealing avarice and indulgence. A number appear to be succumbing to the effects of punch, while Hadfield holds the punchbowl aloft but appears to be also inspecting its base to confirm its worth. Paintings of Bacchus and bawdy Silenus hang alongside a replica of the Uffizi's *Dancing Faun*. Patch included himself in the bust of a faun – a roguish figure of Greek mythology synonymous with wine, music and mischief. It potentially includes additional un-decoded in-jokes alluding to sodomy.

Detail: *Dancing Faun* – originating from the Greek mythological figure Pan, fauns and satyrs were a recurrent motif in Antiquity and continue to capture queer imaginations in subsequent centuries. In Roman mythology, they were traditionally seen as drunken, eccentric companions of Bacchus, the god of wine.

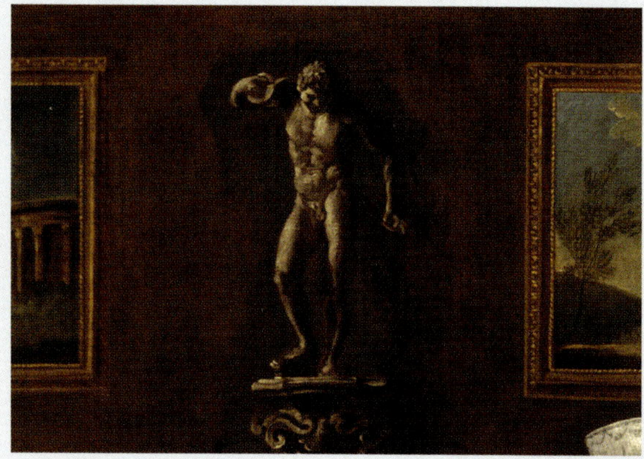

NEOCLASSICISM **p.15**

After being accused of homosexual indiscretions, Patch was banished from Rome in 1755, settling in Florence. His caricature conversation pieces were in consistent demand for their ribald humour, regardless of comments including painter William Patoun's *Advice on Travel* (c.1766), cautioning that 'A Certain Mr Patch at Florence is a _____'.

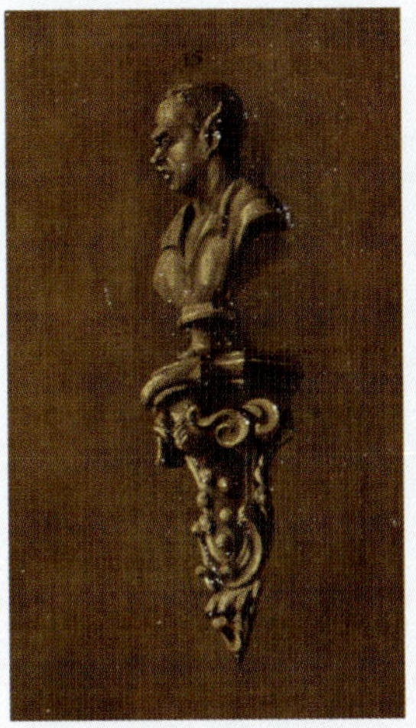

Detail: Patch depicts himself as the bust of a faun, implicating himself as encouraging the scene. Fauns were often depicted dancing but also shown suffering consequences of their excessive lifestyle, making it a fitting form for Patch in Florence.

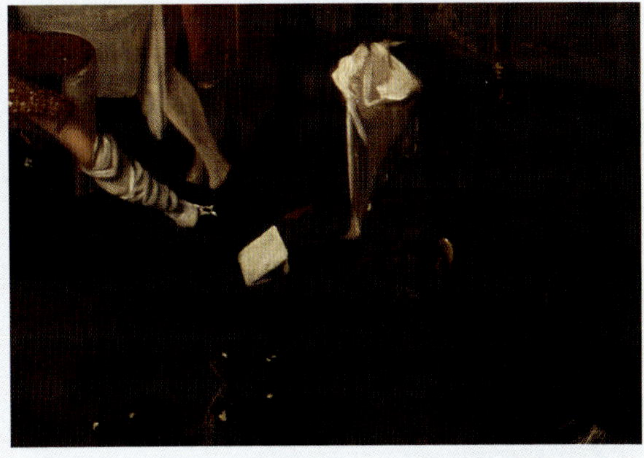

Detail: Stockings were symbolically loaded with sexual suggestion. This fallen one could suggest sexual excess or undoing, or perhaps a comment on Britain's 'masculine health'.

THOMAS PATCH

Patch left England for Rome in 1747 and forged a career as an art dealer, painter and engraver. He garnered a reputation for painting views before becoming famous for caricatures of British Grand Tourists. Patch was also renowned for his sexual predilections. He appears in *The Tribuna of the Uffizi* (1772–1778) by Johan Zoffany (1733–1810), ostensibly admiring Titian's *Venus of Urbino* but pointing to *The Wrestlers*, a statue of muscly entangled men.

PRESENTING THE ARTIST **p.167** RISING CAMP **p.180** DESIRE FOR ANTIQUITY **p.194**

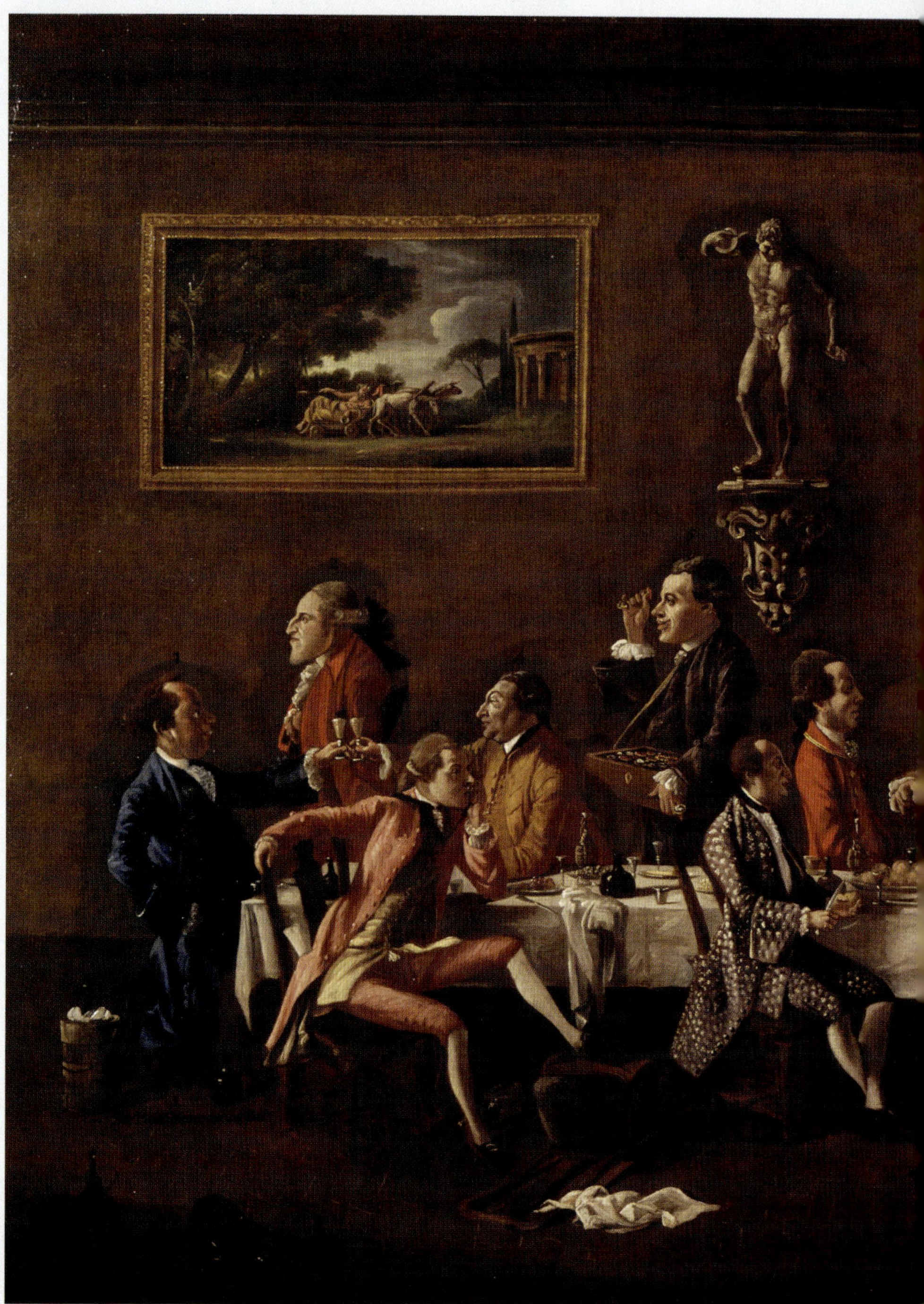

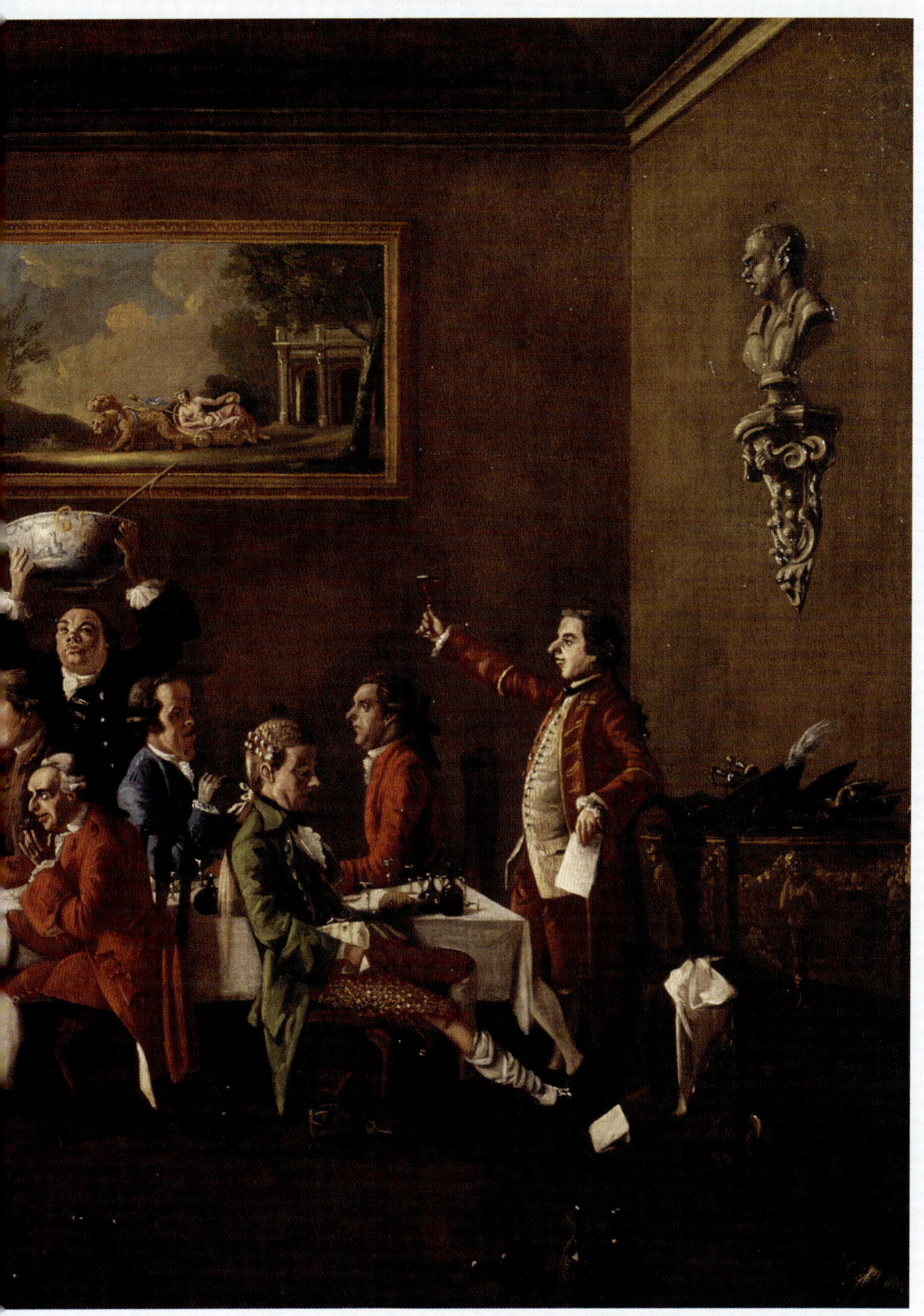

Bacchus

SIMEON SOLOMON: WATERCOLOUR AND GOUACHE ON PAPER • 50 X 37 CM (19⅔ X 14½ IN) • PRIVATE COLLECTION

OTHER KEY WORKS

Babylon Hath Been a Golden Cup, 1859, Birmingham Museums Trust, UK

Sappho and Erinna in a Garden at Mytilene, 1864, Tate, UK

The Bride, Bridegroom and Sad Love, 1865, Victoria and Albert Museum, London, UK

Bacchus, is also known as Dionysus, the Greek god of wine, festivity and fertility. His sexual availability is often tinged with ambiguity making his appeal highly fluid. In the hands of Simeon Solomon (1840–1905), the young god's sensuousness is unleashed, with curling lip, shapely muscles and diaphanous drapery suggesting a generous member. Poet Algernon Charles Swinburne (1837–1909) likened Solomon and Bacchus to one another, having 'the stamp of sorrow; of perplexities unsolved and desires unsatisfied'.

Solomon and Swinburne were once close, with Solomon illustrating Swinburne's erotic novel *Lesbia Brandon*, written in the 1860s but unpublished until the 1950s. With his deeply androgynous figures and stories of same-sex love from the ancient world, Solomon's paintings seemed infused with innate queerness throughout his career. This did not go unnoticed in the Victorian age. An 1870 *Illustrated London News* article declared his work as finely imaginative and a 'triumph', while at the same time mocking his 'effeminate inanity'.

Collectors of originals included Oscar Wilde (1854–1900), and John Addington Symonds (1840–1893) purchased twenty-one photographs of Solomon's drawings in 1868. His works were widely reproduced photographically by Frederick Hollyer (1838–1933), who also included portraits of the artist in his long-spanning series *Portraits of many persons of note*. Tellingly, these included him as a young man in the 1860s and post-scandal in the 1890s, making the extent of his ostracization in later life less clear-cut.

SIMEON SOLOMON

Solomon was born in London, the son of a successful businessman. As a teenager at the Royal Academy Schools, he was swept up by the heady Pre-Raphaelite circles of Dante Gabriel Rossetti (1828–1882), exhibiting regularly until 1873 when he was twice arrested for sex with men in public toilets. Although he later returned to exhibiting, his career had suffered greatly and he died in St. Giles' Workhouse.

PRE-RAPHAELITES **p.17**

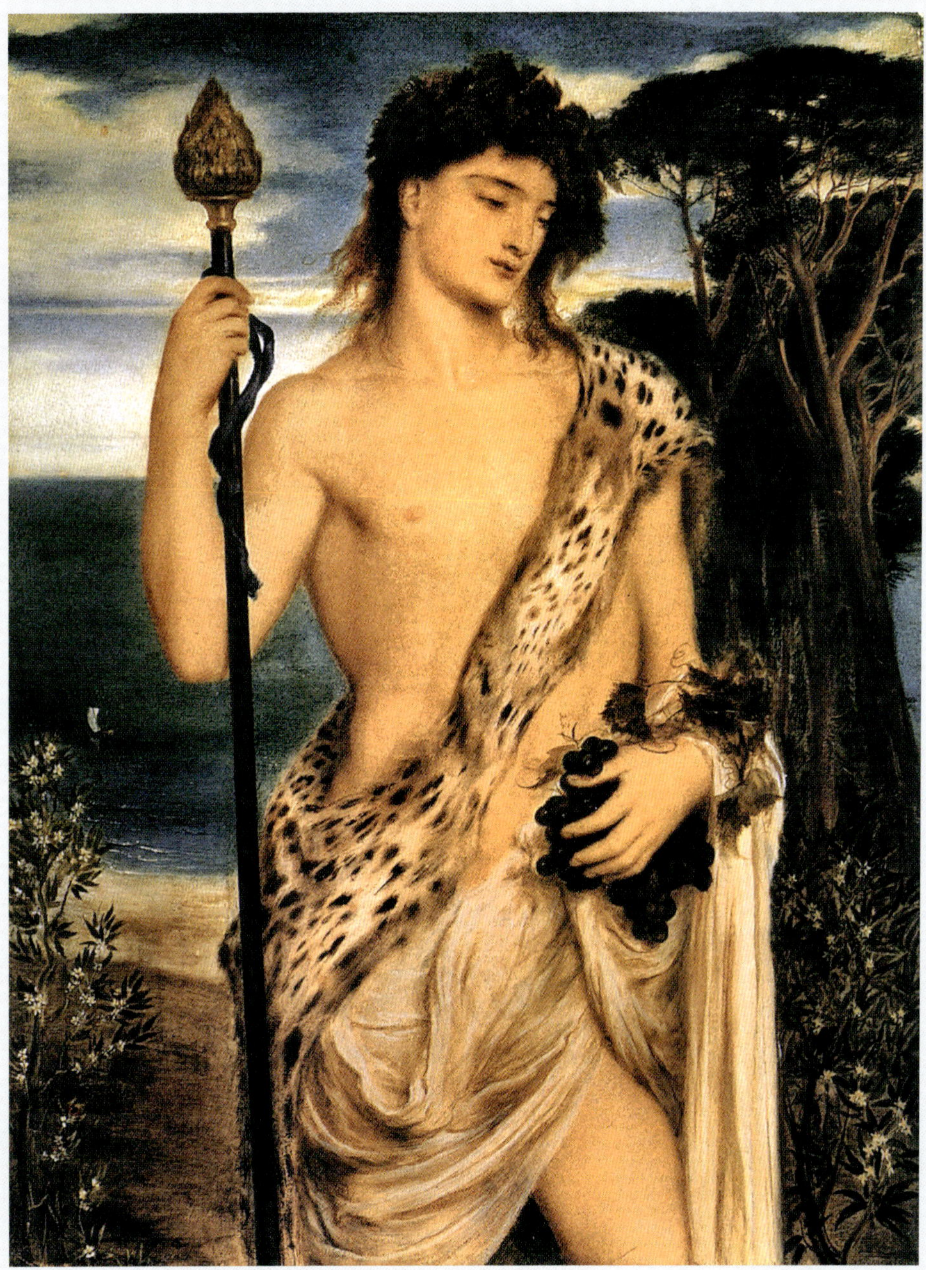

QUEER EYE **p.182** DESIRE FOR ANTIQUITY **p.194**

Polychrome Bowl

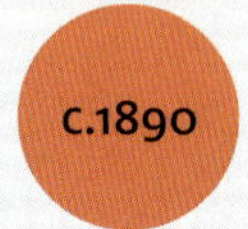

(PROBABLY) WE'WHA: CERAMIC AND PIGMENT • 16.5 X 42 CM (6½ X 16½ IN)
ART INSTITUTE OF CHICAGO, USA

OTHER KEY WORKS

Terraced Bowl, c.1880–84, Smithsonian National Museum of Natural History, Washington D.C., USA

Dough Bowl, c.1880, Private Collection

Earthen Pitcher, 1884, Smithsonian National Museum of Natural History, Washington D.C., USA

At a time when settlers continued aggressive expansion across the United States, suppressing and erasing Indigenous cultures, We'wha (1849–1896) broached and bridged traditional Zuni culture with the rapidly shifting outside world.

Recognized in their own community for skills in weaving and pottery, We'wha created work that garnered admiration from others who shared appreciation for their exuberant and confident decorative hand. We'wha was among the first Zuni to sell their textiles and pottery, helping elevate awareness of Indigenous arts. Collector George Wharton James (1858–1923) noted that We'wha's 'pottery fetched twice the price of that of any other maker' and their weaving demonstrated 'a delicate perception of colour-values that delighted the eye of the connoisseur'.

We'wha was *lhamana* – a male-bodied person who takes on social and ceremonial roles usually performed by women and serves as a mediator within the community. Zuni were among many Native North American tribes who recognized existence of what today would be termed 'two-spirit' people, who were often granted special status.

As wider awareness of Indigenous genders grows, We'wha has increasingly been recognized as a figure of connection for two-spirit and LGBTQ+ individuals. They have been celebrated by artists including non-binary Native American Demian DinéYazhi' (1983–) and Franciscan friar and religious icon painter Robert Lentz (1946–) who depicted them putting on the sacred mask of 'third-gender' spirit Kolhamana.

WE'WHA

Respected for their creative skills and insights, Whe'wha educated anthropologists and wider audiences about Zuni culture, advocating for this community's interests and concerns. They were part of the 1886 Zuni delegation to Washington, D.C. and assisted the Smithsonian National Museum with research, donating objects to the collections. The modern-day Two-Spirit movement has recognized them as an inspirational trailblazer as they endeavour to restore cultural knowledge, pride and resilience.

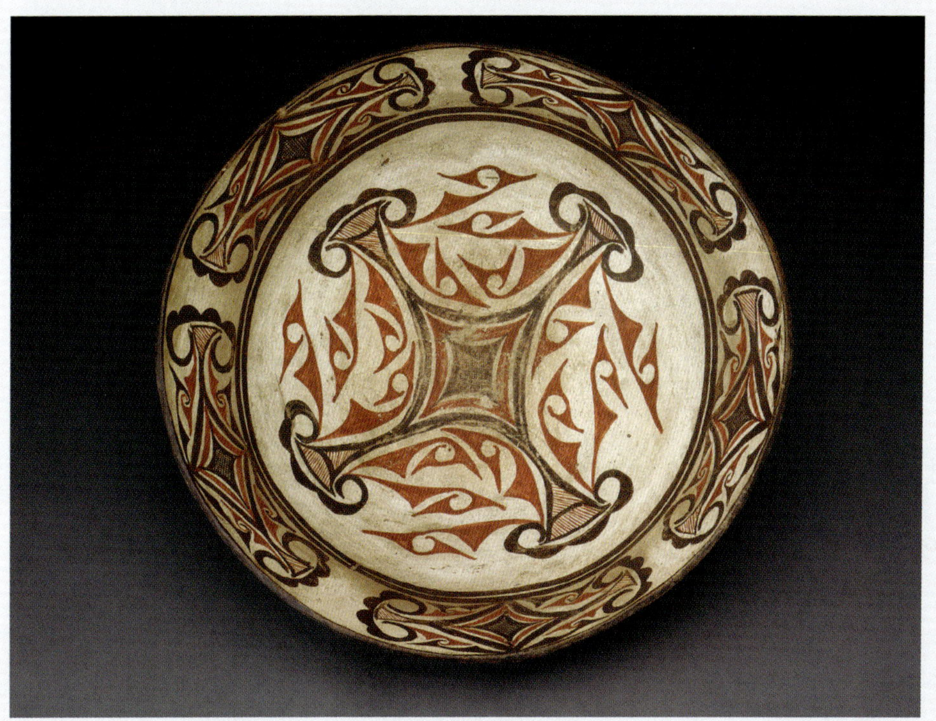

A DOCUMENTED HISTORY **p.162** QUEER ICONS **p.184** INDIGENOUS QUEER LOVE **p.215**

The Peacock Skirt

1893

AUBREY BEARDSLEY: INK DRAWING ON PAPER • 23 X 16.8 CM (9 X 6½ IN)
PRIVATE COLLECTION

OTHER KEY WORKS

Le Morte d'Arthur, 1893, Victoria and Albert Museum, London, UK

Lysistrata, 1896, Victoria and Albert Museum, London, UK

Mademoiselle de Maupin, 1898, Victoria and Albert Museum, London, UK

The sexuality of Aubrey Beardsley (1872–1898) has long been speculated, as his work is infused with an unabashed sense of queerness. From his fey, kinky self-portrait bound to a herm, *A Footnote* (1896), to the tethering of his story to Oscar Wilde (1854–1900), his letters flesh out the wider gay coterie of the *fin de siècle*. Writing to André Raffalovich (1864–1934), a leading writer on homosexuality, Beardsley expresses excitement to receive a copy of his *Annales de l'unisexualité*, an ambitious tome aiming to catalogue everything ever published on homosexuality.

His sumptuous illustrations of Wilde's *Salome* (1891) were first published by John Lane as an edition of 13 plates. Three further plates, suppressed from the original for their outrageousness, were added to a 1904 Melmoth & Co. edition, the pseudonym of Beardsley and Wilde's notorious publisher Leonard Smithers (1861–1907).

A lesbian history is linked to the Salome legend, notably through Maud Allan (1873–1956). Between 1906–1917 she toured *The Vision of Salome* around the world with her jewelled topless dancing as the 'daughter of Sodom'. She was accused by MP Noel Pemberton Billing of being 'a member of the cult of the clitoris', unleashing a press frenzy about female sexuality.

A 1966 retrospective at the Victoria and Albert Museum saw his influence spread to the psychedelic era. Beardsley-esque illustrations feature in many magazines of the gay liberation era including Suzun David's illustrations for *Mirage Magazine – A Voice of Transexual Consciousness.*

AUBREY BEARDSLEY

Beardsley exhibited precocious self-taught talent from a young age. In four frenzied years, while battling against tuberculosis, he became so influential that the era was dubbed 'The Beardsley Period'. He was art editor of a bold new periodical, *The Yellow Book*, and his style was out to shock, propelling him and the magazine to enduring fame. He dazzled the world illustrating exceptional editions of Arthurian legend, ancient Greek comedies and gender transgression in French Romanticism.

AESTHETICISM **p.19** ART NOUVEAU **p.20**

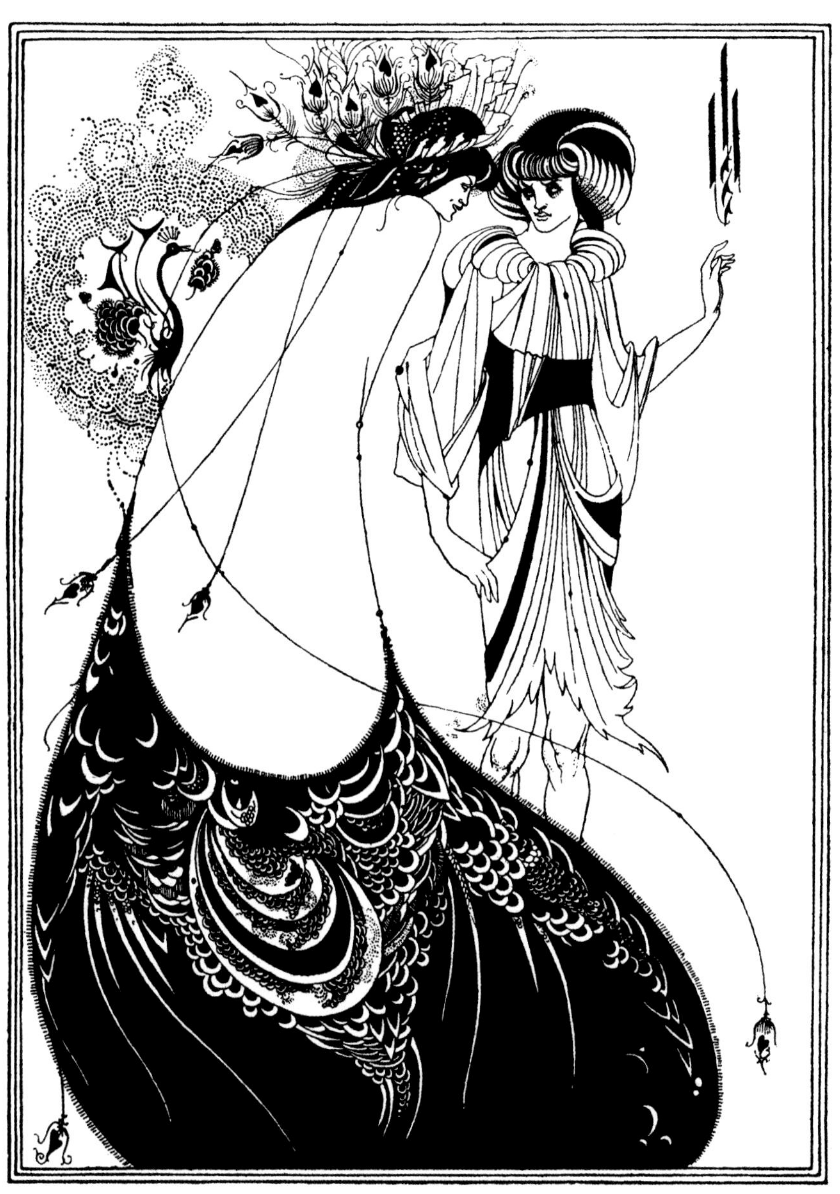

DIVINE CONNECTION **p.178** THEATRICAL TYPES **p.181** EROTIC EXCHANGES **p.183**

Pegasus Drinking from the Fountain of Hippocrene

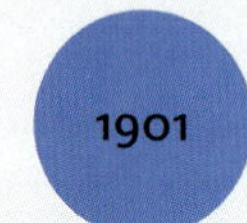

CHARLES DE SOUSY RICKETTS: LOCKET, GOLD, ENAMEL, GARNETS, PEARLS, MADE BY CARLO & ARTHUR GIULIANO, JEWELLER, LONDON • 10.1 X 5.1 X 3.4 CM (4 X 2 X 1⅓ IN)
THE FITZWILLIAM MUSEUM, CAMBRIDGE, UK

OTHER KEY WORKS

'Daphnis and Chlöe', with Charles Shannon, c.1893, Private Collection

Silence, 1905, Private Collection

Don Juan Challenging the Commander, c.1924–28, Royal Academy of Arts, London, UK

Charles de Sousy Ricketts (1866–1931) and his life partner Charles Haslewood Shannon (1863–1937) met at the City and Guilds Technical School of Art in 1882. Part of an intoxicatingly creative congregation in Chelsea, they moved into James McNeill Whistler's old house in 1888. Oscar Wilde (1854–1900) remarked that theirs was 'the one house where you will never be bored'. The two Charleses were great admirers of the Arts and Crafts movement and its connections with Medievalism, and Edmund Dulac (1882–1953) painted them as medieval saints.

They had a close friendship with poets Katherine Bradley (1846–1914) and Edith Cooper (1862–1913), known by their pen-name Michael Field. First simply a *nom de plume* for their poetry, it transformed into a singular masculine identity, using male pronouns and acting as one. Aunt and niece, their relationship was incestuous, prompting sexologist Havelock Ellis (1859–1939) to make enquiries. They responded, 'Let no man think he can put asunder what God has joined'.

PRE-RAPHAELITES **p.17** AESTHETICISM **p.19** ART NOUVEAU **p.20** ←

As niche literary celebrities of their day, Ricketts and Shannon printed and bound a number of beautifully illustrated volumes for them. Ricketts also crafted intricate jewellery designs, such as this pendant. Created as a gift for Bradley, it contains a miniature portrait of Cooper by Ricketts. The front is decorated with Pegasus drinking from the fountain of Hippocrene. In Greek mythology, this spring on Mount Helicon was a site of reverie for the nine Muses, formed when the winged horse struck the ground. The water was considered to bring poetic inspiration.

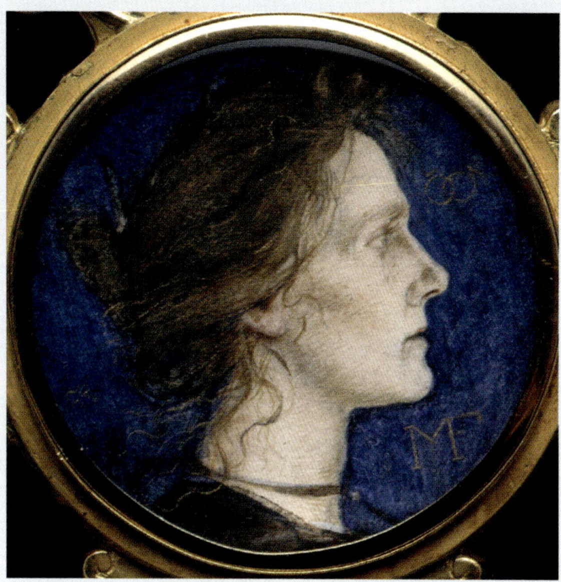

Detail: Bradley recorded her reaction at first seeing the miniature portrait: 'I look down – her face is there: my eyes grow wet as I look, then I turn to the painter & look long, not speaking. Indeed one cannot speak or write.' A celebration of their union, it is monographed MF for Michael Field – Bradley and Cooper's joint identity and includes entwined rings.

CHARLES DE SOUSY RICKETTS

Ricketts achieved prowess in many veins, as a painter, sculptor, author, typographer and theatrical scenographer. Born in Geneva, the only son of artistic parents, he was raised in England, France and Switzerland. Aged 16, he enrolled in art school in London and took up wood engraving. Here he met fellow student Shannon. The two became inseparable, living and working together in Chelsea, producing their own art periodical, *The Dial*.

→ TEXTUAL POWER **p.166** CHOSEN FAMILY **p.170**

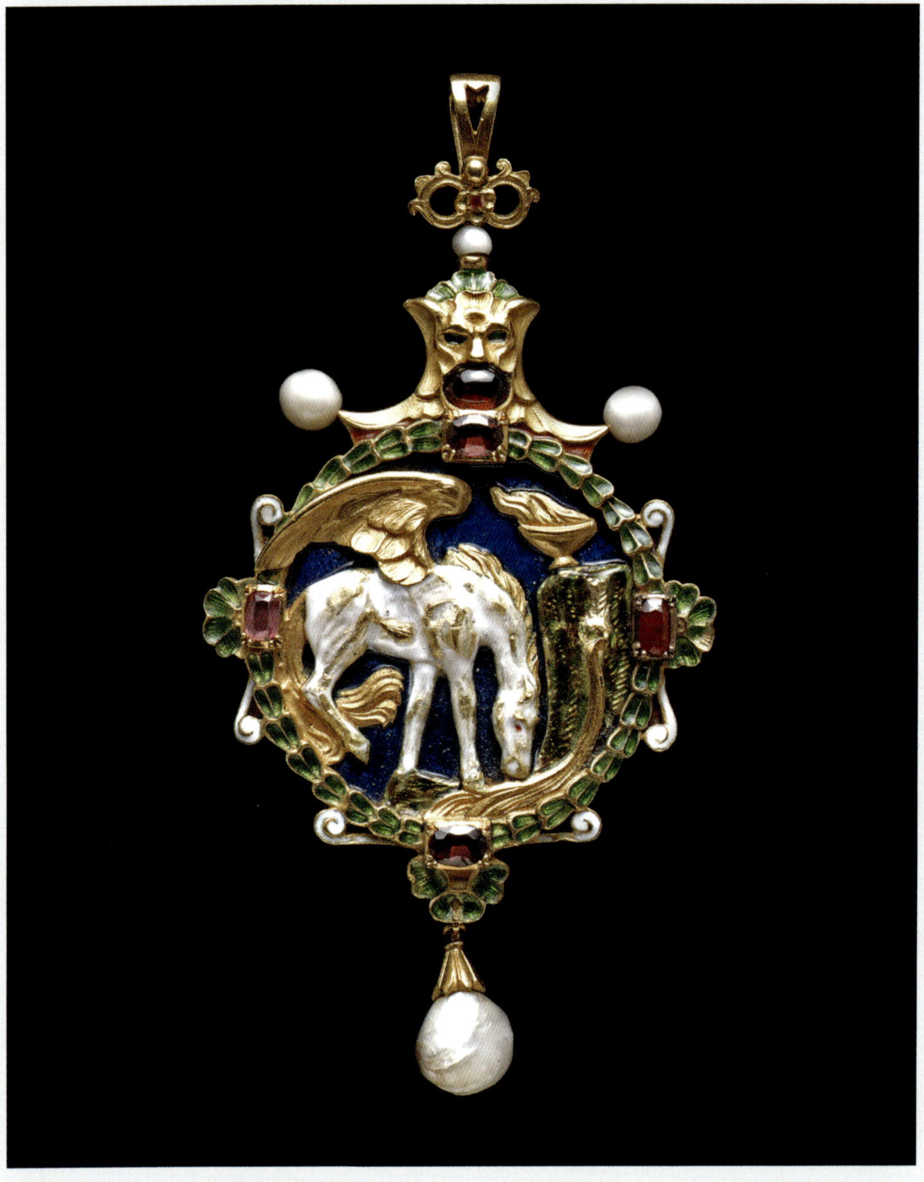

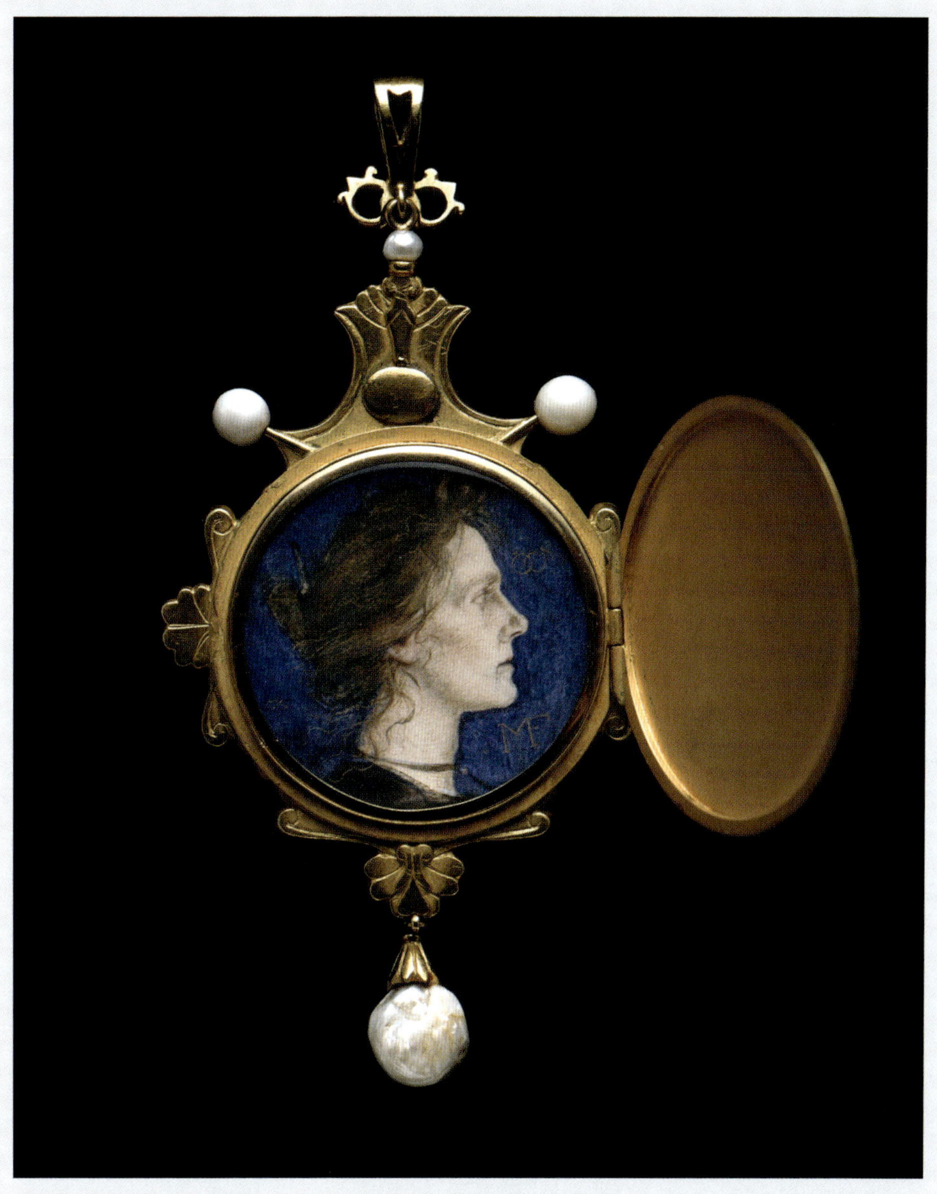

La vie pensive (Pensive Life)

LOUISE CATHERINE BRESLAU: OIL ON CANVAS • 175.7 X 160 CM (69¼ X 63 IN)
MUSÉE CANTONAL DES BEAUX-ARTS, LAUSANNE, SWITZERLAND

OTHER KEY WORKS

The Friends (Les Amies), 1881, Musée d'art et d'histoire, Ville de Genève, Switzerland

La Toilette (Madeleine Zillhardt), 1898, Private Collection

The Artist and Her Model, ca.1910, Musées d'art et d'histoire, Switzerland

Louise Breslau (1856–1927) was famed for her skill at capturing the spirit of her sitters with an intimate directness. A frequent subject were the women in her life, creating portraits with her red-haired partner Madeleine Zillhardt (1863–1950). Classmates at the Académie Julian, they started living together two years later in 1886, and opened a studio.

This painting shows the pair at home in Neuilly-sur-Seine. There is a soft, welcoming light yet an unnerving sense of rumination. Their expressions are unclear, yet Zillhardt has an air of slight exasperation, while Breslau's could be read as interrogative, holding a letter containing what news? The borzoi dog seemingly seeks reassurance among the tension. The viewer is drawn into their space with its palpable energy and atmosphere. The evocative title probably references philosophical ideas around *vita activa* (active life) versus *vita contemplativa* (contemplative life) first tackled by Aristotle.

Breslau was admired in the Parisian artworld and the first female artist from another country to be awarded the Légion d'honneur, France's highest order of merit. Recognition in her home country was slower to realize. This painting was accepted at the 1908 National Fine Art Exhibition in Basel only after Breslau railed against the misogyny of the selection committee (the Association of Swiss Painters and Sculptors) who had repeatedly voted to reject women's inclusion.

LOUISE CATHERINE BRESLAU

The German-born Swiss painter, printmaker and pastel artist left Switzerland at 19 to study her craft, recalling: 'My thirst for knowledge was unquenchable, and I knew that I would find ways to learn in Paris.' She trained at the Académie Julian in Paris and at just 23, was the only female student from the Academy to exhibit at the highly esteemed salon of the Société Nationale des Beaux-Arts in Paris.

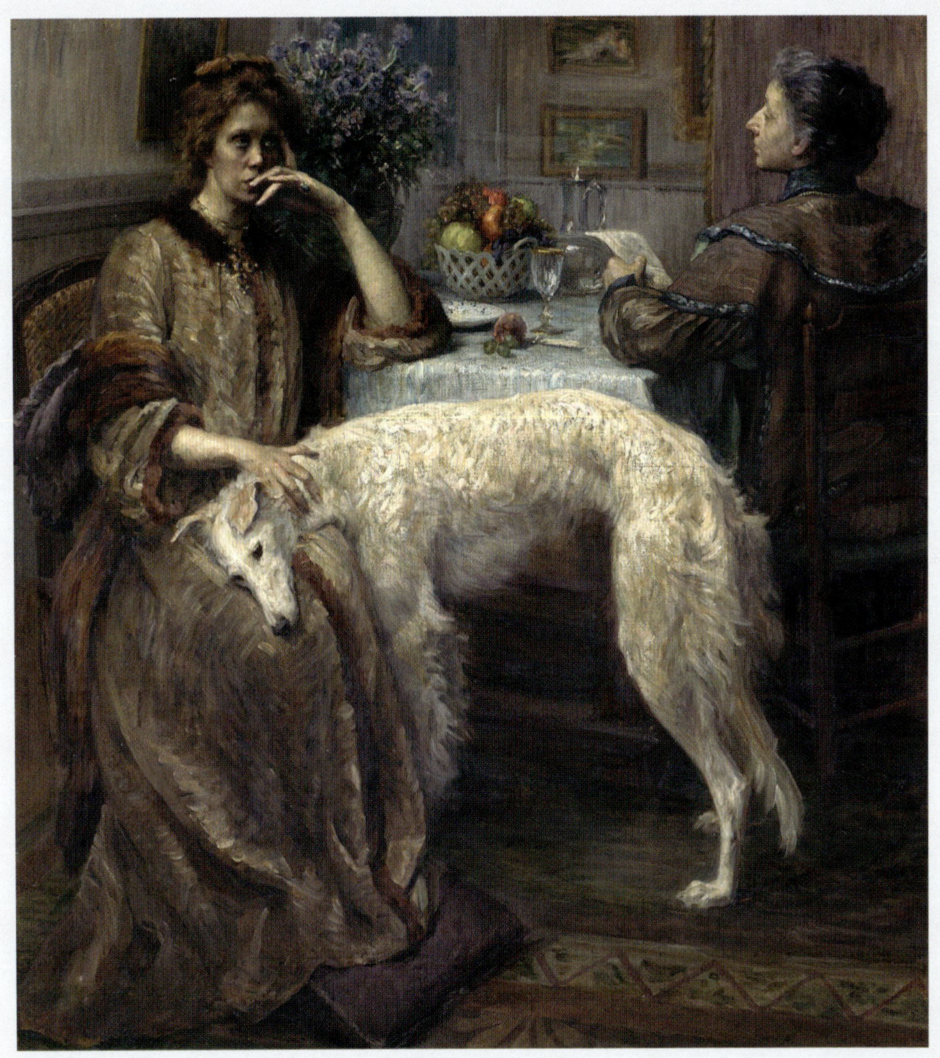

PRESENTING THE ARTIST **p.167** CHOSEN FAMILY **p.170** PLACES TO BE **p.189** GAY PARIS **p.204**

Loge de Théâtre

1912

ERTÉ: SERIGRAPH PRINT, AFTER ORIGINAL 1912 GOUACHE DESIGN, 1980S

OTHER KEY WORKS

Symphony in Black, 1923, Private Collection

Costume design for 'L'Océan Pacifique', George White's Scandals, New York, 1928, The Metropolitan Museum of Art, New York, USA

The Alphabet Suite, 1976, Private Collection

Although synonymous with Art Deco, Erté (1892–1990) didn't welcome association with a particular style saying: 'I belong to no school of art ... I am individualistic in art.' Born Romain Petrovich de Tirtoff in Saint Petersburg, Erté emigrated to Paris in 1912. Throwing himself into Parisian café society, he met his distant cousin, the Prince Nicolas Ouroussoff (1879–1933), who became his lover until the Prince's premature death. Erté's autobiography illuminates 1920s gay nightspots in Paris hosting washed-up cabaret stars performing bawdy tricks for tips.

Moving into designing costumes and stage sets for theatre and film, he became the premiere costume designer at the Folies-Bergère, making costumes for: dancer-turned-spy Mata Hari (1876–1917); Sarah Bernhardt (1844–1923); and Anna Pavlova (1881–1931). He entered the lavish world as a designer for the Ziegfeld Follies in New York and stints in Hollywood saw him create sets for major films like *Ben Hur* (1925), and costumes for stars including Josephine Baker (1906–1975) and Joan Crawford (?–1977).

Returning to Paris and experiencing a 'bracing change' of values towards industrial art, he collaborated with French magazine *Art et Industrie*, making lamps, furniture and other household utilities. A 1967 exhibition at the Metropolitan Museum of Art New York rejuvenated his stardom. A more recent resurgence in his homeland of Russia saw a 2016 exhibition at the Hermitage titled 'Erté: Art Deco Genius'.

ERTÉ

Famed for his elegant Art Deco designs, Erté pursued his chosen career with unflagging zest for almost 80 years. His fashion, costume and set designs are instantly recognizable. His 'Erté woman' was slender, opulent and languid, and based on what he wanted to be like if he was female. In 1915 he started at *Harper's Bazaar* and designed over 250 covers for them.

ART DECO **p.24**

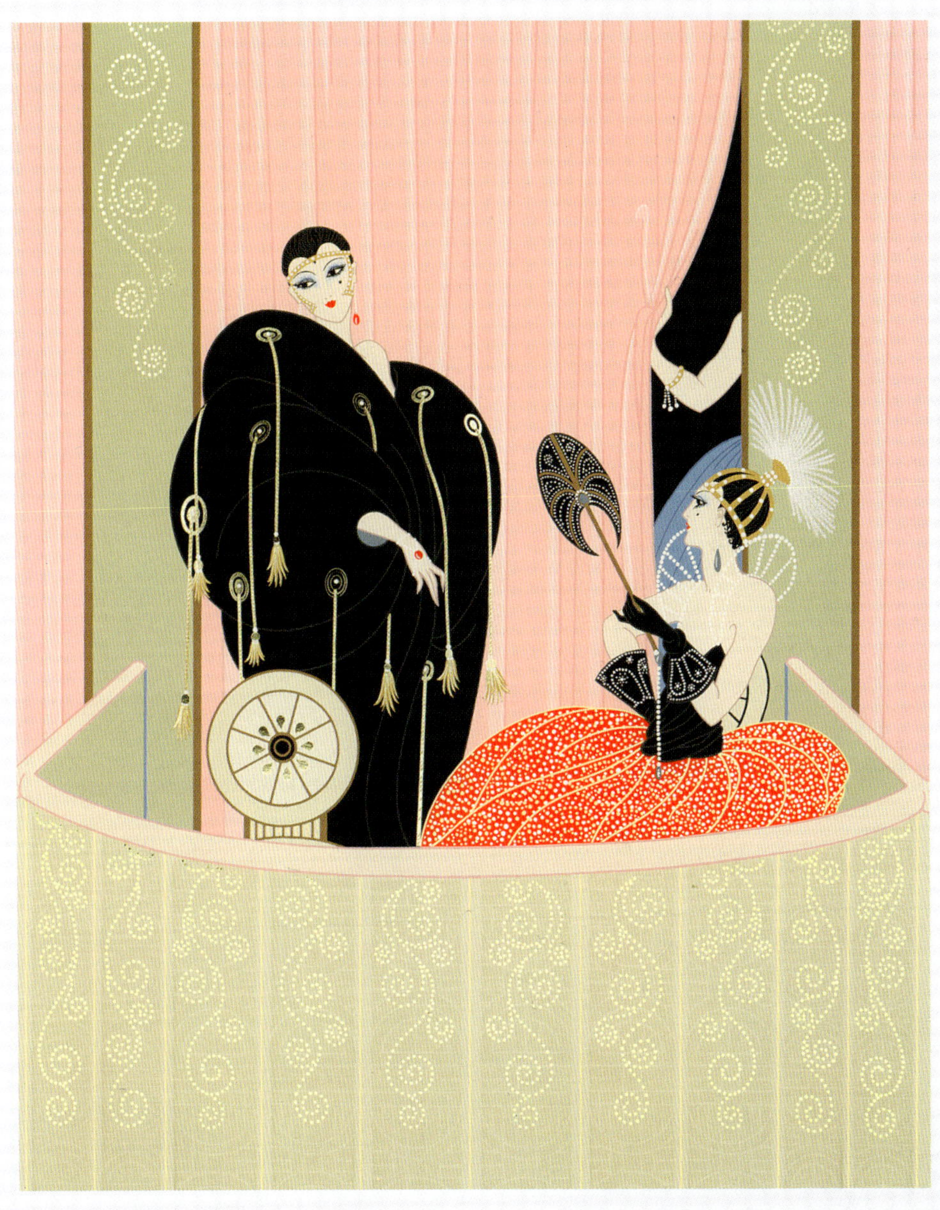

SUMMONING SAPPHO **p.176** RISING CAMP **p.180** THEATRICAL TYPES **p.181** GAY PARIS **p.204**
FASHIONING STYLE **p.206**

Handsome Drinks

1916

MARSDEN HARTLEY: OIL ON BOARD • 61 X 50.8 CM (24 X 20 IN) • BROOKLYN MUSEUM, NEW YORK, USA

OTHER KEY WORKS

Portrait of a German Officer, 1914, The Metropolitan Museum of Art, New York, USA

American Indian Symbols, 1914, Amon Carter Museum of American Art, USA

Madawaska—Acadian Light-Heavy, 1940, Art Institute of Chicago, USA

Marsden Hartley (1877–1943) was a devotee of poet Walt Whitman (1819–1892) whom he described as a giant with a 'burning desire to enlarge the general scope of vision, and the finer capacity for individual experience.' Like many gay men of his era who risked severe persecution, Hartley used Whitmanian wisdom to navigate towards acceptance of his own desires for 'manly love'.

Many elements of queer desire are sublimated into his work, which despite his insistence that they bore no symbolic meaning whatsoever, cannot help but shimmer. From more overt male nude sketches to larger paintings of hulking men like *Flaming American (Swim Champ)* (1940), others appear understated at first glance but are loaded with coded meaning. *Portrait of a German Officer* (1914) is a Cubist melding of military insignia and national flags in commemoration of Karl von Freyburg (1889–1914), a young Prussian he fell in love with, killed in war.

Hartley's many landscapes and still life paintings are considered to conceal phallic imagery and more veiled meanings connected to esoteric spirituality. This painting is thought to reference Gertrude Stein (1874–1946) as a chalice with a mandorla (an aura of light surrounding a holy figure) emerging at the top. She had encouraged Hartley to write as well as paint, purchasing four of his paintings and bringing him warmly into her avant-garde orbit. A similar painting, *One Portrait of One Woman* (1916), is also thought to honour Stein.

MARSDEN HARTLEY

Born in Maine, Hartley held his first solo exhibition in 1909 at Alfred Stieglitz's famed gallery 291 in New York. Expressing a need to escape American conservativism saying 'they are such conventional cats', he sailed for Europe in 1912. Enamoured by Paris and Berlin, he was deeply inspired by Paul Cézanne (1839–1906) as well as German Expressionism. His Modernist oeuvre encompassed landscape, still life and portraiture, and he was one of the first Americans to experiment with abstraction.

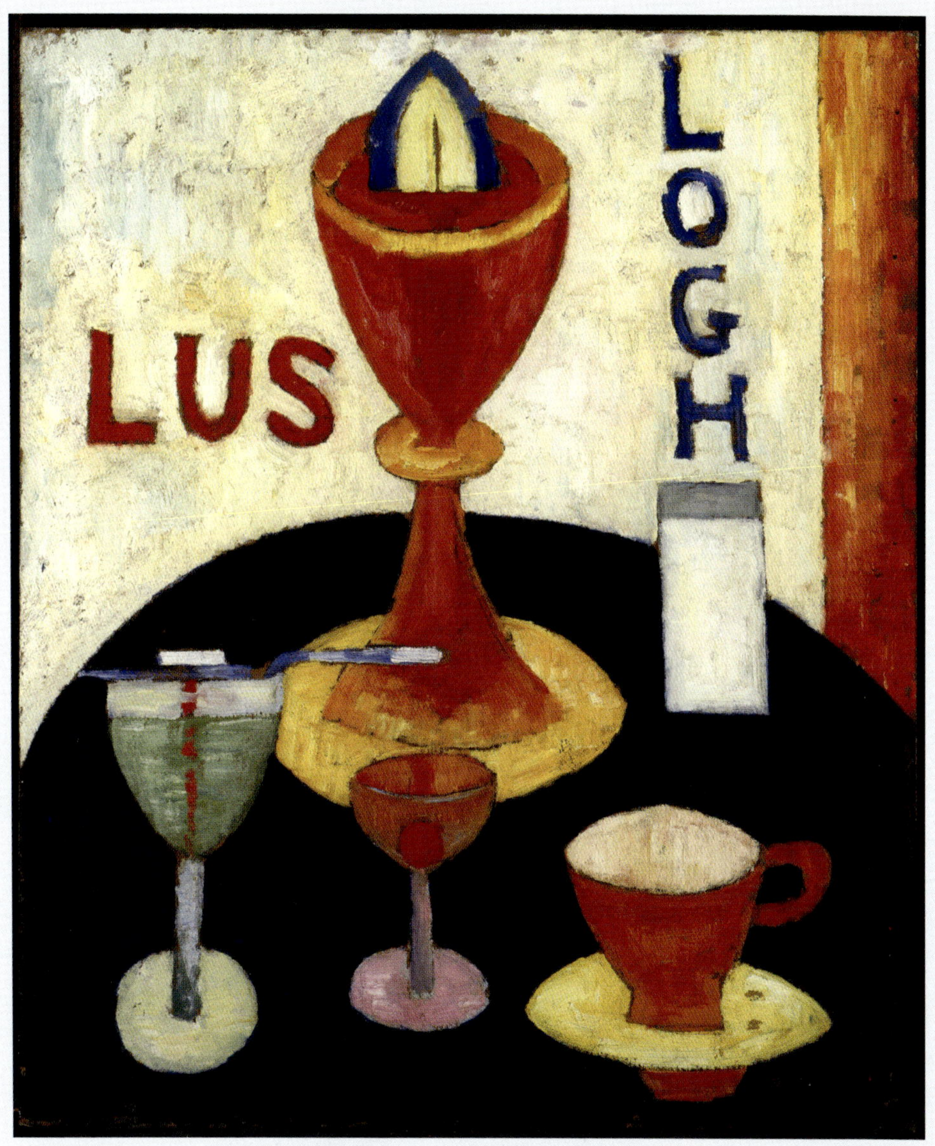

TEXTUAL POWER p.166 QUEER CODING p.168 GAY PARIS p.204

Da-Dandy

HANNAH HÖCH: COLLAGE • 30 X 23 CM (11 13/16 X 9 1/16 IN) • PRIVATE COLLECTION

OTHER KEY WORKS

Cut with the Kitchen Knife Dada through the Last Weimar Beer-Belly Cultural Epoch of Germany, 1919–20, Nationalgalerie, Staatliche Museen, Berlin, Germany

The Beautiful Girl, 1921, Private Collection

Around a Red Mouth, c.1967, Collection of IFA, Stuttgart, Germany

Hannah Höch (1889–1978) was noted for shrewd social and political critiques of the Weimar period. Her work frequently challenged dichotomies between the concept of the idealized, energetic aspirational Weimar 'New Woman' in a modernizing society and the reality of social structures continuing to deny women agency and liberation. Höch parodied elements of bourgeois living and femininity in post-First World War media culture, showing a recurring interest in the cultural commodification of women and their representation as dolls, puppets and mannequins. At the first International Dada Fair (1920) she displayed hand-crafted dada dolls alongside photomontages – a technique in which she was credited as a key originator.

Photomontage was partly inspired by oleograph prints hung in many German homes as a memento of military service – with the head of a family member naïvely cut-and-pasted onto a pre-printed figure. It became a favoured medium for Höch as she explored the subversive power of cutting and pasting to disrupt and alienate images and create layered, discombobulating wonderlands. In some she depicted same-sex couples and explored androgyny by fusing together male and female bodies. In *Da-Dandy*, the silhouette of a man (both a Dadaist and a dandy) has either consumed, or been fashioned from, fragmented images of 'New Women'. Notably, for a portrait of her lover, Dutch writer Mathilda Brugman (1888–1958), Höch opted to collage using plain coloured paper thus removing elements of satiric critique.

HANNAH HÖCH

Removed from school at fifteen to care for her sister, Höch later enrolled in the School of Applied Arts in Berlin-Charlottenburg to study glass design. Part of the Berlin Dada scene, she was among artists whose works the Nazis denounced as 'degenerate'. Her 1932 exhibition at the Bauhaus was cancelled and she was unable to show in Germany until after 1945. She continued creating art and producing photomontages until her death.

DADA **p.21**

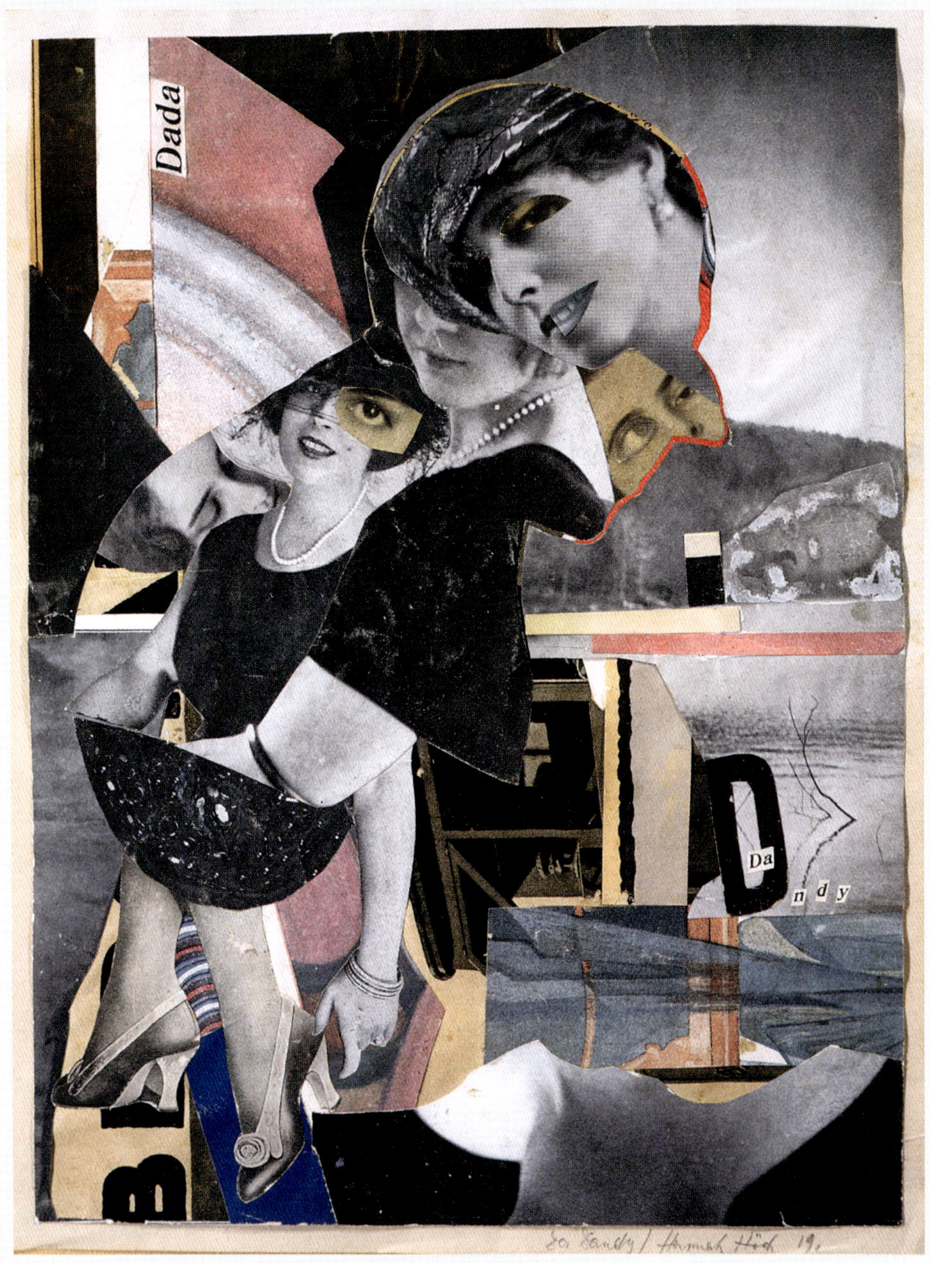

ASSEMBLING p.171 SPACE OF THE BODY p.172 THEATRICAL TYPES p.181 STRAIGHT EXPECTATIONS p.185
WEIMAR BERLIN p.201

Asbury Park South

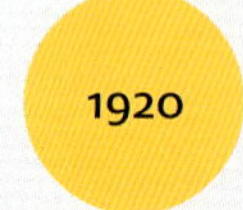

FLORINE STETTHEIMER: OIL ON CANVAS • 127 X 52.4 CM (50 X 60 IN)
COLLECTION OF HALLEY K. HARRISBURG AND MICHAEL ROSENFELD, NEW YORK, USA

OTHER KEY WORKS

A Model Nude Self-Portrait, 1915, Columbia University in the City of New York, USA

The Cathedrals of Art (series), 1929–42, The Metropolitan Museum of Art, New York, USA

Love Flight of a Pink Candy Heart, 1930, Detroit Institute of Arts, Detroit, USA

Born into a wealthy New York family, Florine Stettheimer (1871–1944) and her sisters lived a charmed life, spending years travelling through Europe before the First World War. In Paris they saw the Ballets Russes and probably attended the First International Feminist Congress (1896). Upon her return to New York, Stetheimer threw herself into depicting the rapidly changing city as a pleasure dome. She became part of a cultural avant-garde inclusive of many gay, lesbian and bisexual creatives, including painters Charles Demuth (1883–1935) and Romaine Brooks (1874–1970), photographers Cecil Beaton (1904–1980) and Baron Adolph de Meyer (1868–1964), the composer Virgil Thomson (1896–1989) and his partner Maurice Grosser (1903–1986).

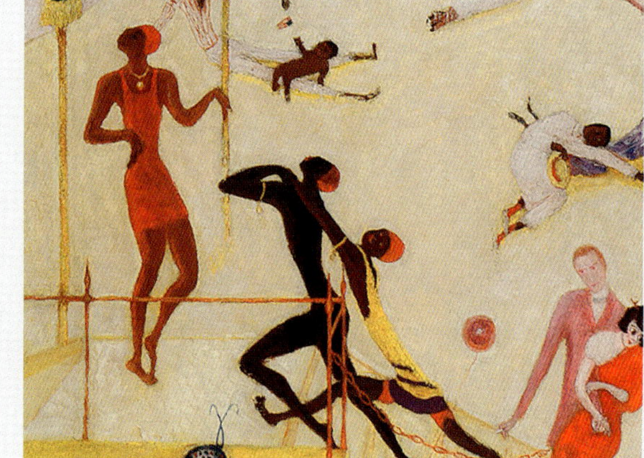

Detail: Virgil Thompson called Stettheimer's style 'high camp'. Linda Nochlin (1931–2017) later dubbed her a 'rococo subversive'.

FLORINE STETTHEIMER

Stettheimer was at times tentative about sharing her work, saying: 'Letting people have your paintings is like letting them wear your clothes.' With its wry, controlling gaze, her *Nude Self-Portrait* (1915) has been termed 'the first overtly feminist self-portrait in Western art' but wasn't publicly displayed during her lifetime. Duchamp's retrospective of her work at the Museum of Modern Art in 1946 was the museum's first for a woman artist.

HARLEM RENAISSANCE **p.22** FEMINIST ART **p.30**

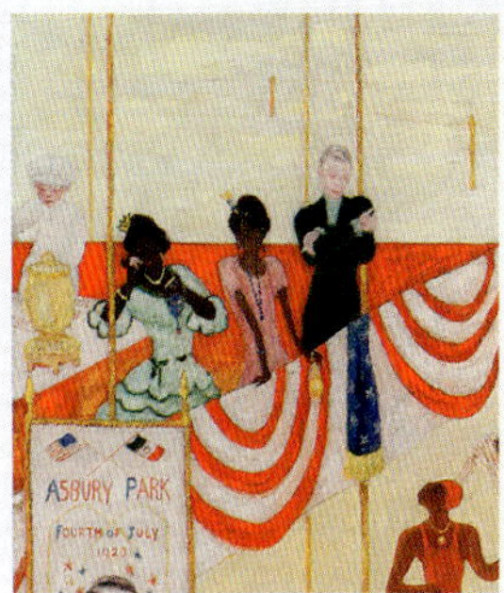

Detail: Van Vechten stands alongside women wearing Edwardian and 'flapper' fashions, looking on as his wife, actress Fania Marinoff (1890–1971), is escorted by Duchamp. A 1922 portrait by Stettheimer shows him sporting a red tie and purple socks, in coded reference to queerness.

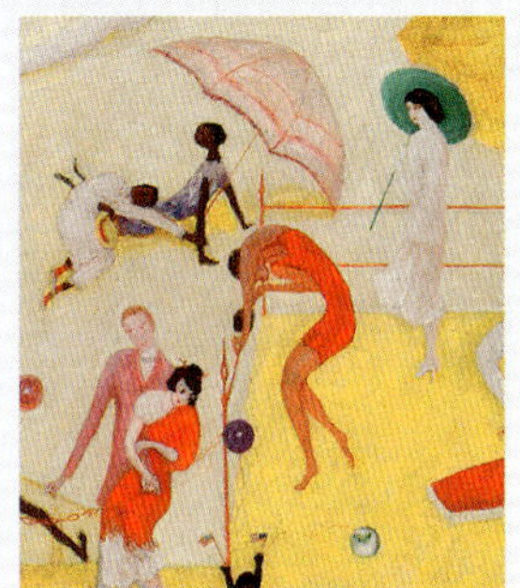

Detail: Stettheimer shows herself standing with a green parasol. Duchamp wears a pink suit like one she depicted his alter-ego Rrose Sélavy wearing in a 1923 portrait. Her three friends appear in other paintings including *La Fete a Duchamp* (1917).

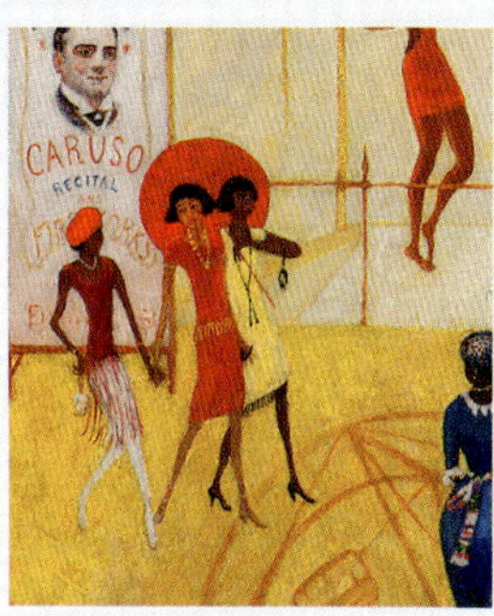

Detail: Van Vechten called her work 'quality jazz' describing her as 'both the historian and the critic of her period ... telling us how some of New York lived in those strange years after the First World War, telling us in brilliant colors and assured designs, telling us in painting that has few rivals'.

With a fondness for delicate satire, she set out scenes as if in mid-performance on a brightly lit stage. A celebration of summer at the seaside, *Asbury Park South* (1920) records a visit to the segregated section of a New Jersey beach with Harlem Renaissance patron Carl Van Vechten (1880–1964) and Marcel Duchamp (1887–1968) mixing with African Americans. She hoped positive joyful scenes would spur a greater sense of togetherness and equality. It was included in the Museum of Modern Art's first exhibition of American art in Europe in 1938. Stettheimer was also responsible for the innovative (if risky because flammable) cellophane sets for Gertrude Stein (1874–1946) and Virgil Thomson's (1896–1989) opera *Four Saints in Three Acts* (1928) which featured an all-Black cast, including Ruby Mae Greene (1909–2002).

PRESENTING THE ARTIST **p.167** THEATRICAL TYPES **p.181** PLACES TO BE **p.189** THE BALLETS RUSSES **p.199** *FIRE!!* MAGAZINE **p.203**

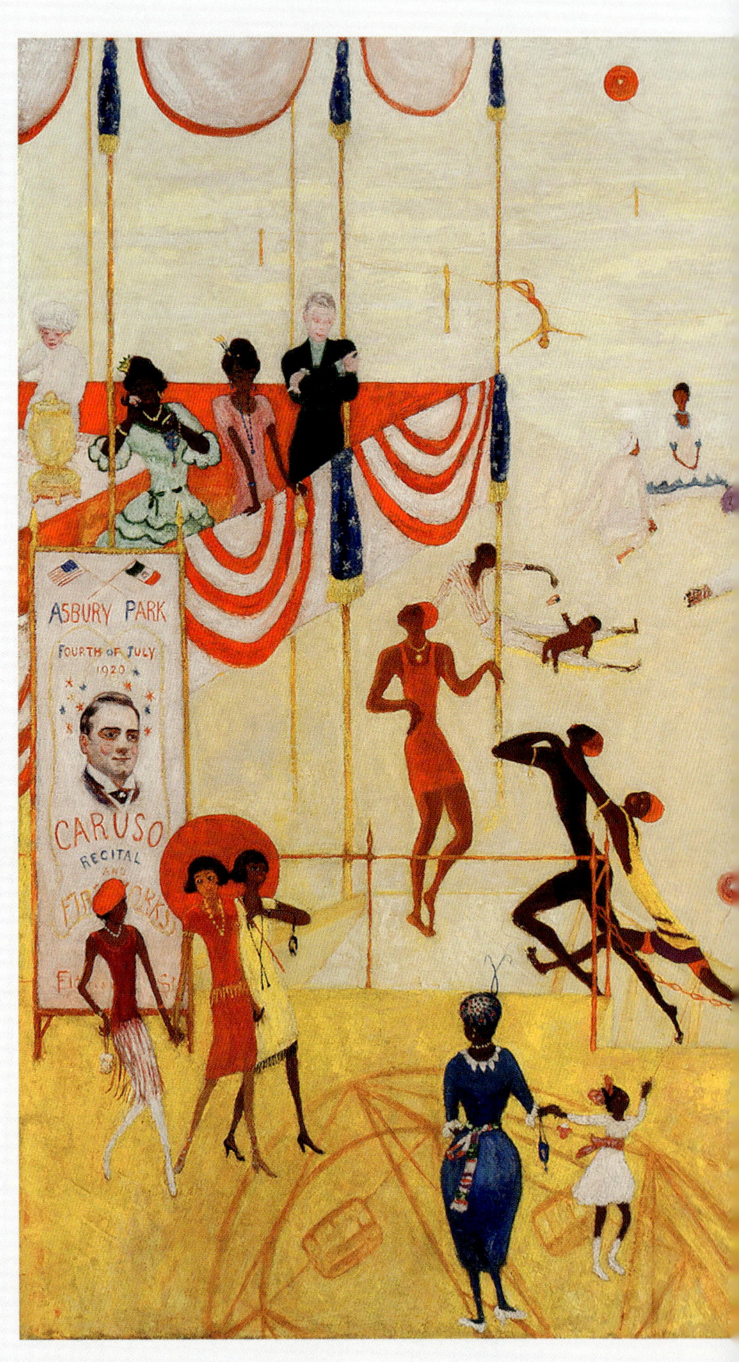
ASBURY PARK
FOURTH OF JULY
1920
CARUSO
RECITAL
AND

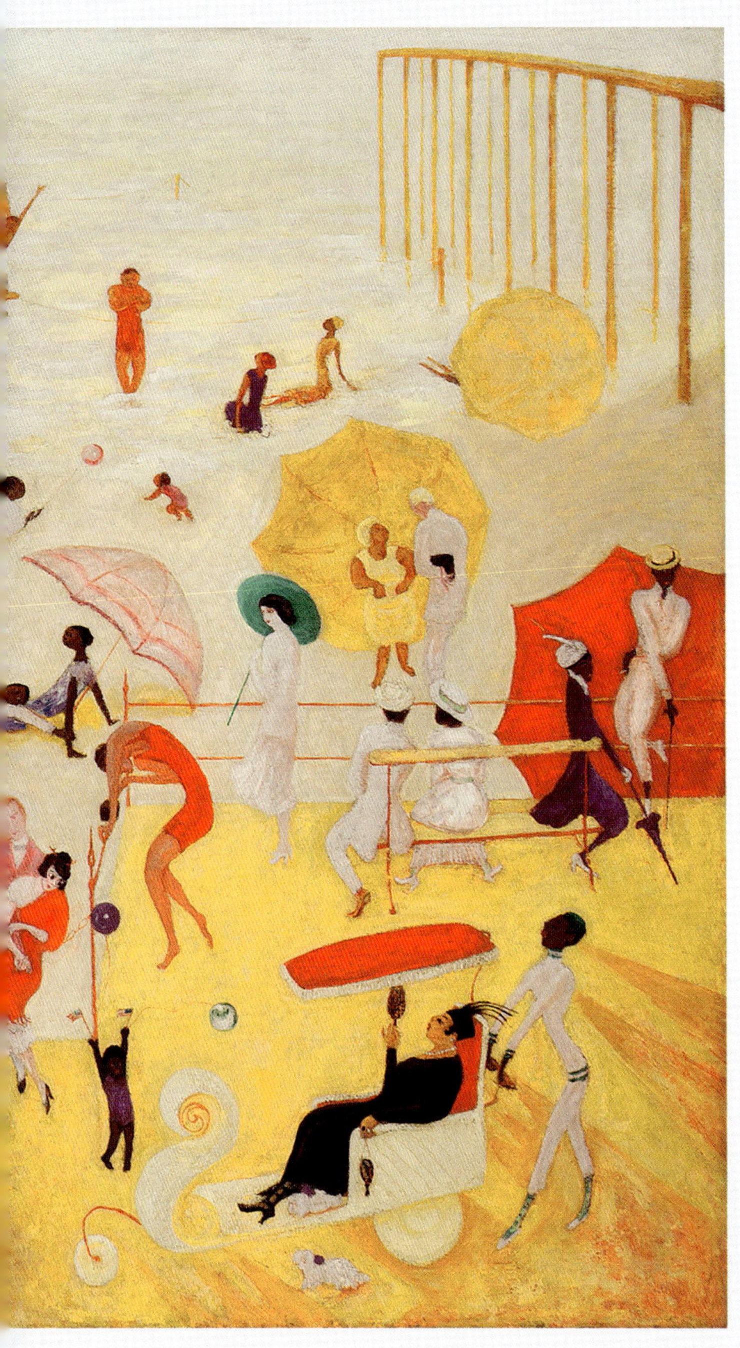

Les Amazones

1921

MARIE LAURENCIN: OIL ON CANVAS • 72.5 X 91 CM (28½ X 35⅞ IN)
PRIVATE COLLECTION

OTHER KEY WORKS

Chanson de Bilitis, 1905, Art Institute of Chicago, USA

Stage curtain design for the ballet *Les biches* (*The Does*), 1923, Private Collection

Illustrations for *Poèmes de Sapho* (*Poems by Sappho*), translated by Édith de Beaumont, 1950, The Metropolitan Museum of Art, New York, USA

MARIE LAURENCIN

Laurencin studied drawing and trained as a porcelain painter at Sèvres before enrolling in the independent Parisian art school Académie Humbert. Her partner Suzanne Moreau kept much of Laurencin's work after her death. As works came to auction in the 1970s, Japanese collector Masahiro Takano became a prolific purchaser. Their collection of hundreds of paintings, drawings and prints was the basis for the Marie Laurencin Museum, Japan.

Marie Laurencin (1885–1956) developed a distinct style early on, producing book illustrations, prints, poetry and designs for ballet costumes and theatre sets. Often centring dreamy, gauzy groupings of diaphanous women in soft pinks and greys, she employed a deliberate flatness connected to her roots in Cubism but using pastel colours and rounded shapes to suggest femininity.

This conscious naiveté was not fully embraced, seen by some as overdelicate and one-dimensional. Here, the Amazons, legendary strongwomen of lore, become slender, hyper-feminine waifs under her brush. Playing with perceptions of girlishness (and concealing her intellect), Laurencin humorously proclaimed herself 'the queen of airheads' according to noted French bookseller Adrienne Monnier (1892–1955).

Men are mainly absent from Laurencin's work. She was one of few women within the Cubist movement, her work featuring in the first group exhibition at the Salon des Indépendants, 1911. In *The Cubist Painters* (1913), his only book on art, Guillaume Apollinaire (1880–1918) commended her for successfully expressing 'an entirely feminine aesthetic'. She later reflected: 'Cubism has poisoned three years of my life, preventing me from doing any work.' Noting the lack of emotional connection, she said: 'I get from Cubism the same feeling that a book on philosophy and mathematics gives me.'

Laurencin enjoyed relationships with men and women and circulated in sapphic circles of 1920s Paris. Gertrude Stein (1874–1946) was an early patron and she socialized with Jean Cocteau (1889–1963), Erik Satie (1866–1925) and Francis Poulenc (1899–1963).

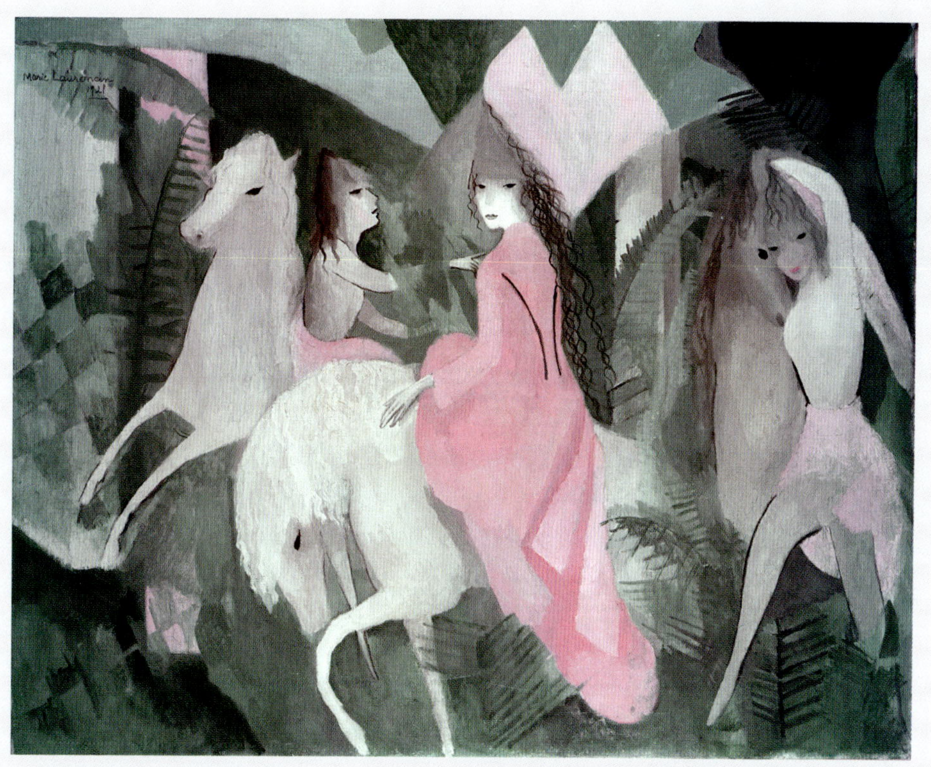

GLIMPSES OF UTOPIA **p.163** DIVINE CONNECTION **p.178** GAY PARIS **p.204**

Semi-Nude in Front of Prickly Pear Cactus

1922 – 1925

ANITA RÉE: OIL ON CANVAS • 66 X 53.3 CM (26 X 21 IN) • HAMBURGER KUNSTHALLE, GERMANY

A sense of dislocation often infuses the work of Anita Rée (1885–1933). Viewed collectively, they suggest the eclecticism or restlessness of an artist. Conveying a reflective take on expressionism, this composition could be presented, in other hands, as humorous or lewd innuendo. However, Rée's stance and lowered eyes bring an unsettling weight to the scene.

She was skilled at using the direction of a subject's gaze to powerful effect. Her somewhat static pose suggests physical disconnection. Encouraging comparison of her breasts to ripe fruit, her downcast, possibly resigned, expression suggests an unaccepted offering or unrealized fertility. Perhaps, like the cactus, she is resigning herself to adapting to arid conditions. Rée's body indicates a sense of hesitancy and caution, suggesting sensual joy holding a threat of danger – evoking the care needed to remove the small spines from prickly pear fruits before they can be eaten.

Having returned to Hamburg in 1926, she was commissioned to paint several well-received murals in the city, but upon delivering her triptych for the new Ansgarkirche in Langenhorn in 1932, the Church elders considered it unsuitable, offensive and 'too Jewish'. Rée was reported to the authorities as 'a Jew' and denounced by the Hamburg Art Group as an 'alien'.

She fled to the German island of Sylt. Amid depression, she committed suicide, leaving a note attributing it to antisemitic harassment and 'disappointments on the personal level', which have been interpreted as struggling with expectations of heterosexual conformity.

OTHER KEY WORKS

Weiße Bäume in Positano (White Trees in Positano), 1925, Hamburger Kunsthalle, Germany

Self Portrait, c.1929, Hamburger Kunsthalle, Germany

Vision des heiligen Antonius zu Padua (Vision of Saint Anthony at Padua), 1930, Private Collection

ANITA RÉE

Notions of identity were a recurring interest for Rée who was born to a Jewish father and Venezuelan Catholic mother and raised in Hamburg as a Protestant. An independent woman of the art world, she briefly studied in Paris, mixing with the likes of Picasso and Matisse, and lived in Italy. In 1926 she was a founding member of GEDOK (Community of German and Austrian Women Artists' Associations of all Arts).

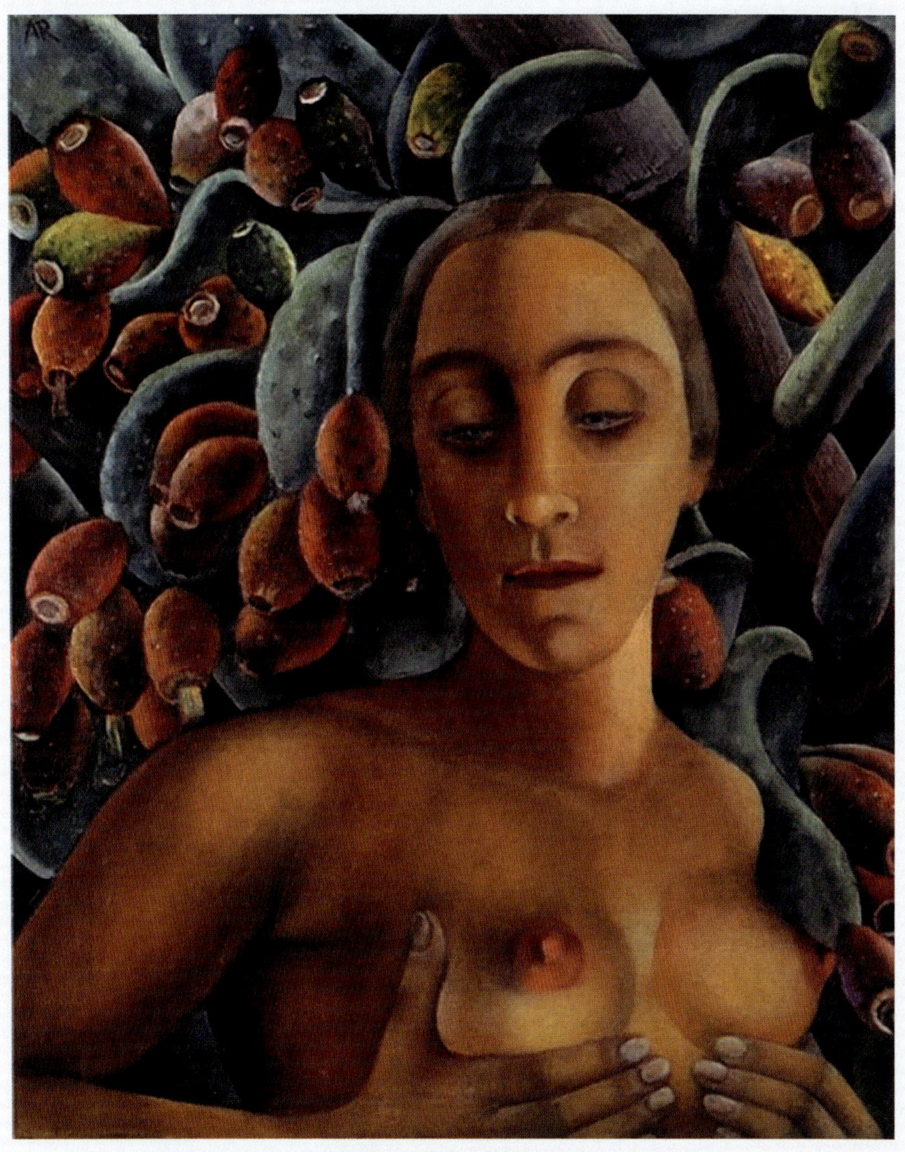

PRESENTING THE ARTIST p.167 SPACE OF THE BODY p.172 STRAIGHT EXPECTATIONS p.185

La Bague Symbolique

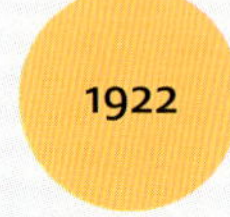

GEORGE BARBIER: POCHOIR PRINT • PRIVATE COLLECTION • ILLUSTRATION FROM *LES CHANSONS DE BILITIS*, PIERRE LOUYS, PUB. 1922

OTHER KEY WORKS

Designs on the dances of Vaslav Nijinsky, 1913, Victoria and Albert Museum, London, UK

Lady with a Panther, 1914, Private Collection

Falbalas et Fanfreluches, 1924, Victoria and Albert Museum, London, UK

George Barbier (1882–1932) was hugely successful and well-connected in his day, but much of his life remains shrouded in mystery. With a luxurious studio neighbouring Man Ray (1890–1976) in Montparnasse, Paris, he was part of a group of printmakers nicknamed by French *Vogue* as 'Beau Brummels of the Brush' for their dandyish attire. Also dubbed 'the knights of the bracelet', they turned heads with their flamboyant mannerisms and common practice of wearing bracelets.

They included André Marty (1882–1974), Erté (1892–1990) and Georges Lepape (1887–1971). The pochoir (stencil) technique they favoured was popular for its intense colour but labour-intensive and expensive. Some of Barbier's best prints appear in *Falbalas et Fanfreluches* (*Frills and Flounces*), a small edition magazine with a high price tag. His male figures are usually depicted as dainty wallflowers, with nipped waists and tiny feet, while his 'New Women' are assertive and appear to only have eyes for each other. The clothes depicted were usually of Barbier's own design, rather than copied from couturiers.

In 1922, Barbier produced 42 illustrations for a reissue of *Les Chansons de Bilitis* (*The Songs of Bilitis*), first published in 1894 by Pierre Louys (1870–1925). Bilitis was a courtesan of Sappho, and Louys falsely claimed he translated the text from Ancient texts found on the wall of a tomb in Cyprus. It later inspired the name of the first lesbian rights organization in the USA, the Daughters of Bilitis (est. 1955).

GEORGE BARBIER

Barbier was one of the leading Art Deco illustrators of the 1910s and 1920s. He was celebrated for his lavish fashion plates, his work dripping with camp, androgyny and same-sex activity. Also a jewellery designer, he created more than 100 pieces for Cartier, and in 1914 devised the panther which remains a symbol of the company. Tellingly, Louys described Barbier as *vraiment grec* (really Greek), then code for gay.

ART DECO **p.24**

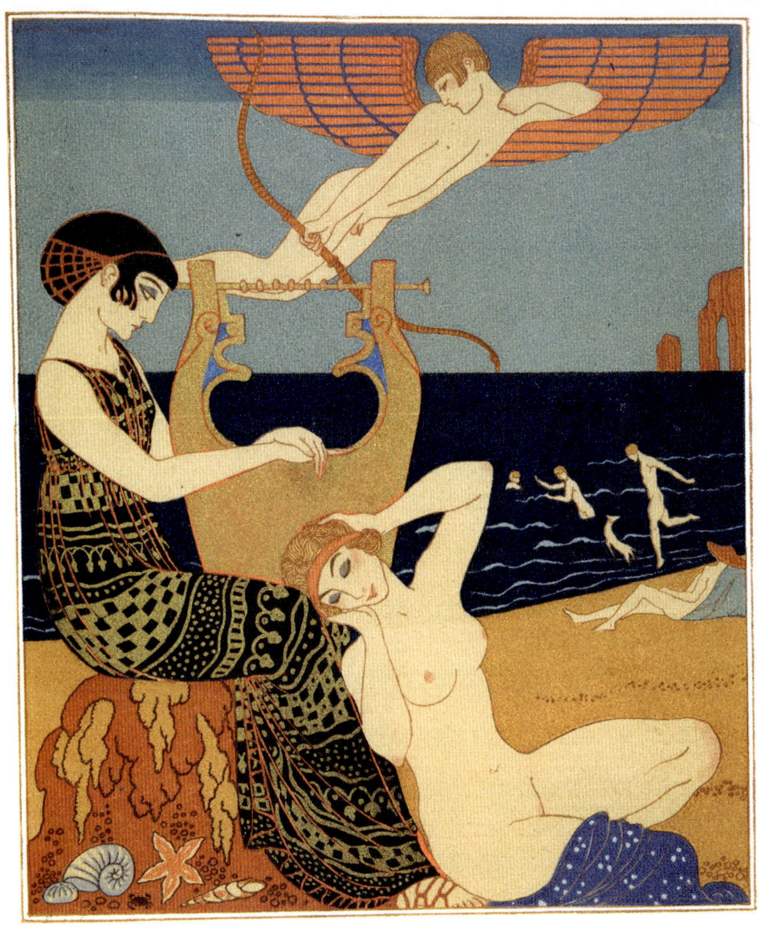

SUMMONING SAPPHO p.176 RISING CAMP p.180 THE BALLETS RUSSES p.199 GAY PARIS p.204
FASHIONING STYLE p.206

The Critics

HENRY SCOTT TUKE: OIL ON BOARD • 41.2 X 51.4 CM (16¼ X 20¼ IN)
LEAMINGTON SPA ART GALLERY AND MUSEUM, UK

OTHER KEY WORKS

All Hands to the Pumps, 1888–89, Tate, London, UK

Midsummer Morning (Lovers of the Sun), 1908, Private Collection

Bathing Group (Noonday Heat), 1911, Private Collection

An industrious painter of maritime scenes, Henry Scott Tuke (1858–1929) is most admired for his shimmering paintings of young men and boys swimming, boating, and sunbathing. One of his earliest works is a seated male in a studio, wearing just a slip, c.1877, but he quickly hit his stride out of doors, saying he moved back to Falmouth not to paint the sea or be a marine painter 'but primarily to paint the nude in the open air'.

He excelled in capturing light on the water and the rippling muscles of sailors and fishermen, the freedom of boyish youth, diving and cavorting or catching moments of couples reclining on the sands, centimetres from touching. *The Critics* is one of his more tantalizing titles, as two young men on the beach appraise another blushing in the water.

Historian Marcia Pointon (1943–) described his reputation by the mid-twentieth century as 'like Georgian poetry, monocles and parasols … too securely lodged in the forgettable compartment of Edwardianism to merit serious attention'. Partly resurrected during the 1970s as more artists came out during the gay liberation movement, keen to seek out their forebears in queer art history, Tuke embodies the so-called Uranian period. Also penning poems in this vein, he published a sonnet anonymously which praised 'Youth standing sweet, triumphant by the sea'.

HENRY SCOTT TUKE

Tuke was a cornerstone of English Impressionism, and his sparkling coastal scenes, enlivened by the nude male form, endure as glimpses of homoerotic idealism before the First World War. After studying at the Slade School of Art in the late 1870s, Tuke spent two formative years in France (1881–83) taking up plein-air painting. Enamoured with the sea, he resettled in Cornwall in 1885 in the 'congenial brotherhood' of the artist colony at Falmouth.

IMPRESSIONISM **p.18**

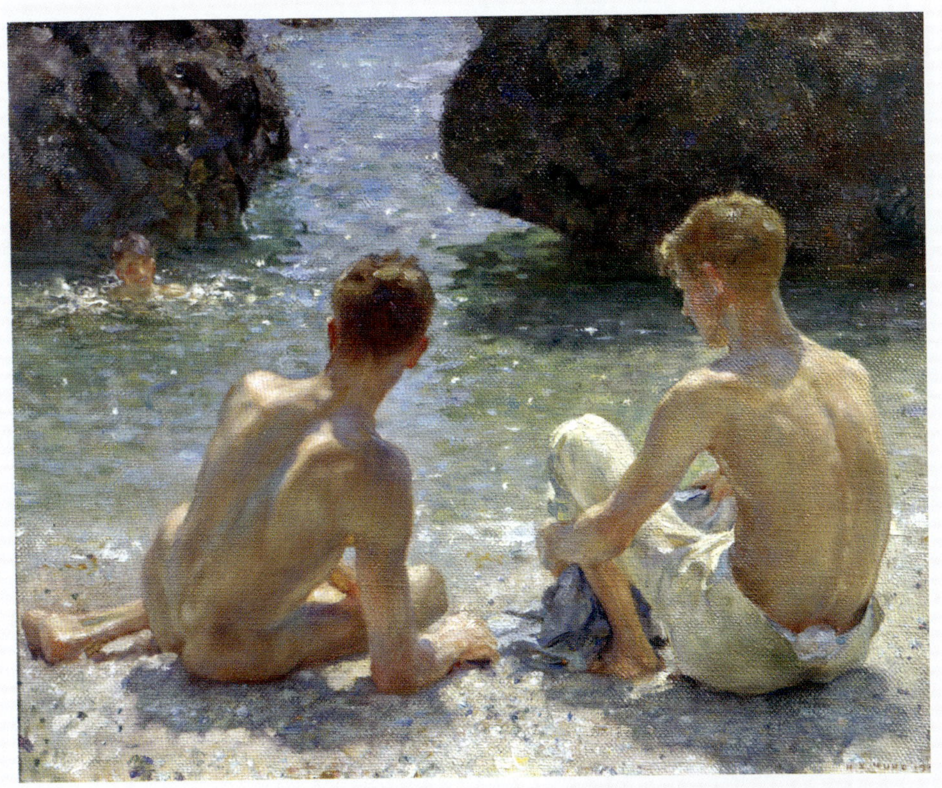

I.O.U. (Self-Pride)

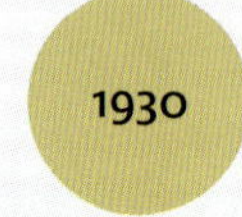

CLAUDE CAHUN: IN *AVEUX NON AVENUS* • PHOTOMONTAGE/GELATIN SILVER PRINT
15.24 X 10.48 CM (6 X 4⅛ IN) • LOS ANGELES COUNTY MUSEUM OF ART, USA

OTHER KEY WORKS

Self-Portrait (I am in Training Don't Kiss Me), 1927, Jersey Heritage Trust, UK

I Reach Out My Arms, 1932, Jersey Heritage Trust, UK

Le Coeur de Pic, cover design I, 1936, The Israel Museum, Jerusalem, Israel

An enigmatic presence in the history of twentieth-century art, Claude Cahun (1895–1954) is revered today as a photographer. During their lifetime, however, they were primarily known as a literary figure, using the camera as a personal tool to experiment quite privately with their experience of being between genders. Describing striving for a new sort of vocabulary used to 'divide myself to rule myself, multiply myself so I can make my mark', Cahun gives new layers of meaning to collage and repetition. This work includes one of their now oft-repeated phrases about the wearing of many masks, inscribed in French around the teetering tower of their stacked heads.

With an array of self-portraits in this one work, seemingly severe and a touch vampiric, it also includes one of their 1927–1929 series as a fey weight-lifter-in-training, replete with fake nipples, barbell and camp, heart-shaped rouge on their cheeks. One of a series titled *Aveux non avenus*, it is typical of Cahun, whose visual work and words revel in dichotomy. Darkly oscillating between comedy and tragedy, their surrealist memoir muses on the masturbatory habits of 90-year-old virgins and Sappho's socks, alongside 'gender confusion', pleasure and pain, God and the meaning of democracy.

They fell towards obscurity after their death, but new generations have been wowed by their uniquely rich body of work, with Cindy Sherman (1954–), David Bowie (1947–2016) and Gillian Wearing (1963–) all paying tribute to Cahun's influence.

CLAUDE CAHUN

Cahun and Marcel Moore (1892–1972) began a life-long relationship and creative collaboration in their teens. Living together in Paris in the inter-war years, as queer Jewish people, they sought refuge in Jersey in 1937 and joined the resistance movement. Famously declaring 'Neuter is the only gender that always suits me', Cahun also wrote about making these photographs with Moore to help better understand their gender identity.

SURREALISM **p.23**

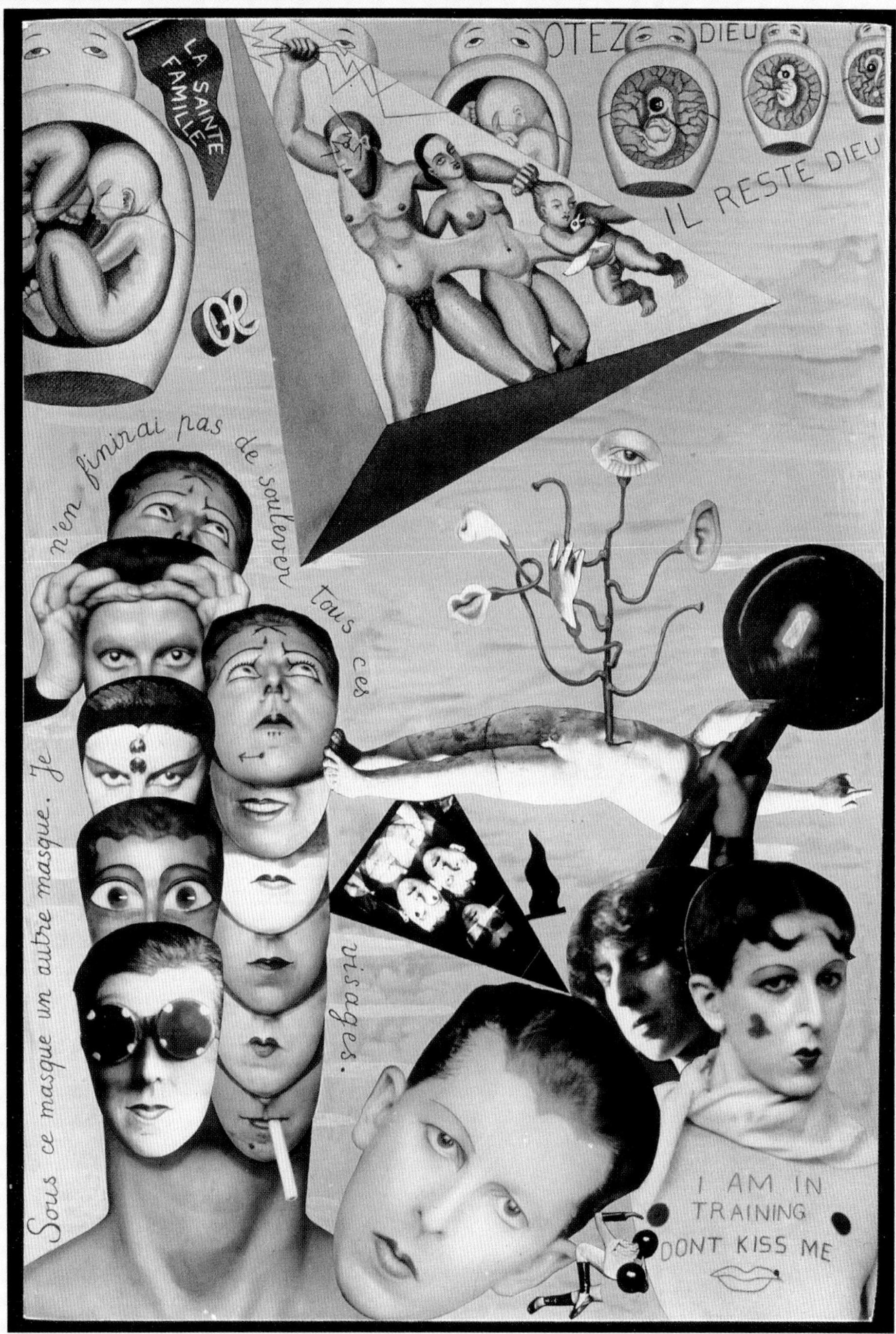

PRESENTING THE ARTIST **p.167** ASSEMBLING **p.171** SPACE OF THE BODY **p.172** MASKS **p.174**
STRAIGHT EXPECTATIONS **p.185**

Stephen Tennant in Costume as Prince Charming

1927

CECIL BEATON: BROMIDE PRINT • 19 X 26.4 CM (7⅝ X 10⅜ IN) • NATIONAL PORTRAIT GALLERY, LONDON, UK

OTHER KEY WORKS

The Bright Young Things at Wilsford, 1927, The Cecil Beaton Studio Archive

Oliver Messel in his costume for Paris in Helen!, 1932, The Cecil Beaton Studio Archive

Greta Garbo at the Hotel Plaza, New York, April, 1946, National Portrait Gallery, London, UK

The Bright Young Things epitomize the Roaring Twenties, a hedonistic period between the two World Wars where people threw caution to the wind. A group of fashionable young aristocrats and their bohemian friends, well-oiled with money and champagne, made news with details of their wild parties around the country. Fancy dress was all the rage and many of the best-known images show them keen on drag for all genders.

This is Stephen Tennant (1906–1987) in his princely costume for a Pageant of Romantic Historical Lovers in 1927, laying on the floor with eyes closed and hands held in prayer at his chest. His mother was the writer Pamela Wyndham (1871–1928), painted by John Singer Sargent (1856–1925) with her sisters in 1899. Upon her husband's death in 1920, Tennant inherited Wilsford Manor where high camp shenanigans and a decadent lifestyle segued into reclusive eccentricity as the decades rolled. He passed the time writing and illustrating an unfinished novel – *Lascar: A Story of the Maritime Boulevard*. Its lust for sailors shares similarities with *Querelle of Brest* (1947) by Jean Genet (1910–1986).

In 1965 Cecil Beaton (1904–1980) described visiting 'haunting and haunted Wilsford' as 'Stephen had not continued to be interested from the moment the last war started' in 1939. Beaton moved with the times into the Peacock Revolution of the 1960s. However, he described himself as a 'terrible homosexualist and try so hard not to be', exposing the weight of a thoroughly gay life lived almost entirely under homophobic legislation.

CECIL BEATON

Beaton came of age in the interwar period at the heart of a group of young socialite party animals, affectionately termed the Bright Young Things. His lavish homes hosted streams of celebrities like Truman Capote (1924–1984), David Hockney (1937–) and Greta Garbo (1905–1990), and he kept notoriously frank diaries about the rich and famous. From the 1940s to the 1970s he was an official photographer to the British Royal Family.

ART DECO **p.24**

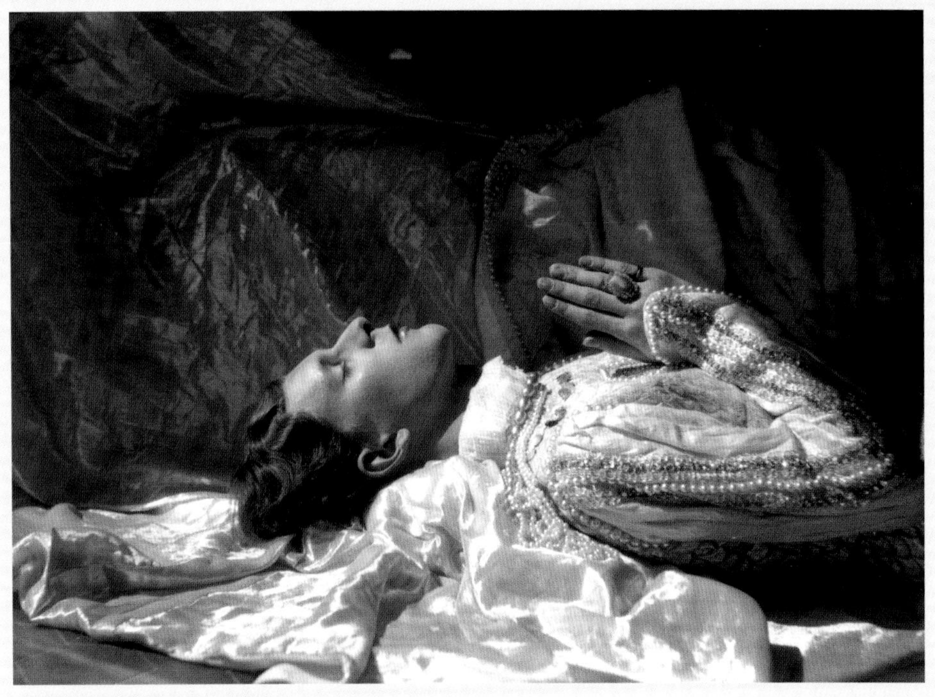

CHOSEN FAMILY **p.170** RISING CAMP **p.180** THEATRICAL TYPES **p.181** TO BE SEEN **p.186**

A Summer Day

1927

GERDA WEGENER: OIL ON CANVAS • 130 X 200 CM (51¼ X 78¾ IN)
PRIVATE COLLECTION

OTHER KEY WORKS

Lili with a Feather Fan, 1920, Private Collection

Illustrations for the erotic book Les Délassements de l'Éros, 1925, Beate Uhse Erotik-Museum Berlin, Germany

On the Banks of the Loire (the artists' colony at Beaugency) Paris, 1926, Private Collection

Gerda Wegener (1886–1940) is rated as one of the finest proponents of Danish Art Deco, standing out for her gay gaze and embrace of flirtatious female beauty rarely attempted as boldly by other women during her lifetime. Lene Schneider-Kainer (1885–1971) is a notable exception, with clearer stylistic crossovers found in the fashionable figures of other queer artists of the Deco age such as George Barbier (1882–1932) and Erté (1892–1990).

This is one of Wegener's most accomplished works. It has been proposed that the sensuous supine nude in the centre is the artist's partner Lili Elbe (1882–1931), with Elbe in her pre-transition form as Einar Wegener wearing a floppy sunhat at the easel, painting the scene from the other side. Their relationship was the subject of widespread scrutiny as they were open about Elbe's transition, together giving many of the world's first media interviews on the subject while seeking pioneering surgical and hormonal interventions through leading German sexologists including Magnus Hirschfeld (1868–1935).

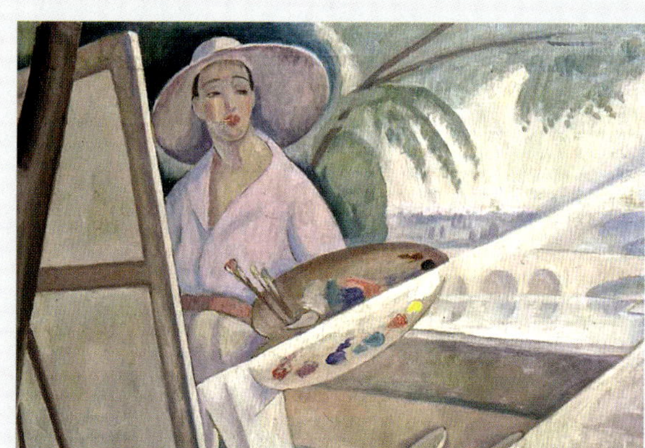

Detail: The composition including the bridge calls to mind Wegener's *On the Banks of the Loire (the Artists' Colony at Beaugency)* (1926). It has been proposed that this figure is Lili in her pre-transition form.

ART DECO **p.24**

The others seated on the ground are the painter Elna Tegner (1889–1976), a recurring sitter for Wegener who is shown gaily playing the accordion, and a Madame Guyot, married to a publisher who co-created a 1924 book with Elbe on ancient Scandinavian sagas. Wegener was entirely supportive of Elbe's identity, and in picturing their wider social circle in this scene of tranquil reverie, advances notions of acceptance and allyship.

Details: Rouge heels suggested a fun, fashionable and bold yet coquettish character. With awareness of historic cordwainer credentials, reference could be made to The Sun King (Louis XIV) who also sported such heels.

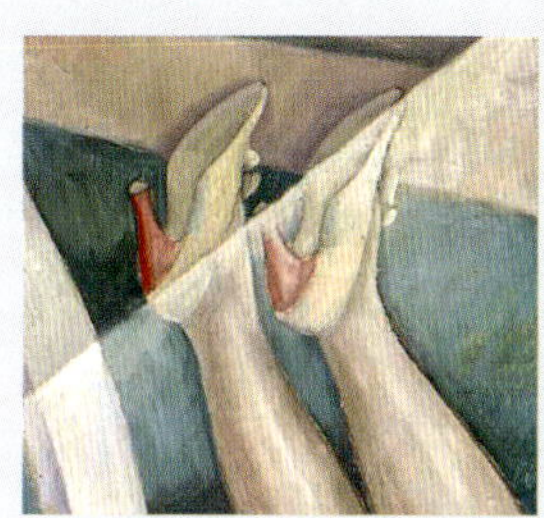

Details: Light rays are replicated in reflections from the rings worn by both women, possibly indicating a particular connection.

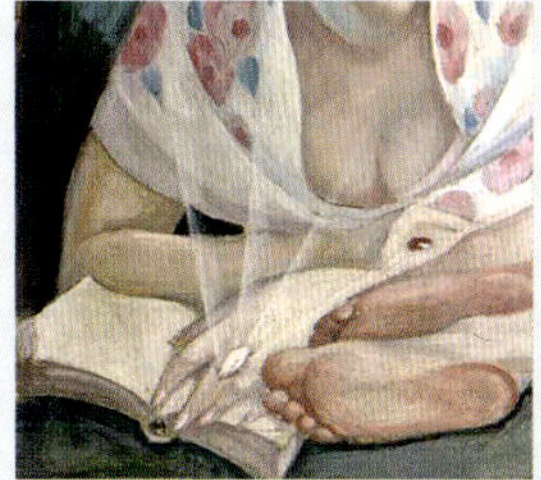

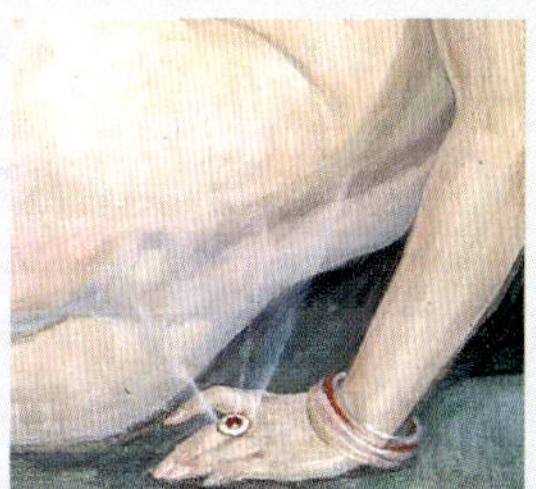

GERDA WEGENER

Wegener courted controversy in her lifetime for lesbian leanings, frequently painting erotic images of women. In 1904 she married her muse, the painter Lile Elbe (1882–1931), and together they relocated to Paris in 1912 where Elbe was freer to live as a transgender woman. Wegener was primarily a portraitist and illustrator with a chic yet highly kitsch style associated with commercial art of the Deco era.

CHOSEN FAMILY **p.170** EROTIC EXCHANGES **p.183** PLACES TO BE **p.189** GAY PARIS **p.204**

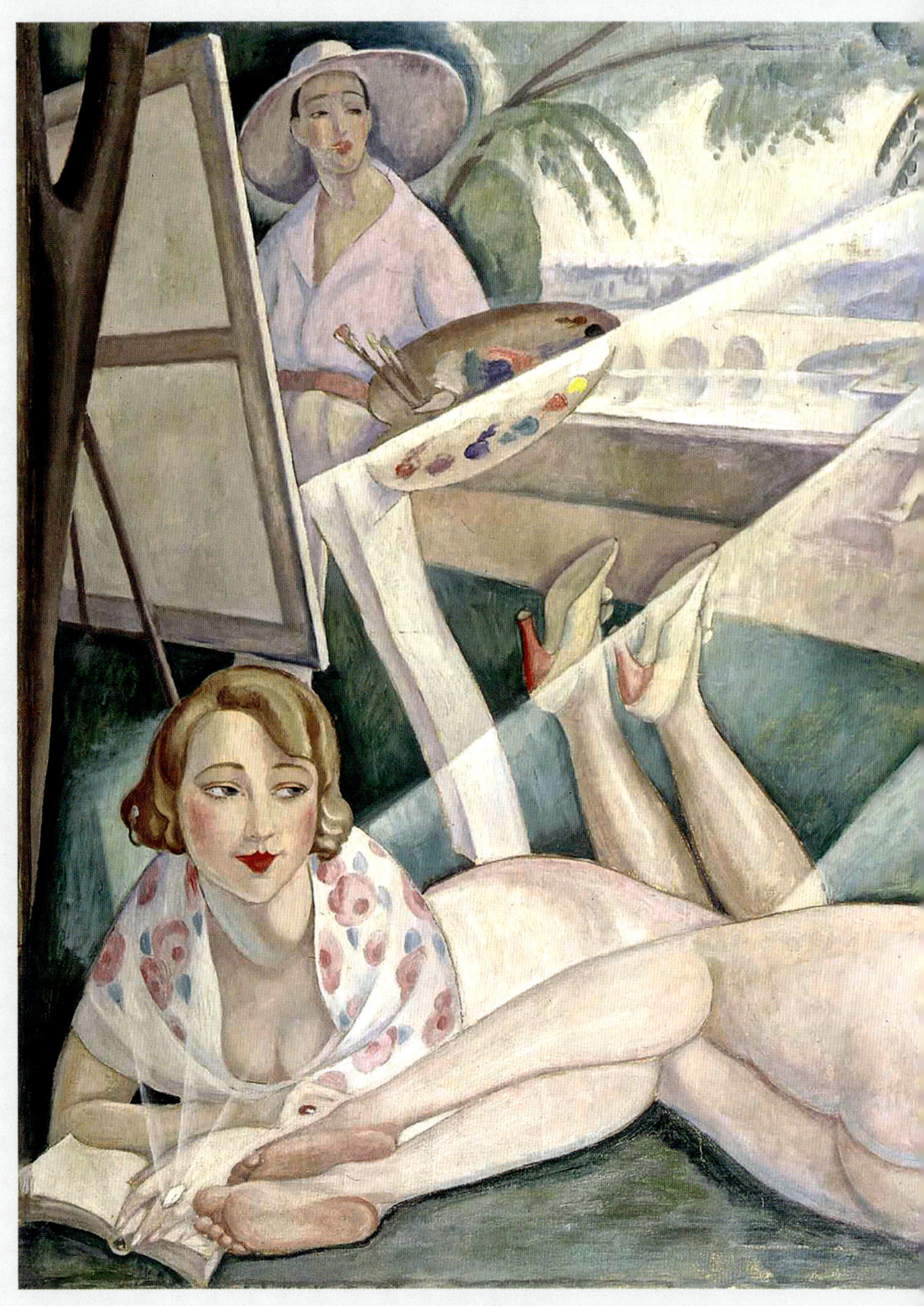

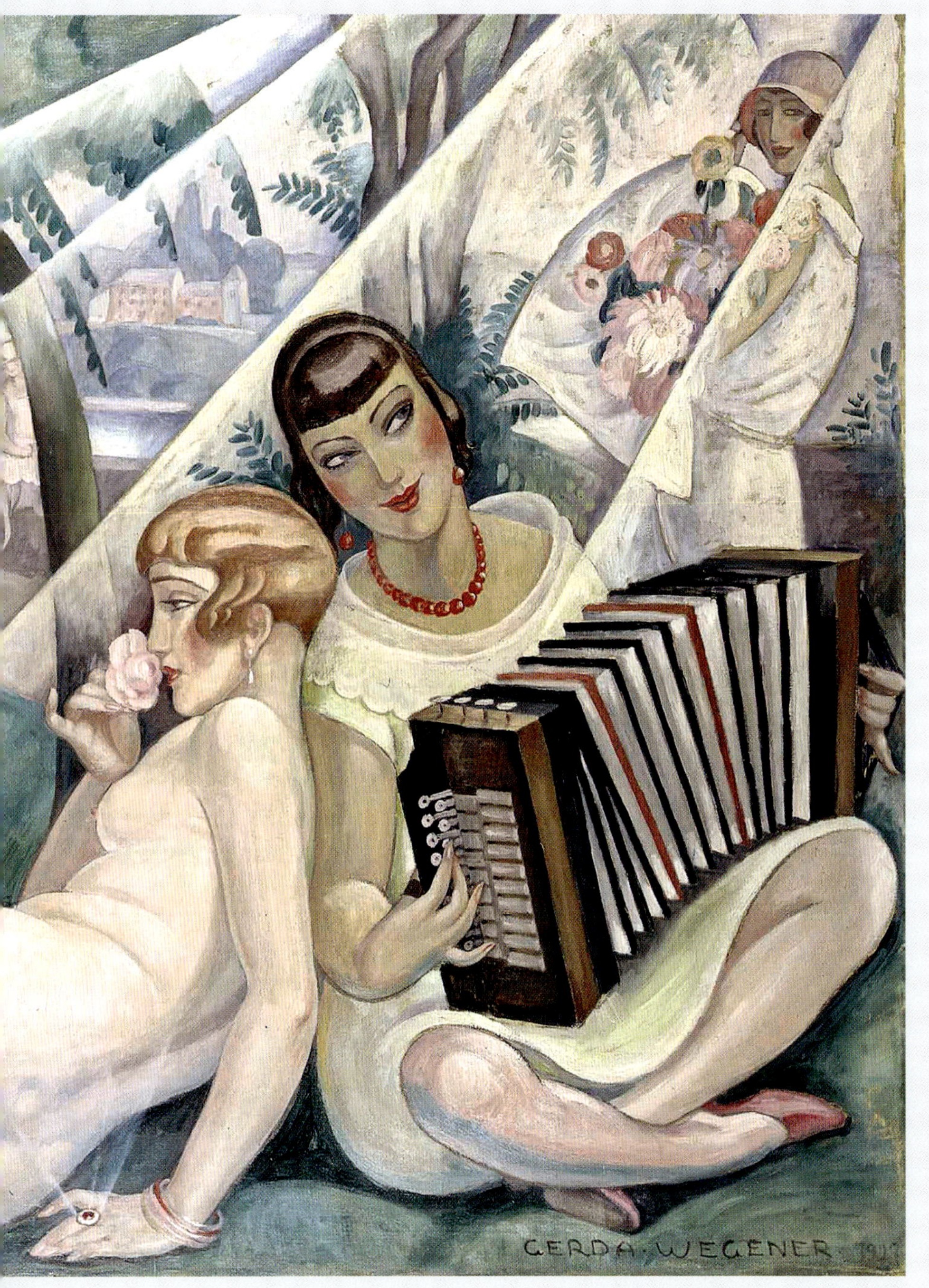
GERDA · WEGENER

Autoportrait (Tamara in a Green Bugatti)

TAMARA DE LEMPICKA: OIL ON PANEL • 35 X 27 CM (13¾ IN X 10⅝ IN)
PRIVATE COLLECTION

OTHER KEY WORKS

Portrait of the Duchess of La Salle, 1925, Private Collection

Group of Four Nudes, 1925, Private Collection

Portrait of Suzy Solidor, 1933, Private Collection

Art Deco has ricocheted through extreme highs and lows of popularity, and de Lempicka's career mirrors its giddy trajectories. Her work exemplifies the opulence of the Machine Age, and her breakthrough came with the legendary 1925 Paris world fair from which Art Deco derives its name.

Chiming with the Futurist manifesto that 'the splendour of the world has become enriched with a new beauty: the beauty of speed', this self-portrait was commissioned by the fashion director of *Die Dame* (*The Lady*). She had seen de Lempicka in Monte Carlo parking a yellow and black Renault outside Chanel, and exiting to reveal an ensemble matching her car. Upgrading into to a top-of-the-range Bugatti, this aligned with the artist's motto: 'There are no miracles. There is only what you make.'

Orgiastic scenes of muscular women such as *Group of Four Nudes* elucidate her bisexuality, and she was a regular attendee of the soirees of Natalie Barney (1876–1972), having affairs with many of her models including the singer Suzy Solidor (1900–1983). Solidor was tried for Nazi collaboration. De Lempicka too, while Jewish, professed an admiration for Mussolini (1883–1945) during the 1930s as she cornered a glittering market in modern portrait commissions from aristocrats across Europe, many similarly fascist sympathizers. In 1939, as Europe collapsed into war, she moved with her second husband to Los Angeles, but her career swiftly declined until the Deco revivals of the 1960s and a major retrospective of 1972.

TAMARA DE LEMPICKA

Born in Warsaw into a wealthy, culturally connected Jewish family, De Lempicka had a talent and lust for adventure that were both apparent from an early age. She married a lawyer at 18, fleeing the Russian Revolution to settle in Paris in 1918. In the pulsating heart of the international art world, she studied with Cubist André Lhote (1885–1962) before branching out to become a keystone of emerging Art Deco style, epitomizing interwar glamour and gaiety.

SURREALISM **p.23** ART DECO **p.24**

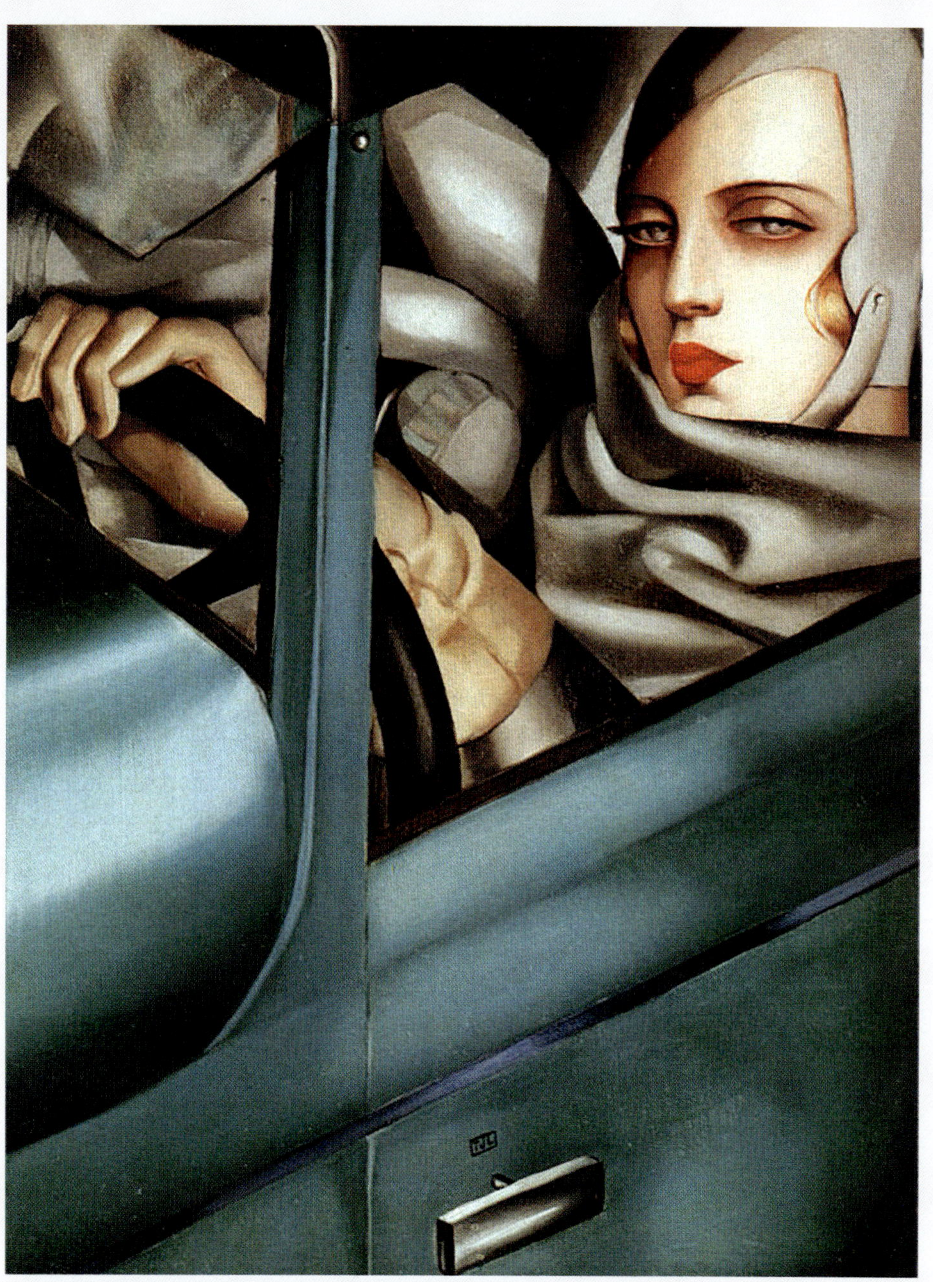

PRESENTING THE ARTIST **p.167** EROTIC EXCHANGES **p.183** COMMERCIAL ALLURE **p.200** GAY PARIS **p.204**

The Fleet's In!

1934

PAUL CADMUS: TEMPERA ON CANVAS • 94 X 170.2 CM (37 X 67 IN) • NAVY ART COLLECTION, WASHINGTON D.C., USA

OTHER KEY WORKS

Greenwich Village Cafeteria, 1934, Museum of Modern Art, New York, USA

Stone Blossom: A Conversation Piece, 1939–40, Museum of Fine Arts Boston, USA

What I Believe, 1948, McNay Art Museum, Texas, USA

The Fleet's In! by Paul Cadmus (1904–1999) came to public attention in 1934 when a letter by retired Navy General Admiral Hugh Rodman (1859–1940) was published in multiple newspapers, complaining: 'It represents a most disgraceful, sordid, disreputable, drunken brawl' and 'Apparently a number of enlisted men are consorting with a party of streetwalkers and denizens of the red-light district.' The painting caught his eye in a preview of The Corcoran Gallery of Art, Washington, D.C. and on his orders was removed before the exhibition opened.

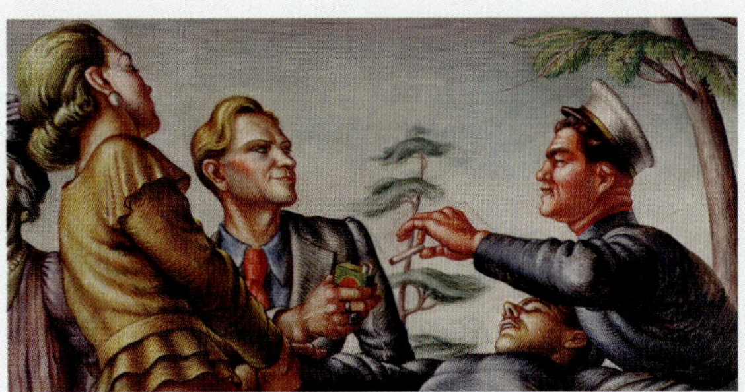

Detail: Waterfronts such as Riverside Park, New York (the likely setting here) were well-known pick-up spots for gay men at the time. The blond gentleman's appearance includes characteristics of 'fairy' or 'pansy' characters, seen in other works by Cadmus. The offer of a cigarette has obvious phallic connotations.

Rodman's description is nevertheless fitting for a decidedly unheroic depiction of sailors and a marine on shore leave. Two figures especially draw the queer eye: the svelte woman in red with the prominent Adam's apple, and the blond-haired gentleman whose hair, red tie, plucked eyebrows and rouge evoke a gay male archetype of the time. He is strikingly similar to a man seen entering the men's lavatories in the equally cacophonous *Greenwich Village Cafeteria* (1934). *Shore Leave* (1933) also includes a similar man cruising a sailor.

Cadmus cannily contoured ensuing conversations circulating his censorship. He provided comments for newspapers, alongside reproductions of the painting, remarking to the *New York Times*: 'I don't think admirals have much sense of humor' and noting that the controversy had propelled him to fame. He was not deterred from pursuing this form of 'naval gazing', and *Sailors and Floosies* (1938) was a further scene of portside debauchery and ambiguity.

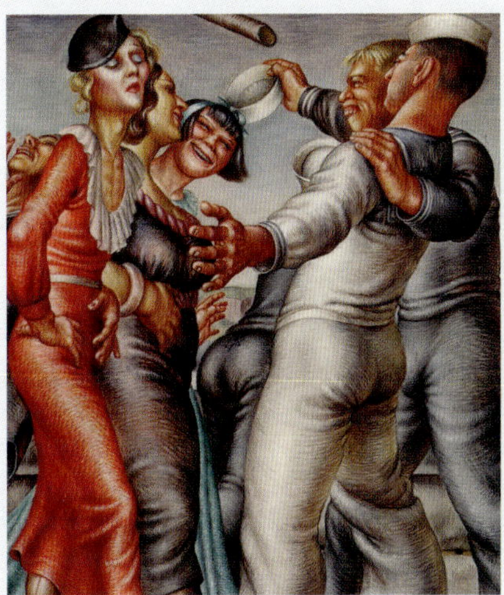

Detail: The sailors are shown as being in pursuit and subject of varying desires. The visible chest bones and Adam's apple of the figure in red suggest some gender ambiguity.

PAUL CADMUS

Cadmus was intrigued by human foibles, and his work often has an informality. Homosexuality became an increasingly dominant element within his carefully rendered images of implied and explicit sexual symbolism. In the 1930s and 1940s, Cadmus formed the PaJaMa collective with his sister Margaret (1906–1998) and her husband Jared French (1905–1998) (with whom he had an intimate friendship), sharing a studio as well as philosophies. Their circle included George Platt Lynes (1907–1955), who shared interests in figurative homoerotica.

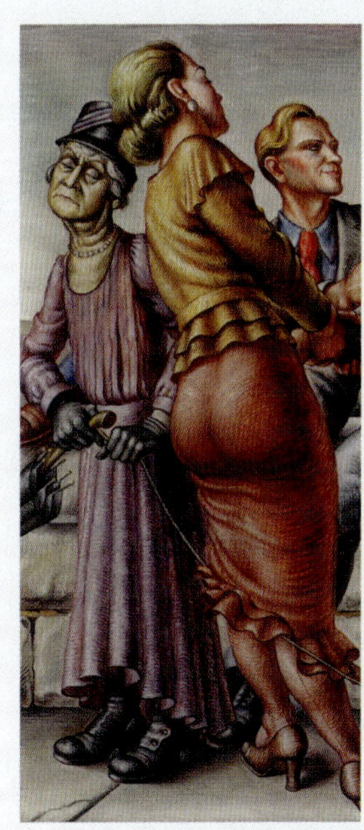

Detail: Tight clothing is used to sexualize most participants. As the figure in the tight skirt attempts to pull a drunk sailor up off the wall, their hemline is raised by a dog lead. The older woman's grip on the umbrella handle and its position could also be read into.

CALL OF THE SEA **p.179** QUEER EYE **p.182** EROTIC EXCHANGES **p.183**

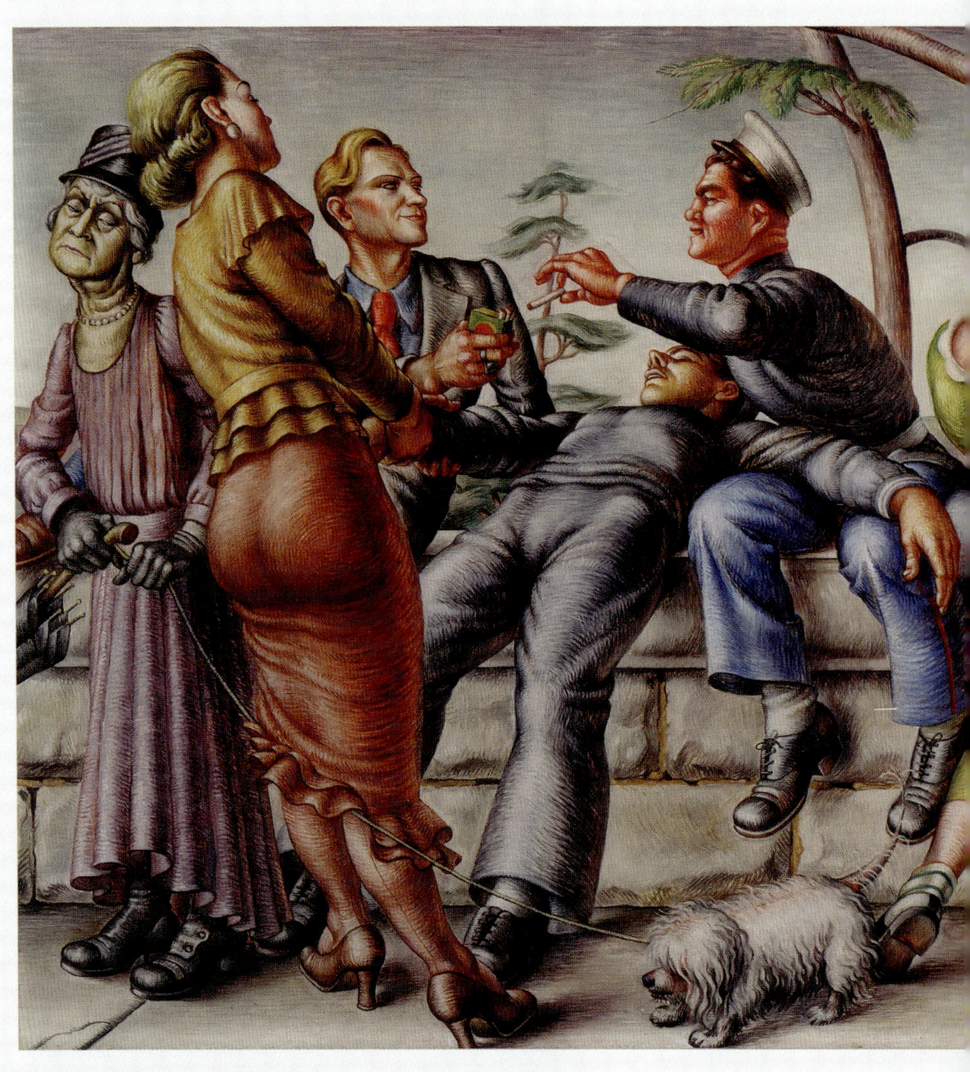

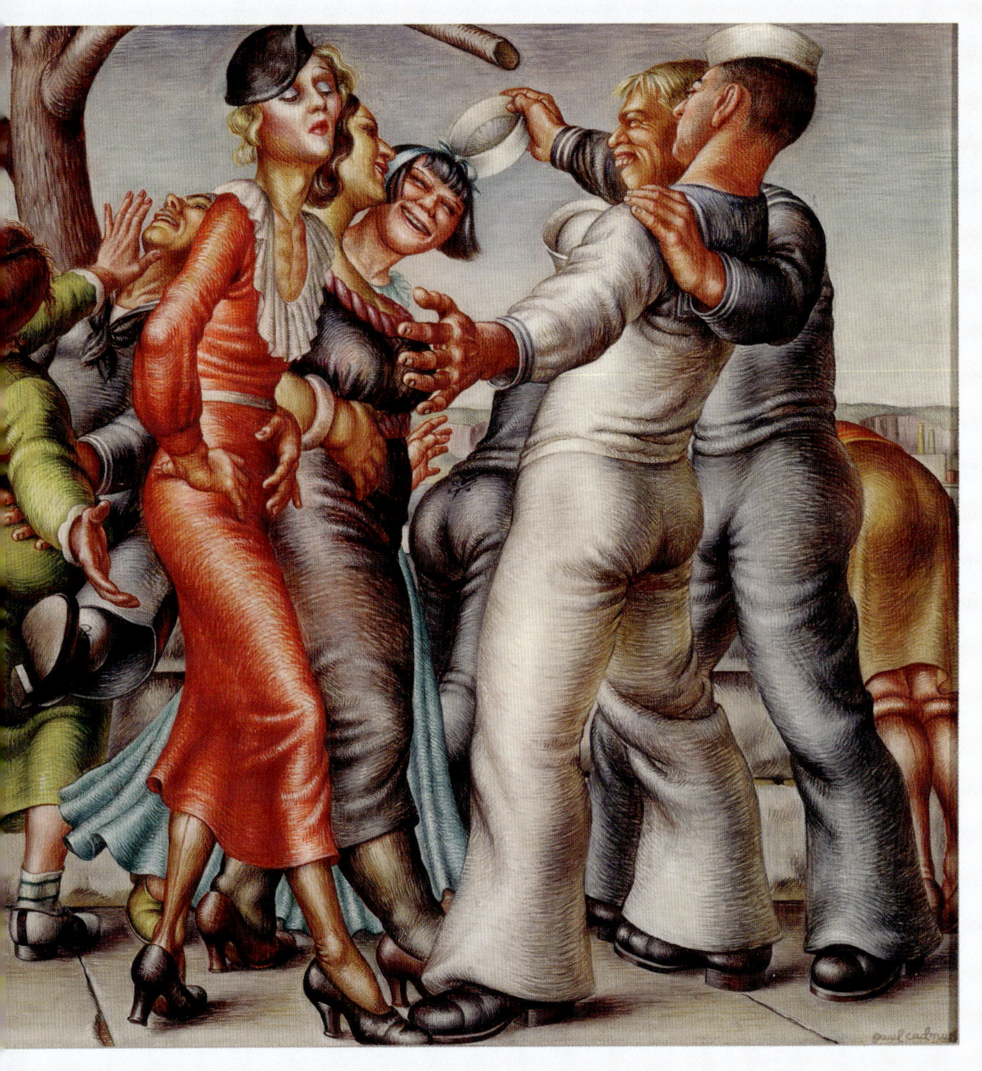

Feral Benga

1935

JAMES RICHMOND BARTHÉ: BRONZE • 48.3 X 17.1 X 11.4 CM (19 X 6¾ X 4½ IN)
MUSEUM OF FINE ARTS, HOUSTON, TEXAS, USA

OTHER KEY WORKS

Black Narcissus, 1929, Courtesy Childs Gallery, Boston, USA

Fallen Aviator, 1945, Tuskegee Institute, Tuskegee, Alabama, USA

Africa Awakening, 1959, Museum of Art, University of Southern Mississippi, Hattiesburg, USA

James Richmond Barthé (1901–1989) was committed to figurative art: 'All my life I have been interested in trying to capture the spiritual quality I see and feel in people, and I feel that the human figure as God made it, is the best means of expressing this spirit in man.'

Adopting motifs of Classicism to depict (mainly) African American male figures, he aspired for his work to be regarded in the context of classical masterpieces, rather than critiquing their restrictive traditions. He painted several portraits but intermittently noted unrealized intentions to 'give up sculpture and get back to my painting'. In 1971 he recorded feeling validated by reception to his work: 'The Italians like my work … They compare it with the best of the Renaissance.' However, Barthé is more known for involvement with the Harlem Renaissance, forming close relations within its bi and homosexual circles including photographer and patron Carl Ven Vechten (1880–1964) and writer Alain LeRoy Locke (1885–1954).

A 1934 trip to Paris introduced him to performers including François Benga (1906–1957), a famous gay Senegalese dancer who starred for a time at the Folies Bergère (where he gained his fetishized stage name 'Féral'). Barthé's bronze of Benga performing his signature 'Danse Du Sabre' was noted at the time as possessing a sexual charge. Barthé's gaze complicates the eroticized racial 'exotic primitives', stereotypes that Benga had to perform amidst.

JAMES RICHMOND BARTHÉ
Born in Mississippi, Barthé showed early artistic promise but was unable to enrol at art schools in the South due to racial segregation. He entered the Art Institute of Chicago in 1924 with aspirations as a portrait painter. Introduced to sculpture in his senior year, he gained recognition for figurative sculpture, with male physiques evoking aspects of the Black experience. After moving to New York he became a leading figure in the Harlem Renaissance.

HARLEM RENAISSANCE **p.22**

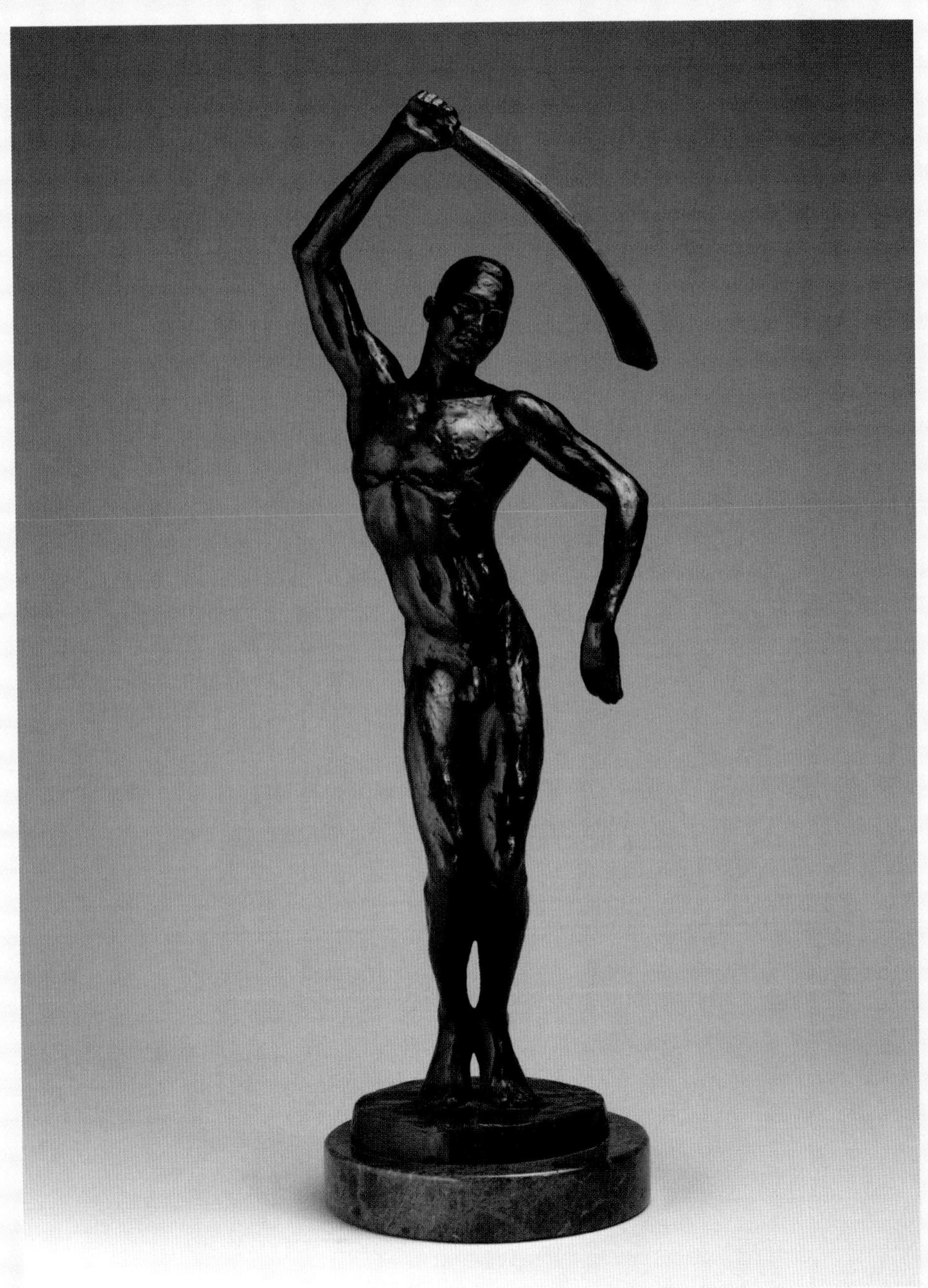

SPACE OF THE BODY **p.172** DANCE **p.188** DESIRE FOR ANTIQUITY **p.194**

Dancing Figures

1935

RICHARD BRUCE NUGENT: BLACK INK AND GRAPHITE ON PAPER • 37.5 X 26.7 CM (14¾ X 10½ IN) • BROOKLYN MUSEUM, NEW YORK, USA

OTHER KEY WORKS

Drawings for Mulattoes, Numbers 2 and 3, 1927, Fales Library and Special Collections, New York University, USA

Black Gum, illustration from *Opportunity* magazine, 1928, Beinecke Rare Book & Manuscript Library, Yale University, New Haven, USA

Salome Dancing, c.1925–1930, Brooklyn Museum, New York, USA

RICHARD BRUCE NUGENT

Dubbed the 'Gay Rebel of the Harlem Renaissance' Nugent had a long, productive career as an author, actor, dancer and artist, becoming an influential bridge between the Harlem Renaissance and Black gay movements of the 1980s. He helped create and edit *FIRE!!*, an avant-garde magazine devoted to African American artists [see *FIRE!!* Magazine] and in the 1960s was one of the founders of the Harlem Cultural Council.

Silhouettes encompass associations with Ancient Greek pottery, rulers on coins, Asian shadow theatre, and European portraiture fashions of the eighteenth and nineteenth centuries. Its peak corresponded with the international slave trade and there are records of enslaved people's silhouettes being used as ownership documents.

Several Harlem Renaissance artists adopted Art Deco silhouette aesthetics to create scenes often linking African histories with diasporic futures. The work of Richard Bruce Nugent (1906–1987) featured in *Ebony and Topaz* (1927), by Charles S. Johnson (1893–1956). Here depicting two dancers, Nugent had acute appreciation of the expressive power of moving bodies, being a dancer himself.

Nugent's poem *Shadow* (1925) conveys the personal significance of silhouettes: 'A dark shadow in the light. / A silhouette am I / On the face of the moon / Lacking color / Or vivid brightness / But defined all the clearer / Because / I am dark, / Black on the face of the moon. [...]'. He later explained that rather than alluding to racial stigmatization, 'I intended it to be a soul-searching poem of another kind of lonesomeness ... You see, I am a homosexual.' Posthumously published in 2008, Nugent's novel *Gentleman Jigger*, which follows Stuart, a defiantly queer artist amid the Harlem Renaissance, is celebrated for its candid exploration of Black sexuality.

Kara Walker (1969–) has cut-out a subsequent renaissance of the silhouette, with panoramic paper-cut friezes that reveal and confront brutality of American racism, slavery and inequality.

HARLEM RENAISSANCE **p.22**

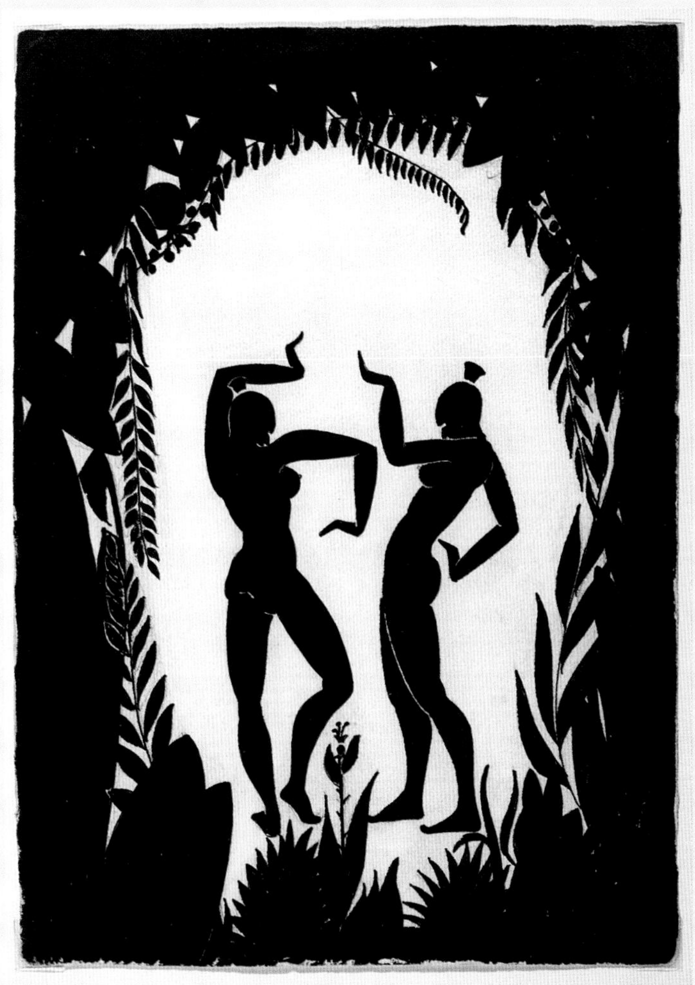

SPACE OF THE BODY **p.172** TO BE SEEN **p.186** DANCE **p.188** *FIRE!!* MAGAZINE **p.203**

Medallion (YouWe)

GLUCK: OIL ON CANVAS • 30.5 X 35.6 CM (12 X 14 IN) • PRIVATE COLLECTION

OTHER KEY WORKS

Flora's Cloak, c.1923, Tate, London, UK

Lilac and Guelder Rose, 1932–37, Manchester Art Gallery, UK

Gluck, 1942, National Portrait Gallery, London, UK

Adopting the name Gluck, they specified on the backs of publicity photographs: 'please return in good condition to Gluck, no prefix, suffix or quotes'. Gluck referred to *Medallion* as the 'YouWe' painting and considered it a marriage picture to artist and philanthropist Nesta Obermer (1893–1984), writing: 'Darling Heart, we are not an "affair" are we – We are husband and wife. I have never said or written "Eternity" before.' Fused together, Gluck looks directly into the immediate future with a steady eye and Obermer raises their gaze to the sky. Biographer Diana Souhami (1940–) has suggested it reflects Gluck's difficulties with boundaries in relationships noting that Gluck 'In love, melted willingly, if dangerously' into a woman.

While producing work for a 1937 exhibition at the Fine Arts Society, London, Gluck wrote to Obermer 'nothing but happy pictures since YouWe', and painted *Noel* (1937) to hang alongside it in the exhibition – a scene of festive detritus from celebrating their first Christmas together.

Journalists covering Gluck's exhibitions frequently remarked on them being 'very unconventional in regard to dress'. In the 1950s Gluck became exasperated by the attention consistently given to their appearance and destroyed several early self-portraits. Romaine Brooks' famous portrait of Gluck, *Peter, a Young English Girl* (1923–24), captures their natural androgyny. It was probably among the portraits in Brooks' studio where Truman Capote (1924–1984) famously exclaimed it 'the all-time ultimate gallery of famous dykes', 'an international daisy chain'.

GLUCK

Gluck was born in London to a wealthy family, and a musical career and marriage was their expected route. Keen to escape the restrictive reins of family and convention, they left home, cropped their hair, donned 'male clothing' and set to establish themselves as an artist. Their oeuvre incorporated an eclectic selection of subjects, including portraits, vaudeville acts, racetracks, flowers and fish. In later years they championed the cause of ensuring the quality manufacture of oil paints.

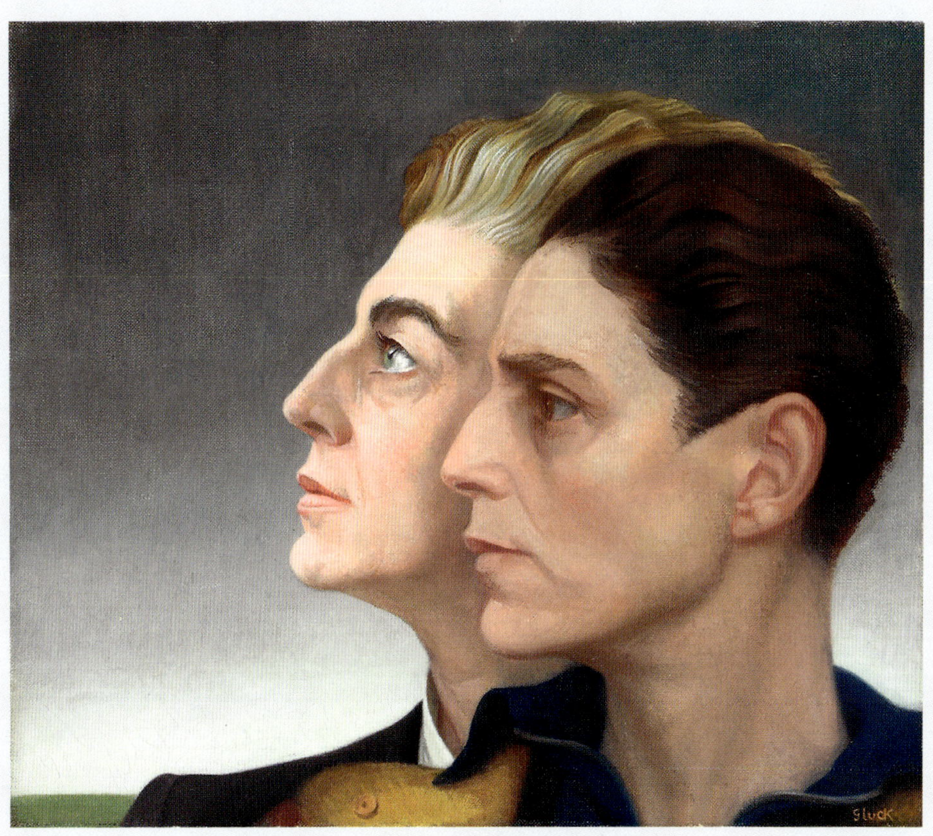

PRESENTING THE ARTIST **p.167** TO BE SEEN **p.186** ON THE COVER **p.207**

Object (Le Déjeuner en Fourrure)

MÉRET OPPENHEIM: FUR-COVERED CUP, SAUCER AND SPOON • CUP 10.9 CM (4⅜ IN) DIAMETER; SAUCER 23.7 CM (9⅜ IN) DIAMETER; SPOON 20.2 CM (8 IN) LENGTH, OVERALL HEIGHT 7.3 CM (2⅞ IN) • MUSEUM OF MODERN ART, NEW YORK, USA

OTHER KEY WORKS

Ma gouvernante – My Nurse – Mein Kindermädchen, 1936/1967, Moderna Museet, Stockholm, Sweden

Red Head, Blue Body (Roter Kopf, blauer Körper), 1936, Museum of Modern Art, New York, USA

Das Paar (The Couple), 1956, Private Collection

At a Parisian café in 1936, Dora Maar (1907–1997) and Pablo Picasso (1881–1973) admire Méret Oppenheim's (1913–85) bracelet – a design of brass coated with ocelot fur she created for fashion designer Elsa Schiaparelli (1890–1973). Picasso remarks that everything could be covered with fur. 'Even this cup and saucer,' quips Oppenheim, and jokingly calls for a fur to warm her tea. So runs the oft-repeated origin story of this iconic artwork.

Oppenheim returned to this image when invited to contribute to the *Surrealist Objects* exhibition (1936), Paris – producing a cup, saucer and spoon covered in fur. André Breton (1896–1966) designated the tile *Breakfast in Fur*, alluding to the notorious *Le Déjeuner sur l'herbe* (1863) by Édouard Manet (1832–1883), and Leopold von Sacher-Masoch's sadomasochistic novella *Venus in Furs* (1870) – starkly arousing erotic insinuations.

Sexual connotations are obvious – both fur and cups being associated with female genitalia and 'drinking from the furry cup' used to describe oral sex – often insinuating lesbianism. The combination also evokes a sensual frisson of simultaneous oral pleasure and repulsion.

Oppenheim's work is significant as women were largely regarded as subjects the and muses of the men who dominated Surrealism. She struggled with the work's fame arising from its appearance in MoMA's *Fantastic Art, Dada, Surrealism* (1936–37) and only regained creative confidence in the mid-1950s. Increasingly concerned with concepts of female creativity, she advocated for an 'androgyny of the spirit'.

MÉRET OPPENHEIM

Born in Berlin and raised in Switzerland, Oppenheim left to attend the Académie de la Grande Chaumière, Paris. Here she fell into Surrealist circles and posed for one of Man Ray's most famous photographs, *Erotique Voilée* (1933), nude and covered in ink at a printing press. She had her first solo exhibition in Basel, in 1936 and returned to live there the following year.

SURREALISM **p.23** FEMINIST ART **p.30**

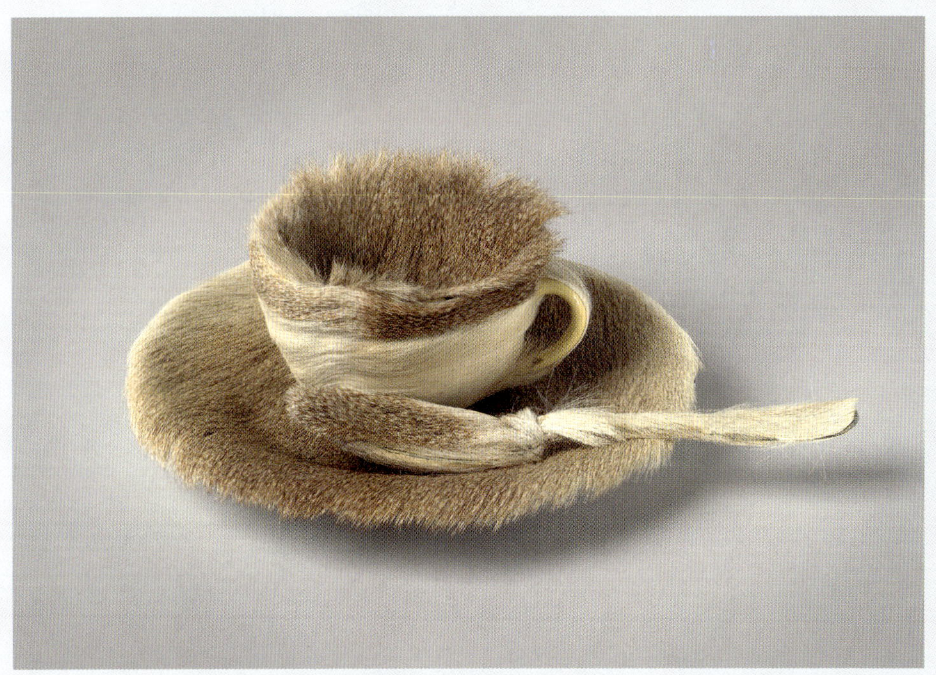

ASSEMBLING **p.171** SPACE OF THE BODY **p.172** QUEER EYE **p.182**

Self Portrait with Cropped Hair

FRIDA KAHLO: OIL ON CANVAS • 40 X 27.9 CM (15¾ X 11 IN) • MUSEUM OF MODERN ART, NEW YORK, USA

OTHER KEY WORKS

Self-portrait on the Border between Mexico and the United States of America, 1932, Detroit Institute of Arts, USA

The Two Fridas, 1939, Museo de Arte Moderno, Mexico City, Mexico

Roots, 1943, Private Collection

Here Frida Kahlo (1907–1954) eschews the traditionally feminine Tehuana dresses and flowers donned in other self-portraits. Wearing a suit, with cut hair strewn across the ground, she presents a more androgynous figure. The inclusion of lyrics from a popular Mexican song ('Look, if I loved you it was because of your hair. Now that you are without hair, I don't love you anymore') suggests disdain for the superficiality of attraction.

Kahlo and her husband, artist Diego Rivera (1886–1957), had divorced the previous year. The loose-fitting suit (probably Rivera's) suggests usurpation of another's role in newfound autonomy. The painting implies both the brutality of separation and determination to reclaim agency and has also been read as indicating her bisexuality.

Kahlo's influence is felt through subsequent generations of artists. Collective Las Yeguas del Apocalipsis (The Mares of the Apocalypse) describe their *Las Dos Fridas* (1989) as 'a becoming of Frida Kahlo', linking to the power and politics of blood during the AIDS crisis. Mexican artist Nahum B. Zenil (1947–) similarly uses self-portraiture to offer cultural critiques of Mexico touching upon gender and sexuality and Kahlo appears in works imprinted on his heart or alongside him on the bus. Yasumasa Morimura (1951–) takes on her appearance in the series of self-portraits *An Inner Dialogue with Frida Kahlo* (2001), describing Kahlo's work as an inspirationally 'fierce and intense manifestation of human sentiments and universal themes.'

FRIDA KAHLO

Kahlo famously stated, 'I paint self-portraits because I am the person that I know best.' A revolutionary communist, feminist, bisexual, disabled Mexican – Kahlo has an appeal and resonance (particularly to marginalized groups) that could be ascribed to her ability to present herself as a distinctively multifaceted individual. Introspective but with an acute eye on sociopolitical themes, she challenged machismo and gendered expectations of Mexican society.

SURREALISM **p.23** FEMINIST ART **p.30**

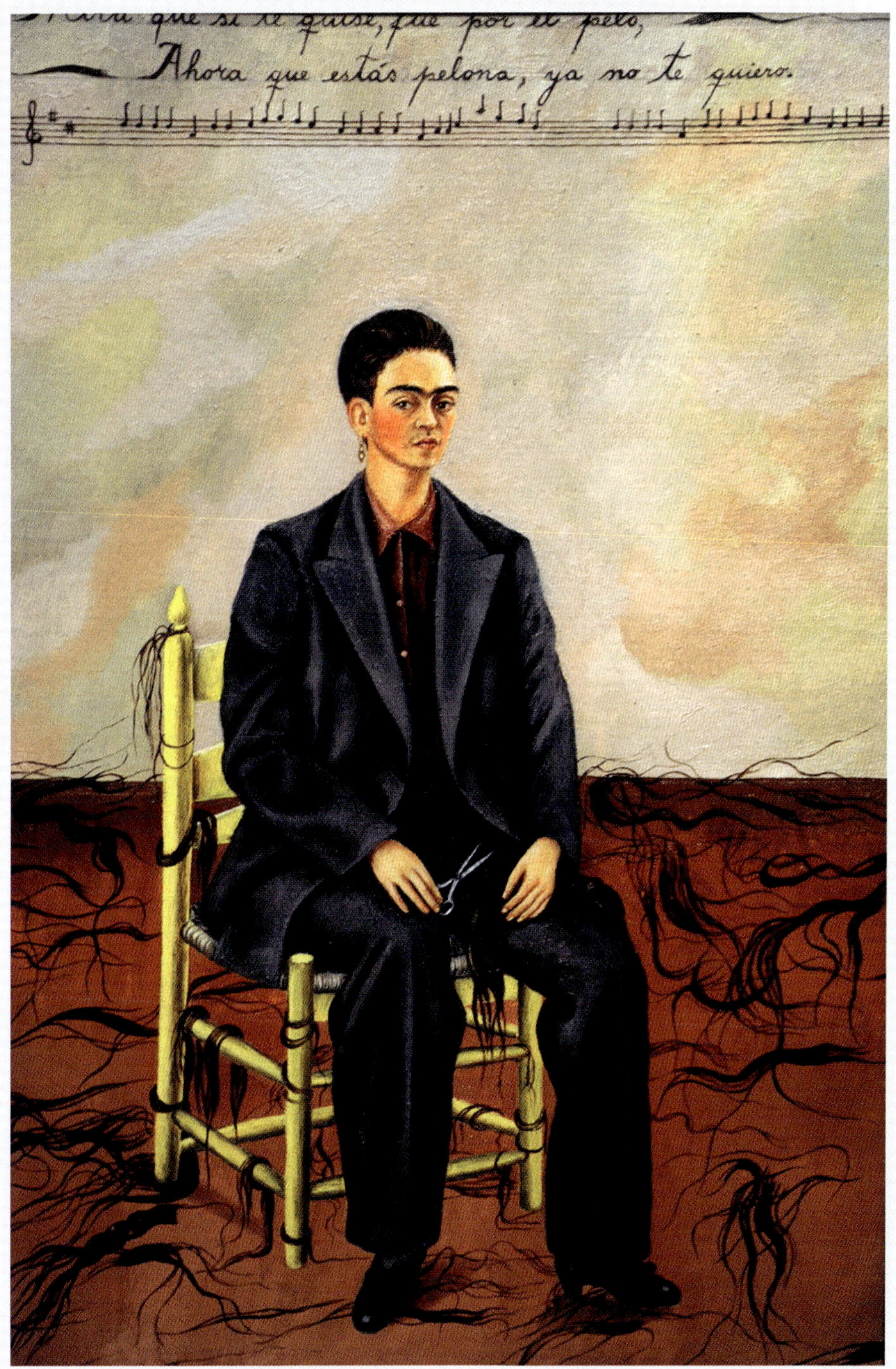

PRESENTING THE ARTIST **p.167** STRAIGHT EXPECTATIONS **p.185** TO BE SEEN **p.186**

Untitled

1962

TOM OF FINLAND (TOUKO LAAKSONEN): GRAPHITE ON PAPER • 30.48 X 25.4 CM (12 X 10 IN) • SAN FRANCISCO MUSEUM OF MODERN ART, USA

OTHER KEY WORKS

Untitled **(biker and sailor)**, 1962, San Francisco Museum of Modern Art, USA

Untitled **(biker and two men)**, 1973, Private Collection

Untitled **(policeman and construction workers)**, 1988, Art Institute of Chicago, USA

In the mid-twentieth century, mainstream stereotyping of homosexual men as 'effeminate' sissies was widespread. Tom of Finland was at the core of a group of emerging artists challenging this homogeny by depicting gay men as strong, assertive and hyper-masculine. Influenced by precursors like Etienne (1933–1991) and George Quaintance (1902–1957), Touko Laaksonen (1920–1991) refined the look with expressive hyperbolic men whose superlative musculature and enormous appendages pushed boundaries between erotica, fetishism and art. He commented: 'I know my "dirty little drawings" are never going to hang in the main salons of the Louvre, but it would be nice if … our world learns to accept all the different ways of loving. Then maybe I could have a place in one of the smaller side rooms.'

Attributing his fetish for uniforms to time serving in the Second World War, from all-American sailors to leather-clad Nazi officers, after the war he turned his attention to emerging biker subcultures. This was stimulated by photographer Scott of London (Tom Nicholls), a specialist in leather-clad bikers, whom Laaksonen met on a 1957 London trip. Initially skirting censorship laws by drawing 'physique scenes', they became more explicit as restrictions eased – and increasingly pirated.

Laaksonen's influence can be seen in the works of many who have modified motifs and expanded representation, including Sadao Hasegawa (1945–1999), Go Mishima (Tsuyoshi Yoshida) (1924–1988) and G. B. Jones (1965–), whose *Tom Girls,* defiant leather dykes, are both erotic tribute and critique.

TOUKO LAAKSONEN (TOM OF FINLAND)

Raised in south-western Finland, Laaksonen studied advertising at Helsinki, his famed homoerotic pencil drawings first appearing publicly in the American magazine *Physique Pictorial* in 1957. Its editor, photographer Bob Mizer (1922–1992), is credited with creating the name Tom of Finland. In 2014 the Finnish postal service published a set of three stamps featuring Laaksonen's work and reported a record amount of global interest with pre-orders from 178 countries.

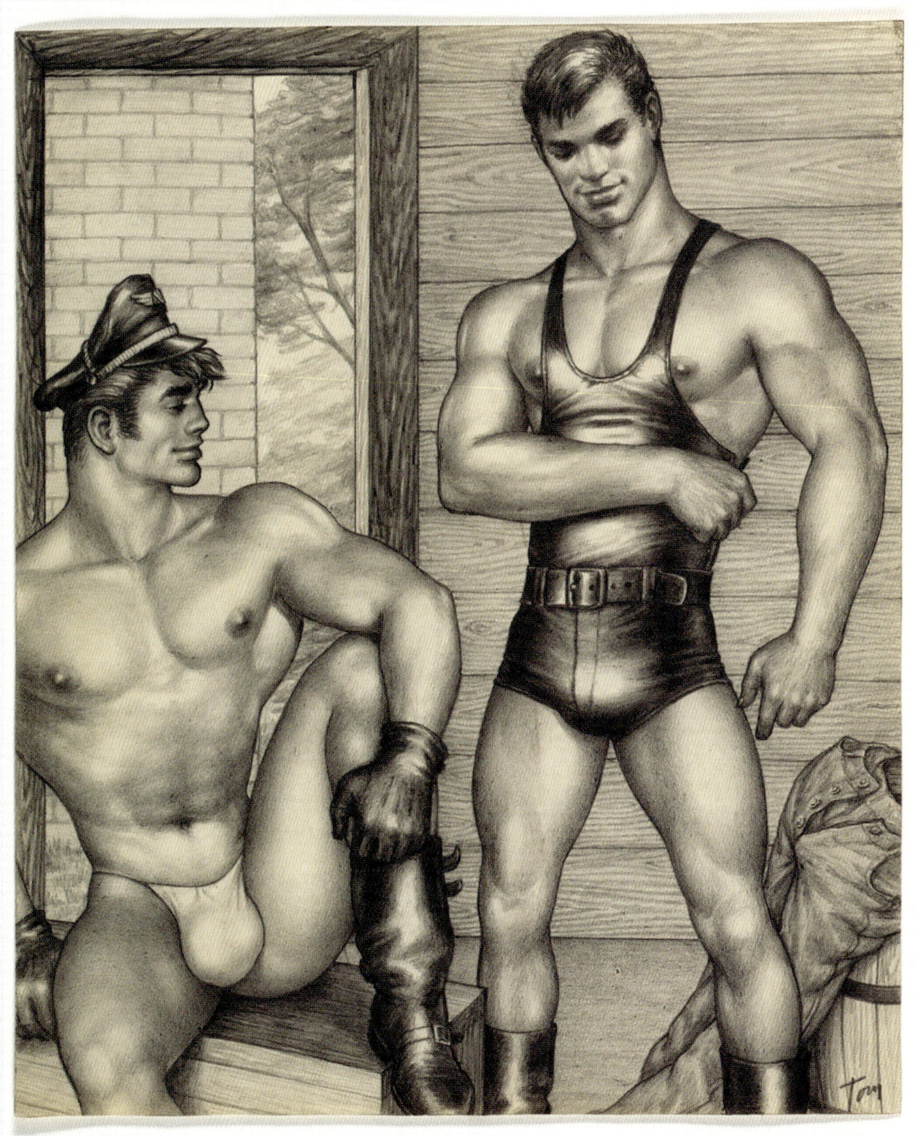

EROTIC EXCHANGES **p.183**

Ladies and Gentlemen (Marsha P. Johnson)

ANDY WARHOL: SCREENPRINT • 110.5 X 71.9 CM (43½ X 28⅓ IN)
PRIVATE COLLECTION

OTHER KEY WORKS

Campbell's Soup Cans, 1962, Museum of Modern Art, New York, USA

Marilyn Diptych, 1962, Tate, London, UK

Exploding Plastic Inevitable, series of events, 1966–67

Transvestites, drag queens and transgender individuals formed the core of Andy Warhol's (1928–1987) 'Superstars', including Holly Woodlawn (1946–2015), Candy Darling (1944–1974) and Jackie Curtis (1947–1985), described by Warhol as a 'pioneer without a frontier'. In 1974, art dealer Luciano Anselmino commissioned 'a series on drag queens', *Ladies and Gentlemen*. Warhol's response was illuminating as, according to associates, he declared drag queens 'were out' and had tired of his trans subjects. Deciding upon a collection of 'nutty-looking drag queens' who frequented The Gilded Grape, participants were offered $50 an hour to have their Polaroid taken.

Despite Warhol's initial disrespect, it became one of the biggest series he produced. Participants included Marsha P. Johnson (1945–1992) who variably identified as gay, transvestite and a drag or street queen. Famously involved in the 1969 Stonewall uprising, Marsha is now recognized as a heroic figure in LGBTQ+ liberation.

The *Altered Image* series (1981) by Chris Makos (1948–) contains 365 shots of Warhol himself made-up, wearing various wigs, but retaining a shirt and tie, evoking a Robert Mapplethorpe (1946–1989) self-portrait of the previous year. Deborah Kass (1952–) identified with Warhol as 'the first queer artist'. Her *The Warhol Project* series (1992–2000) adopts his icon-creating aesthetics, in simultaneous homage and critique, to celebrate figures she thought Warhol would have chosen had he been a forty-something Jewish lesbian. In *Jewish Jackie* (1992), Warhol's Jackie O (1929–1994) becomes Barbra Streisand (1942–) and Chairman Mao becomes Gertrude Stein (1874–1946) in *Chairman Ma* (1993).

ANDY WARHOL

Having worked as an illustrator and commercial artist, Warhol primarily played with dichotomies of power and superficiality in depicting 'real life'. Embracing smooth impersonal surfaces and detaching himself from physical production by employing assistants in his 'factory' he deliberately eluded embedded meanings, advising: 'If you want to know all about Andy Warhol, just look at the surface of my paintings and films and me, and there I am. There's nothing behind it.'

POP ART **p.27** POSTMODERNISM **p.33**

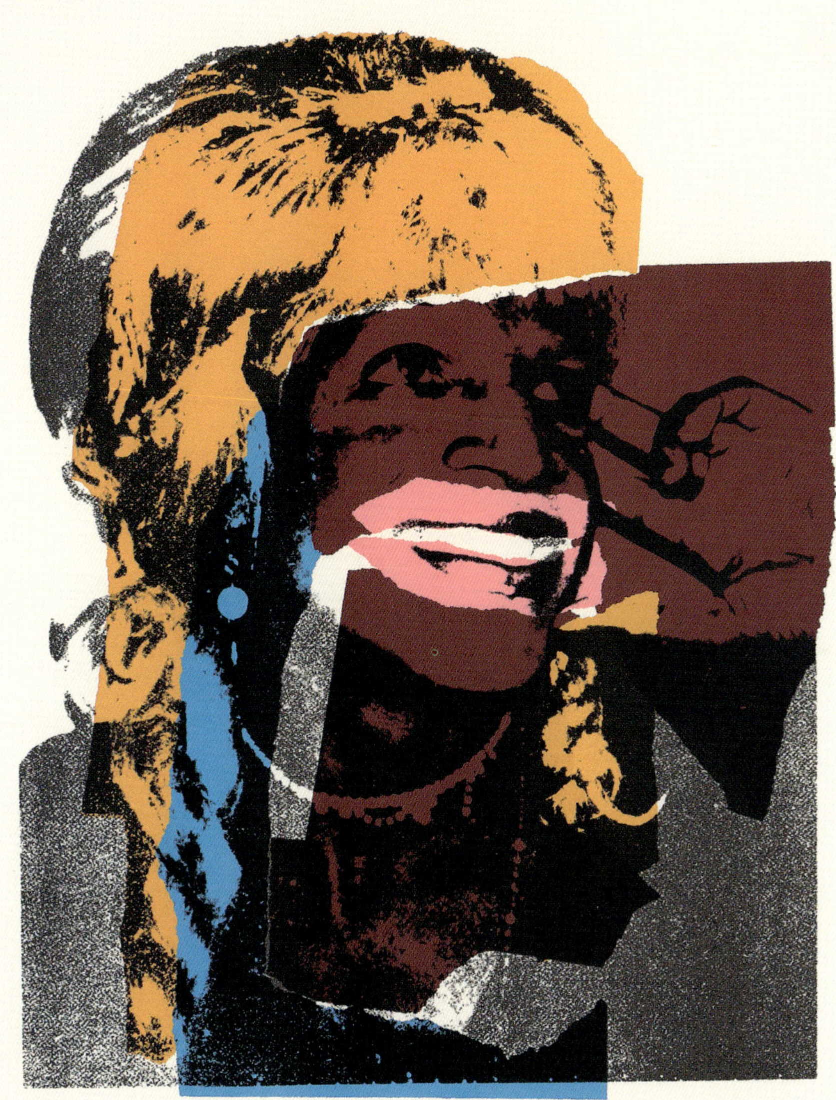

QUEER ICONS **p.184** ON SCREEN **p.187**

Cunt Coloring Book

1975

TEE A. CORINNE: PRINT ON PAPER, • 21.6 X 27.95 X 0.6 CM (8½ X 11 X ¼ IN)
PUBLISHED BY LAST GASP

OTHER KEY WORKS

***Yantras of Womanlove: Diagrams of Energy* photobook**, 1982, University of Oregon, USA

Isis series, 1986, University of Oregon, USA

Intimacies, 2001, hardcover book published by Last Gasp

With a devotion to sex positivity, erotic imagery and lesbian visibility, Tee A. Corinne (1943–2006) worked to broaden lesbian sexual language and imagery. Corinne conceived of the *Cunt Coloring Book* while working at the San Francisco Sex Information Switchboard. Noting a lack of access to images of women's genitals, beyond pornography for straight men, Corinne sought to demystify bodies in an educational and affirmational manner.

First self-published in 1975, it features 41 pages of black-and-white drawings from life, with an introductory image labelled with anatomical names. The publication proved popular, but amid shifting feminist ideologies, the content and title proved challenging. The women's print shop that produced the first run later refused to reprint it. A revised edition retitled *Labiaflowers* (1981) saw sales plummet. Last Gasp took over publication with the original title and it remains in print to this day.

Corinne's work further explored sexual education and lesbian eroticism. She illustrated Joani Blank's *Good Vibrations: The Complete Guide to Vibrators* (1976) and collaborated with photographer Honey Lee Cottrell (her then partner) on *I Am My Lover* (1978) about female masturbation. Feminist concerns of erotic art objectifying women were ongoing.

Corinne is celebrated for her kaleidoscopic collages of sexually intimate women and experiments with solarization, a technique she felt preserved her model's privacy while also creating the magical effect of making 'bodies look lit from within'. She is also notable for making consistent efforts to broaden the types of women included in sexual imagery.

FEMINIST ART **p.30**

TEE A. CORINNE

Corinne researched and published on the history of lesbian imagery in fine art, describing the lack of a publicly accessible history as a form of oppression faced constantly by lesbians. Keen to support women exploring their creativity in women-centred-spaces, she co-established the Feminist Photography Ovulars (1979–1982) workshops in Oregon woodland and co-founded *The Blatant Image, A Magazine of Feminist Photography* (1981–1983).

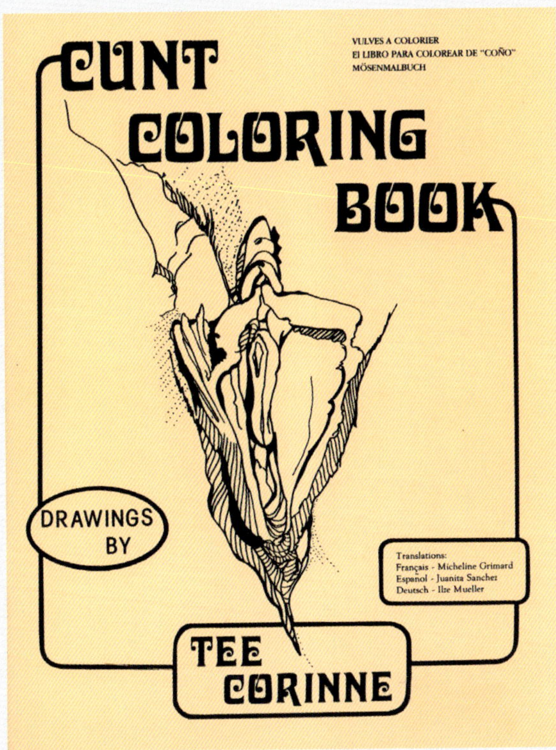

Detail: Bold contouring brought an element of graphic abstraction, and the process of colouring them in prompts a more considered gaze and sensual experience. Some drawings include models' fingers touching their genitals (see overleaf), challenging taboos against women being (literally) in touch with their bodies.

SPACE OF THE BODY **p.172** TO BE SEEN **p.186**

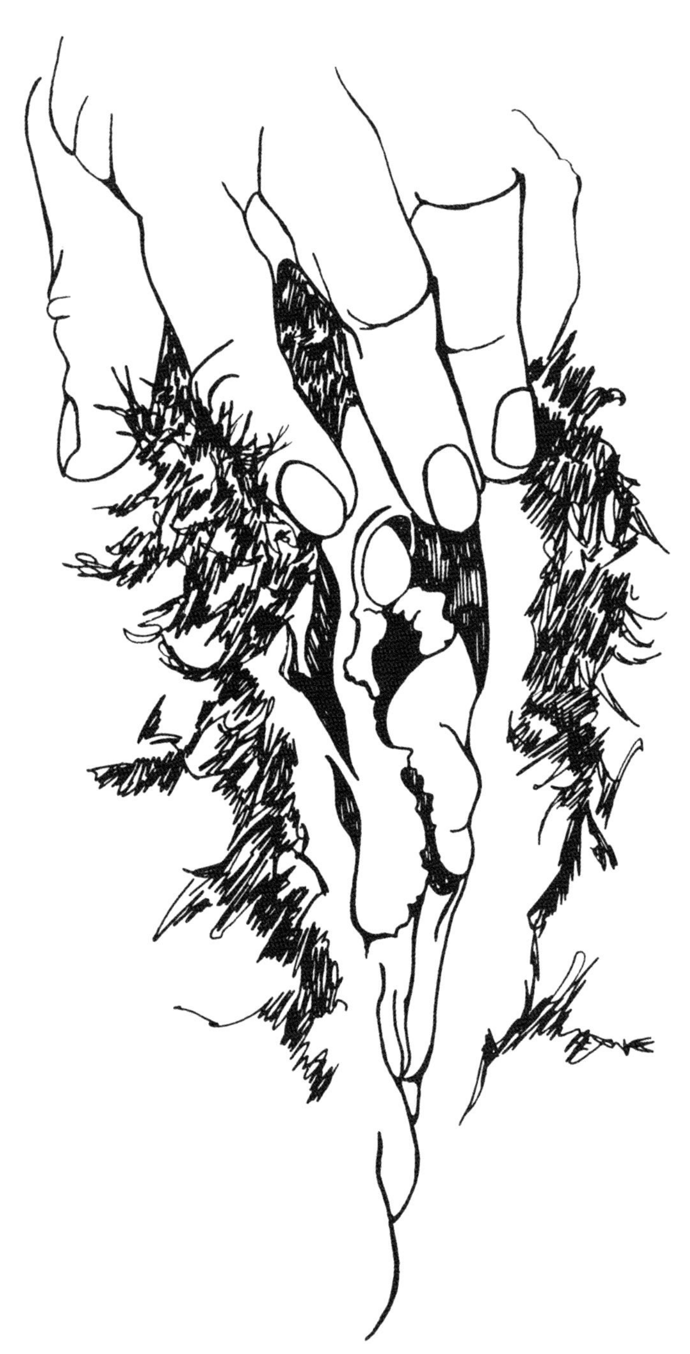

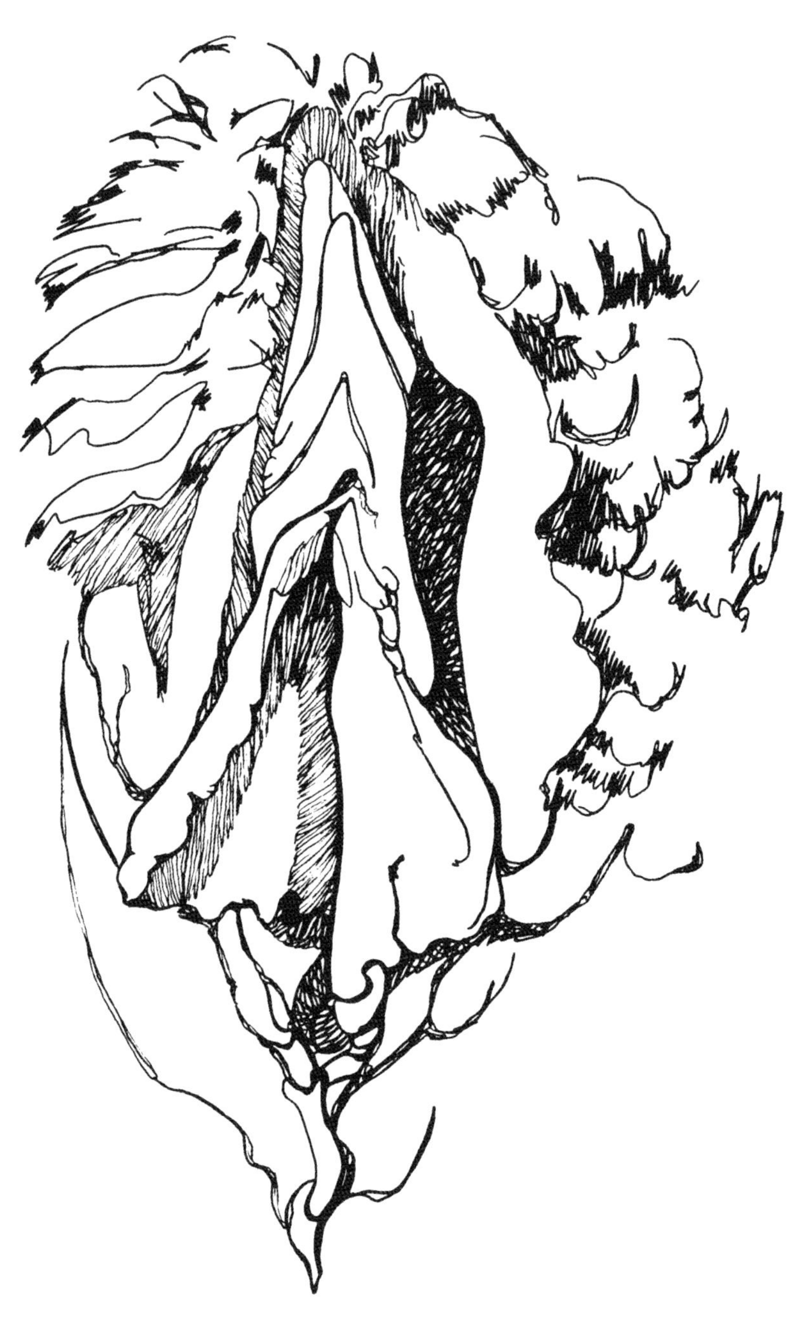

Ranchodbhai Relaxing in the Winter

1977

BHUPEN KHAKHAR: OIL ON CANVAS • 134.5 X 134.5 CM (53 X 53 IN)
PRIVATE COLLECTION

OTHER KEY WORKS

Man with Plastic Flowers, 1975/76, National Gallery of Modern Art, Delhi, India

You Can't Please All, 1981, Tate, London, UK

Two Men in Benares, 1982, Private Collection

'One can't hide oneself behind a painting. It is standing naked in front of everyone—what you are.' Bhupen Khakhar (1934–2003) forged an influential role in modern Asian art, interweaving observations of Indian society and sexuality in his original, figurative style. A keen observer of urban spaces and everyday life, he was drawn to streetscapes, workplaces and domestic interiors. Often picturing mundane scenes in humble and homosocial spaces, he infused a certain romance amid the realism.

His work characteristically featured saturated beds of colour with figures who appear to glow. *Ranchodbhai Relaxing in Bed* (1975) is an example of employing a strikingly pale ground to create a pseudo-solarizing effect around the figures.

He eclectically drew from modern and traditional visual cultures, including 1960s American pop, Bollywood posters, Indian miniature painting (particularly the Nathdwara school) and eighteenth–nineteenth century 'Company Style'. Meticulous early works shifted towards a looser, more expressive and energetic style.

Later titles make playful use of language including *You Can't Please All* (1981) – which Khakhar revealed represented his 'coming-out' as a gay man. He simultaneously considered homosexuality as just another facet of life to depict: 'Though I have never tried to hide my sexuality, I have not gone out of my way to announce it either. I am not a gay activist and the depiction of the man-to-man intimacy in paintings was not really meant to be a social statement'.

BHUPEN KHAKHAR

An accountant-turned-artist, Khakhar was born in Baroda and grew up in Mumbai. A self-taught painter, he was part of a vibrant vanguard of narrative painting in India and achieved international recognition. Considered the first Indian painter to openly express his homosexuality, he lived his whole life under the threat of prosecution due to a British colonial law (Section 377) created in 1861 and not repealed until 2018.

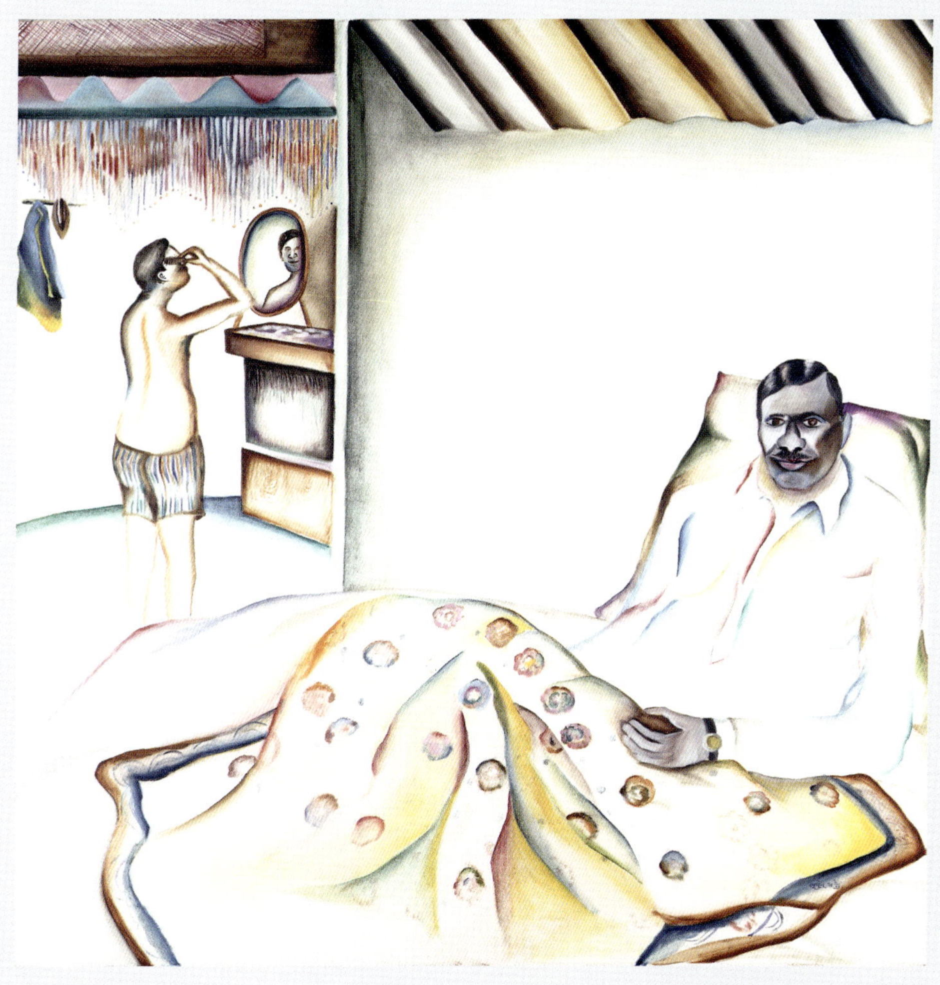

PERSONAL REALIZATION **p.164** INTIMACIES **p.165** CHOSEN FAMILY **p.170** PLACES TO BE **p.189**

Hunkertime

1979
–
1980

HARMONY HAMMOND: CLOTH, WOOD, ACRYLIC, GESSO, LATEX RUBBER, RHOPLEX AND METAL • 205.7 X 487.7 X 73.7 CM (81 X 192 X 29 IN) • ELIZABETH A. SACKLER CENTER FOR FEMINIST ART, BROOKLYN MUSEUM, NEW YORK, USA

OTHER KEY WORKS

Presence series, 1971–72, Private Collections

Inappropriate Longings, 1992, Private Collection

Bandaged Grid #1, 2015, Private Collection

The work of Harmony Hammond (1944–) straddles feminism, abstraction and sexual politics – notably lesbian visibility. *Hunkertime* (1979–80) is an example of her 'Wrapped Sculptures' of the late 1970s and early 1980s. Seemingly anthropomorphic, short, plump ladders are bound with layers of fabric suggesting muscle or flesh. Grouped together, supporting each other, and holding space, they evoke ideas of feminist collectivity, the fabric alluding to women's 'traditional' artistic practices. Hammond likes ladders as 'things that have a purpose' and they appear in other works. Knowing that Hammond described her wrapped sculptures as her first 'consciously lesbian' body of work inspires reference to *The Ladder* (1956–72), the first nationally distributed lesbian publication in the United States.

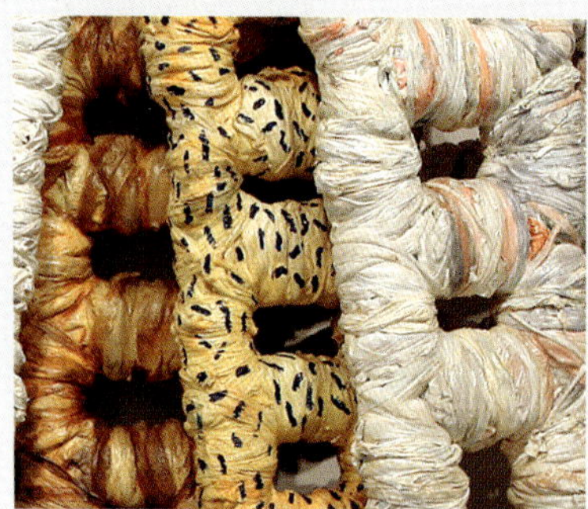

Detail: 'Like our bodies, the ladders are hard and soft, and lumpy and bumpy, with all kinds of marks,' Hammond reflected. Using materials collected from friends 'meant I was literally putting all these women in the work.'

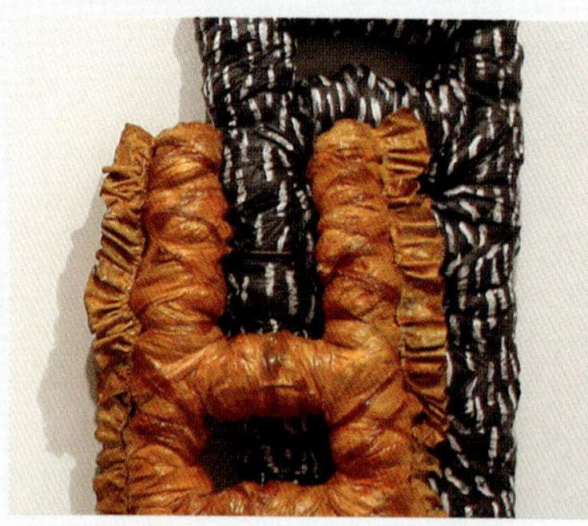

Detail: Describing the work's positioning as 'frontal and formal – almost theatrical', she also recalled getting 'perverse pleasure' from adding ruffles to intentionally feminize elements and 'mess with the serious minimal ladder form'.

FEMINIST ART **p.30**

Material that appears to simultaneously cover/censor and support/heal also feature in her *Bandaged Grid* series (2015–). Acutely attuned to the physicality of materials, she explains that their manipulation is an important pleasurable element for her – 'Piecing, patching, fraying, layering, suturing are loaded with meaning.'

Hammond has emphasized the importance of documenting and preserving artwork to avoid erasure. Her publication *Lesbian Art in America: A Contemporary History* (2000) was an effort to address this. In it she cautioned 'We cannot afford to … let our creative work be ignored, "straightened," dehistoricized, decontextualized, or erased.' The refusal of some artists to be included inspired a series of artworks including *Erasure #1* and *Erasure #2* (2002).

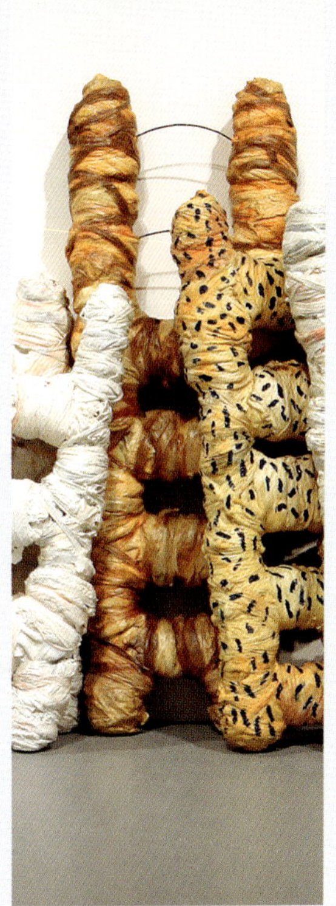

Detail: In addition to being abstract stand-ins for bodies 'hunkering down, leaning on each other … waiting for their moment of action', the ladders interested Hammond 'as metaphors for states of being or planes of enlightenment, vertical bridges between ground and spirit'.

HARMONY HAMMOND

Hammond moved to New York in 1969, where involvement in the women's movement guided her to coming out as a lesbian. A central figure of the 1970s feminist art movement, she co-founded A.I.R. (Artists in Residence) Gallery and *Heresies: A Feminist Publication on Art and Politics*. She curated *A Lesbian Show* (1978), the first exhibition of lesbian artists in the United States and participated in the Great American Lesbian Art Show (1980).

POWERFUL PROTEST **p.169** SPACE OF THE BODY **p.172** STRAIGHT EXPECTATIONS **p.185** TO BE SEEN **p.186**

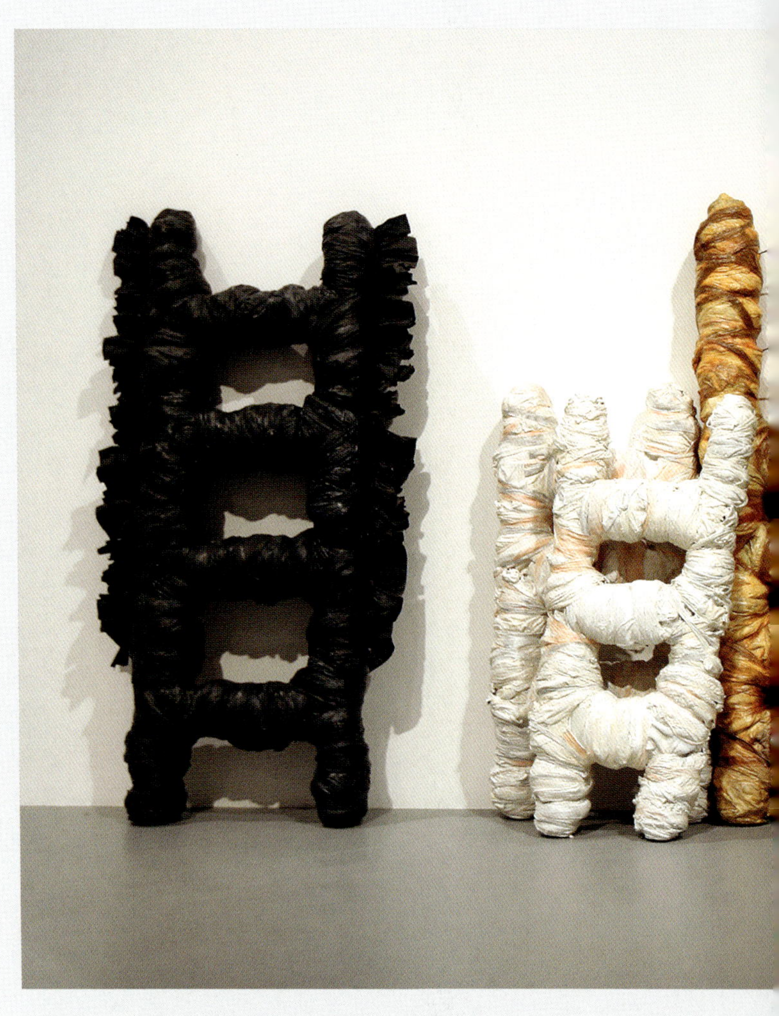

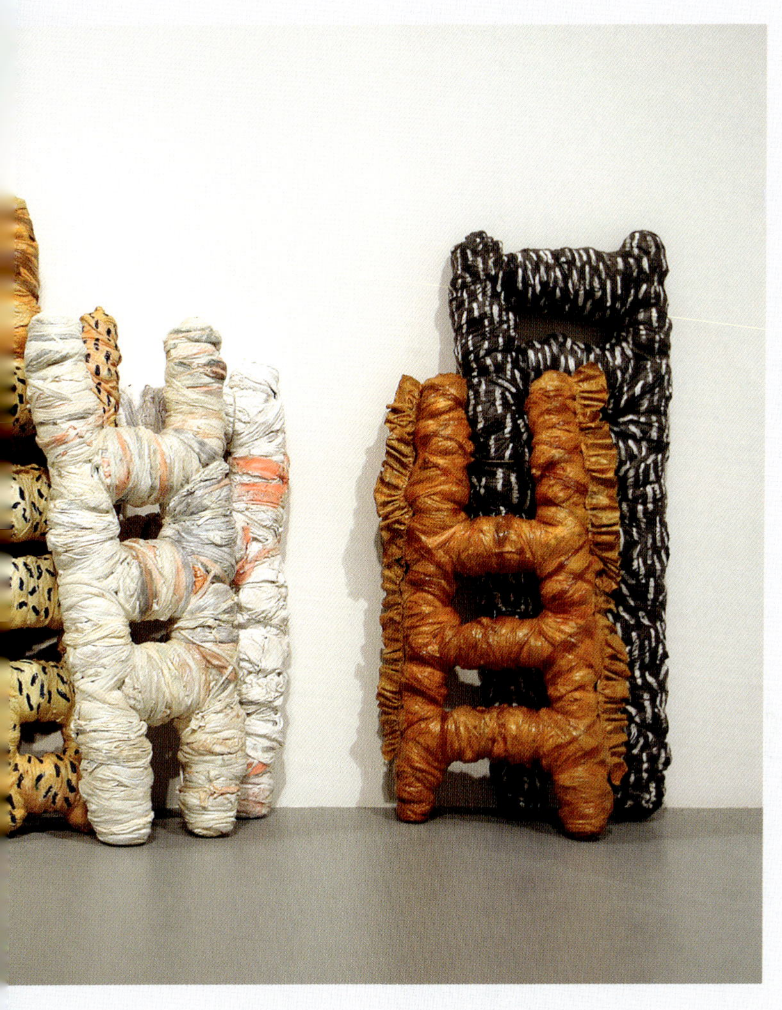

The Wrestlers after Muybridge

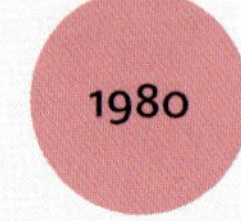

FRANCIS BACON: OIL, AEROSOL PAINT AND DRY TRANSFER LETTERING ON CANVAS
198.1 X 148 CM (78 X 58¼ IN) • LOS ANGELES, USA

OTHER KEY WORKS

Three Studies for Figures at the Base of a Crucifixion, 1944, Tate, London, UK

Three Studies of Lucian Freud, 1969, Private Collection

In Memory of George Dyer, 1971, Fondation Beyeler, Riehen/Basel, Beyeler Collection

Francis Bacon (1909–1992) took figurative painting to new and contorted heights. This wrestling scene follows in a long lineage of sporting subjects designed to impress with athletic prowess. However, Bacon metamorphoses the concept into something brutally unsettling, the face of the vanquished figure reduced to a screaming mouth being driven into the canvas. This figure went on to inspire the design of the horrific creatures in the seminal film *Alien* (1979).

Bacon was stirred by film, citing early classics including *Battleship Potemkin* (1925) as a recurring stimulus in his compositions. Eadweard Muybridge (1830–1904) paved the way for the existence of film with his chronophotographic breakthroughs capturing the locomotion of the human body and animals. Muybridge's figures were usually nude to emphasize muscle motion, and his nude wrestlers swiftly found a keen homoerotic audience.

Heavily inspired by a string of destructive and physically punishing relationships, Bacon channelled his sadomasochistic desires and lust for dangerous men into a viscerally loaded string of paintings. One lover, George Dyer (c.1933–1971), was the subject of many works. Two days before Bacon's career-defining retrospective was due to open at the Grand Palais in 1971, Dyer killed himself in their Paris hotel room. Through his bereavement of the following years, Bacon created 'The Black Triptychs' (1972–74), some of his most revered paintings, interpreting the moments immediately before, during and after Dyer's departure from life.

FRANCIS BACON

Born in Dublin in 1909, the young Bacon was drawn to bohemia, spending his late teens drifting through the gay underworlds of London, Berlin and Paris. He did not find success until around 1945 when his triptychs of monstrous anguished figures seemed to capture a shaken imagination in the post-war period. His reputation and infamy grew through the decades to earn the moniker of 'greatest living painter'.

BAROQUE **p.13** FILM AND VIDEO ART **p.28**

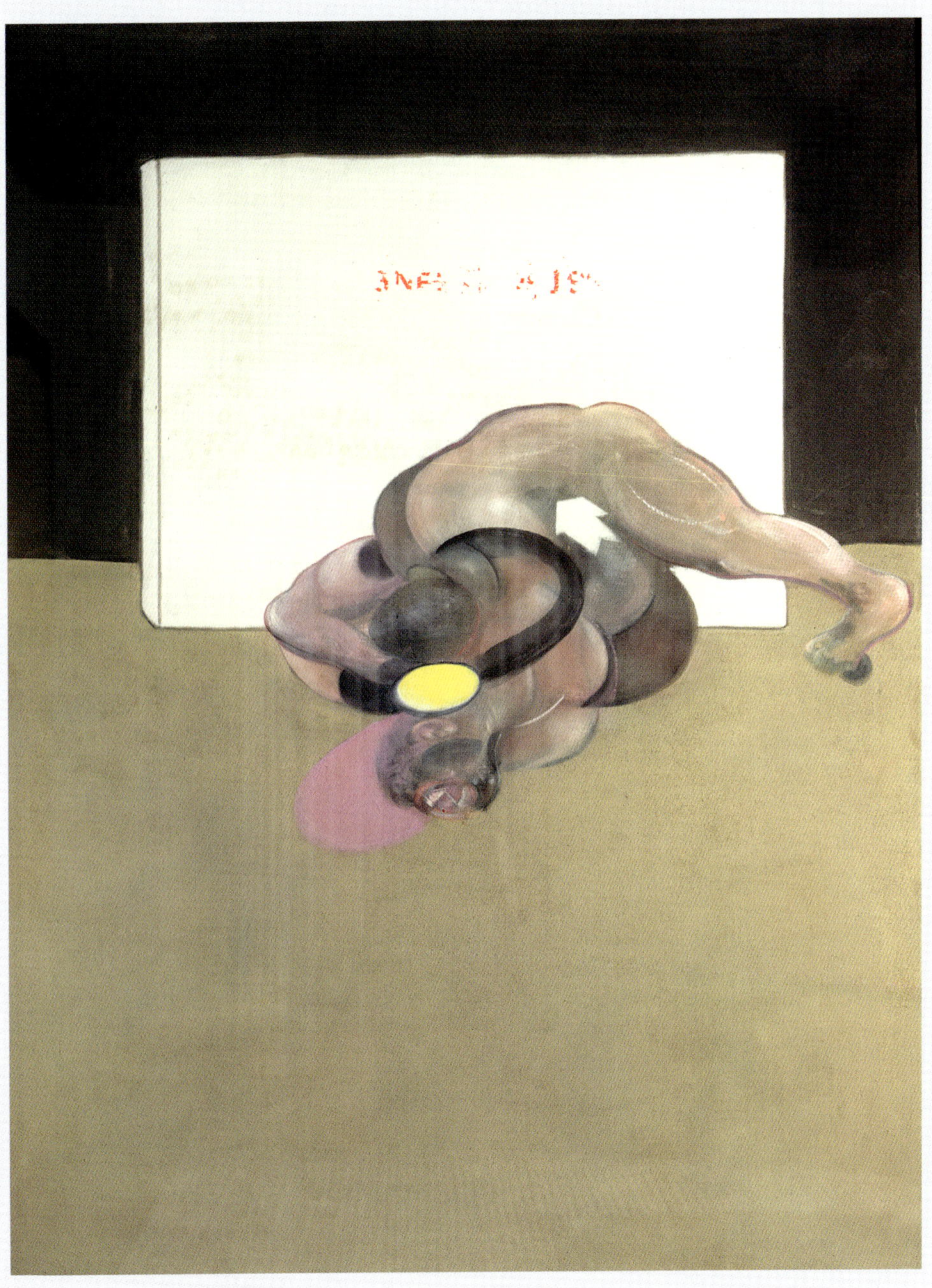

SPACE OF THE BODY **p.172** IN THE STUDIO **p.173**

Freedom and Change

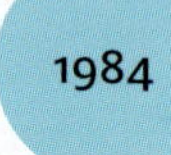
1984

LUBAINA HIMID CBE, RA: WOOD, TEXTILES, CARDBOARD, PAINT, GRAPHITE, COLOURED PENCIL, CHALK AND INK • 282.5 X 578 X 6 CM (111¼ X 227½ X 2⅓ IN) TATE, LONDON, UK

OTHER KEY WORKS

Ankledeep, 1991, Tate, London, UK

Naming the Money, 2004, Private Collection

Ball on Shipboard, 2018, Rennie Collection, Vancouver, Canada

One of Britain's most celebrated contemporary painters, Lubaina Himid (1954–) was accused in her early career of being 'a cultural terrorist' for creating exhibitions like 'The Thin Black Line' (1985) at the Institute of Contemporary Arts. Recently commissioned to create a print celebrating 75 years of the ICA, it is 'a letter to the doubters to remind everyone that the exhibition is important now and was important then'.

Among these burgeoning networks Himid was helping to forge in the 1980s, she met others who similarly centred gender and lesbian identities in their artistic practice, including Maud Sulter (1960–2008). Together they created *Passion: Discourses on Blackwomen's Creativity* (1990), the first UK published book to exclusively celebrate work of Black women artists.

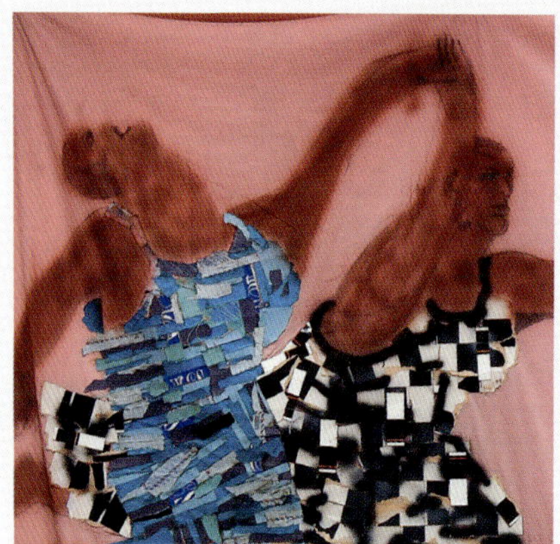

Detail: The symbol of the goddess Venus was particularly popular among feminists and lesbians in the 1970s. Two interlocking Venus symbols came to be used to specifically represent lesbians or sex between women.

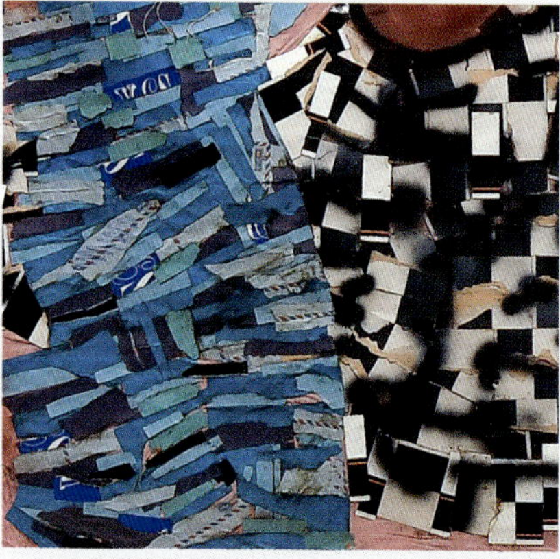

Detail: The women's dresses are pieced together from card and paper, including scraps of airmail envelopes. Himid later commented: 'I am constantly exploring the notion that textile design could be a secret and yet visible language between women.'

FEMINIST ART **p.30**

LUBAINA HIMID

Himid came to the fore as an artist and curator while at university in London, linking with the BLK Art Group formed in 1982. Blazing a trail organizing back-to-back exhibitions such as 'Black Woman Time Now' (1983), these delivered new platforms for marginalized talent to break through. A noted painter and teacher, she won the 2017 Turner Prize and in 2018, was awarded a CBE and elected a Royal Academician.

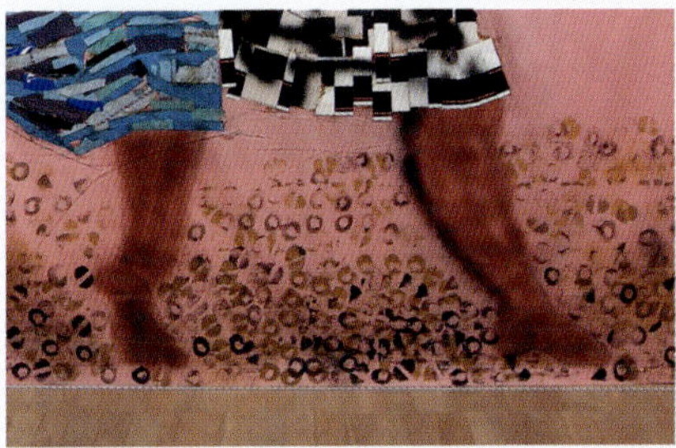

Detail: The beach surface is suggestive of cowrie shells, which traditionally carry an economic and cultural significance.

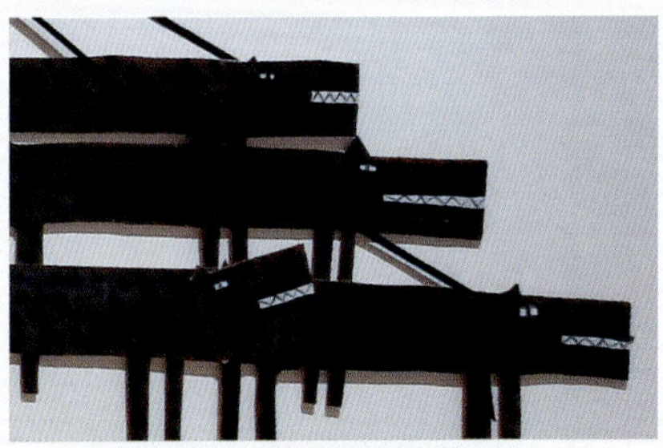

Detail: Baring their teeth in protection for the women, the dogs reflect Himid's use of painted cut-outs in early artworks she described as 'large political installations' that challenged and satirized aspects of British history and colonialism.

Himid's first degree was in theatre design. The imaginative resourcefulness of this background is reflected in works like *Freedom and Change*. Painted on a pink sheet, with two further extensions of a pack of black dogs tethered in front, and two bald, white men buried to their necks behind, the central composition shows two Black women in patchwork dresses, holding hands and running barefoot with gay abandon. One sports a Venus symbol earring, a popular lesbian emblem at the time. At its base is a 1922 painting by Picasso (1881–1973) subtitled 'The Race', making this installation a welcome reversal of his misogynistic treatment of women, and the persistent trope of European artists appropriating African influences.

GLIMPSES OF UTOPIA **p.163** POWERFUL PROTEST **p.169** STRAIGHT EXPECTATIONS **p.185**
PLACES TO BE **p.189** REWORKING ART HISTORY **p.191**

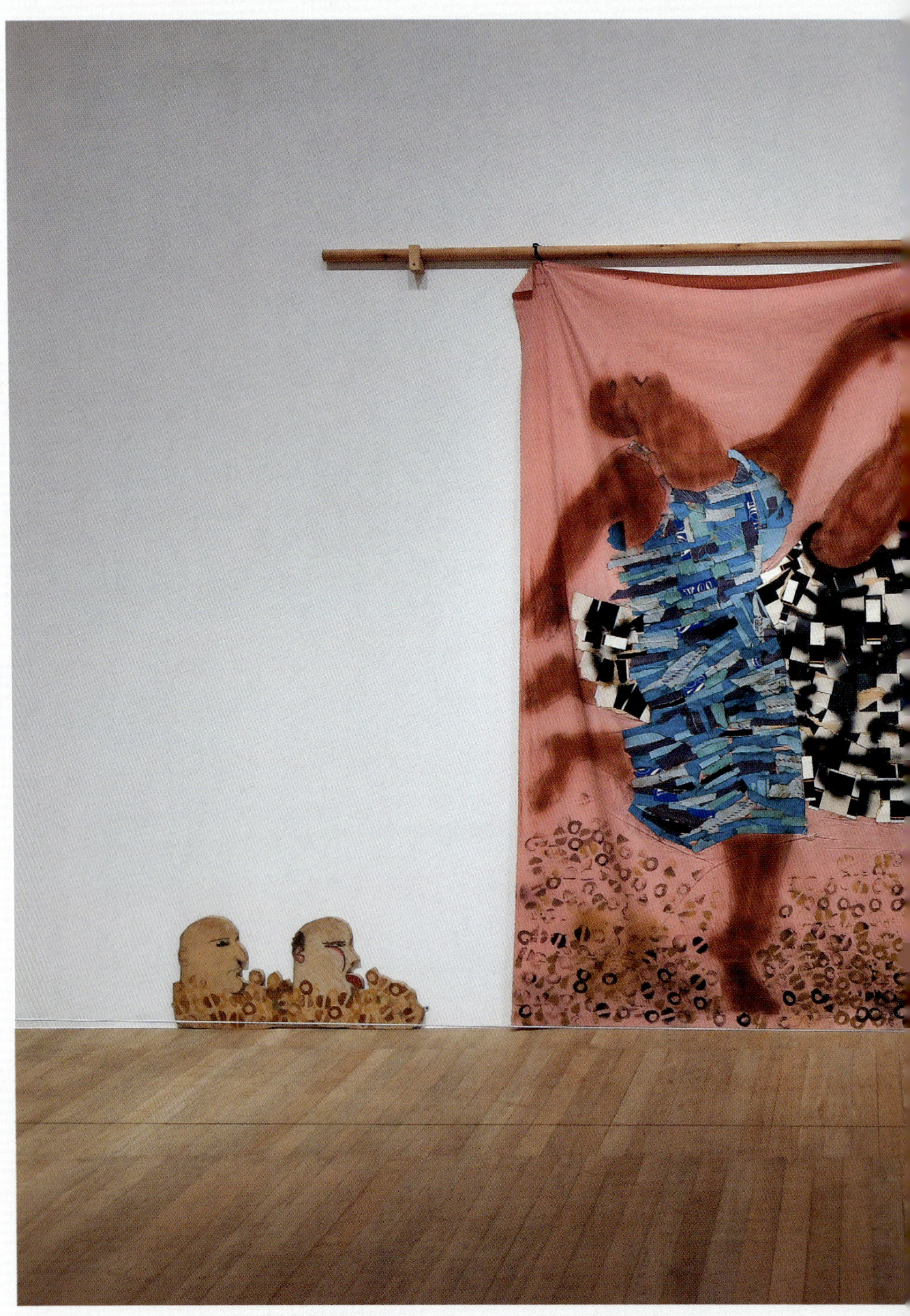

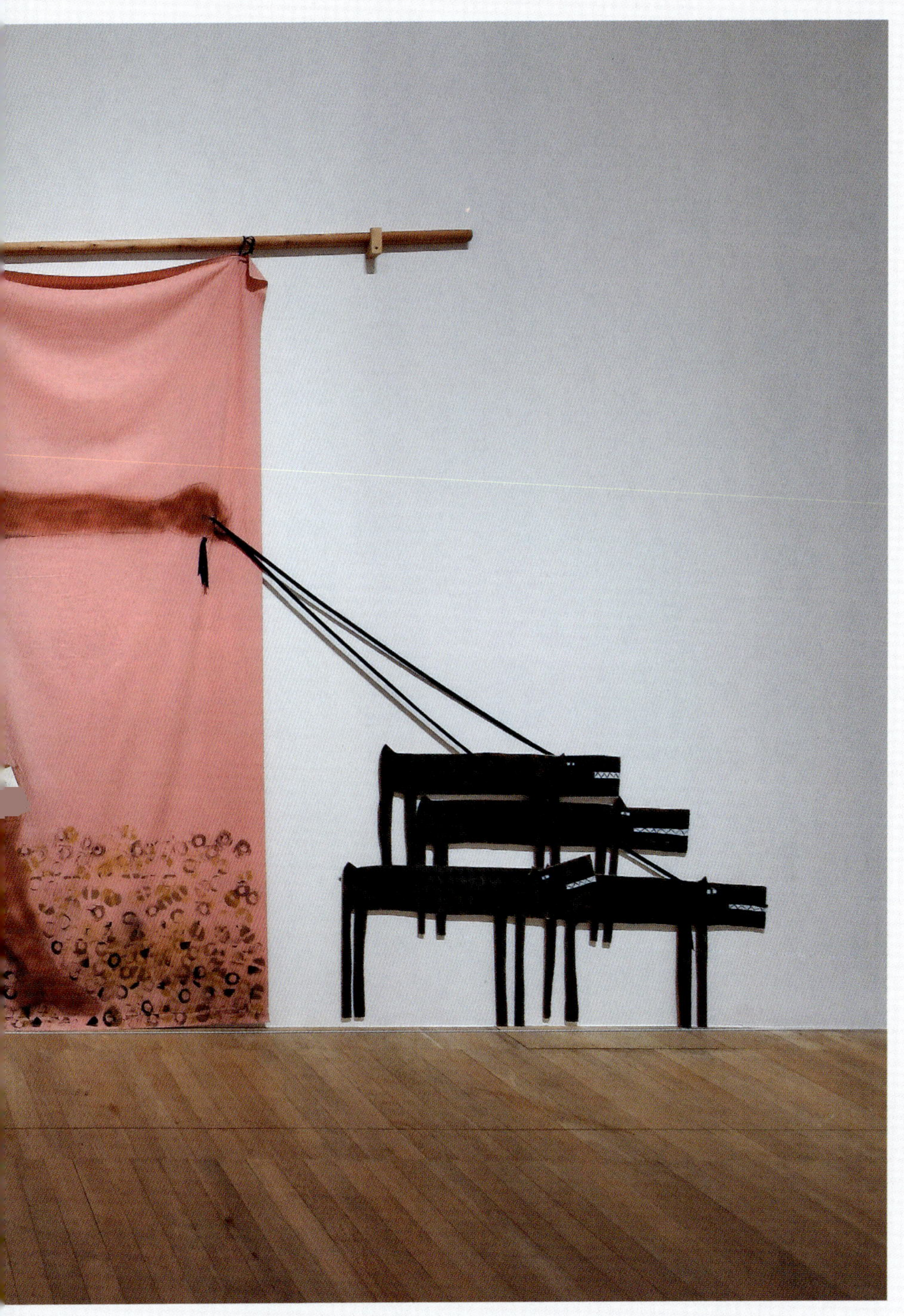

Jama Masjid

SUNIL GUPTA: FROM THE SERIES *EXILES* • COLOUR PRINT

OTHER KEY WORKS

'Pretended' Family Relationships (series), 1988, Museum of London, UK

The New Pre-Raphaelites (series), 2008

Sun City (series), 2010

This photograph bears the text 'I love this part of town. It's got such character and you can have sex just walking in the crowd.' It is a quotation from someone in the photograph, immediately opening the door to the frisson of feeling we may otherwise have simply imagined existing between the couple in the foreground, or the men seated in a half embrace with knowing smiles in the background. On the origins of *Exiles*, Sunil Gupta (1953–) wrote: 'It had always seemed to me that art history seemed to stop at Greece and never properly dealt with gay issues from another place.' Countering this cultural commandeering, Gupta's compassionate extensive body of work set out to change this.

Reflecting in 1987, he said: 'exploring the Indian gay scene as an adult I found an intimidating wall of silence'. Concerned, however, about losing his Indian identity and eager to contribute to positive change, he returned for several years in 2007 to begin the series *Mr Malhotra's Party* (2007–12). Participants were photographed where they lived and worked, as opposed to hidden away in secret clubs, embedding people into the wider worlds they occupy as a powerful visual act against marginalization.

'Pretended' Family Relationships (1988) was another ground-breaking series titled after an odious speech by British prime minister Margaret Thatcher (1925–2013) when Section 28 was enacted, which 'mobilized a vigorous response from the gay and lesbian community as it brought men and women together'.

SUNIL GUPTA

Gupta was born in India and moved to Canada as a teenager, where he discovered the gay liberation movement. He settled in London in 1983, and many of his photographic series focus on LGBTQ+ communities globally, from exercising his gay gaze in New York for *Christopher Street* (1976) to *Women in Love* (2018) depicting a lesbian couple's quotidian in New Delhi. His heartfelt documentation of queer lives over the past half a century is unmatched.

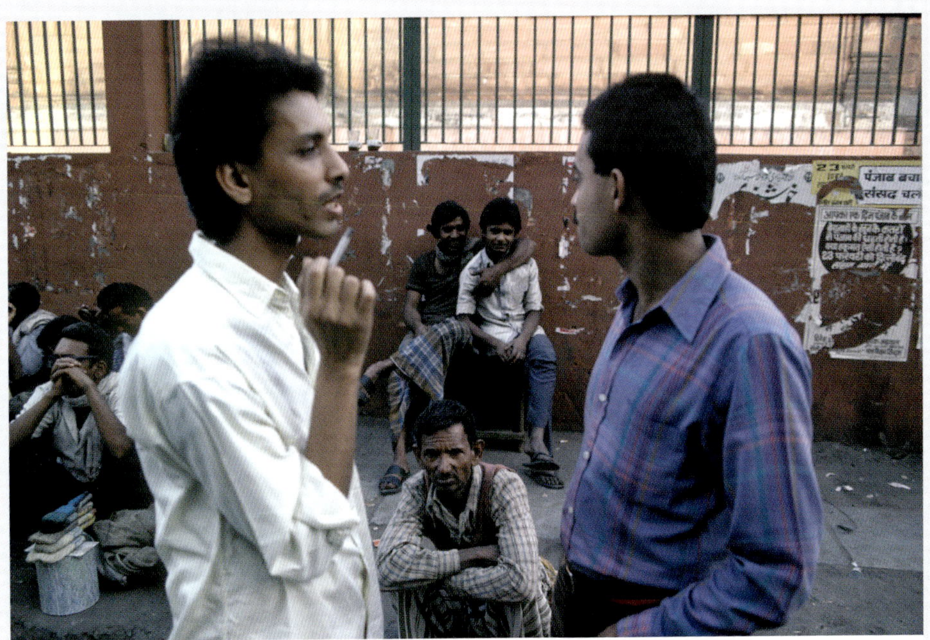

Jama Masjid
I love this part of town. It's got such character and you can have sex just walking in the crowd.

QUEER EYE **p.182** TO BE SEEN **p.186** PLACES TO BE **p.189**

Every Moment Counts (Ecstatic Antibodies)

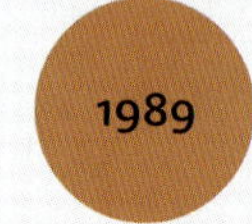

ROTIMI FANI-KAYODE: C-TYPE ARCHIVAL PRINT • 122 X 122 CM (48 X 48 IN)
PRIVATE COLLECTION

OTHER KEY WORKS

Bronze Head, 1987, Tate, London, UK

Sonponnoi, 1987, Tate, London, UK

Golden Phallus, 1989, National Science and Media Museum, Bradford, UK

'My identity has been constructed from my own sense of otherness, whether cultural, racial or sexual … Photography is the tool by which I feel most confident in expressing myself … Black, African, homosexual photography.' The photographs of Nigerian-born Rotimi Fani-Kayode (1955–1989) explore complex personal and politically engaged notions of desire, displacement, sexuality, spirituality, race and cultural dislocation.

He was a leading voice among Black British artists amid the AIDS crisis and flourishing queer culture of the late 1980s. Alongside his romantic and creative partner Alex Hirst (1951–1993), he sought to: 'translate my rage and my desire into new images which will undermine conventional perceptions and which may reveal hidden worlds'.

At a time when erotic touch was connected to heightened risk for gay men, he centred the body to explore relationships between fantasy and spirituality. Infusing Christian and Yoruban imagery with homoerotic sensibility, he characterized his subjects as: 'my smallpox Gods, my transexual priests, my images of desirable Black men in a state of sexual frenzy, or the tranquility of communion with the spirit world'.

This is an example of his later work – large-scale, colour-saturated dramatic tableaux with Baroque-esque chiaroscuro lighting. Inspired by masks in African traditional art, he often evoked Yoruban ritual masquerades for ancestral reverence. Here a *Commedia dell'Arte* mask brings an additional charge, referencing the theatric mischief of seventeenth- and eighteenth-century European entertainments amid an era of aggressive colonization.

ROTIMI FANI-KAYODE

Born in Lagos, to a prominent Yoruba family, Rotimi Fani-Kayode moved to England following the outbreak of civil war in Nigeria. He later studied at Georgetown University and the Pratt Institute in the USA, before settling in London in 1983. Within his brief six-year career he produced a complex body of work. A significant figure in the Black British art scene, he was a founding member and early chairman of Autograph.

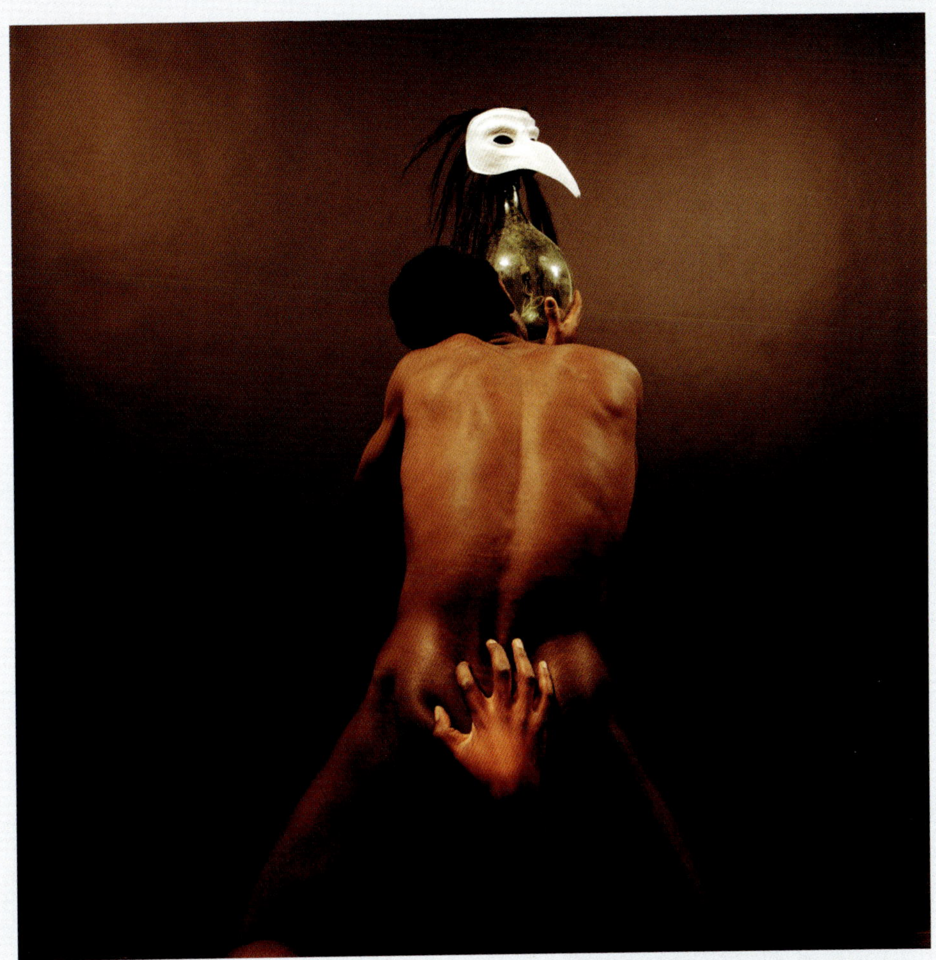

INTIMACIES **p.165** MASKS **p.174** DIVINE CONNECTION **p.178** FACING AIDS **p.208**

Once Upon a Time

1989

KEITH HARING: PAINTED MURAL AT THE NYC LGBT COMMUNITY CENTER, NEW YORK, USA

OTHER KEY WORKS

Heritage of Pride logo, 1986

Crack is Wack, 1986, 128th Street and 2nd Avenue, New York, USA

Ignorance = Fear, 1989, poster, Whitney Museum of American Art, New York, USA

Wrapping around four walls of what was once a men's bathroom, the trippy orgiastic figures in the signature chunky line drawings of Keith Haring (1958–1990) make for surely one the most sex-positive murals ever created. Commissioned for 'The Center Show' marking the 20th anniversary of the Stonewall Uprising, the figures metamorphose into fantastical phallic forms and tumble orgiastically above the tiles. Restored and reopened to the public in 2015, it is a paean to the more carefree days of cruising and group sex in the pre-AIDS era.

Haring applied his bold freehand style with a preference for free-flowing creativity and chance, noting: 'I never sketch a plan … even for huge murals.' Between 1982 and 1989 Haring created around 50 public works in cities around the world, including several for orphanages and hospitals. Tseng Kwong Chi (1950–1990) took over 40,000 photographs of Haring, forming a vast record of the artist at work and play.

As Haring's fame rapidly grew, he was highly sought after to collaborate with celebrities including Madonna (1958–), Grace Jones (1948–) and Andy Warhol (1928–1987). Orbiting multiple worlds of graffiti, art galleries, fashion, commercial commissions and protest iconography, he broke down such silos, noting: 'The use of commercial projects has enabled me to reach millions of people.' He described selling affordable artworks in his 1986 Pop Shop as 'an extension of what I was doing in the subway stations, breaking down the barriers between high and low art'.

KEITH HARING

Haring produced a spectacular amount of work within his lifetime. Initially on track to become a commercial graphic artist, he abandoned study at Pittsburgh's Ivy School of Professional Art and instead moved to New York. Here he found a place in burgeoning downtown alternative art communities, becoming friends with artists including Jean-Michel Basquiat (1960–1988), and developing his distinctive palette of cartoon-ish pop art 'radiating' figures that gained worldwide fame.

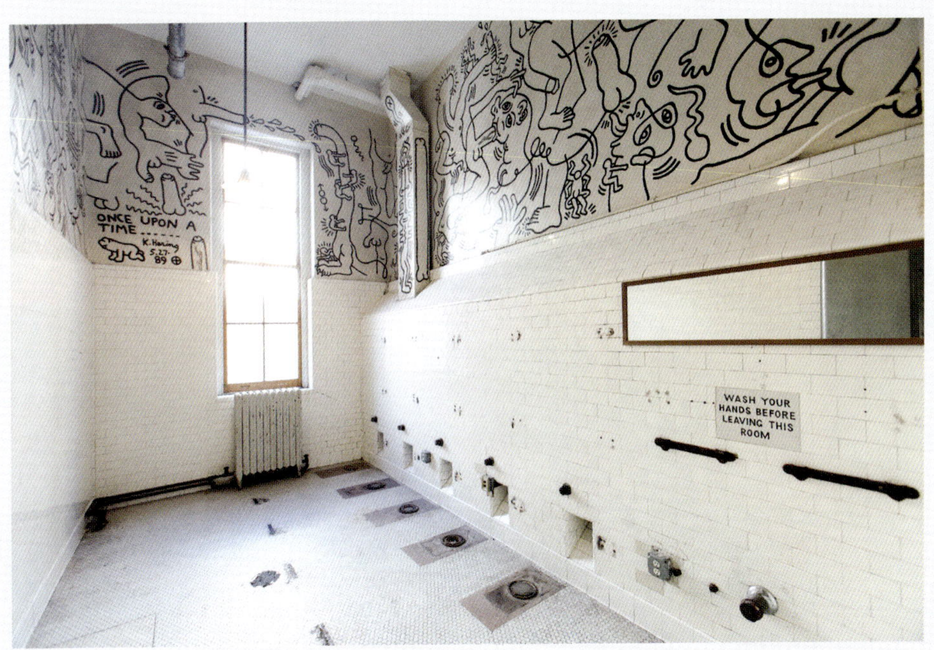

POWERFUL PROTEST **p.169** TO BE SEEN **p.186** PLACES TO BE **p.189** PUBLIC PRESENCE **p.197**
FASHIONING STYLE **p.206** FACING AIDS **p.208**

Untitled, from Dream Girls

1990

DEBORAH BRIGHT: PHOTOMONTAGE • 28 X 35.5 CM (11 X 14 IN)
LESLIE-LOHMAN MUSEUM, NEW YORK, USA

OTHER KEY WORKS

The Management of Desire, 1994, Artist's Collection

Being & Riding, 1996–99, Artist's Collection

Passiflorae, 2002–08, Artist's Collection

Well-known for her photographic work and writing on queer desire and politics, American artist and educator Deborah Bright (1950–) gained renown for her series *Dream Girls* (1989–90). Using an analogue process of photomontage, Bright inserted herself into Hollywood film stills, taking the place of romantic male leads. Here lighting Audrey Hepburn's cigarette in *Breakfast at Tiffany's* (1961), she disrupts male-female interactions and 'heteronormative identities propagated by Hollywood', introducing lesbian desire.

Having come out as a lesbian in 1985, Bright said: 'I had grown up watching old movies on TV and loved particular actors who displayed androgynous or gender-nonconforming signs when the Hollywood Code forbade any positive images of queer life. I recalled how freely my child's imagination roamed among male and female personae … I had no names for these feelings at the time but in re-enacting a few of these roles using old film stills, I could make explicit what was at stake.' Similar strategies can be seen in the works of Risk Hazekamp (1972–), with *Giant* and *Movie Stars*, and Laurence Jaugey-Paget's *Hollywoodn't* (1995).

Bright used photomontage again in *The Management of Desire* (1994), reimagining *The Agnew Clinic* (1889), the painting by Thomas Eakins (1844–1916) which depicts mastectomy surgery. Reflecting on 'intertwined histories of medical pathology, patriarchy and bigotry vis-à-vis women who desire other women', she introduces her own post-mastectomy-surgery body under the gaze of Eakin's female nurse.

DEBORAH BRIGHT

Following her retirement from Chair of Fine Arts at the Pratt Institute, New York, in 2017, Bright has produced a number of non-photographic works, including *Small Appliances* (2019), a series of vibrant coloured-pencil studies drawing on the aesthetics of sex toys and human pleasure. She has also maintained a strand of work on landscape photography over the decades.

FEMINIST ART **p.30**

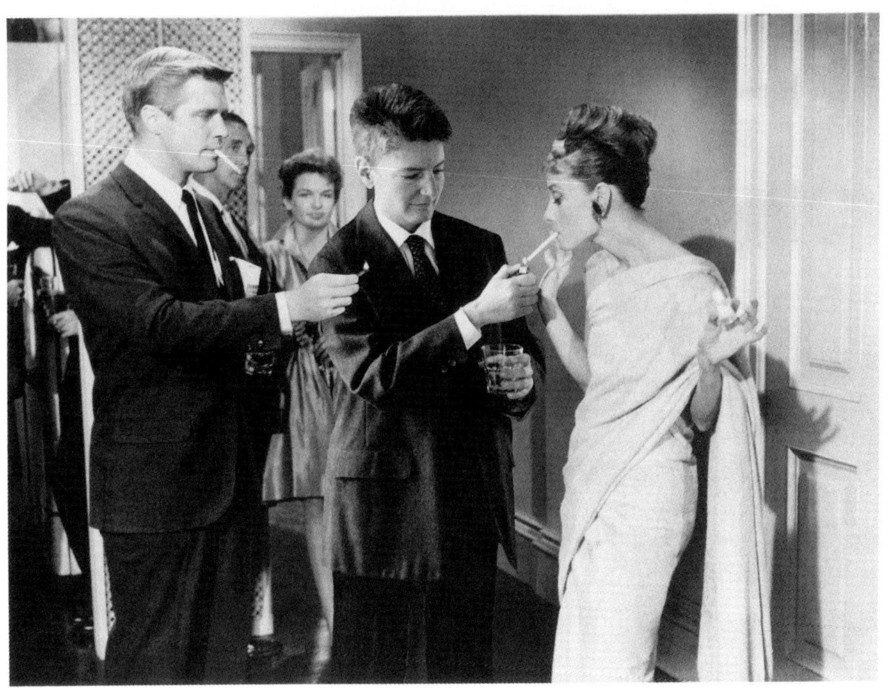

PERSONAL REALIZATION **p.164** PRESENTING THE ARTIST **p167** STRAIGHT EXPECTATIONS **p.185**
TO BE SEEN **p.186** ON SCREEN **p.187**

Notes on the Margin of the Black Book

1991 – 1993

GLENN LIGON: DETAILS FROM INSTALLATION OF OFFSET PRINTS AND TEXT • 91 OFFSET PRINTS, FRAMED: 29.2 X 29.2 CM (11½ X 11½ IN) EACH; 78 TEXT PAGES, FRAMED: 13.3 X 18.4 CM (5¼ X 7¼ IN) EACH • SOLOMON R. GUGGENHEIM MUSEUM, NEW YORK, USA

OTHER KEY WORKS

Untitled (I'm Turning Into a Specter before Your Very Eyes and I'm Going to Haunt You), 1992, Philadelphia Museum of Art, USA

Condition Report, 2000, Tate, London, UK

Untitled (I Live on my Shadow), 2009, Private Collection

Glenn Ligon (1960–) has created many pivotal works challenging the evolution of American history and contemporary culture. Hot on the heels of 'The Black Book' (1986) by Robert Mapplethorpe (1946–1989) came Ligon's response, literally deconstructing the book by cutting it up and inserting around seventy texts foregrounding how these homoerotic photographs of the Black male nude are consumed and sensationalized. Having annotated his own copy of the notorious book, he also added many other voices in the final installation from a broad church of artists, writers, activists and thinkers. Filmmaker Marlon Riggs (1957–1994), whose own work aimed to 'shatter [America's] brutalizing silence on matters of sexual and

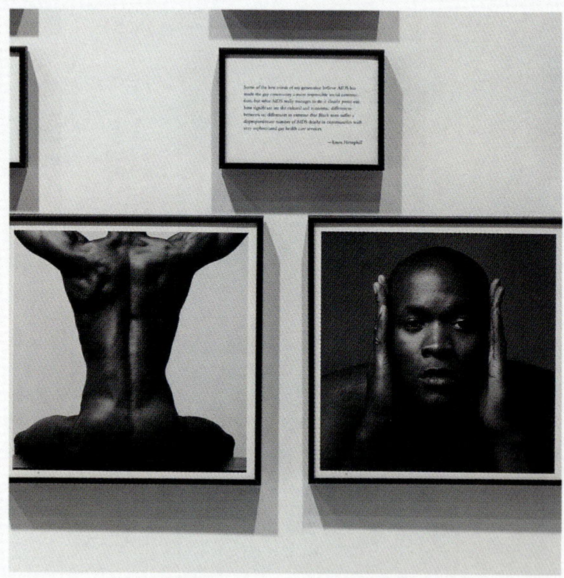

Detail: Framed and positioned in double-rows among the images, quotations range in tone and focus – collectively expanding and 're-framing' how Mapplethorpe's work may be viewed. Some connect with broad sociopolitical issues while others concentrate on specific images.

HARLEM RENAISSANCE **p.22**

GLENN LIGON

Starting as an abstract painter in the 1980s, Ligon began incorporating text early on by African American luminaries including James Baldwin (1924–1987) and French queer renegade Jean Genet (1910–1986). Early 1990s large-scale commissions and installations incorporate sound, photography and print, confronting the history of slavery and ongoing racial injustice. Working with neon since 2005, he has challenged the belittling white gaze upon the Black body in many pieces, including *Warm Broad Glow* (2005), which quotes Gertrude Stein.

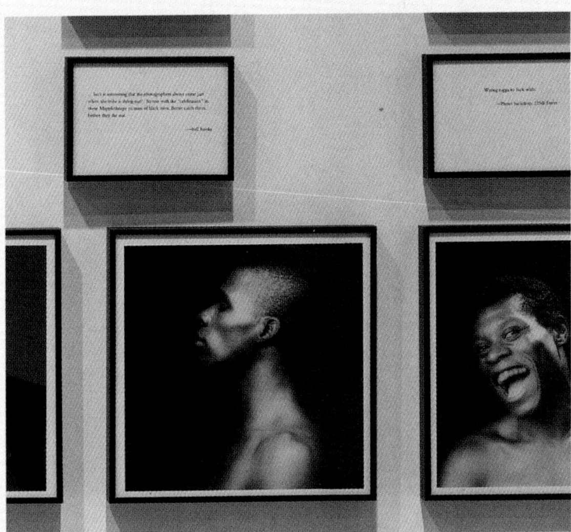

Detail: Quotations from poet Essex Hemphill (1957–1995), author bell hooks (1952–2021) and Mapplethorpe himself note how *The Black Book* coincided with AIDS. hooks reflected: 'Isn't it interesting that the photographers always come just when the tribe is dying out? So too with the "celebration" in these Mapplethorpe pictures of black men. Better catch them before they die out.'

racial difference' mused on the need to go beyond 'Are you gay? Are you het? Are you bi?'. Gender studies and queer theory heavyweight Judith Butler (1956-) considered the 'racist romanticism of Black men's excessive physicality', while a bar patron called Micheal is also given a platform to drool over which figure he would most favour fellating. Sweeping through many concepts from desire to disdain, fantasy and fear, *Notes on the Margin of the Black Book* is a seminal work operating on many levels to both critique and compliment Mapplethorpe's own.

In 1998, Ligon elaborated on racial and gender stereotyping with a pair of identical full-length 3 m (10 ft) portraits titled *Self Portrait Exaggerating My Black Features* and *Self Portrait Exaggerating My White Features.*

TEXTUAL POWER **p.166** SPACE OF THE BODY **p.172** EROTIC EXCHANGES **p.183** TO BE SEEN **p.186**
OUT IN THE GALLERY **p.211** INSTITUTIONAL CRITIQUE **p.212**

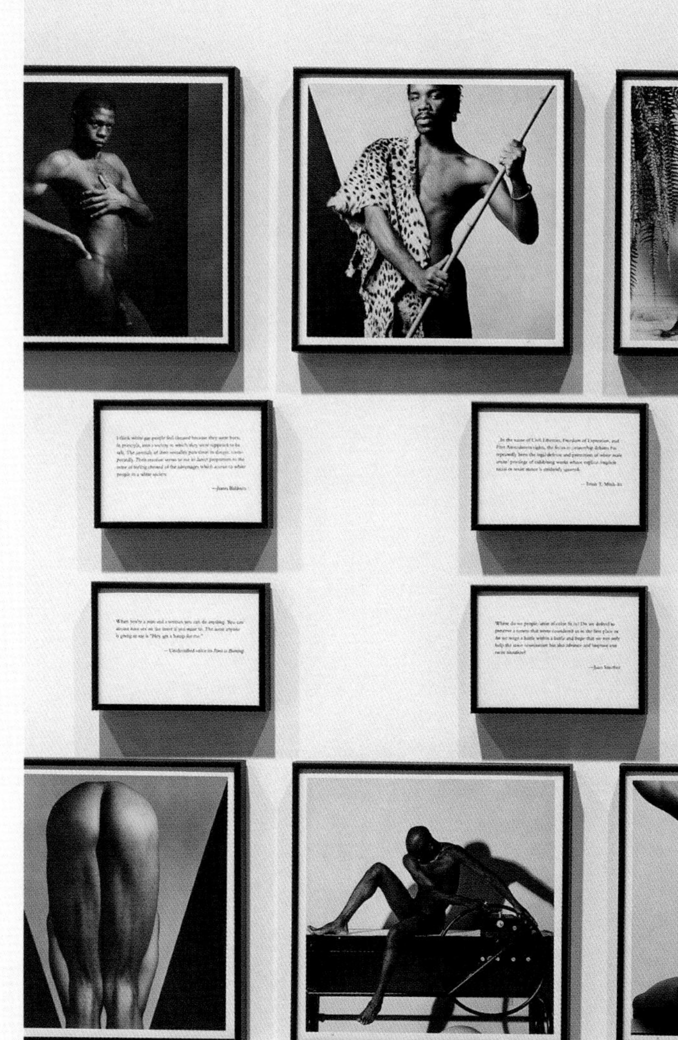

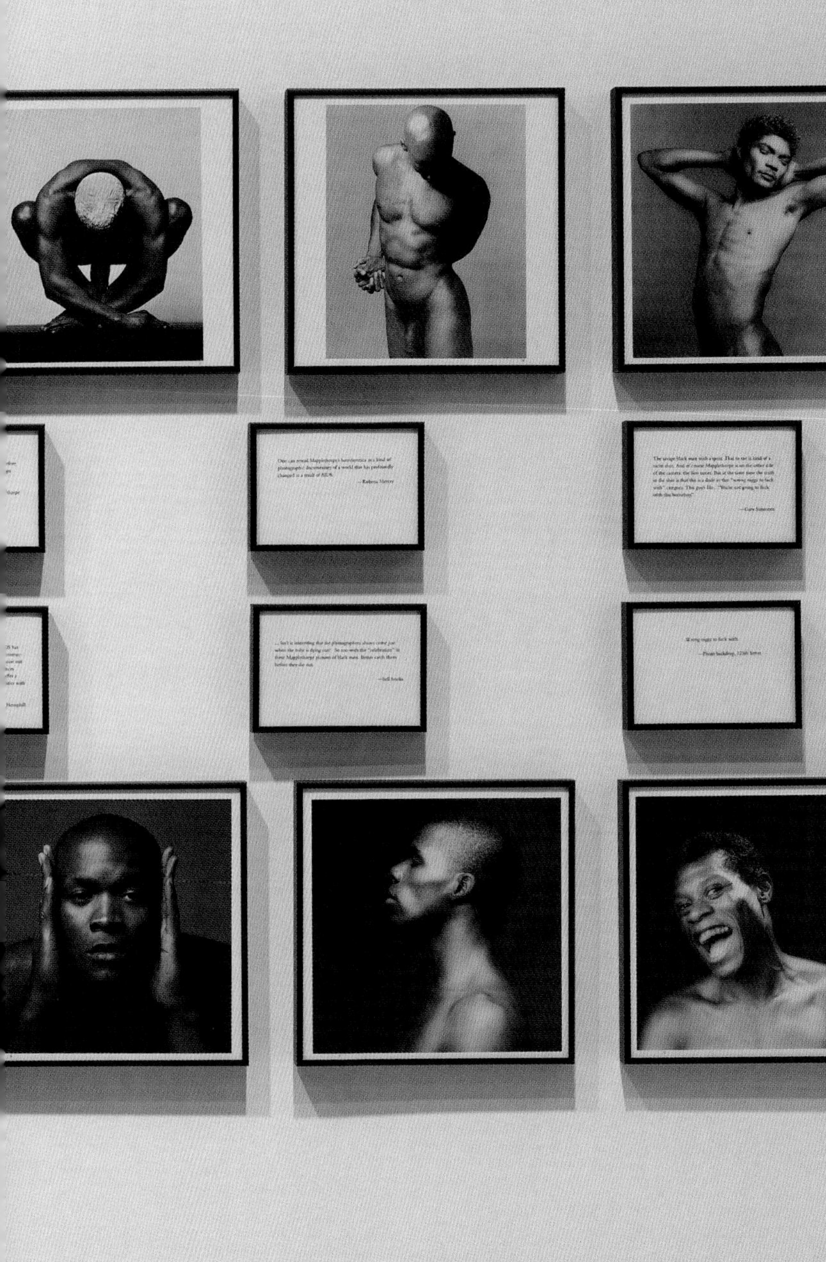

Gate 门

XIYADIE: PAPER-CUT WITH WATER-BASED DYE AND CHINESE PIGMENTS ON XUAN PAPER • 176 X 176 CM (69⅓ X 69⅓ IN)

1992

OTHER KEY WORKS

Train, 1985–86, Tate, London, UK

Fun, 2001, Tate, London, UK

Fish on a Chopping Board, c.2001, Tate, London, UK

'This is my stage. Here I can dance with abandon, I can give free rein to my thoughts, I can live out my fantasies.' Xiyadie (1963–) literally cuts out and creates spaces to express and celebrate queer experiences and fantasies using the traditional art of paper-cutting. Vignettes of entangled male lovers, decorative imagery and Chinese symbols are formed in Xuan paper (thin rice paper) and vibrantly coloured with traditional Chinese pigments.

Largely the domain of women, paper-cut decorations are believed to bring prosperity and fortune into households displaying them. Xiyadie learned the art from his mother and initially made them for family celebrations but described, 'as I grew and changed and my sexuality developed, my paper-cuts changed with me'. They provided a source of relief from social pressures, a retreat: 'I fantasized about eloping with a man to the moon, where there was no one to discriminate against us … My paper-cuts focus on this desire for love and freedom.' He worked on them secretly at home in fear of being punished for them.

He adopted the pseudonym Xiyadie (Siberian Butterfly), to protect his identity as a gay man married to a woman with children. He appears to be the first known Chinese paper-cut artist to visibly engage with queer themes. Recurring motifs include doors, as shown here, which he describes as representing both a sense of safety and feeling trapped.

XIYADIE

Xiyadie grew up in Weinan, a city in the Shaanxi Province of Northwest China, a region known for the ancient art of paper-cutting. In the 1990s, as a migrant worker, he moved to Beijing where he was able to connect with gay subcultures. Most notably he attended the LGBTQ Centre in Beijing, where he was first encouraged to display and share his artwork in exhibitions and online.

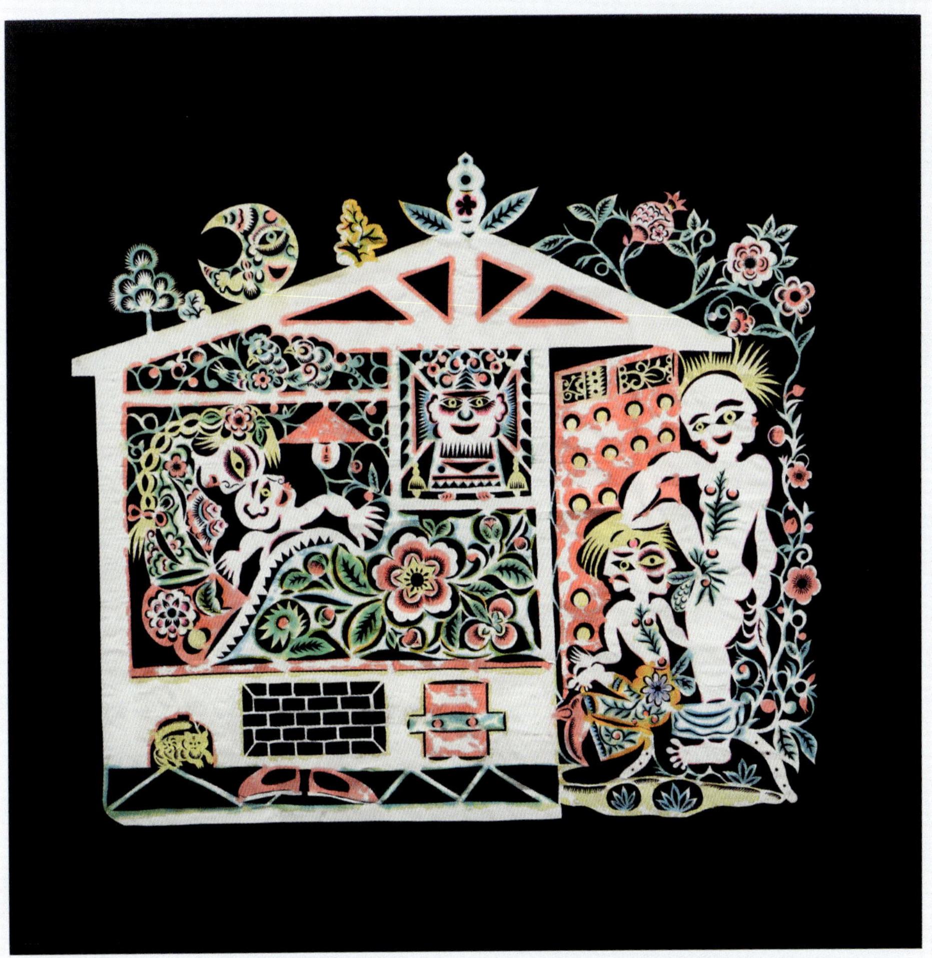

GLIMPSES OF UTOPIA **p.163** PERSONAL REALIZATION **p.164** PRESENTING THE ARTIST **p.167**
EROTIC EXCHANGES **p.183** STRAIGHT EXPECTATIONS **p.185**

Blue

1993

DEREK JARMAN: 35MM FILM SHOWN AS VIDEO, HIGH DEFINITION, COLOUR/SOUND
DURATION: 79 MINS • TATE, UK

OTHER KEY WORKS

Queer, 1992, Manchester Art Gallery, UK

Ataxia – Aids is Fun, 1993, Tate, London, UK

Prospect Cottage garden, 1987–1994, Creative Folkestone, UK

Derek Jarman (1942–1994) applied the eye of an artist and art historian to his films, frequently acknowledging the artifice of filmmaking by mixing past and present with a hearty dose of anachronisms.

Jarman considered *Blue* 'the first film made by someone with AIDS as opposed to one made about the situation'. It boldly consists of an unchanging blue image – a key inspiration being the monochromatic paintings made by Yves Klein (1928–1962) using International Klein Blue (IKB). Jarman noted, 'Since the virus is essentially invisible, the Blue reflects it more accurately.' The colour provided a seductive space to immerse in a soundscape of intercutting narratives: one telling adventures of Blue, as a character and colour, the other relating Jarman's day-to-day life, as a gay man living with AIDS in 1990s London.

Much of his later work was informed by involvement in HIV/AIDS activism, notably the painting series *Queer* and *Evil Queen*. Jarman embraced the term 'queer', explaining, 'For me to use the word "queer" is a liberation; it was a word that frightened me, but no longer', and took it for the title of his 1993 Manchester City Art Gallery exhibition.

Screened in cinemas, broadcast on television, presented as art installations and in 2023 as a live performance *(Blue Now), Blue* has continued to realize Jarman's hope for his work to resonate with successive generations of LGBTQ+ viewers and beyond.

DEREK JARMAN

Growing to become a multifaceted creative – painter, poet, filmmaker, set designer, diarist, author, activist and gardener – Jarman described first discovering painting at school as 'self-defence' and that it became 'my secret garden ... an escape out of Heterosoc [heterosexual society]'. One of Jarman's recurring interests was queer connections across time – recovery and remembrance of the past and conscious creation of testimony and evidence for future significance.

FILM AND VIDEO ART **p.28** CONCEPTUAL ART **p.32**

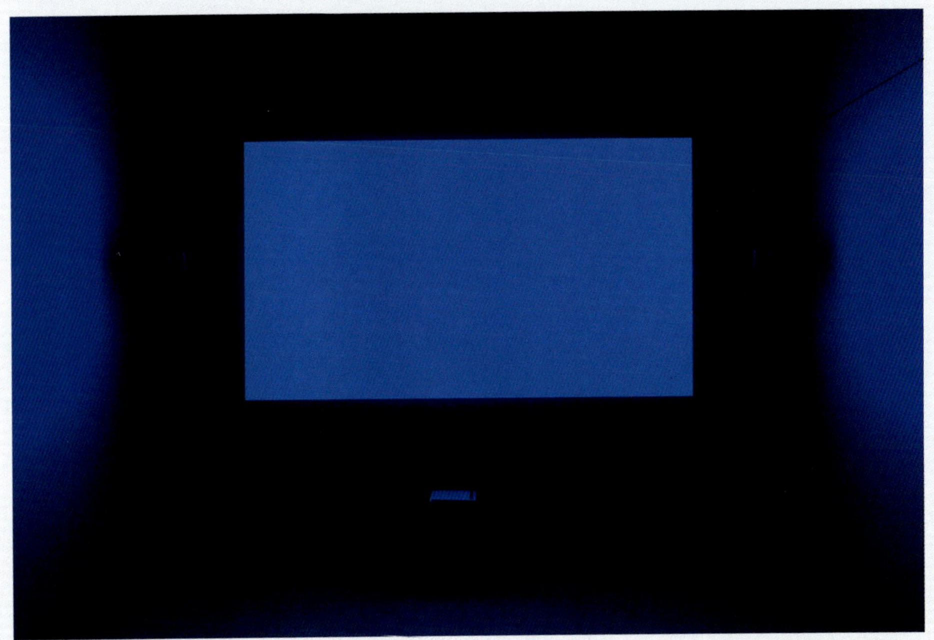

A DOCUMENTED HISTORY **p.162** PRESENTING THE ARTIST **p.167** POWERFUL PROTEST **p.169**
SPACE OF THE BODY **p.172** TO BE SEEN **p.186** REWORKING ART HISTORY **p.191**

Memorial to a Marriage

2002

PATRICIA CRONIN: BRONZE • 68.5 X 107 X 213 CM (27 X 42 X 84 IN)

OTHER KEY WORKS

Tack Room, 1997, Artist's Collection

Harriet Hosmer: Lost and Found, A Catalogue Raisonné, 2009

Shrine for Girls, 2015, site-specific temporary installation, Venice Biennale, Italy

The 'dream piece' by Patricia Cronin (1963–) is a 3-tonne, over life-size, marble mortuary sculpture of herself and her partner, the artist Deborah Kass (1952–). Created for their burial plot in Woodlawn Cemetery in the Bronx, New York, it was the first Marriage Equality monument in the world. Completed when same-sex marriage was still illegal across the United States, it marries political protest with visual poetry to convey broader issues including status, love, loss, lesbian invisibility and the paucity of real women represented in public sculpture.

It is visually both homage and appropriation of *The Sleepers* (1866), the infamous lesbian painting by Gustave Courbet (1819–1877) – which previously inspired her 1990s series of erotic watercolours. Cronin consciously opted to emulate nineteenth-century American Neoclassical sculpture, with its nationalist associations, to fittingly address what she considered 'a federal failure'. 'In death I make official my "marriage" which is still not legal while we are alive.'

To protect it from the elements and enable its inclusion in exhibitions, the original marble version was replaced with a bronze in 2011. Interested in how visitors to Parisian cemeteries often touch tombs with personal significance, Cronin embraced the potential of bronze to 'extend the performative nature' of the tomb, eager to see which areas become polished down through touch.

Researching the history of sculpture in preparation for this work, Cronin discovered the work of American-born Harriet Hosmer (1830–1908), who had been a highly regarded, self-supporting sculptor with international clients and a notorious lesbian. She reflected, 'While I was thinking about my own death … I found someone else's life.' The discovery inspired her to compile a catalogue raisonné of Hosmer's work which served as a broader corrective comment on the omission of women, feminists and lesbians from art-historical records.

PATRICIA CRONIN

Frequently mining and subverting sources from art history, the Brooklyn-based artist makes work that encompasses a variety of media to address social justice issues of gender, sexuality and class. Inequalities and precariousness of visibility and recognition in life and death are recurring concerns – as are the conditions that can cause some individuals and their achievements to be lost to history. Cronin notably seeks to give presence to female and lesbian absence.

NEOCLASSICISM **p.15**

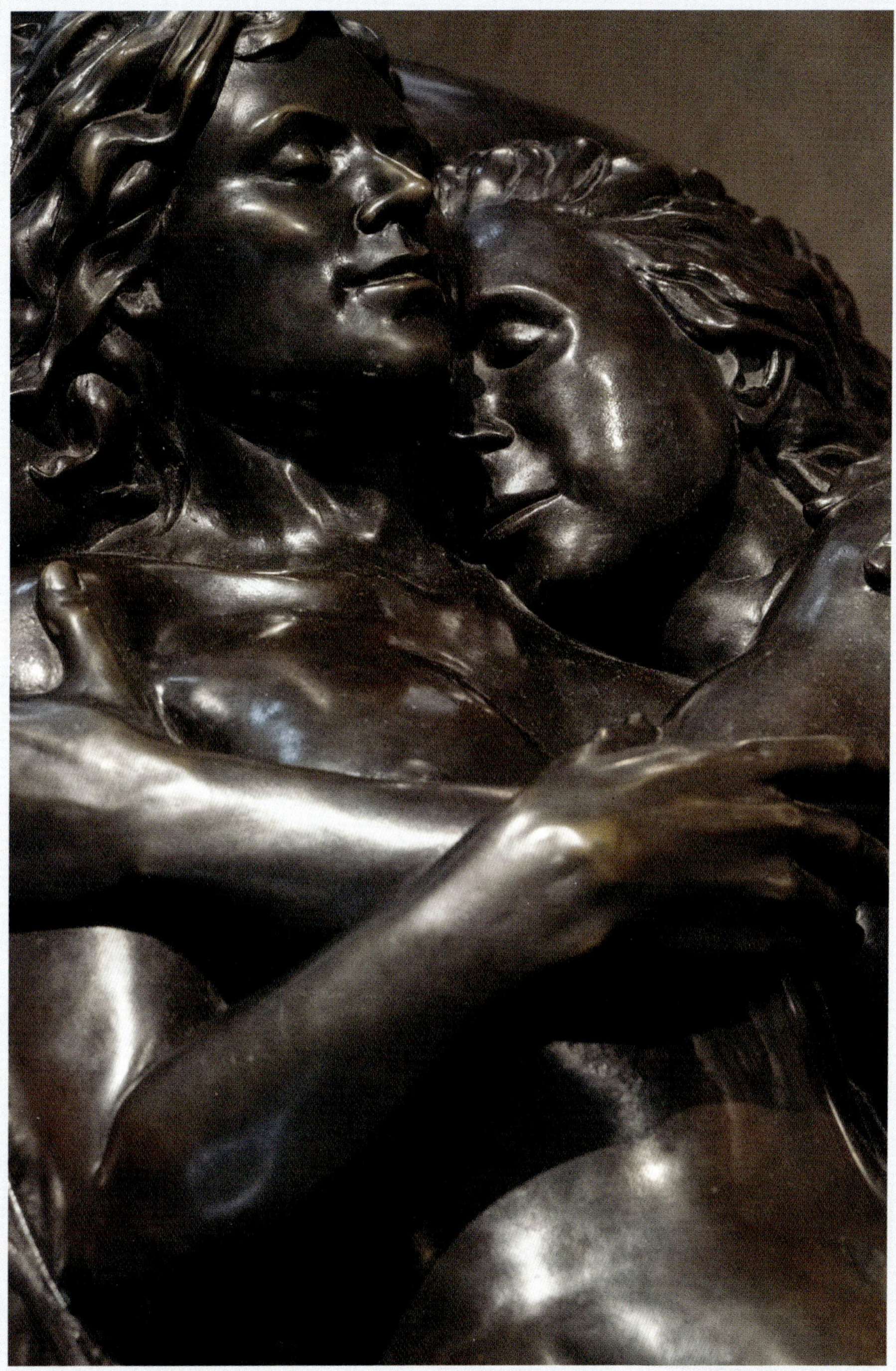

FEMINIST ART **p.30** A DOCUMENTED HISTORY **p.162** POWERFUL PROTEST **p.169** TO BE SEEN **p.186**
PUBLIC PRESENCE **p.197**

Passing / Posing, from Coronation of the Virgin

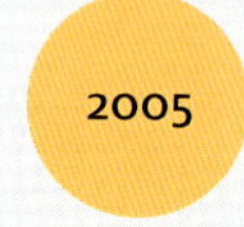

KEHINDE WILEY: OIL AND ENAMEL ON CANVAS • 207 X 175.2 CM (81½ X 69 IN)
PRIVATE COLLECTION

OTHER KEY WORKS

Napoleon Leading the Army over the Alps, 2005, Brooklyn Museum, New York, USA

President Barack Obama, 2018, Smithsonian's National Portrait Gallery, Washington, D.C., USA

***Tahiti* (series)**, 2019

Kehinde Wiley (1977–) has cited influences including Thomas Gainsborough (1727–1788) and Jacques-Louis David (1748–1825), whose portraits of regal, aristocratic and governmental people have bolstered the grandeur and power of their white sitters, not just in their lifetime but continuing through the ages.

Reappropriating such overblown scenes as David's five versions of *Napoleon Crossing the Alps* (1801–1805), making the heroic horseman a young Black man wearing camo and Timberland boots, Wiley uses his work to redress the erasure of people of colour in the historical narrative and arouses 'the desire to be seen and to be taken seriously'. Sperm are deftly incorporated into the painting's background and corners of the frame (shaped like testes) to indicate the propaganda of hypermasculinity in the long history of this exaggerated form of status-elevating portraiture.

The *Passing / Posing* series of paintings all utilized street casting. The artist and model would then look through Renaissance, Rococo and Neoclassical artworks, selecting a pose to adopt from a particular historic painting and incorporating its name into the title. Here, an unnamed model in an Atlanta Hawks basketball jacket takes the place of the Virgin Mary in the moment she is crowned the Queen of Heaven. The artist explains this carves out 'space for people who don't often occupy that space'. The words 'passing' and 'posing' also have complex meanings and intersections with race, sexuality, class and gender fluidity.

KEHINDE WILEY
Wiley is one of most sought-after portrait painters of the twenty-first century. Incorporating a broad church of the decorative arts such as stained glass, wallpapers and botanical backgrounds, he engages the visual conventions of historic European and American portraiture to portray people of the African diaspora. Predominantly discovering his sitters in the street, he has also been commissioned to capture famous faces including Barack Obama (1961–) (2018) and fellow artist Mickalene Thomas (1971–) (2017).

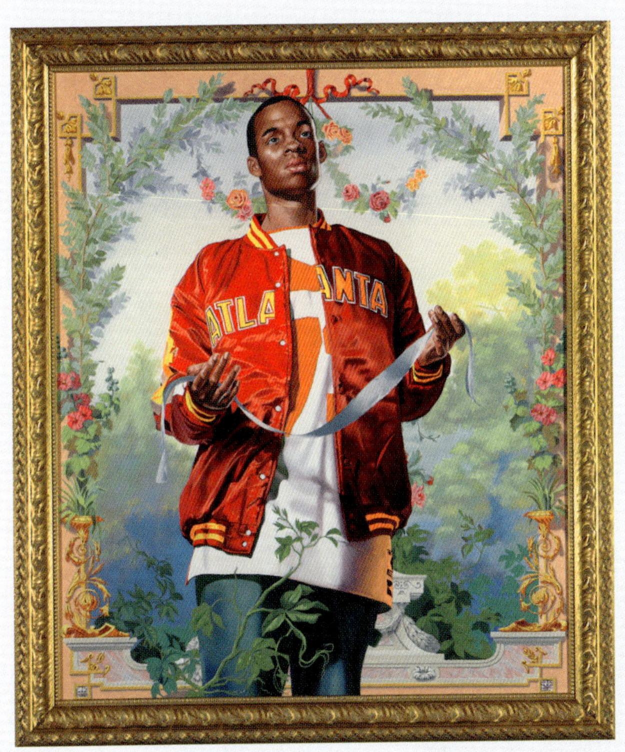

TO BE SEEN **p.186** REWORKING ART HISTORY **p.191**

Becoming an Image

2013

CASSILS: PERFORMANCE STILL NO. 1 (EDGY WOMEN FESTIVAL, MONTREAL)
C-PRINT FACE MOUNTED TO PLEXIGLASS • 91.4 X 61 CM (36 X 24 IN) • PHOTO: CASSILS WITH ALEJANDRO SANTIAGO

OTHER KEY WORKS

Tiresias, 2011

CUTS: A Traditional Sculpture, 2011–2013

Human Measure, 2021–

Cassils (1975–) describes themselves as 'disciplinarily promiscuous', employing a dizzying array of methods and mediums. From ancient materials like clay and bronze to punishing performances harnessing the elements, they have self-immolated in *Inextinguishable Fire* (2007–2015) and melted ice sculptures representing classical ideals of the binary body with their nude trans body in *Tiresias* (2011).

Mining the meaning of corporeality, they made a wall of their own urine to rubbish anti-trans legislation prohibiting public bathroom usage, and sold cans of their faeces as non-fungible tokens, mocking hollow novelties of the capitalist art world.

Becoming an Image illustrates Cassils' staggering multidimensionality. Each performance generates a unique suite of photographs. Taking place in the dark, a cloak of safety yet vulnerability, the artist's exertions are heard as they punch a 2000-pound block of clay, amplified with a soundscape titled 'Ghost' incorporating their pulse and breathing. Illuminated periodically by the stark light of flash bulbs, this creates a temporary 'retinal burn' effect in the eyes of the audience, disallowing passive spectatorship. The pulverized clay from the first performance was cast into a bronze sculpture, *The Resilience of the 20%*, highlighting the horrendous fact that murders of trans people increased by this percentage worldwide in 2012. Furthermore, a film and collaborative four-hour performance, *Monument Push* (2017), took the bronze to Omaha to be collectively hauled 'with allies and advocates' in a visceral visualization of the burden of struggle.

CASSILS

Bursting out c.2000, Cassils has an impressive frame that filled a void of trans-masculine representation in the art world. Inspired by feminist artists who tore the gender-binary apart, including Lynda Benglis (1941–) and Carolee Schneemann (1939–2019), they also reference gay physique aesthetics to create often physically gruelling work condemning the violence and scrutiny the trans body is subjected to in society. They defy categorization as a sculptor, photographer, performance artist, activist and more.

FILM AND VIDEO ART **p.28** PERFORMANCE ART **p.29** FEMINIST ART **p.30**

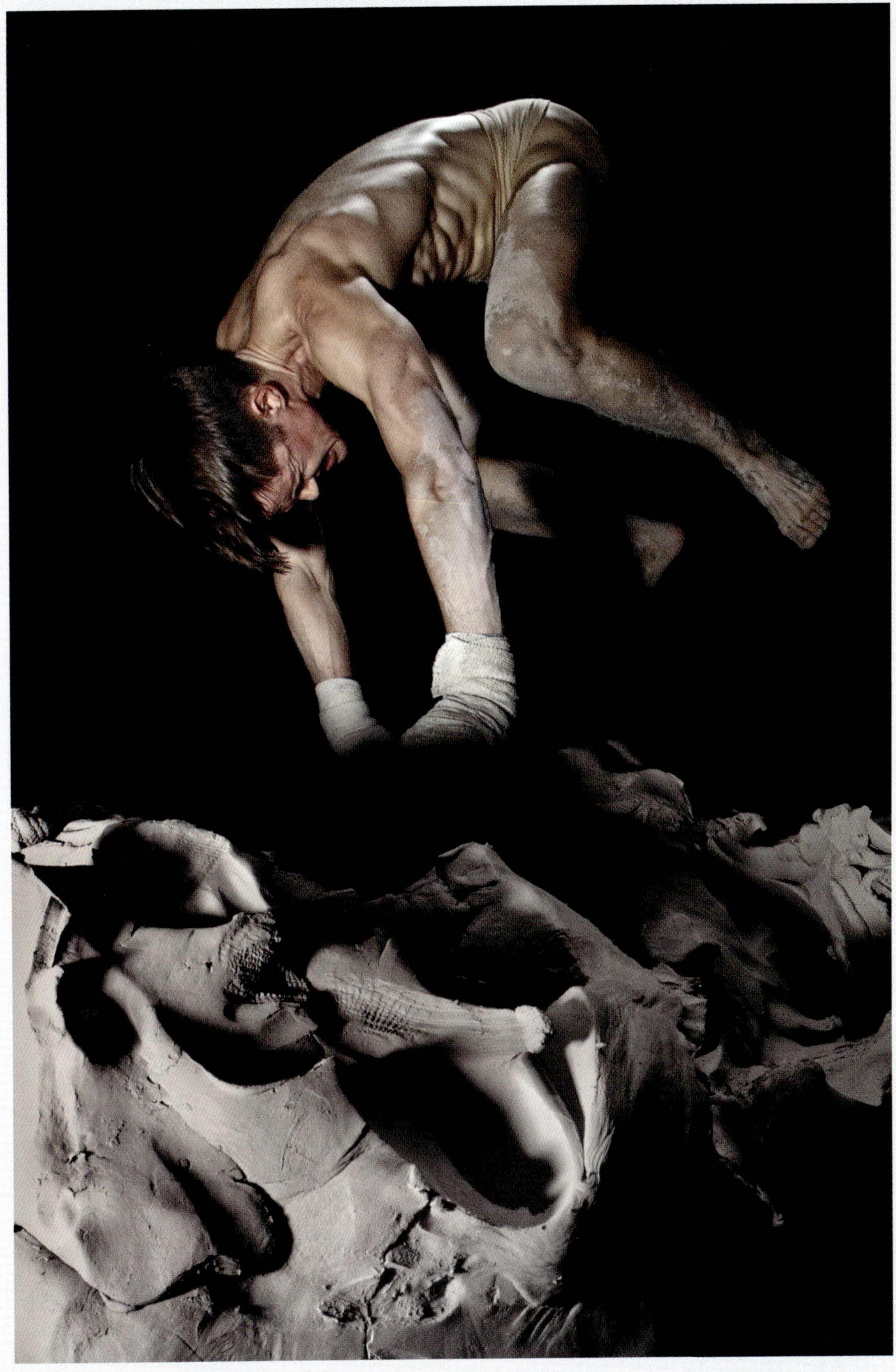

POWERFUL PROTEST **p.169** SPACE OF THE BODY **p.172** TO BE SEEN **p.186** TRANSFORMING **p.190**

Night of the Long Knives I

2013

ATHI-PATRA RUGA: ARCHIVAL INK-JET PRINT ON PHOTORAG BARYTA • 150 X 190 CM (59 X 74¾ IN) • EDITION OF 5 + 2AP • PHOTOGRAPHER: HAYDEN PHIPPS

OTHER KEY WORKS

The Naivete of Beiruth, 2007

Beatification of Feral Benga, 2017–

Things we lost in the Rainbow, 2018

Athi-Patra Ruga (1984–) crafts responses to post-apartheid South Africa, evoking myths to explore notions of nationalism and utopia. Ruga's multimedia series create thriving worlds of creativity and queer liberation populated with vivid characters that disrupt historical and contemporary narratives of xenophobia, misogyny and homophobia. Ruga has reflected that creating myths or alternative realities allows for a level of detachment often needed to face such issues. *Future White Women of Azania* (2012–) envisions the semi-mythical lands of East Africa first recorded in GrecoRoman texts and adopted by the Pan Africanist Congress (PAC) in 1965 to signify a future South Africa.

Engulfed by balloons, evoking connotations of cocoons or a fertility goddess, the Futurewhitewomenofazania character reappears in multiple works – 'a frivolous, light apparition that disturbs the burden of fear people have with black men … [and] the notion of white women as aspirational characters'.

During performances Ruga pops the balloons 're-writing the pomp and ceremony of how nations are founded as a feminine character … I'm deflating all of these constructed ideas.' Here they contrast with the title, *Night of the Long Knives*, which Ruga used to highlight that 'Apartheid is inextricably linked to the Third Reich and international fascism.' Funeral procession meets pantomime, Ruga describing it as a camp and sarcastic comment on 'unfounded settler panic'. 'South Africa was built on processions. Those are all the ways that we perform real issues. It also bursts open places that are shut, reclaiming it somehow'.

ATHI-PATRA RUGA

Growing up in South Africa, Ruga described the 'Rainbow Nation' vision that accompanied Nelson Mandela (1918–2013) becoming the country's first democratically elected Black president as appearing 'an Eldorado of sorts, a utopian tomorrow'. However, as Black, gay and non-Christian he felt he could only 'look at the rainbow from the outside'. In response, his work frequently focuses on ideas of nationhood and reinserting and elevating the exiled or excluded.

PERFORMANCE ART **p.29** AFROFUTURISM **p.34**

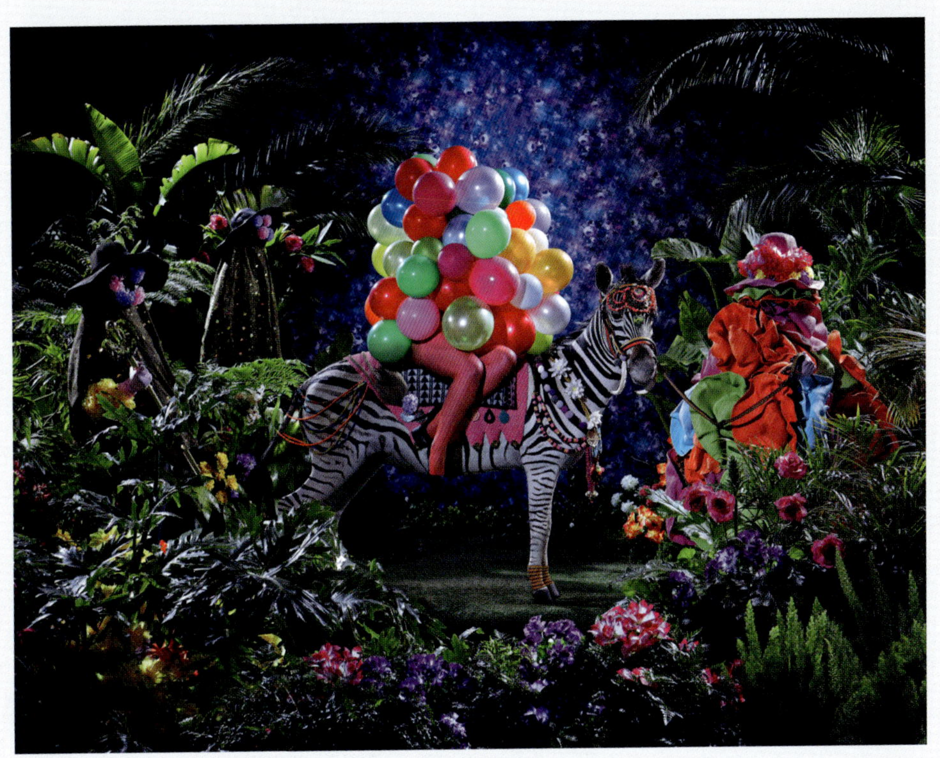

A DOCUMENTED HISTORY **p.162** GLIMPSES OF UTOPIA **p.163** POWERFUL PROTEST **p.169** TO BE SEEN **p.186**

Vanishing Point

2014

ANNA CAMPBELL: BALSA WOOD, MYLAR HELIUM BALLOON, RIBBON, NYLON HARDWARE • 244 X 91 X 5 CM (96 X 36 X 2 IN) • ARTIST'S COLLECTION

OTHER KEY WORKS

Passing, 2014, Artist's Collection

Convent of Pleasure (edition of 50), 2022, Artist's Collection and Private Collections

Transmission Spell, 2023, Artist's Collection

Anna Campbell's (1979–) work both cites and sites a range of signifiers and queer histories with a confident clarity and often wry sense of humour. Interested in exploring 'queer relationality' and expanding queer representation in ways that don't rely on foregrounding a body, Campbell's endeavours take the form of sculpture, installation, video projection, found objects and more. Keenly reconnoitring 'the erotics of the archive', she has noted the need to incorporate pleasurable elements when evoking difficult stories.

In Campbell's *Vanishing Point*, a multitude of references and ideas converge. A reflective silver balloon floats as a beacon tethered to a balsa wood maquette. Over time the balloon deflates, before crumpling to rest upon the structure. With a visible lifecycle, it amplifies notions of impermanence and the chance timing of encounters. It nods to Andy Warhol's (1928–1987) floating metallic pillows in *Silver Clouds* (1966) and shares acknowledged links with works by Felix Gonzalez-Torres (1957–1996).

Vanishing Point also references the old piers of Manhattan, which were spaces for congregating and cruising in the 1970s and 1980s, with the Christopher St Piers notably featuring in *Paris is Burning* (1990). By evoking this scene, Campbell prompts consideration of historical queer spaces more broadly. *Vanishing Point* simultaneously suggests the joys of 'coming together' and a deflating sense that 'the party is over', be it due to the AIDS epidemic, gentrification or community fractures. Whilst conjuring notions of loss, it also provides encouragement to regroup, reinflate, reconfigure and construct new horizons, evoking the words of José Esteban Muñoz (1967–2013): 'We may never touch queerness, but we can feel it as the warm illumination of a horizon imbued with potentiality.'

ANNA CAMPBELL

A significant focus of Campbell's time at college was 'structured around feminist and queer activism', which has held enduring influence on their artwork. Attracted to 'the chaotic, utopic, world-making, authorial voice that can be expressed through an art practice', Campbell has described 'mining' sites of history and queer desire, in both physical and imaginary senses. Artwork titles often tactically 'crowbar in' inescapably queer meanings, preventing potential erasure in future display or interpretation.

CONCEPTUAL ART **p.32**

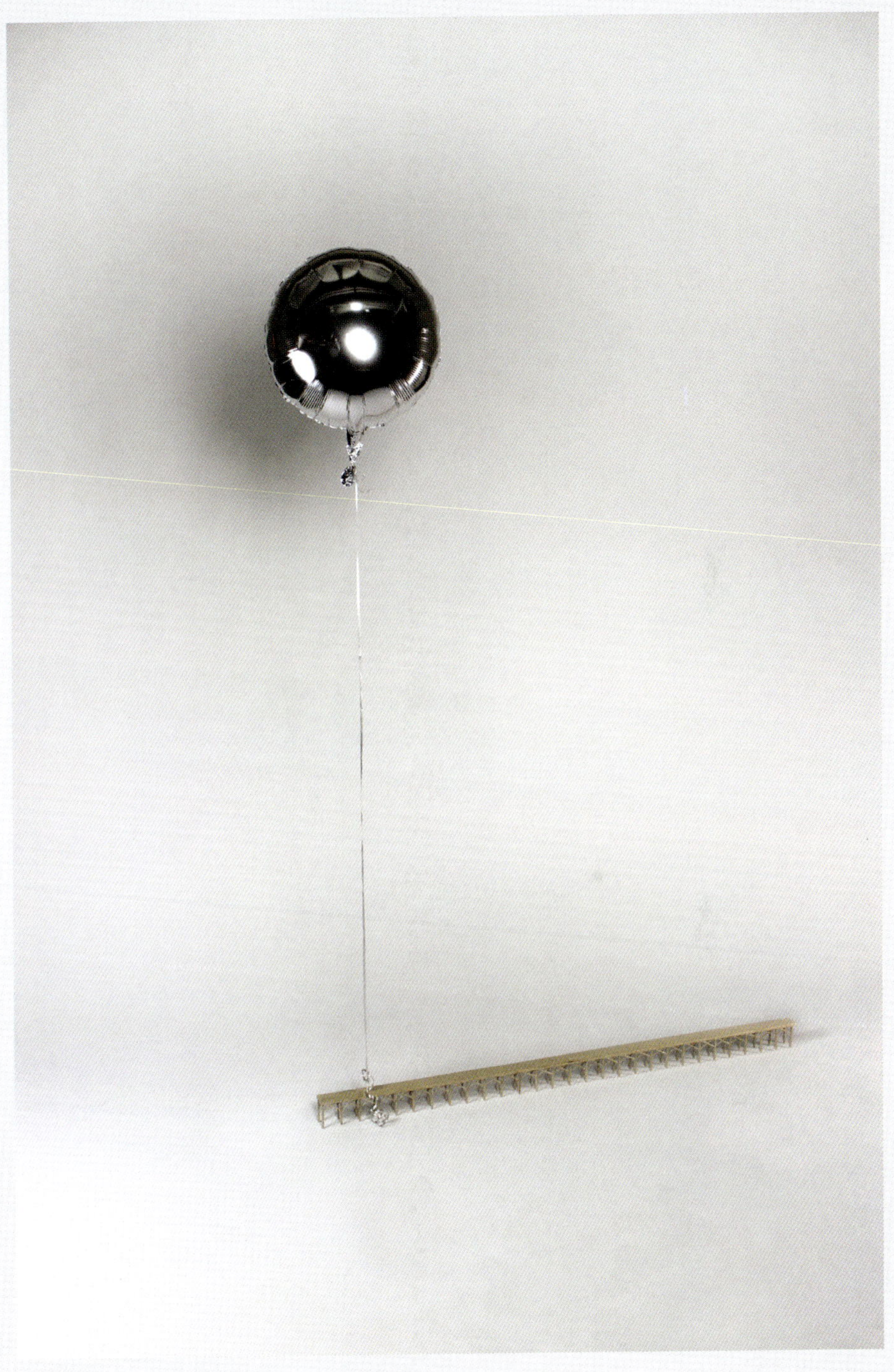

INTIMACIES p.165 FACING AIDS p.208

Qusuquzah Lounging with Pink + Black Flower

2016

MICKALENE THOMAS: RHINESTONES, ACRYLIC AND OIL PAINT ON WOOD PANEL
243.8 X 304.8 CM (96 X 120 IN)

OTHER KEY WORKS

Afro Goddess With Hand Between Legs, 2006, The Studio Museum in Harlem, New York, USA

Le déjeuner sur l'herbe: Les Trois Femmes Noires, 2010, Baltimore Museum of Art, USA

A Little Taste Outside of Love, 2007, Brooklyn Museum, New York, USA

Mickalene Thomas (1971–) is one of the most innovative painters and printmakers working today, hybridizing serigraphy, woodblock, photography and textured elements with flocking, fabrics, glitter and embossing, alongside utilizing a wide palette of digital tools. Thomas has reflected, 'There are not enough images of Black women loving Black women, specifically, so I feel I have a responsibility to contribute positive images for those who don't know anywhere else to go.' Thomas' work is actively trans-inclusive and she has depicted Qusuquzah as muse multiple times, celebrating the beauty of Black trans womanhood.

Reflecting also on a Western art history dominated by white men, Thomas has reworked canonical paintings as 'a way of claiming that space, of aligning my voice and art history and entering this discourse'. *Olympia* (1863) by Édouard Manet (1832–1883) was the basis for *A Little Taste Outside of Love* (2007) where the nude figure is a Black woman reclining upon a visual feast of

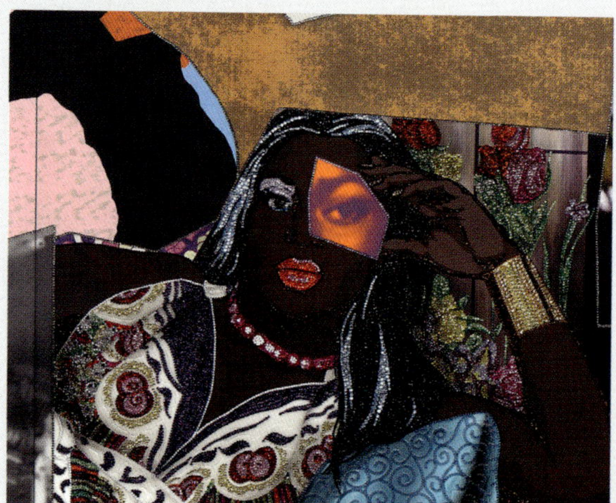

Detail: Qusuquzah looks confidently out at the viewer. Thomas has explained, 'all of my muses possess a profound sense of inner confidence and individuality'.

POP ART **p.27**

monochromatic patterned cushions and wallpaper, replete with rhinestones.

Victorine Meurent (1844–1927), Manet's model for *Olympia* and *Le Dejeuner sur l'Herbe*, was a lesbian artist herself, accepted into the 1876 Salon when Manet's works were rejected. Her narrative, however, has been reduced to that of a part-time sex worker. Thomas' work critiques this misogynistic reduction of female sexuality, expanding space for it to define and exist on its own terms, free of judgement and censorship.

Detail: A hybrid of materials and textures, Thomas' work often blurs distinctions between recording a scene and creating imaginary scenarios, with energetic combinations of photography, paint, textiles, fabrics, glitter and diamantés.

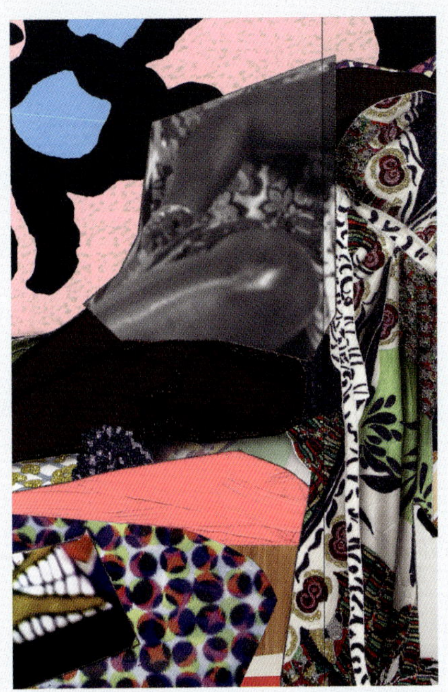

MICKALENE THOMAS

Thomas is a New York-based artist reenergizing art historical tropes and genres of portraiture, still life and landscape. With inspirations transcending time, borders and identities, her complex and richly layered paintings and prints incorporate bold and brilliant Black fashions and interior design from 1970s family photographs. Inspired by her personal life, she is driven to fill the void that persists around lack of representation of queer women of colour.

INTIMACIES **p.165** CHOSEN FAMILY **p.170** ASSEMBLING **p.171** TO BE SEEN **p.186** REWORKING ART HISTORY **p.191**

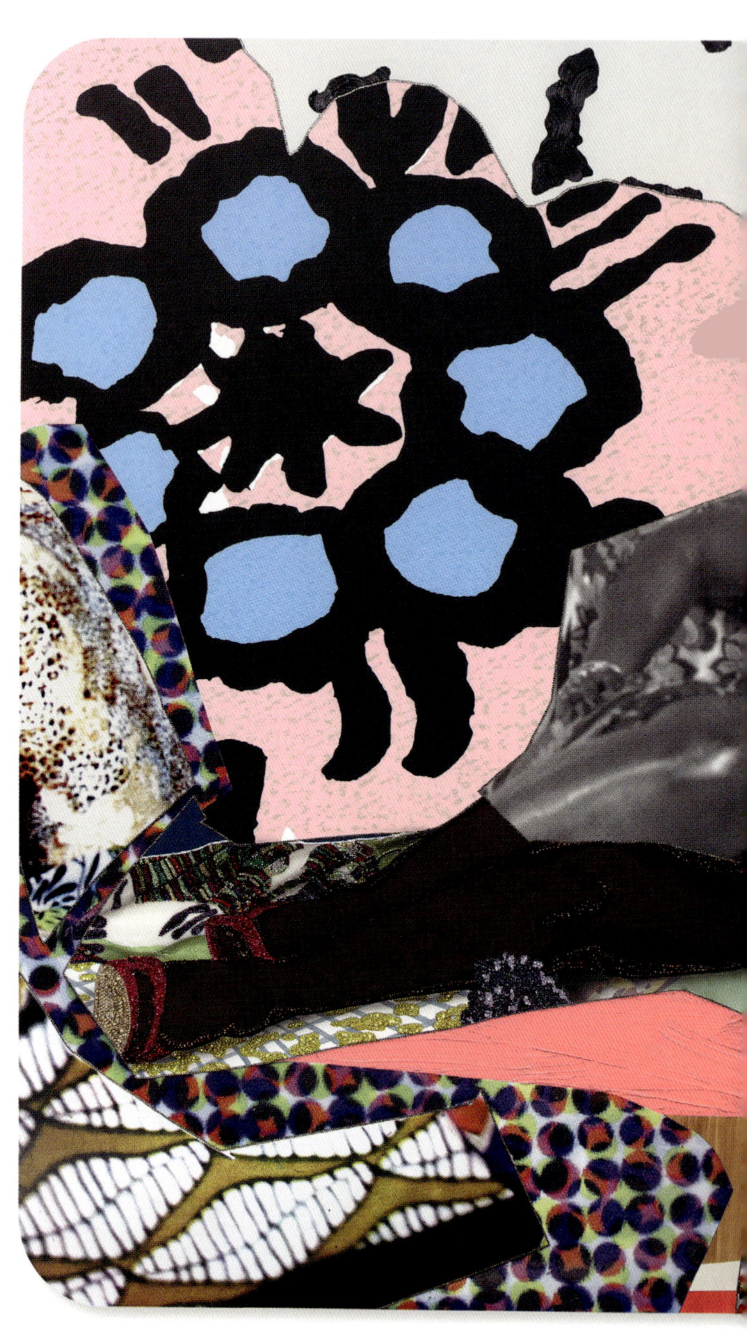

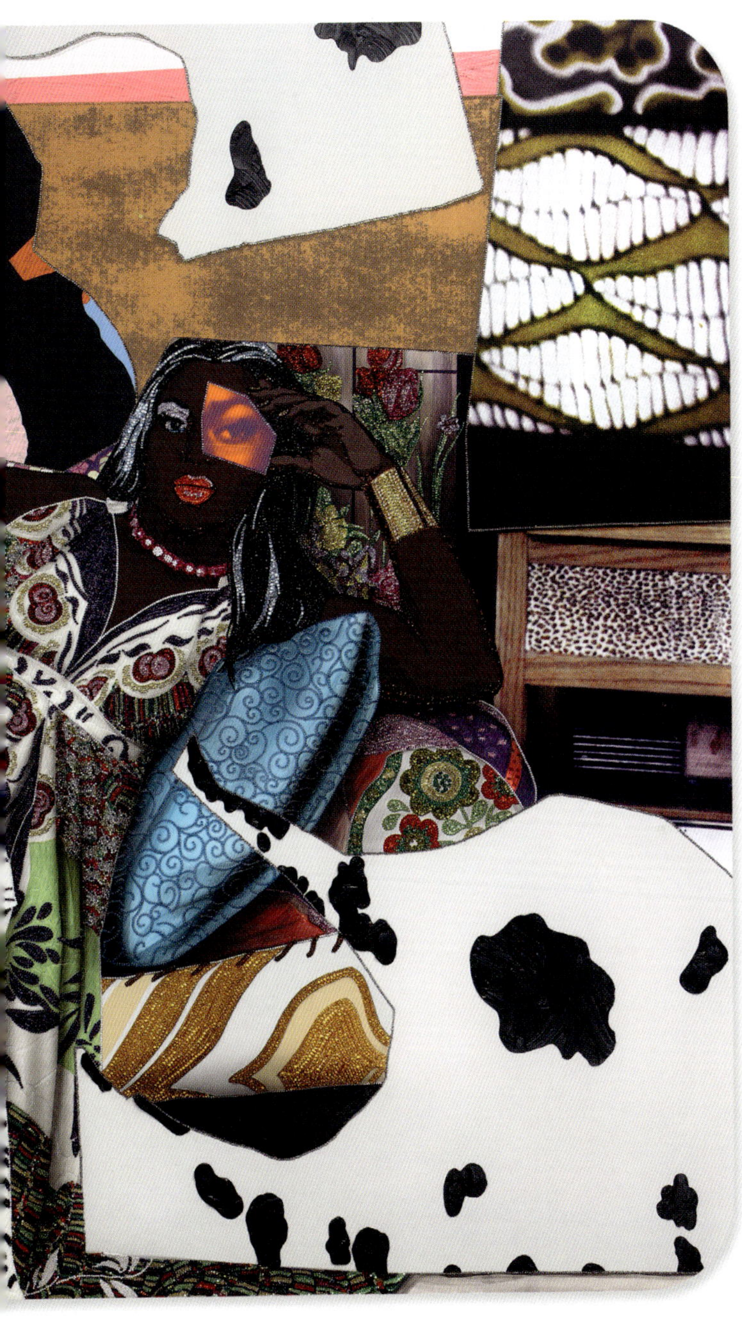

Phila I, Parktown

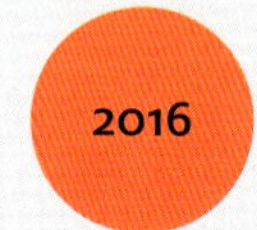

ZANELE MUHOLI: GELATIN SILVER PRINT ON PAPER • 80 X 53.5 CM (31½ X 21 IN)
PRIVATE COLLECTION

OTHER KEY WORKS

ID Crisis, 2003, Tate, London, UK

Lebo Leptie Phume, Daveyton, Johannesburg, 2013, Nottingham Castle Museum and Art Gallery, UK

Qiniso, The Sails, Durban, 2019

Zanele Muholi (1972–) has steadily become a towering presence in the artworld over the past two decades, on a mission 'to re-write a black queer and trans history of South Africa (SA) for the world to know of our resistance and existence at the height of hate crimes in SA and beyond.'

Participants in *Faces and Phases* (2006–2016) were all born into horrors of apartheid which officially came into force in 1948 following centuries of colonial oppression. Many of their personal stories of survival, defiance and queer visibility are recorded in a community lifeline with an online platform founded by the artist (www.inkanyiso.org), made by, and primarily for, queer people in South Africa. The network's ethics and productions encapsulate the power of art to generate positive change and fightback against homophobic and transphobic violence. *Brave Beauties* (2014) is another series picturing drag queens, trans women and other queer participants in gay beauty pageants popular 'especially in the townships, as a way of creating awareness through cultural activities'.

Muholi has recently turned the camera on themself to create incredibly arresting self-portraits. This photograph is part of the ongoing series entitled *Somnyama Ngonyama: Hail the Dark Lioness*. Refashioning household items like pegs, hoovers and, in this instance, latex gloves, these frame the artist's form as reminders of the labour of people of colour forced into positions of domestic servitude.

ZANELE MUHOLI

Muholi is a visual activist, describing their primary tool of the camera as 'the weapon with which I speak'. In 2006 they began the long-running series *Faces and Phases*, photographing hundreds of black lesbians, intersex, non-binary and trans masculine people from across South Africa. Founding the Inkanyiso network in the same year, Muholi is the pulsating heart of a thriving queer community and a virtuoso of the photographic medium.

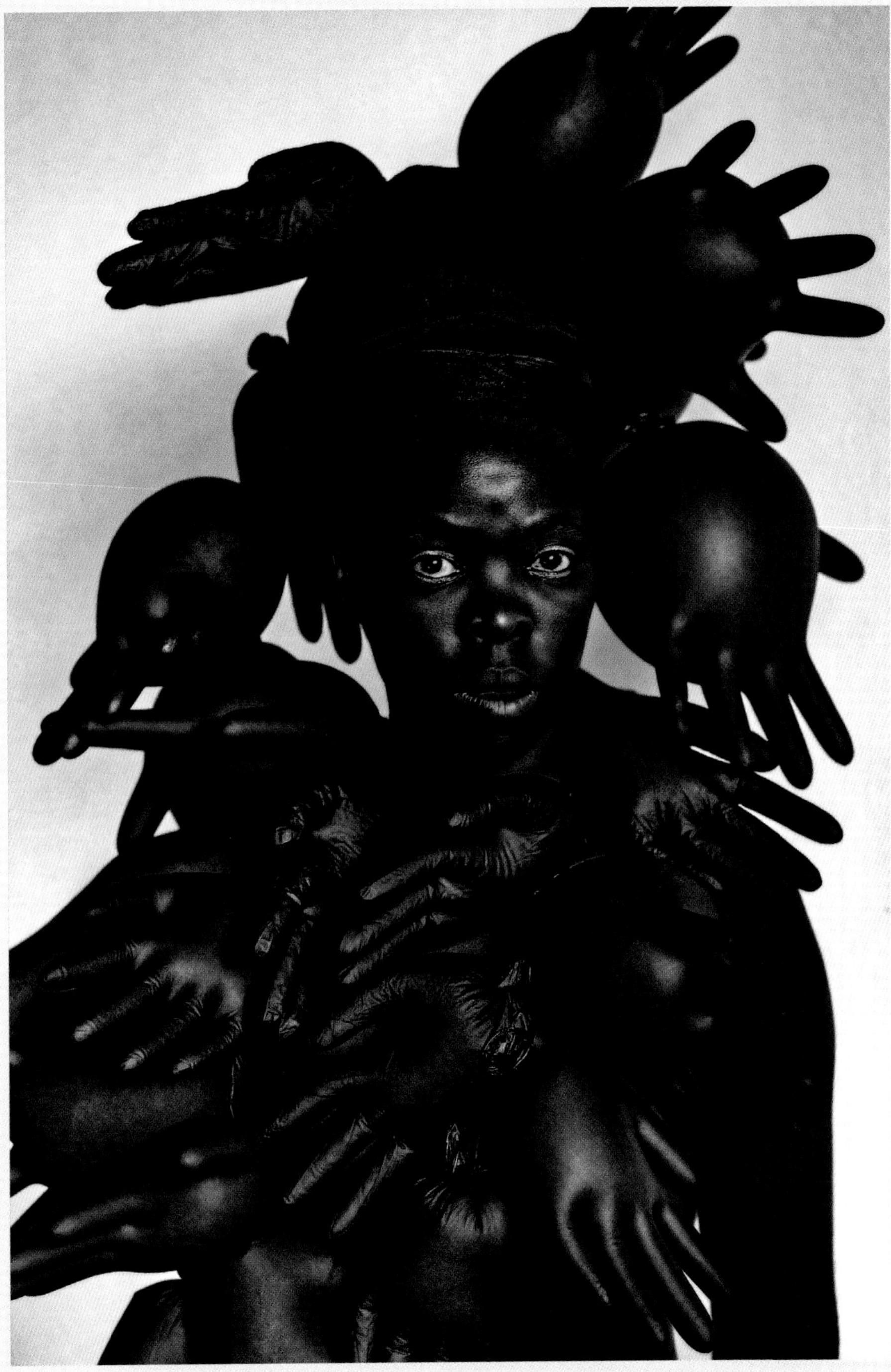

INTIMACIES **p.165** PRESENTING THE ARTIST **p.167** CHOSEN FAMILY **p.170** TO BE SEEN **p.186**

Resurgence of the People

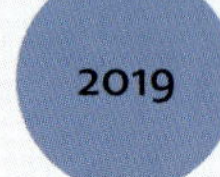

KENT MONKMAN: ACRYLIC ON CANVAS • 335.28 X 670.6 CM (132 X 264 IN)
COLLECTION OF THE METROPOLITAN MUSEUM OF ART, NEW YORK, USA

OTHER KEY WORKS

The Academy, 2008, Art Gallery of Ontario, Canada

Gender Splendour, 2021

The Mystery of mistapew (After Carr, Haring and Picasso), 2022

Kent Monkman (1965–) has a time-travelling, Two-Spirit persona/alter-ego Miss Chief Eagle Testickle, who makes recurring appearances in the artist's films, paintings and performances. Describing her as 'a legendary being, she comes from the stars', Monkman created her 'to offer an Indigenous perspective on the European settlers and to also present a very empowered point of view of Indigenous sexuality pre-contact.' At times she allows him to introduce touches of camp playfulness even when considering disturbing chapters of history.

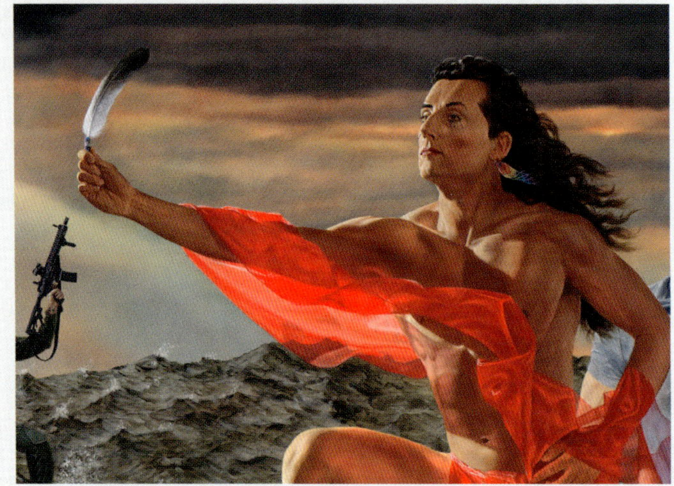

Detail: With a rainbow-coloured feather fluttering from her ear, Miss Chief Eagle Testickle holds an eagle feather aloft. The feather is powerfully symbolic in indigenous cultures, and its position here implies it could plug the barrel of a gun.

Personifying Cree values and traditions, she takes on the 'hero' position here – usurping that of George Washington (1732–1799) in *Washington Crossing the Delaware* (1851), by Emanuel Leutze (1816–1868), which this painting reimagines. It is one of a pair of large-scale paintings Monkman was commissioned to create for The Metropolitan Museum of Art's Great Hall. Their shared title *mistikôsiwak* derives from a Cree word meaning 'wooden boat people' – originally denoting French settlers, it here encompasses all colonizing Europeans. The first, *Welcoming the Newcomers*, depicts their arrival, along with institutions of religion and slavery. Here, Miss Chief Eagle Testickle leads a resurgence of people resilient in the face of displacement, returning to their languages and traditions. Both feature references to works in The Met collection, and here the central figures in blue nod to Titian's *Venus and Adonis* (1500s). While evoking various specific references the works speak to broader subjects of 'migrations and displacements of people around the world'.

Detail: Both paintings include figures referencing the frequently depicted scene in the tale of Venus and Adonis – where Venus implores Adonis to stay with her rather than hunt, correctly fearing that he would be killed.

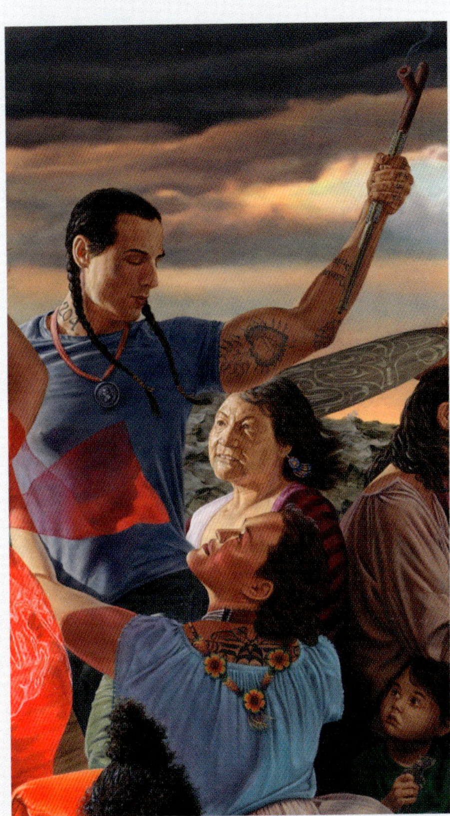

KENT MONKMAN

Monkman is a multidisciplinary Cree artist whose work frequently references classical traditions of art history, to craft critical interventions that highlight colonial violence, resistance and resilience in ways that link pasts, presents and futures. A core concern is nineteenth-century European depictions of Indigenous people of North America, refuting their frequent romanticization of a 'disappearing race'. Monkman also foregrounds Indigenous traditions of gender and sexuality distinct from colonial binaries.

A DOCUMENTED HISTORY **p.162** QUEER ECOLOGIES **p.177** REWORKING ART HISTORY **p.191**
INDIGENOUS QUEER LOVE **p.215**

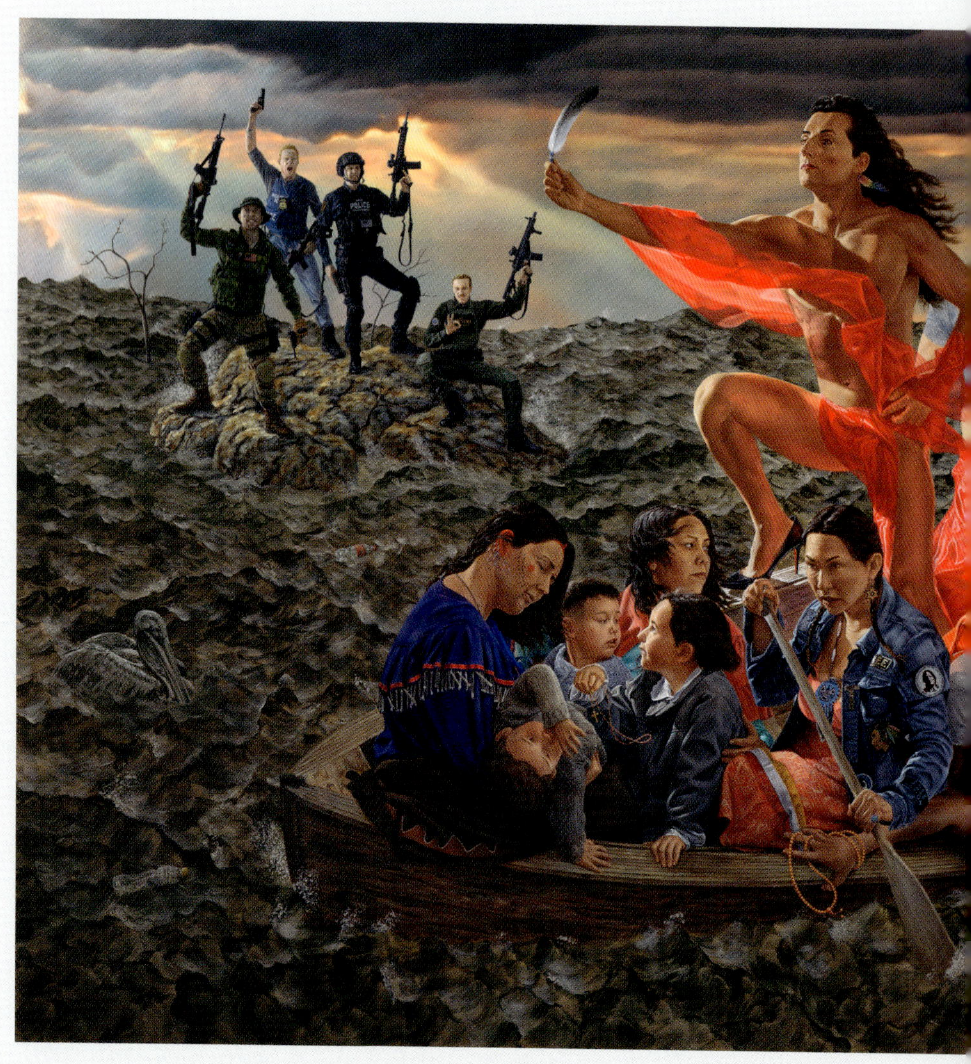
POLICE

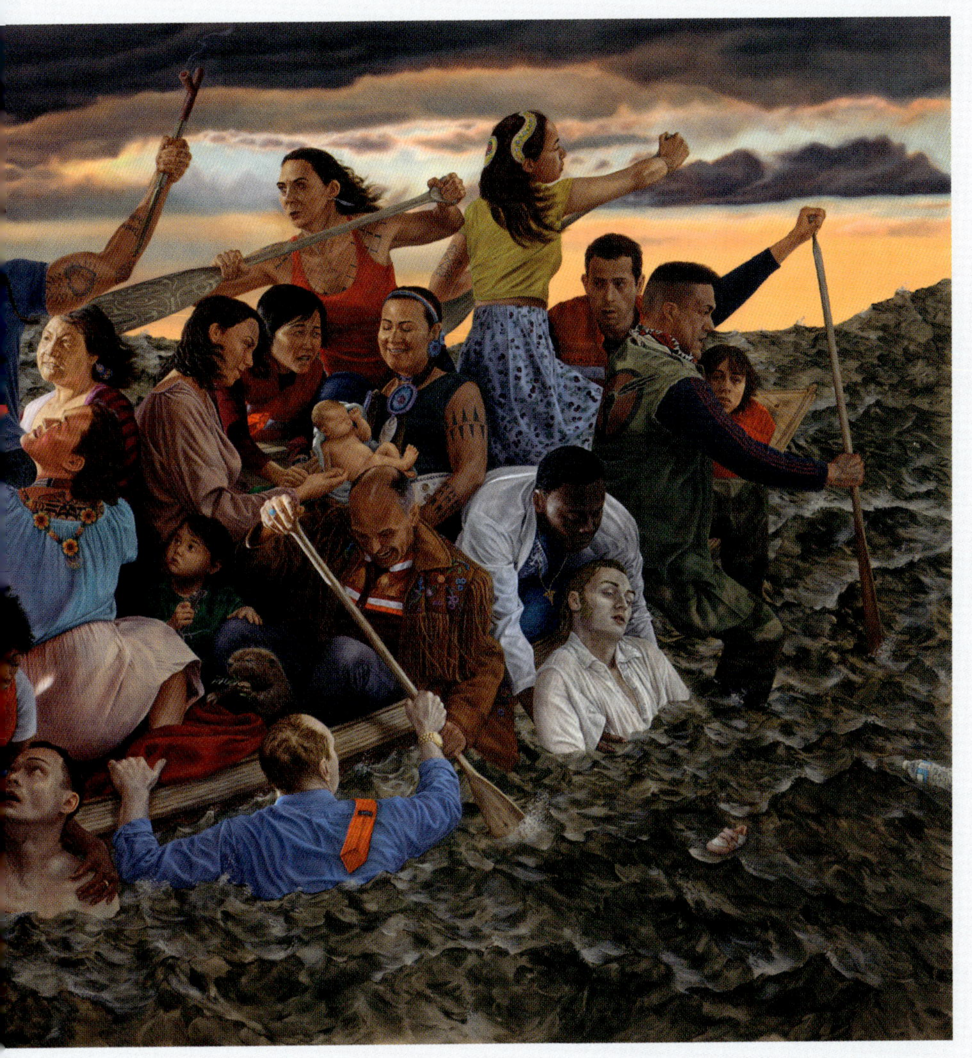

The Latecomer

2021

SALMAN TOOR: OIL ON PANEL • 121.9 X 152.4 CM (48 X 60 IN)

OTHER KEY WORKS

The Star, 2019, Whitney Museum of American Art, New York, USA

Museum Boys, 2021

Four Friends, 2019

'I paint figures to enhance my context as a queer man living between cultures … to mythologize my life, define my relationship to power, but also to laugh at myself and have fun.' Salman Toor (1983–) uses fluid brushstrokes to create a distinctive world of in-between spaces and moments rooted in diasporic experience. Combining inviting intimacy with disorientating separation, Toor has explained that he is 'trying to draw a line between growing up in a conservative Islamic country and being an authentic inheritor of the liberation movements of gay men' of the 1970–1980s which existed where he now lives in New York.

The Latecomer captures that disconcerting moment of arrival in a space before you feel welcomed or 'at home'. Appearing spotlit the figure makes his nervous exploratory passage across what appears to be a queer-friendly club, visually separate from those around him who possess intriguing ambiguities.

It makes bold use of what has become Toor's signature sea-green palette, which he described as evoking 'the nocturnal allure and fantasy of a freely queer life'. Suggestive of emeralds and absinthe, it calls to mind the heady depictions by Toulouse-Lautrec (1864–1901) of urban leisure in La Belle Époque, Paris and the rich Art Deco portraits by Tamara de Lempicka (1898–1980).

A contemporary jolt is provided by another of Toor's tropes – faces lit by the glow of a mobile phone, a pervasive technology that both connects and alienates.

SALMAN TOOR

Born and raised in Lahore, Pakistan, Toor moved to Ohio to study painting before settling in New York. Intensely influenced by European art history and fascinated by how multiple moments and places can coexist within a painting, he sees himself as 'part of a multiethnic generation of painters in the US who are taking on art history to update, critique, and tweak it, to write ourselves into its rich story'.

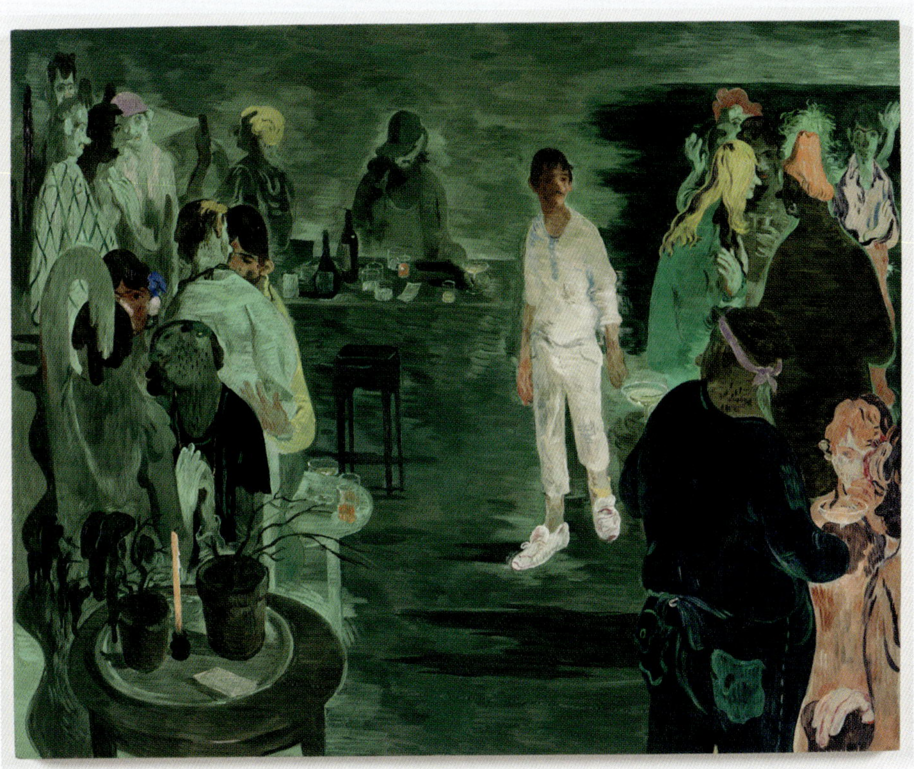

INTIMACIES **p.165** CHOSEN FAMILY **p.170** PLACES TO BE **p.189** REWORKING ART HISTORY **p.191**

Sous le ciel de Shiraz (PaykanArtCar)

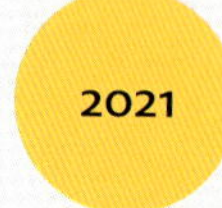

ALIREZA SHOJAIAN: MULTIMEDIA INSTALLATION AND ACRYLIC PAINTING ON HILLMAN HUNTER CAR • 430.5 X 161.3 CM (169½ X 63½ IN)

OTHER KEY WORKS

Hexagon Series, 2015

Hamed Sinno et un de ses Frères, 2018

Sous le ciel de Shiraz (series), 2022

A consistent concern in the work of Alireza Shojaian (1988–) is connecting queer histories of West Asia with present day concerns to challenge anti-LGBTQ+ prejudices. He frequently uses coloured pencils, which are light and inexpensive, and have proved practical for an exiled artist on the move. Subjects are often intimate and vulnerable, frequently nude or semi-nude, giving an affecting gentle but powerful directness.

The poignant *Hexagon Series* (2015) depicts cropped, close-ups of the final moments of a murdered gay friend – 'the details belonging to a time which has been stopped by a bullet' delicately rendered in pencil and acrylic.

Shojaian switched pencils for an airbrush in his treatment of the inaugural *PaykanArtCar*. Using characters from ancient Persian literature, it includes imagery from the painting *Sohrab and Shaban*, by Hossein Qollar-Aghasi (1902–1966) and inspired by the *Shahnameh* ('The Book of Kings'). The figure of Shaban relates the story of Ali Fazeli Monfared (2002–2021), who was beheaded by family members for his homosexuality. It includes a recording of Monfared reading a note to his boyfriend, who had fled to Türkiye days earlier. Conscious of persistent claims that homosexuality is a Western import, Shojaian did not use well-known Western LGBTQ+ symbols but included an iris flower – subtly referencing the Greek Goddess of the Rainbow.

In 2021 an invitation to exhibit the car at the Paris art fair *Asia Now* was retracted, citing fears of endangering the safety of the people working with the fair.

ALIREZA SHOJAIAN

The Iranian self-described visual activist was born in Tehran, Iran, where the censorship and suppression of LGBTQ+ people prompted him to move to Beirut to be able to create work. In 2019 he was offered an art residency by the French embassy in Lebanon with the Académie des Beaux-Arts and now resides in Paris. He seeks to create space for non-heteronormative masculine identities and fight societal prejudice against LGBTQ+ people.

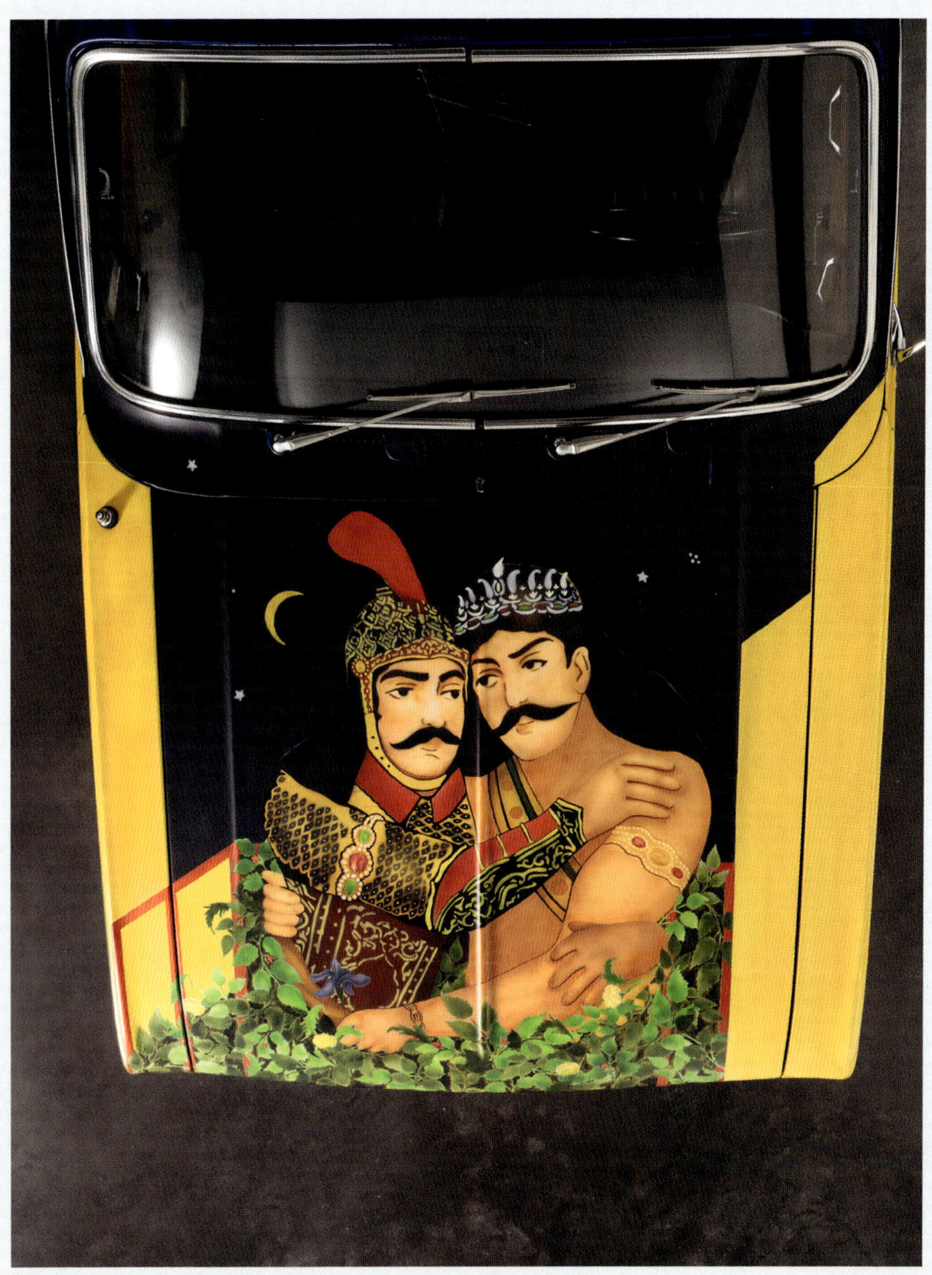

A DOCUMENTED HISTORY **p.162** INTIMACIES **p.165** POWERFUL PROTEST **p.169** CHOSEN FAMILY **p.170**
REWORKING ART HISTORY **p.191**

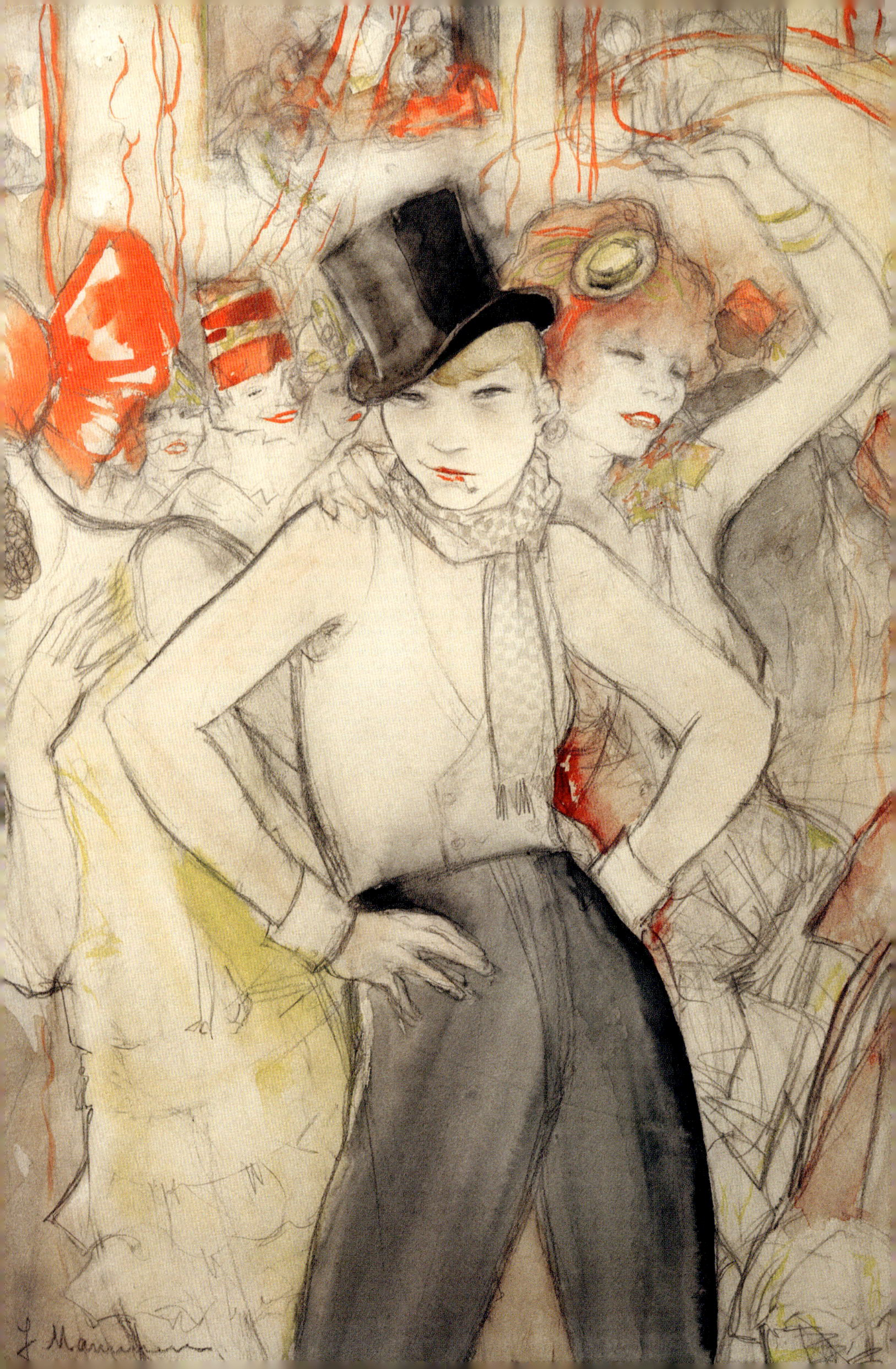

Themes

A DOCUMENTED HISTORY 162 • **GLIMPSES OF UTOPIA** 163 • **PERSONAL REALIZATION** 164 • **INTIMACIES** 165 • **TEXTUAL POWER** 166 • **PRESENTING THE ARTIST** 167 • **QUEER CODING** 168 • **POWERFUL PROTEST** 169 • **CHOSEN FAMILY** 170 • **ASSEMBLING** 171 **SPACE OF THE BODY** 172 • **IN THE STUDIO** 173 • **MASKS** 174 • **CRAFTING THREADS** 175 • **SUMMONING SAPPHO** 176 • **QUEER ECOLOGIES** 177 • **DIVINE CONNECTION** 178 **CALL OF THE SEA** 179 • **RISING CAMP** 180 • **THEATRICAL TYPES** 181 • **QUEER EYE** 182 **EROTIC EXCHANGES** 183 • **QUEER ICONS** 184 • **STRAIGHT EXPECTATIONS** 185 • **TO BE SEEN** 186 • **ON SCREEN** 187 • **DANCE** 188 • **PLACES TO BE** 189 • **TRANSFORMING** 190 • **REWORKING ART HISTORY** 191

A Documented History

KEY ARTISTS: JOAN E. BIREN (JEB) • DEREK JARMAN • PAULINE BOUDRY & RENATE LORENZ GIUSEPPE CAMPUZANO • RIA BRODEL • CARLOS MOTTA

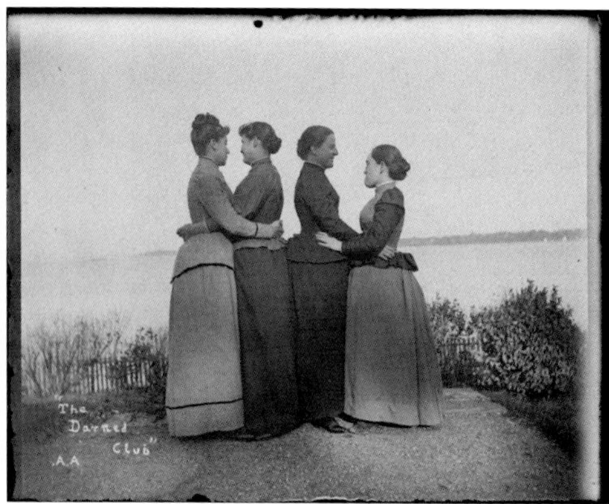

The Darned Club, Alice Austen, 1891, photograph, collection of Staten Island Historical Society, Alice Austen House Museum, New York, USA

KEY DEVELOPMENTS

Photographer Joan E. Biren (JEB) (1944–) committed to improving visibility of lesbian communities. She disseminated her own images with publications including *Eye to Eye: Portraits of Lesbians* (1979) and travelled around America presenting the slideshow 'Lesbian Images in Photography: 1850–the present' (1984). It included *The Darned Club* (1891) by Alice Austen (1866–1952) whose photography included intimate depictions of her 'larky life' with Gertrude Tate (1872–1962).

Derek Jarman declared 'The Absence of the Past was a Terror' and described how in the 1960s 'I began to read between the lines of history. The hunt was on for forebears who validated my existence.' Countless LGBTQ+ individuals have actively searched for threads of connection to queer lives of the past amid a historic landscape of frequent suppression and erasure [see also *To Be Seen*].

The work of video and visual artists Pauline Boudry (1972–) and Renate Lorenz (1963–) has been termed 'queer archaeology' as they 'unearth' and reframe historic objects through a queer feminist lens. Ria Brodell (1977–) views their series *Butch Heroes* (2010–) as an effort to reclaim and document the history of LGBTIQA communities, with portraits presented alongside biographies like Catholic holy cards, subversively venerating lives.

Many have turned their attention to art history. Artist and author Emmanuel Cooper (1938–2012) hoped his landmark publication *The Sexual Perspective – Homosexuality and Art in the Last 100 Years in the West* (1986) would help 'make the homosexual presence in art more public and encourages artists to take it as their subject matter'. Artists and activists have increasingly acknowledged the role of archives in safe-keeping histories. Projects merging art, activism and archiving include the travelling Museo Travesti del Perú (2004–2013) by Giuseppe Campuzano (1969–2013), the virtual QUEER ARCHIVE INSTITUTE by Karol Radziszewski (1980–) and The Museum of Transgender Hirstory & Art (MOTHA) (2015–).

REALISM **p.16** FILM AND VIDEO ART **p.28** INTERNET ART **p.37**

Glimpses of Utopia

KEY ARTISTS: ATHI-PATRA RUGA • ELISÀR VON KUPFFER • SIN WAI KIN
AMARYLLIS DEJESUS MOLESKI • KLÁRA HOSNEDLOVÁ

Throughout time people have invoked ideal worlds or alternate realities they long to create, discover or return to. They may be speculative, practical or satirical and look to the past or imagined futures for inspiration. Introduced in *Utopia* (1516) by Sir Thomas More (1478–1535), the word derives from the Greek eutopia ('good place'), an ideal that can exist, but is also suggestive of utopos ('no place') an escapist's fantasy. When living within restrictive social and legal landscapes, visions of utopia can provide spaces for imagining and working towards more equitable futures. Depictions of male-homosexual utopias frequently referenced Ancient Greece and Italy as places of 'classical freedom'. Yevgeniy Fiks (1972–) has asserted that 'Any utopia is queer by nature, because it takes you from the present and directs you to a strange time and place'.

The series *Future White Women of Azania* (2010–) by Athi-Patra Ruga (1984–) presents his vision of Azania – semi-mythical lands of East Africa first mentioned in Greco-Roman texts. Through recurring fantastic characters and fusions of cultural and religious imagery, Ruga works across media including performance and tapestry to convey 'the story of black queer women in South Africa'. Shown here covered by balloons, Ruga explained, 'As much as my utopia is inspired by my own black, queer story [I like] to remove both skin and faces' to prevent assumptions.'

KEY DEVELOPMENTS

The relationship between utopianism and pragmatism has sometimes caused friction in LGBTQ+ communities. *Cruising Utopia: The Then and There of Queer Futurity* (2019), by José Esteban Muñoz (1967–2013), argues for queerness itself as a future-oriented, utopian way of being in the world. Queer utopianism offers the potential to step out of 'this place and time to something fuller, vaster, more sensual, and brighter' – that could drive present real-world change.

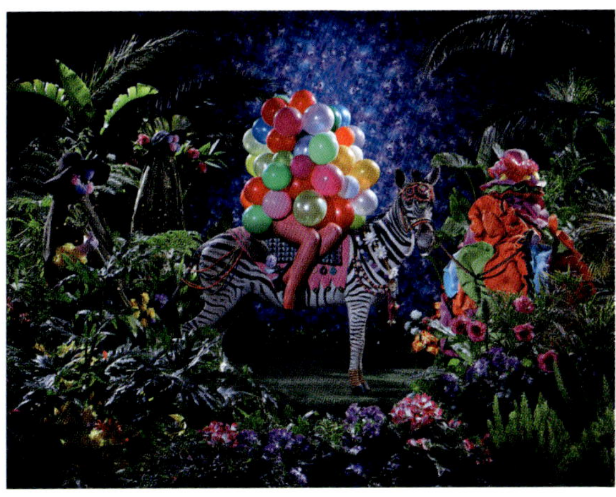

Night of the Long Knives I, from the series *Future White Women of Azania*, Athi-Patra Ruga, 2013, archival ink-jet print on photorag baryta, 150 x 190 cm (59 x 74¾ in), edition of 5 + 2AP, photographer: Hayden Phipps (see Works p.142)

DIGITAL ART **p.31** AFROFUTURISM **p.34** INTERNET ART **p.37** *FREEDOM AND CHANGE* **p.116**
NIGHT OF THE LONG KNIVES I **p.142**

Personal Realization

KEY ARTISTS: SADIE BENNING • DAVID HOCKNEY • TĀRI ITŌ • KARLA DICKENS • JOAN SNYDER XIYADIE

Art can act as a statement of self-reflection, awareness and understanding. It can chronicle an artist's sexual awakening or gender realization. This creative 'coming out' may be publicly direct, privately covert and constantly evolving. Many LGBTQ+ artists reappropriate the visual language of an excluding dominant society to create ways to define and express themselves.

Sadie Benning (1973–) came to prominence for a series of short, auto-biographic films created in their teenage bedroom using a Fisher-Price PXL-2000 (Pixelvision) camera. They later reflected that 'as a transgender queer youth without access at that time to images or language that affirmed my reality, I saw it as urgent to make my own images'. The camera recorded pixelated black-and-white video onto audio cassette tapes, creating visual textures reminiscent of charcoal sketches or photocopied zines – a feature of the 'riot grrrl' movement Benning connected with. The films collage conversations to camera; re-enactments of pop culture films; toys and photographs. Scripted, yet seemingly spontaneous, they explore the challenges of growing up, including Benning's emerging gender and sexual identity.

Their bedroom provided a safe space in which to create, separated from the outside world. In *If Every Girl Had a Diary* (1990) they reflect, 'I guess to be alone is to know yourself for you and not who you're with; and I like that.'

If Every Girl Had a Diary, Sadie Benning, 1990, b&w still from pixelvision video, USA

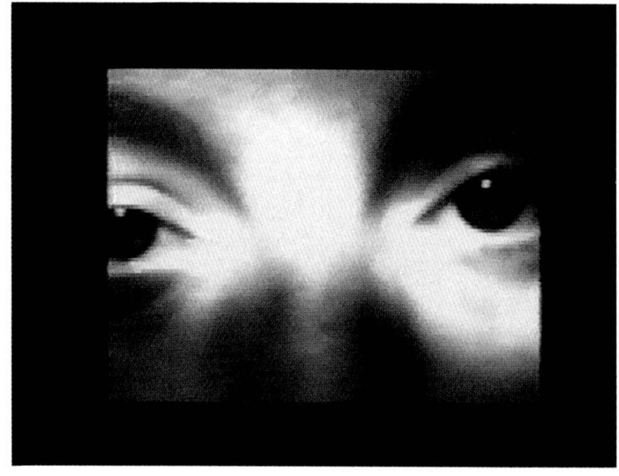

KEY DEVELOPMENTS

Benning's *It Wasn't Love* (1992) featured in the 1993 Whitney Biennial, making them, at 19, the youngest to participate. The catalogue preface 'Know thy self (know your place)' noted it came 'at a moment when problems of identity and the representation of community extend well beyond the artworld'. Notably diverse in terms of race and sexualities, the Biennial was criticized for being too focused on 'identity politics' and experi-ences of marginalization.

FILM AND VIDEO ART **p.28** PERFORMANCE ART **p.29** *I.O.U. (SELF-PRIDE)* **p.76**
UNTITLED, FROM *DREAM GIRLS* **p.126** *GATE* 门 **p.132**

Intimacies

KEY ARTISTS: MICHAEL LEONARD • HUGH STEERS • PAMELA DODDS • TEE A. CORRINE CLIFFORD PRINCE KING • ZANELE MUHOLI

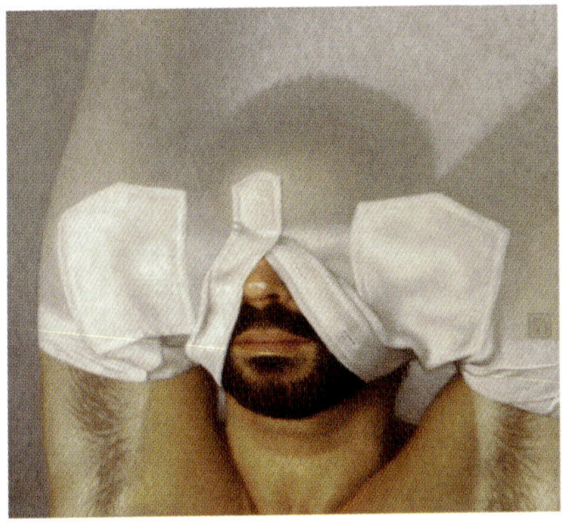

Changing Head, Michael Leonard, 1982, acrylic on rag board, 31.1 x 34.3 cm (12¼ x 13½ in), Private Collection

KEY DEVELOPMENTS

Leonard's depictions of men dressing and undressing suggest sensual, intimate insights rather than intrusive sexual voyeurism. Here, the subject conveys a calm vulnerability as his veil-like shirt reveals his torso and temporarily covers his eyes. Leonard found 'pictorial potential' in everyday actions and figures 'caught on the move'. This image was used as a cover for the iconic novel *Faggots* (1978) by Larry Kramer (1935–2020). Leonard's illustrations also appeared in *The Joy of Gay Sex* (1977).

Acts or gestures of intimacy provide moments of connection, vulnerability and familiarity that help bring meaning to relationships. Legal and social environments have historically restricted how LGBTQ+ individuals can safely publicly express personal relationships.

With an historic emphasis on sexual activity in defining non-heterosexual identities, queer artists have increasingly explored alternative forms of queer connection, including close non-sexual relationships and emotional intimacy. Artist and weaver Diedrick Brackens (1989–) described how intimacy within his artwork is important in trying to 'broaden my own understanding of what queerness looks like without thinking about sex'.

Writer-photographer and intimacy coordinator Raqeeb (1993–) noted a lack of mainstream representation of queer intimacy or vulnerability. In their series *A Day with the Lovers*, Raqeeb spends 24 hours with a couple to document their intimacies and 'everything that encompasses a relationship'.

Social gendering and racializing of certain qualities and expressions, including tenderness, is also alluded to in works by Jarvis Boyland (1995–) and Clifford Prince King (1993–) depicting intimate domestic scenes of friends and lovers.

During the AIDS crisis, physical touch and intimacy became charged with fear and a threat of contamination and death. The paintings of Hugh Steers (1962–1995) document the combination of intimacy, mundanity and harrowing moments of isolation.

Demonstrations of queer intimacy also served as a form of protest within AIDS activism, notably 'kiss-ins' organized by ACT UP (AIDS Coalition to Unleash Power).

ROCOCO **p.14** REALISM **p.16** *LA VIE PENSIVE* **p.56** *RANCHODBHAI RELAXING IN THE WINTER* **p.108** *MEMORIAL TO A MARRIAGE* **p.136**

Textual Power

KEY ARTISTS: RACHAEL HOUSE • GLENN LIGON • FIERCE PUSSY • DAVID HOCKNEY

Words and text can be tools of freedom or oppression. They can help crystallize, define and understand subjects, provide legal protection or political threat. Many queer artists have created works to overcome a lack, or limitation, of words to express themselves. Others have included words to emphasize connection with resonant texts.

Reflecting on the power of words when considering sexuality, the phrase 'Love that dare not speak its name' first appeared in the poem 'Two Loves' (1896) by Lord Alfred Douglas (1870–1945). Its meaning was famously probed at the trial of his lover Oscar Wilde (1854–1900).

Historically, LGBTQ+ visibility predominantly took textual form – often written about rather than by communities. Lesbianism was a notably popular topic of mid-nineteenth century erotic French fiction. In *Mademoiselle de Maupin* (1835), a novel by Théophile Gautier (1811–1872), the title character describes themself as a member of the Third Sex 'which as yet has no name'. Later that century the wider spectrum of sexualities and genders became of great interest to European sexologists – whose attempts at definition would influence the blossoming of identities.

Involved in the world of queer zines and comics since the 1990s, Rachael House (1961–) has developed a sincere directness in using text and image. Hers is a consciously intersectional approach to subjects including LGBTQ+ rights, feminism, bisexual visibility and ageing, and her recent work includes a series of ceramic welcoming wall panels that incorporate several reclaimed derogatory terms.

KEY DEVELOPMENTS

'Lavender Menace' was reportedly first used by feminist activist Betty Friedan (1921–2006) in 1969, to describe the threat she believed associations with lesbianism posed to the women's movement. It was quickly reclaimed in protest by an informal group of lesbian radical feminists and in 1982 adopted by the gay and lesbian Lavender Menace Bookshop, Edinburgh, Scotland. Bookshops have of course been vital in connecting LGBTQ+ communities.

Welcome Lavender Menace, Rachael House, 2022, glazed tiles, 50 x 40 x 1.5 cm (19⅔ x 15¾ x ⅗ in), Artist's Collection

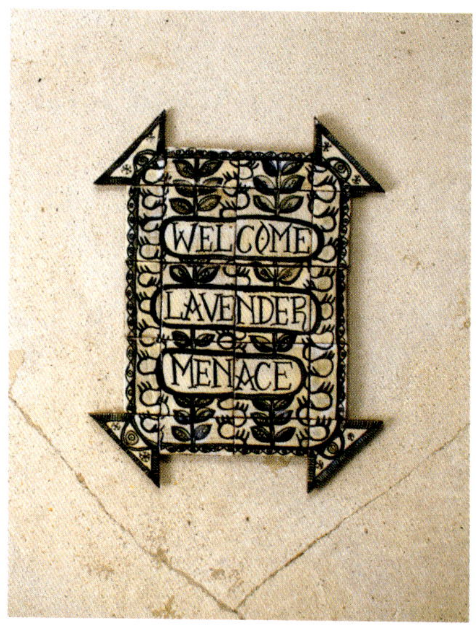

PRE-RAPHAELITES **p.17** AESTHETICISM **p.19** HARLEM RENAISSANCE **p.22** *I.O.U. (SELF-PRIDE)* **p.76**
SELF PORTRAIT WITH CROPPED HAIR **p.98** *NOTES ON THE MARGIN OF THE BLACK BOOK* **p.128**

Presenting the Artist

KEY ARTISTS: LOTTE LASERSTEIN • ALICE AUSTEN • MARIE HØEG AND BOLETTE BERG CLAUDE CAHUN • GLUCK • VLADISLAV MAMYSHEV-MONROE • ZANELE MUHOLI

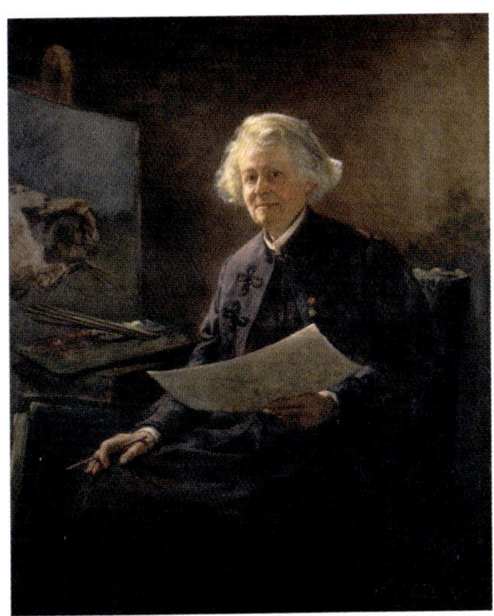

Anna Klumpke, Rosa Bonheur, 1906, oil on canvas, 117.2 x 98.1 cm (46⅛ x 38⅝ in), The Metropolitan Museum of Art, New York, USA

Rosa Bonheur (1822–1899) had to gain police permission to wear trousers so she could work undisturbed in masculine environments like horse markets, frequently also donning them for photographic self-portraits. Such 'cross-dressing' provided practical inroads for women to enter masculine professions. Considerable evidence proves such strategies fulfilled a wider variety of personal aspirations.

In the thriving lesbian and bisexual avant-garde circles of early-twentieth-century Paris and Berlin, portraiture strengthened the visibility of sartorial signifiers and fashions associated with these identities. Visiting the studio of Romaine Brooks (1874–1970) in the 1940s, Truman Capote (1924–1984) declared it, 'the all-time ultimate gallery of all the famous dykes from 1880 to 1935.' Expressionist Marianne Werefkin (1860–1938) wrote of having 'both masculine and feminine qualities united in artistic practice.' Their diary notes: 'I am neither man nor woman – I am I', comparable to the instructions from Gluck (1895–1978): 'No prefix, suffix, or quotes.' Okuhara Seiko (1837–1913) also eschewed a specifically feminine persona and adopted the gender-neutral name Seiko. The self-portraits *NoMan's Land* (1998) by Linn Underhill (1936–2019) 'queered' notions of the sought gaze by appropriating the place of male models photographed by the homo-eroticizing gaze of George Platt Lynes (1907–1955).

Artists have explored presenting multiple imagined personas. Vladislav Mamyshev-Monroe (1969–2013) took on the guise of famous mythical, political and cinematic figures. Described as 'a trickster in drag', he expressed, 'For some people art is art; for me, it's my personal life.'

KEY DEVELOPMENTS

Celebrated as a painter of animals, Bonheur is today also famed as a lesbian artist who commented, 'As far as males go, I only like the bulls I paint.' Presenting what was deemed a 'masculine appearance', Bonheur wore her hair short, smoked and lived openly with female partners including artists Nathalie Micas (1824–1889) and Anna Klumpke (1856–1942) (the artist here), becoming an inspirational reference point for subsequent queer artists.

LA VIE PENSIVE **p.56** *I.O.U. (SELF-PRIDE)* **p.76** *AUTOPORTRAIT (TAMARA IN A GREEN BUGATTI)* **p.84** *MEDALLION (YOUWE)* **p.94** *SELF PORTRAIT WITH CROPPED HAIR* **p.98** *PHILA I, PARKTOWN* **p.150**

Queer Coding

KEY ARTISTS: MARSDEN HARTLEY • PAUL CADMUS • HAL FISCHER

Individuals throughout history have employed visual codes to navigate legal threats and social stigma when expressing queer identities and desires. Codes and symbols allow those familiar with the language to read 'hidden' meanings that would not be recognized by a wider public. They often allowed for an ambiguity that enabled artists to maintain a plausible denial of queerness if needed.

Various symbols of queer identity have emerged and receded as aesthetics and subcultures have changed. Peacock feathers unfurled within the Aesthetic movement and a queer language of flowers bloomed with violets, pansies, lavender and others being adopted by different LGBTQ+ groups.

The photo-text series *Gay Semiotics* (1977) by Hal Fischer (1950–) wryly deconstructed and shared sartorial ciphers used by San Francisco's gay communities, which he described as 'a lexicon of attraction'. Fischer marked up photographs of men with text explaining signifiers including 'The Hanky Code' – the placement of coloured handkerchiefs in back pockets to signal sexual preferences. Other codes may not be part of a distinctly queer language but indicate close and intimate LGBTQ+ relationships, as in works by Marsden Hartley (1877–1943).

Even where queer artists have increased freedoms and less need for protective codes, their use continues as artists are inspired by and pay homage to their predecessors. Painter Roxana Halls (1974–) reflected that 'it does seem to be something of a fascination and something that comes quite naturally.'

Handsome Drinks, Marsden Hartley, 1916, oil on board, 61 x 50.8 cm (24 x 20 in), Brooklyn Museum, New York, USA (see Works p.60)

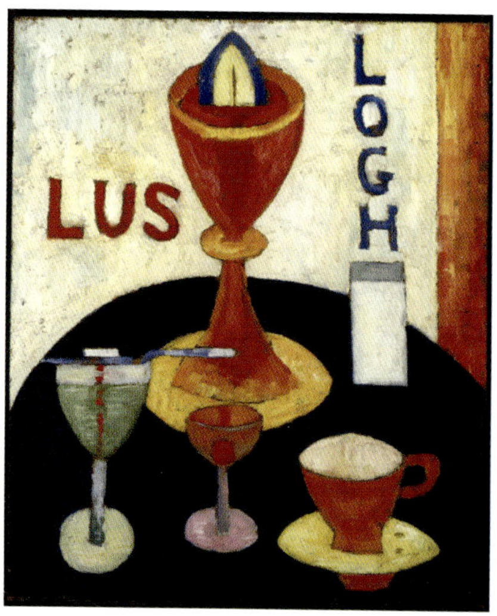

KEY DEVELOPMENTS

Handsome Drinks was Hartley's first painting after having to leave Paris for America. Then in the closet, he was known for using objects to convey relations with people, while also insisting they contained 'no hidden symbolism whatsoever'. The chalice may represent Gertrude Stein (1874–1946) and the absinthe Pablo Picasso (1881–1973). Made in the year of the Easter Rising, *logh* means 'forgive' in Irish; the vessels may also signify sacrifice.

Powerful Protest

KEY ARTISTS: DAVID WOJNAROWICZ • GRAN FURY • FIERCE PUSSY • PUSSY RIOT YEGUAS DEL APOCALIPSIS • ALIREZA SHOJAIAN

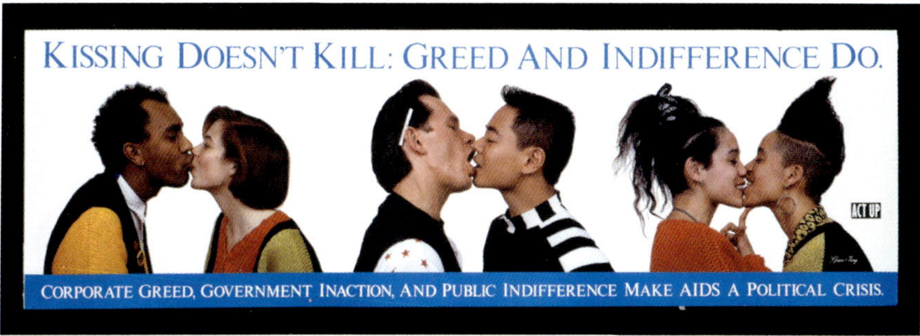

Kissing Doesn't Kill: Greed and Indifference Do, Gran Fury, 1989, poster, 29.3 x 94.1 cm (11½ x 37 in), published by ACT UP, USA

LGBTQ+ communities and artists have needed to take a stand against many issues, frequently forming groups to increase their impact. Gran Fury were an artistic spin-off of the seminal activist group ACT UP (AIDS Coalition to Unleash Power). Formed in 1988 as an autonomous collective, they described themselves as 'a band of individuals united in anger and dedicated to exploiting the power of art to end the AIDS crisis'. Over seven years, their ground-breaking work created some of the most memorable, and therefore highly successful, graphic design campaigns of the modern age.

Many other collectives rose up in New York out of the ACT UP protests such as fierce pussy. Formed in 1991, the four original members describe themselves as 'a queer art collective' who speak with one voice. Low-fi in their practice, they made creative use of Xerox machines, typewriters and cheap flea market photographs to create posters to paste all over the city hard-hitting and humorous messages around lesbian visibility.

New York was also home to the Guerrilla Girls, who started their famed poster campaigns in 1985 attacking museums for their almost non-existent display of women artists. Their campaigning continues by a group who guard their anonymity by wearing gorilla masks. PESTS were a similarly anonymous group who possibly emerged from Guerrilla Girls to concentrate on calling out racism in the art world.

KEY DEVELOPMENTS

This poster has been elevated beyond ephemeral status to a work of art which captured the zeitgeist. Taking back control of the narrative during the AIDS crisis, *Kissing Doesn't Kill* proudly positions three sets of kissing couples including the artist Lola Flash (1959–). Oozing joy, they present a vision of love and inclusion to juxtapose fiercely with the corporate greed and government inaction they stand firmly against.

STREET ART **p.36** *MEMORIAL TO A MARRIAGE* **p.136** *SOUS LE CIEL DE SHIRAZ (PAYKANARTCAR)* **p.158**
FACING AIDS **p.208** INSTITUTIONAL CRITIQUE **p.212**

Chosen Family

KEY ARTISTS: DEREK JARMAN • NAN GOLDIN • SUNIL GUPTA • CATHERINE OPIE

'Chosen Family' is the idea that family is not solely what you are born into, but something you can build yourself. The concept plays a significant role in the lives of LGBTQ+ people and the term has been used as a title, subject and unifying theme of LGBTQ+-focused artworks and exhibitions. Artists have variously recorded, explored and reflected on the challenges and possibilities – including how it can take physical or aesthetic form and notions of queer homemaking and domesticity.

Joan E. Biren (JEB) (1944–) and Catherine Opie (1961–) are among artists who have adopted documentary and portraiture approaches to recording non-heteronormative family lives.

The work and lives of artists in groups and collectives have frequently conveyed 'alternative' communal homes where art and life frequently intertwine, including artists of the Bloomsbury Group, the Red Rose Collective, the Furies Collective and the polyamorous household of artist Clare (Tony) Atwood (1866–1962) with Christopher St John (Christabel Marshall) (1871–1960) and Edith (Edy) Craig (1869–1947) at Smallhythe, Kent.

Chosen Family, Chosen Name, Separatist, Safe Space, Expat, Invert, Homophile, Homestead (2016), by Anna Campbell (1979–), brings together strategies and terms that LGBTQ+ and other marginalized people have used to form a place 'to be'. Amos Gebhardt (1976–) explores concepts of communal care in cinematic tableau *Family Portrait* (2020), from the series *Small acts of resistance*, with two fathers and their baby surrounded by their supporting queer network.

Ladies of Llangollen, after Mary Parker (later Lady Margarette Leighton, 1799–1864), lithograph by R.J. Lane, c.1832, 22.9 x 19.8 cm (9 x 7¾ in)

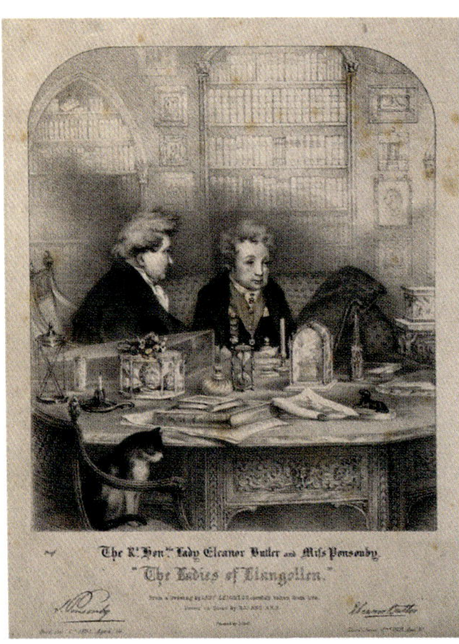

KEY DEVELOPMENTS

The lives and home of Lady Eleanor Butler (1739–1829) and Sarah Ponsonby (1755–1831) became famous through many reproduced depictions. After fleeing Ireland in 1778 to escape conventional marriage, they lived together in Wales with a series of dogs called Sappho. Suggested as a model of perfect friendship, their relationship drew speculation, including by lesbian diarist Anne Lister (1791–1840) – 'surely it is not platonic ... something more tender still than friendship'.

AFROFUTURISM **p.34** STREET ART **p.36** INTERNET ART **p.37** *LA VIE PENSIVE* **p.56** *HANDSOME DRINKS* **p.60** *A SUMMER DAY* **p.80**

Assembling

KEY ARTISTS: NICK CAVE • ANNE SAMAT • JEFFREY GIBSON • RENATE HAMPKE RAMEKON O'ARWISTER • NICHOLAS HLOBO • RASHAAD NEWSOME

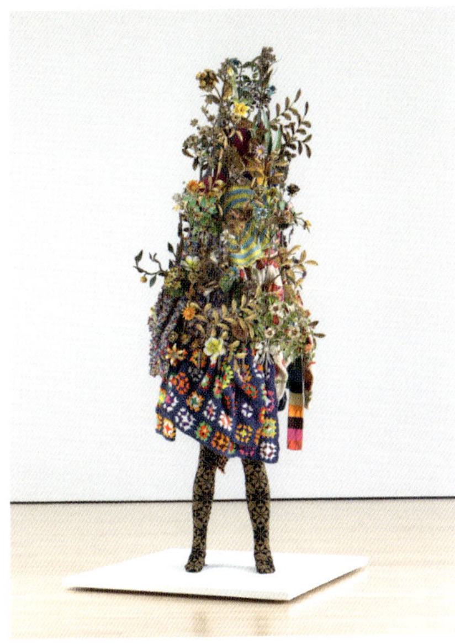

Soundsuit, Nick Cave, 2009, mixed media including metal flowers, beaded and sequined garments, crocheted afghan, fabric, metal, and mannequin, 246.4 x 66 x 66 cm (97 x 26 x 20 in), SFMOMA, San Francisco, USA

David Wojnarowicz (1954–1992) reflected that most of his work was in response to being 'born into something that's invented before we're even conceived'. The impulse to challenge or restructure a surrounding 'pre-invented society' to better articulate experiences and thrive is a recurring thread in LGBTQ+ experiences.

(Re)assembling objects and imagery in different fashions can decontextualize them from their original purpose and challenge the status quo. As Dadaists demonstrated, unexpected combinations of familiar objects can produce surprising, subversive and discombobulating effects. Assemblages can seem paradoxically both destructive and constructive.

They can suggest rescuing lost or overlooked objects, and a crafting of care – mending and healing – 'bandaging' objects together. Cory Perry (1989–) describes his patchworked textiles as a way of archiving and telling stories of communities in flux and 'recovering and rebuilding memory'.

Combinations of imagery and references can allow intersections of identities and cultures to come to the fore. Jeffrey Gibson (1972–) fuses popular and queer culture with traditions of his Cherokee and Choctaw heritage in animated calls for queer and Indigenous empowerment. The stoic yet playful hybrid totems–altars–avatars by Anne Samat (1973–) evoke both her Malaysian lineage and identity as a transgender activist. She has described their creation as collective transformation 'giving new meanings, form, and function' to objects, noting, 'When I put together my work, I always deal with gender.'

KEY DEVELOPMENTS

Nick Cave (1959–) reflected, 'Objects and assemblage have always been the foundation of my practice.' His famed 'Soundsuits' are wearable sculptures crafted from an array of materials and brought to life in performances. First conceived following the beating of Rodney King (1965–2012) by LAPD officers in 1991, Cave noted their 'masquerade' in 'hiding race, gender, class, so you're forced to look at the objects without judgement' and the importance of transformation, transition and conviction when donning them.

DADA **p.21** SURREALISM **p.23** POSTMODERNISM **p.33** *DA-DANDY* **p.62** *I.O.U. (SELF-PRIDE)* **p.76** FACING AIDS **p.208**

Space of the Body

KEY ARTISTS: LORENZA BÖTTNER • R E A • GENESIS BREYER P-ORRIDGE & LADY JAYE • CASSILS VA-BENE ELIKEM FIATSI

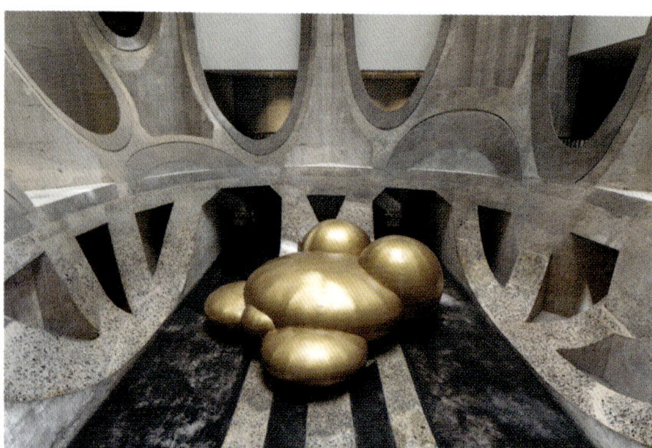

Soft Vxnxs, Goldendean, 2021, commissioned and produced by HetHEM (Netherlands), inflatable sculpture with air-blower, approx. 500 x 450 x 250 cm (197 x 177 x 98½ in), shown installed at Zeitz Museum of Contemporary Art Africa, Cape Town, South Africa, in 2022

KEY DEVELOPMENTS

Seeking to 'affirm the right of all bodies to exist, to be celebrated and protected', Goldendean (Dean Hutton) (1976–) provokes reflection on queer bodies, public space and social justice. Their large inflatable sculptures take up and queer space with a soft and tender boldness – visible and vulnerable. As a 'Fat Queer White Trans body' in South Africa, Hutton questions bodily entitlement to space and being paradoxically hyper-visible and invisible in society.

Our physicality is an inescapable element of the way we experience life – shaping our identity internally and externally through signifiers of gender, ethnicity, health and size, for example – and further subjected to the whims of radically changing fashions and ideals of desirability through history. To quote Barbara Kruger (1945–) 'the body is a battleground', a heavily politicized zone of control with endless governmental attempts to wrest and control bodily autonomy.

Artists have helped destabilize, challenge and expand personal and social expectations of the relationship between body and self. For Cassils (1975–), the body is inherently sociopolitical, a site of challenge and resistance: 'Our bodies are sculptures formed by society's expectations. I am a visual artist, and my body is my medium.' 'I resist the idea that you have to live as a man or as a woman.'

Gamilaraay/Wailwan/Biripi artist r e a, has expressed how their body carries and encompasses time: 'I am always the queer non-binary blak body that I am repatriating in all my work. I carry the past and the present within my blak body.'

Va-Bene Elikem Fiatsi [aka crazinisT artisT] (1981–) takes on a shamanic role and gender-fluid persona, as they question cultural frictions between gender performativity, race and sexual prejudice, explaining, 'I present my body as a violation, taboo and pleasurable object of violence through simple but complexly layered rituals.'

PERFORMANCE ART **p.29** FEMINIST ART **p.30** DIGITAL ART **p.31** CONCEPTUAL ART **p.32** INTERNET ART **p.37**
I.O.U. (SELF-PRIDE) **p.76** *BECOMING AN IMAGE* **p.140**

In the Studio

KEY ARTISTS: FRANCIS BACON • GEORGIA O'KEEFE • ANDY WARHOL

Studios are potent places of intense creativity. From the sequestered inner sanctums of some, to the nonstop party atmosphere of others, they frequently appear as a backdrop in the visual arts as nascent spaces of possibility. Some have been preserved in attempts to guard this magic for posterity, including Francis Bacon's (1909–1992) 7 Reece Mews in London. Painstakingly re-erected in Dublin, the space simmered with sexual tension as he incorporated the lugubrious atmosphere of the place into his distinctive thickly layered oil paintings of sadomasochistic sessions with George Dyer (1934–1971) and others. Beyond this potential as a place for sexual and social connections, studios are also revealing of a wider vulnerability. To show the process of creating, the artist feeling their way and perhaps failing, adds to the complexity and intrigue around spaces of invention.

Elizaveta Sergeevna Kruglikova (1865–1941) was a Russian painter, silhouettist and printmaker who lived in Paris from 1895, with her own studio from 1900 until the outbreak of war in 1914. Portraits depict her somewhat androgynously, often smoking (then taboo for women), and in a 1934 self-portrait silhouette she rendered herself in dandy dress. Here in her studio, she pictures herself wearing large gloves, inking a plate à la poupée beside her own press. These tools are symbolic of her skills and independence.

KEY DEVELOPMENTS

Occasionally the studio becomes a work of art itself. Andy Warhol (1928–1987) had an open-door policy beckoning creative wannabes and dropouts galore to his freewheeling Factory, a production line of screen-printing and low-budget filmmaking. Making 'superstars' of interesting regulars, it was a haven for many trans and gender non-conforming people like Candy Darling and Holly Woodlawn. The heady, drug-fuelled atmosphere was a place of self-discovery, escapism and queer hedonism.

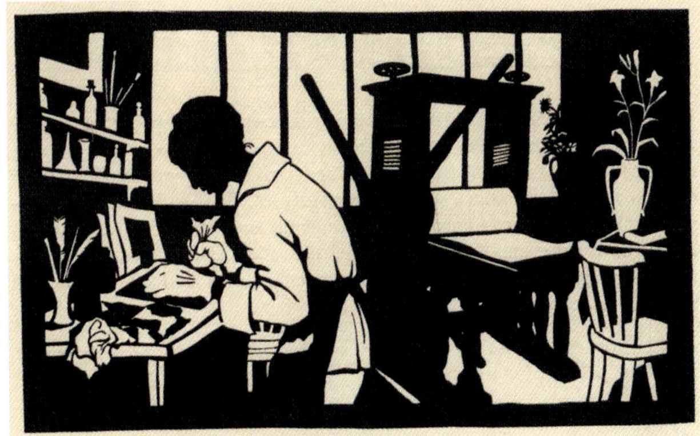

Self-portrait in Studio, Elizaveta Sergeevna Kruglikova, c.1910, yellow paper with ink, brush and pen, State Tretyakov Gallery, Moscow, Russia

THE WRESTLERS AFTER MUYBRIDGE **p.114**

Masks

KEY ARTISTS: CLAUDE CAHUN • KONSTANTIN SOMOV • MARGARET ROSE VENDRYES LYLE ASHTON HARRIS • JONATHAN BALDOCK

Masks paradoxically provide both concealment and revelation. Physical and symbolic, they enhance emotions both external and internal, allowing for an exploration of multiple identities. Globally used for practical and ceremonial purposes, as well as performance and entertainment, they have continued resonance across Africa and Latin America.

Margaret Rose Vendryes (1955–2022) used masks in *The African Diva Project* (2005–2022), considering their ceremonial significance as objects traditionally worn by men. Transposing masks onto Black, predominantly women and gender non-conforming celebrities, she challenged notions of gender, race, sexuality and diaspora legacies.

Joel Hernandez (1984–) draws on Mexican mask traditions and aesthetics, reflecting that, 'I had to wear several masks growing up, whether it was trying to act more Mexican or American, or even having to hide the fact that I was gay.'

The queer theme of masks in Europe is best embodied by the eighteenth-century masquerade ball. Infused with the masked *Commedia dell'arte* characters, they opened up space for intrigue, fantasy, gender theatricality and transgression. Konstantin Somov (1869–1939) repeatedly painted carnivalesque masked figures in erotically charged scenes of this era saying, 'art is unimaginable without an erotic basis'. Such stimulating notions are picked up by Two-Spirit artist Dayna Danger (1987–) whose *Kinship Masks* series (2016–) are beaded BDSM masks, sensually connecting their Indigenous culture with taboos around sex, sexuality and identities in colonial environments.

KEY DEVELOPMENTS

Masks were a recurring motif for Claude Cahun (1894–1954), who often adopted multiple personae. Photomontage *I.O.U. (Self-Pride)* featured in *Aveux non avenus (Unexplained Confessions)*, their Surrealist 'anti-memoir' of fragmentary poems and thoughts grappling with identity and resistance. The increasingly quoted encircling text translates as, 'Under this mask, another mask. I will never be finished with carrying all these faces.'

I.O.U. (Self-Pride) in *Aveux non avenus*, Claude Cahun, 1930, photomontage/gelatin silver print, 15.24 x 10.48 cm (6 x 4⅛ in), Los Angeles County Museum of Art, USA (see Works p.76)

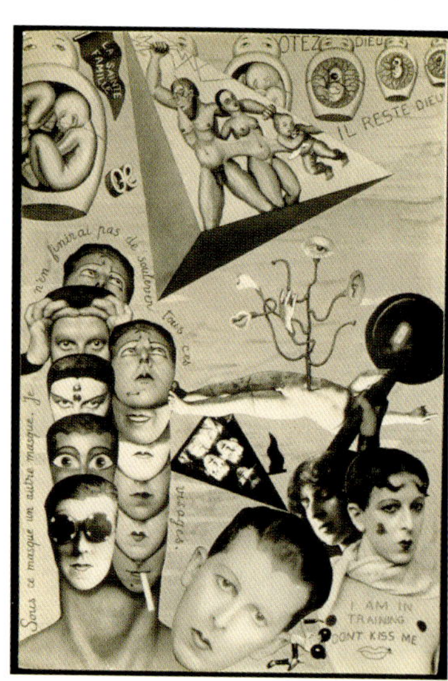

Crafting Threads

KEY ARTISTS: LJ ROBERTS • NICOLAS MOUFARREGE • MALCOM HARRISON
FELICIANO CENTURIÓN • DIEDRICK BRACKENS • MRINALINI MUKHERJEE • JOSÉ LEONILSON

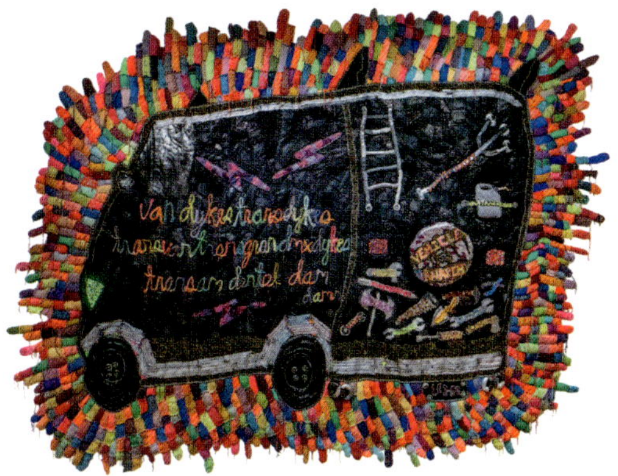

KEY DEVELOPMENTS

The exhibition 'Queer Threads: Crafting Identity and Community' (2014) sought to explore associations between LGBTQ+ identities and fibre textile crafts. Curator John Chaich (1973–) described craft as 'long considered the queer stepchild of fine art.' It notably reflected the recent interest in and reassessment of potent and potential links between textiles, craft and queerness, and featured a range of artists including LJ Roberts.

VanDykesTransDykesTransVanTransGrandmxDykesTransAmDentalDamDamn, LJ Roberts, 2014–2020, yarn, leather, lace, recycled bike inner tubes, thread, poly-fil, metal studs, zippers, lurex, shoelaces and Lite Brites, 426.72 x 609.6 cm (168 x 240 in)

Alla Nazimova (1879–1945) and Marlene Dietrich (1901–1992) used 'Sewing Circle' to euphemistically describe groups of lesbian and bisexual women in Hollywood. It wryly acknowledged connotations of gender and power hierarchies bound up in textile crafts, that later feminist and queer artists have looked to unpick and reweave.

Associated processes hold pertinent symbolism: weaving, knitting and sewing new forms and ways of being, creative resilience of 'make-do-and-mend' and time taken handcrafting indicating care and affection. Two of the most recognizable twentieth-century LGBTQ+ connected artworks – the Rainbow Flag and the AIDS Memorial Quilt – are textile works.

Described as the precursor of Polish queer art, Krzysztof Jung (1951–1998) employed threads in conceptual performative ways, wrapping them around objects, people and spaces to create entangling cocoons. Feliciano Centurión (1962–1996) often used soft fabrics, decorated with decidedly queer or kitsch motifs, described as possessing a 'delicate drama'. He reflected, 'we've lost so much affection and tenderness in today's society, and my work tries to recapture this.'

LJ Roberts (1980–) connects marginalized craft with marginality experienced as a queer, gender non-conforming, non-binary person. '*VanDykesTrans …*' was inspired by the 1970s Van Dykes 'van gang' that travelled North America, becoming a lesbian separatist collective. Celebrating the crafting of alternative kinship, they used materials (including leather, zips and metal studs) that nod to queer subcultures and qualities of resourcefulness.

FEMINIST ART **p.30** HUNKERTIME **p.110** MAKING RAINBOWS **p.205** FACING AIDS **p.208**

Summoning Sappho

KEY ARTISTS: ANGELIKA KAUFFMAN • SIMEON SOLOMON • GEORGE BARBIER

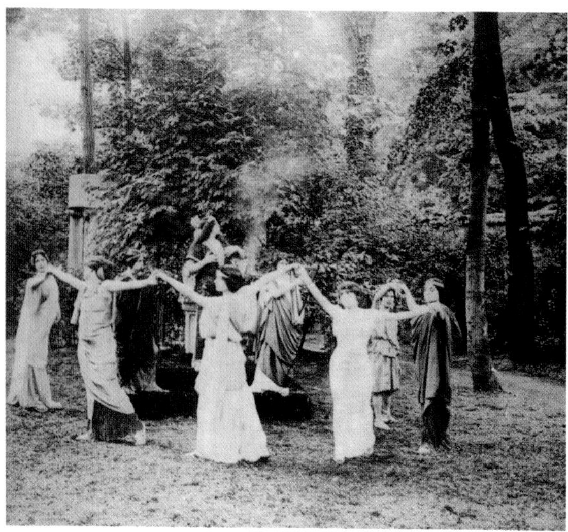

A performance in Natalie Barney's garden, unknown, photograph, c.1906, Private Collection

KEY DEVELOPMENTS

For Natalie Barney living was 'first of all the arts'. She dressed up as 'a page of love sent by Sappho' to woo Liane de Pougy (1869–1950), who later chronicled their relationship in *Idylle sapphique* (1901). This photograph may depict a performance of Barney's play *Équivoque*, a retelling of Sappho's legend. Her landlord reportedly objected to an outdoor performance of a play about Sappho, which he believed 'followed nature too closely'.

'You may forget but let me tell you this: someone in some future time will think of us' – Sappho (seventh century BCE). Described by Plato as the tenth muse, Sappho was a highly regarded poet whose works extolled love for women. She lived on the Greek islands of Lesbos and Leucas (Lefkada) and provided the origin of the terms 'Sapphic' and 'lesbian'.

Only fragments of her verse survive. Their interpretation and Sappho's sexuality continue to be debated, reflecting changing cultural contexts and scholars' personal biases. With details of life lost in myth, Sappho reflects a frequent theme in exploring queer histories – the piecing together of fragments. A compelling thread reaching back into longer lesbian and queer lineages, ripe for reclaiming and reweaving, Sappho has become a recurrent reference and motif.

Seventeenth- and eighteenth-century writers imagined lesbianism as a secret cultural tradition originating with Sappho. She stirred interests of late-nineteenth-century writers and artists, including Simeon Solomon (1840–1905) and Lawrence Alma-Tadema (1836–1912). Connecting to a perceived freedom in the ancient culture of Lesbos, writer Natalie Barney (1876–1972) was inspired to establish her own sapphic community. She cultivated one of the most open-minded salons in Paris, hosting influential figures from accross the creative spectrum. Gatherings included performances and re-creations of ancient Greek dance and music, often with a sapphic focus, conjuring the spirit of Sappho.

NEOCLASSICISM **p.15** PRE-RAPHAELITES **p.17** PERFORMANCE ART **p.29**

Queer Ecologies

KEY ARTISTS: UÝRA SODOMA • FRIDA KAHLO • LAURA AGUILER • ADHAM FARAMAWY
JODY PINTO

Constrained by dominant manufactured social structures, many LGBTQ+ individuals have explored connections with the wider natural world, in all its many variations, often challenging assertions that non-heteronormative behaviours are 'unnatural'. Through scientific, political, spiritual and sensual lenses, artists have responded to the interconnectedness of living organisms and their physical surroundings in various ways.

Frida Kahlo (1907–1954) often alluded to a relationship of mutual nourishing with the Mexican landscape, as in *Roots* (1943). She described bodies as landscapes, and in an intense letter to Diego Rivera (1886–1957) wrote, 'The green miracle of the landscape of my body becomes in you the whole nature. […] I penetrate the sex of the whole earth, her heat chars me and my entire body is rubbed by the freshness of the tender leaves.' In her photography series *Nature Self-Portrait* (1996) and *Grounded* (2006–2007), Laura Aguiler (1959–2018) presents her nude body as both *in* and *part* of the landscape, blurring boundaries between body and earth. Shitou (1969–) and Mingming merge art and life, sharing creative queer visions of everyday organic organizing, including plant-based food and farming experiments. Interested in links between people, the natural environment and the notion of homeland, Shitou aspires to undo the division of genders and binary systems 'in order to see the world differently and reconstruct balance'. Her *Underwater* series explores a literal immersive connection with nature.

Mud, from the *Elementary* series, Uýra Sodoma, photography and editorial by Keila Serruya and Sindri Mendes, 2017, Lagoa Azul, Presidente Figueiredo, AM

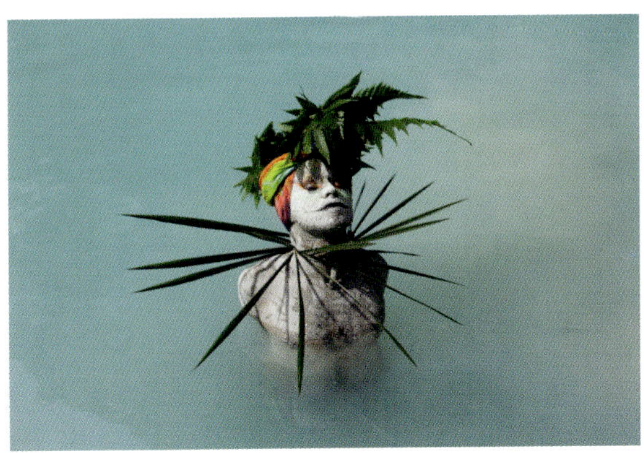

KEY DEVELOPMENTS

Ecologist and human rights activist Emerson Uýra (1991–) describes Uýra Sodoma as, 'an old spirit that has followed me for a very long time'. Through Uýra, the Indigenous nonbinary artist connects key issues in Brazil – environmental destruction, Indigenous erasure, homophobia and transphobia – into a shared struggle to preserve life. They explain, 'I like to see persecuted groups as plants that will grow in violent and abandoned land, like nature does.'

FILM AND VIDEO ART **p.28** PERFORMANCE ART **p.29**

Divine Connection

KEY ARTISTS: ESTER HERNÁNDEZ • ELISÀR VON KUPFFER • JOSÉ PÉREZ OCAÑA GRUPO CHACLACAYO • NAHUM ZENIL • ALMA LÓPEZ

Many religions have tried to mould views around acceptance of LGBTQ+ people. The historic dominance of religious artwork provides a vast gallery of influence and aesthetics. Finding connections with figures including Saint Sebastian and Saint Wilgefortis, 'the bearded virgin', opens complex ideas of love, protection, damnation and martyrdom [see *Queer Icons*]. Many artists have explored how spiritual beliefs align with their identity and desires.

Tony De Carlo (1956–2014) aimed to affirm the 'holiness' of homosexual love, creating 'Adam and Steve' and blending homoeroticism and spirituality in glowing paintings of saints. Yet depicting religious references remains controversial. In 2024 Salustiano García Cruz (1965–) depicted Jesus Christ on a poster for Seville's Holy Week celebrations, causing outcry due to it being perceived as 'camp' and 'effeminate'.

David Wojnarowicz (1954–1992) expressed his fury and complex relationship with the Catholic Church and other power structures in works including *A Fire in My Belly* (1986–87). Peruvian collective Grupo Chaclacayo (1983–1994) publicly parodied Catholic practices in experimental sexual-political performances to exorcise oppression. Others have envisioned and claimed more positive alternatives. In the cyclorama *The Clear World of the Blissful* (1919–29), Elisàr von Kupffer (1872–1942) formed a temple to the arts revering ideals of transcendent sexuality and 'queer mysticism'. With *Queer Temple* (2023), genderqueer Quaker Cai Quirk (1996–) offers a sanctuary embracing intersections of gender, spirituality, mythology and nature.

KEY DEVELOPMENTS

The Virgin of Guadalupe holds a sacred place in Mexican Catholicism. Ester Hernández (1944–) shows the Virgin tattooed across her partner's back – embodying the often-complicated meeting of religious and lesbian love of women. The artist's hand holding out a rose indicates reverence and intimacy with both.

La Ofrenda, from the National Chicano Screenprint Taller, 1988–1989, 1988, Ester Hernández, screenprint on paper, 95.9 x 63.5 cm (37¾ x 25 in), Smithsonian American Art Museum, USA

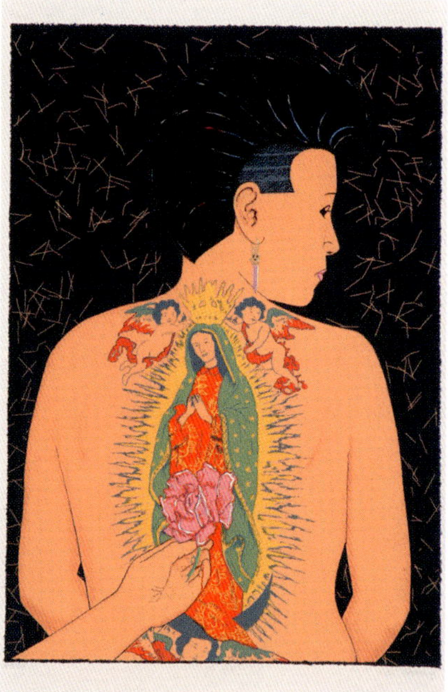

RENAISSANCE **p.12** BAROQUE **p.13** ROCOCO **p.14** PERFORMANCE ART **p.29** AFROFUTURISM **p.34**
EVERY MOMENT COUNTS (ECSTATIC ANTIBODIES) **p.122**

Call of the Sea

KEY ARTISTS: PAUL CADMUS • CHARLES DEMUTH • TOM OF FINLAND • YANNIS TSAROUCHIS GAN (GÖSTA ADRIAN-NILSSON) • PIERRE ET GILLES

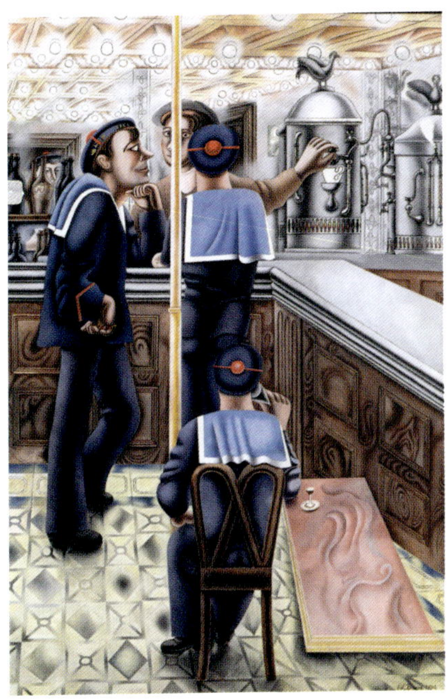

Three Sailors at the Bar, Edward Burra, 1930, watercolour on paper, 67.3 x 48.2 cm (26½ x 19 in), Private collection

Positioned as protectors of a nation's interests, sailors were frequently presented as idealized, nationalistic symbols embodying attributes such as virtue, virility, discipline, bravery and strength. With their 'worldly experience' they were also considered set apart from ordinary civilian life, detached from conventional rules of morality and behaviour.

Muscular physiques in distinctive snug uniforms and male-only environments held obvious appeal for gay cultural imagination and fantasy, with male-presenting sailors a recurring homoerotic motif in the arts and gay pornography.

Writer W. H. Auden (1907–1973) reflected on the attraction of sailors when considering the novel *Querelle de Brest* (1945) by Jean Genet (1910–1986): 'for the sailor on shore is symbolically the innocent god from the sea who is not bound by the law of the land and can therefore do anything without guilt'. *Querelle* (1982), the arthouse film adaptation by Rainer Werner Fassbinder (1945–1982), was stylistically influenced by the erotic works of George Quaintance (1902–1957) and Tom of Finland (1920–1991) and in turn inspired the campy kitsch mariner masculinity of fashion designer Jean Paul Gaultier (1952–1990).

Sailors' real-world reputation for portside promiscuity is portrayed in works by Charles Demuth (1883–1935) and Paul Cadmus (1904–1999), with a coarser and often seedy aesthetic.

KEY DEVELOPMENTS

The homoerotic allure of sailors was a recurrent theme for Edward Burra (1905–1976) amid his social observations of dance halls, bars and cafés. Burra's exaggerated depictions notably lacked moralizing undertones. In *Three Sailors at the Bar*, well-defined buttocks in tight naval trousers are suggestively positioned above the head of a sailor. Amplified perspectives and mirror reflections bring a voyeuristic allure and questions of 'who is making eye contact with whom?'

HARLEM RENAISSANCE **p.22** POP ART **p.27** *THE FLEET'S IN!* **p.86** RISING CAMP **p.180**

Rising Camp

KEY ARTISTS: CECIL BEATON • ANDY WARHOL • PIERRE ET GILLES • DAVID LA CHAPELLE JAMES BIDGOOD • LÉOPOLD L. FOULEM

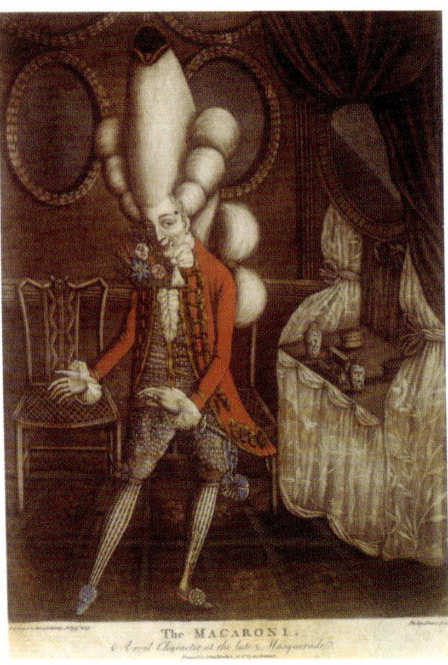

The Macaroni. A Real Character at the Late Masquerade, Philip Dawe, coloured mezzotint, printed for John Bowles, 1773

KEY DEVELOPMENTS

Satiric depictions of 'Macaroni' characters in eighteenth-century Europe highlighted deviating masculinities in a period that saw a move from homosexuality being determined by sexual acts towards notions of distinct social identities. Macaronis' 'excessive' interest in fashions started to indicate a potential lack of sexual interest in women. Their theatrical gestures and interest in 'frivolous trinkets' are now read as early demonstrations of camp sensibilities and behaviour.

A notoriously slippery term to define, 'camp' possesses a distinct element of 'if you have to ask, you'll never know'. A long-term bedfellow of gay culture, the term first appeared in 1671 when playwright Molière (1622–1673) gave a stage direction for a male character to 'camp about on one leg'. In *The World in the Evening* (1954), the novel by Christopher Isherwood (1904–1986), it is summarized into 'High Camp' and 'Low Camp', the former being ballet, Baroque and Mozart, and the latter being a 'swishy little boy with peroxided hair, dressed in a picture hat and a feather boa, pretending to be Marlene Dietrich'. The duo Pierre et Gilles fuse these two orbits together, applying the pomp and pageantry of religious and mythological iconography to pop stars and beautiful boys in crystal-clad vistas of homoerotic fantasy.

Dancer and painter Paul Swan (1883–1972), dubbed by Isadora Duncan (1877–1927) the most beautiful man in the world, gained notoriety for his nearly nude stage performances in the interwar period. Embodying the tragicomedy of camp after slipping into obscurity, he found new fame after his eccentricities were exposed in the film *Camp* (1965) by Andy Warhol (1928–1987).

Susan Sontag's (1933–2004) influential essay 'Notes on "Camp"' (1964) attempted to summarize camp's 'aesthetic sensibility'. While her essay remains a hallmark, it has also been criticized for its attempts to decouple camp from homosexuality.

ROCOCO **p.14** AESTHETICISM **p.19** POP ART **p.27** POSTMODERNISM **p.33** *LOGE DE THÉÂTRE* **p.58** *NIGHT OF THE LONG KNIVES I* **p.142**

Theatrical Types

KEY ARTISTS: GLYN PHILPOT • GEORGE BARBIER • GLUCK • ANGUS MCBEAN LEONARD ROSOMAN • TESSA BOFFIN

The thrill of the theatre has long attracted LGBTQ+ people to the stage and behind the scenes. Engaging in a cyclical relationship with the visual arts, many have attempted to fix the backstage buzz in paintings of actors and stagehands in the wings with the glow of the auditorium beyond, including *Leonide Massine waiting for his cue to go on stage in 'On With the Dance'* (1925) by Gluck (1895–1978). Other viewpoints from the stalls and circles have tried to capture the reverie or scorn of the audience, like *The Wagnerites* (1894) by Aubrey Beardsley (1872–1898) or the obsessive return to the music halls that were a source of inspiration for Walter Sickert (1860–1942) – the theatre holding all walks of life where comedy rubs shoulders with tragedy.

Leonard Rosoman (1913–2012) returned nightly to sketch John Osborne's (1929–1994) play *A Patriot for Me* (1965), which had circumvented a ban by turning the Royal Court Theatre, London, into a private member's club for its run. The play tells the story of a gay spy and requires a cast of around 25 drag queens. Rosoman completed paintings *The Drag Ball, No. 1* and *No.2* in 1968, the year censorship was abolished in British theatres.

Actors have also turned from the drama of the stage to work in other mediums. A true diva of the theatre, immortalized in fin-de-siecle works by Alphonse Mucha (1860–1939), Sarah Bernhardt (1844–1923) 'gave myself up to another art, and began working at sculpture with frantic enthusiasm.'

KEY DEVELOPMENTS

The posturing portraits of performers by Glyn Philpot (1884–1937) include Glen Byam Shaw (1904–1986), here oozing flamboyant, melodramatic charm as Laertes in Shakespeare's *Hamlet*. Associations between homosexuality and the stage were recorded in the Elizabethan and Jacobean theatre. Cross-dressing provoked Puritans and in *Skialetheia* (1598), Edward Giulpin described a sodomite as someone 'who is at every play and every night sups with his ingles' (slang for youths used for sexual purposes).

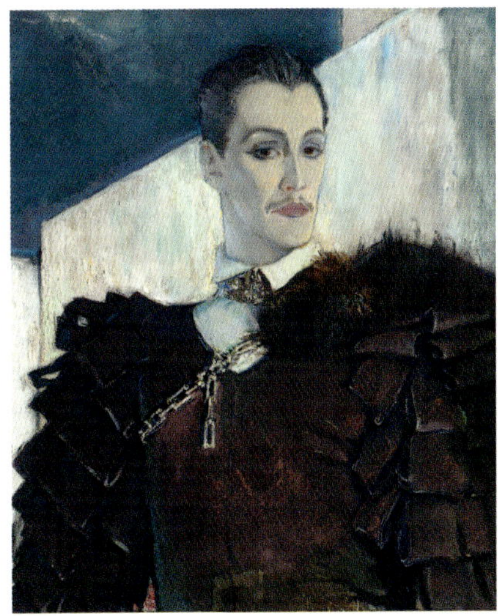

Glen Byam Shaw as 'Laertes', Glyn Philpot, 1934–35, oil on canvas, 76.2 x 63.5 cm (30 x 25 in), Private Collection

HARLEM RENAISSANCE **p.22** SURREALISM **p.23** PERFORMANCE ART **p.29** *LOGE DE THÉÂTRE* **p.58**
STEPHEN TENNANT IN COSTUME AS PRINCE CHARMING **p.78** *NIGHT OF THE LONG KNIVES I* **p.142**

Queer Eye

KEY ARTISTS: CARAVAGGIO • CHARLES DEMUTH • ED BURRA • CHRISTOPHER WOOD

The 'queer eye' starts to develop at the first inkling of difference, and sharpens over time into a well-honed machine, combing culture for clues of others. This 'gay gaze' naturally gets to work in galleries, often looking back at past worlds through paintings potently holding their maker's desires and intentions. While some artworks employ recognizable symbolism and iconography [see *Queer Coding*], the queer eye can be equally drawn to ambiguities or nuances that suggest shared 'sensibilities' or sensualities, or create a space in which to find queer possibilities, regardless of an artist's intention.

Once belonging to Cecil Beaton (1904–1980), this painting later sold under the title 'Battersea Park'. The original and more suggestive title is *'Dogs at Play'* by Christopher Wood (1901–1930). Wood had already pictured sailors and wrestlers to hint at homoerotic interests, and these soldiers (with another pair in the distance) may be subtle to the untrained eye but to the queer eye it screams cruising.

Jean Cocteau (1889–1963) described Wood's work as having 'a frankness, a naivety of a young dog who has not had the illness of time'. Mining the annals of art history for his own inspiration and queer visions, Cocteau eroticized the 'Creation of Adam' by Michelangelo (1475–1564) in his own drawings and further 'queered' the already languidly inviting Barberini Faun of the second century BCE.

Dogs at Play, Christopher Wood, 1927, oil on canvas, 81.3 x 85 cm (32 x 33½ in), Private Collection

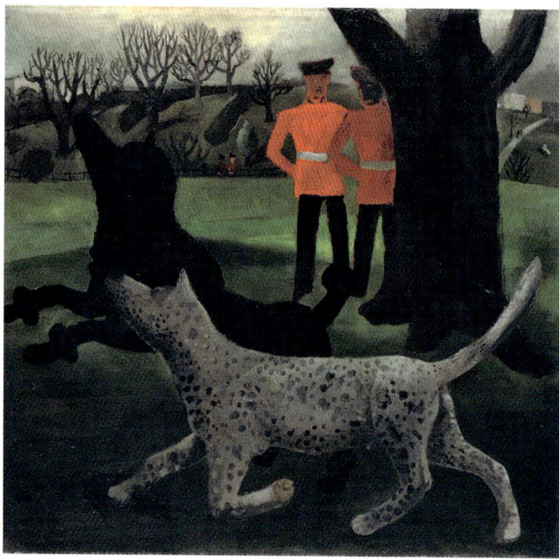

KEY DEVELOPMENTS

Recently increasing numbers of galleries and museums have started acknowledging (even embracing) 'queer readings' of artworks and curations. Concepts like 'queering the collections' can challenge dominant 'assumed-straight', cis-centric, heteronormative narratives – not solely by raising awareness of LGBTQ+ biographies and content but also by encouraging people to 'read' and connect with works on their own terms, challenging perceptions that there are limited 'legitimate' ways to interpret and connect with art.

BAROQUE **p.13** NEOCLASSICISM **p.15** HARLEM RENAISSANCE **p.22** ART DECO **p.24** AFROFUTURISM **p.34**
LOGE DE THÉÂTRE **p.58** *THE FLEET'S IN!* **p.86** *THE WRESTLERS AFTER MUYBRIDGE* **p.114**

Erotic Exchanges

KEY ARTISTS: KATSUSHIKA HOKUSAI • BARON WILHELM VON GLOEDEN • GERDA WEGENER TOM OF FINLAND • GO MISHIMA (TSUYOSHI YOSHIDA) • G. B. JONES • DEL LAGRACE VOLCANO

Far East Asia mastered the art of paper-making and printing centuries before the rest of the world and quickly turned these revolutionary inventions to the production of pornography. Intended for different gazes, and created in large quantities, they depicted all manner of positions and practices, forming a world of visual titillation which appeared to be free of shame and small-mindedness. Lesbian scenes were rarer and female artists themselves had little or no access to the tools to make these prints, so the majority were made by and for men. However, homoerotic male scenes and gender beyond the binary were widely and subtly surveyed.

Such works were created for an open market, but other examples reveal much more personal narratives of private expression. A cache of 400 erotic drawings by Duncan Grant (1885–1978) were discovered in 2020. Given to Edward le Bas (1904–1966) in 1959, the folder was marked 'these drawings are very private'. Created when sex between men risked imprisonment in England, they were preserved by four gay men and passed down for safekeeping.

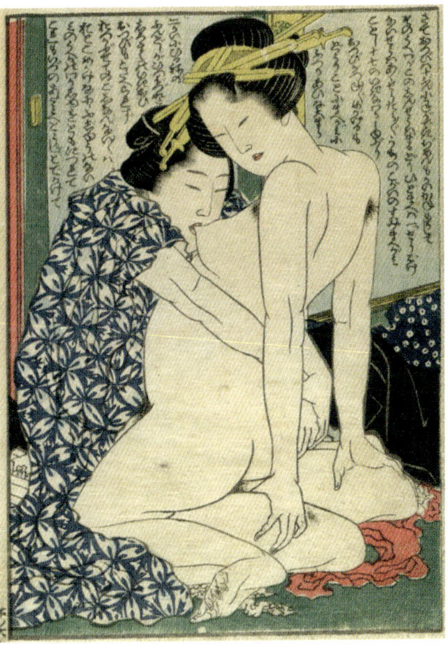

Lesbian Lovers, from the series 'Manpoku Wago-Jin' (The Gods of Conjugal Delights), Katsushika Hokusai, colour woodblock print, 1821, Private Collection

In parallel, the drawings by Tom of Finland (1920–1991) debuted in softcore homoerotic magazine *Physique Pictorial* in 1957. Unleashing a new underground of fetishism and fantasy, they entered the mainstream as a driving force in sex positivity in the 1970s. Women and non-binary artists have increasingly created erotic imagery on their own terms, with notable visibility within Weimar Germany and 1970s' and 1990s' lesbian circles.

KEY DEVELOPMENTS

With roots stretching back over a millennium, *shunga* (meaning 'spring pictures'), explored erotic adventures of all persuasions. Same-sex scenes were widespread at the peak of the artform's popularity during the Edo period (1603–1868), and Hokusai (1760–1849) is the best remembered of all the *ukiyo-e* printmakers. Intertwining sex with spirituality, religious shrines were often adorned with explicit decoration. The unsealing of Japan in 1859 somewhat snuffed out such open reverence and tolerance towards erotic enjoyment.

ROCOCO **p.14** AESTHETICISM **p.19** PERFORMANCE ART **p.29** *UNTITLED* **p.100**

Queer Icons

KEY ARTISTS: ANDY WARHOL • ROBERT LENTZ • CARL GRAUER • PIERRE ET GILLES • RIA BRODELL

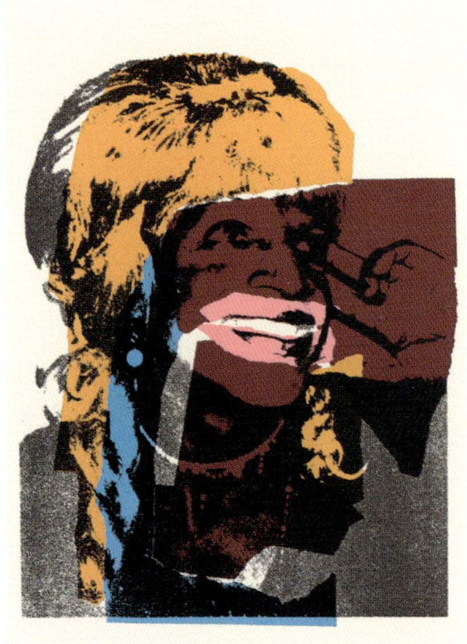

Ladies and Gentlemen (Marsha P. Johnson), Andy Warhol, 1975, screenprint, 110.5 x 71.9 cm (43½ x 28⅓ in), Private Collection (see Works p.102)

The adoption and creation of queer icons using emblematic language of religious painting and sculpture is a rich and complex area of study. Projecting queer visibility into realms where it has often been excluded provokes underlying questions of who is valued and recognized, and how we visually denote concepts of idealization and spiritual connection or enlightenment.

Saint Sebastian has been widely adopted as a figure of erotic divinity, inspiring numerous artists including Derek Jarman (1942–1994), Ron Athey (1961–), Catherine Opie (1961–) and Kehinde Wiley (1977–). *Saint Sebastian* by Guido Reni (1575–1642) had a powerful effect on Oscar Wilde (1854–1900) and prompted the sexual awakening of writer Yukio Mishima (1925–1970), who was photographed posing as the martyr shortly before his death.

Franciscan friar Brother Robert Lentz (1946–) came to prominence in the 1990s for paintings of biblical figures interpreted as having LGBTQ+ significance, including Perpetua and Felicity, as well as depicting modern gay heroes and pillars of the community such as Harvey Milk (1930–1978).

The Sisters of Perpetual Indulgence formed in 1979 as a street performance and activist network who dress as nuns and canonize inspiring individuals for services to the queer community, including Milk's friend Armistead Maupin (1944–) and drag performer and filmmaker Peaches Christ (1974–), whose retrospective *Cattychism* (2007) at the de Young Museum, San Francisco, and *Midnight Mass* live film-screening events continue to queerly blend the sacred and profane.

KEY DEVELOPMENTS

Dubbed the 'Pope of Pop', Andy Warhol (1928–1987) amplified the kitsch side of Catholic iconography to elevate celebrities, drag queens and others into a new constellation of stars – here joined by activist Marsha P. Johnson (1945–1992). Religious yet queerly subversive, Warhol merged obsessions of religion and celebrity, famously posing Marilyn Monroe (1926–1962) in a diptych format, taking the place of the Virgin Mary as a figure of reverence.

POP ART **p.27** PERFORMANCE ART **p.29** *LADIES AND GENTLEMEN (MARSHA P. JOHNSON)* **p.102**

Straight Expectations

KEY ARTISTS: KATE MILLET • LEONOR FINI • TRUONG TAN • XIYADIE

Leonor Fini (1907–1996) described, 'I always imagined I would have a life very different from the one that was imagined for me, but I understood from a very early time that I would have to revolt in order to make that life. Now I am convinced that in any creativity there exists this element of revolt.'

Historically, art has frequently been employed to emphasize and endorse the legitimacy and power of familial lineage. Posited as crucial anchor points on which to build identities, art has reflected how society has measured lives in terms of marriage and the production of descendants. People who find themselves outside of these systems have formed new lineages of celebration. *Beginning of a Dynasty* (2013) by Truong Tan (1963–) immediately conjures these ideas. Depicting three figures floating on a flattened visual plane, it is painted using lacquer on wood, evoking traditional, highly prized techniques and links to respected lineages within art and craft heritage.

In her critique of patriarchy within Western literature, *Sexual Politics* (1970), Kate Millett (1934–2017) describes 'the gnawing suspicion which plagues any minority member, that the myths propagated about his inferiority might after all be true.' Many LGBTQ+ individuals and artists have grappled with the presence of this 'gnawing suspicion' as the source of personal insecurities when negotiating their own path, taking the form of introspective struggles, or scathing direct critiques on societal oppression.

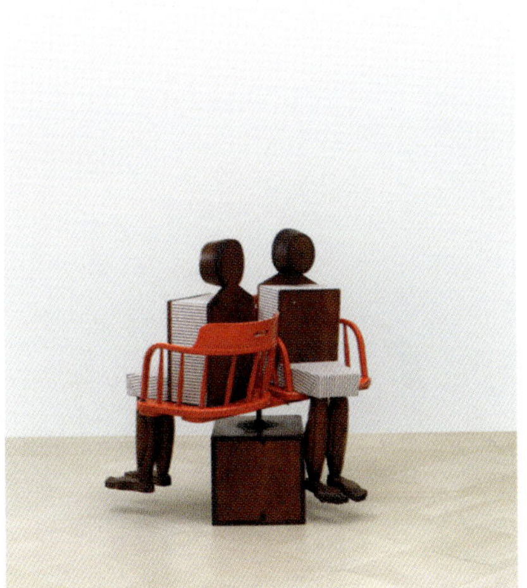

KEY DEVELOPMENTS

Feminist Art from the 1960s onwards vividly questioned and confronted restrictive gendered roles and limitations of heteronormative frameworks across various societies. The issues raised have been increasingly recognized as detrimentally affecting a broad spectrum of identities. Millett's *Sexual Politics* (1970) outlined both sexism and hetero-sexism and advocated challenging patriarchal power dynamics and reverence of the 'patriarchal family unit' to make way for the sexual revolution.

Love Seat, Kate Millett, 1965, carved wood, milliner's form, ticking fabric, desk chairs, paint (1965) 91.4 x 121.9 x 121.9 cm (36 x 48 x 48 in), Private Collection

FEMINIST ART **p.30** *LA VIE PENSIVE* **p.56** *DA-DANDY* **p.62** *SEMI-NUDE IN FRONT OF PRICKLY PEAR CACTUS* **p.70** *GATE* 门 **p.132**

To Be Seen

KEY ARTISTS: SUNIL GUPTA • GON BUURMAN • JOAN E. BIREN (JEB) • CATHERINE OPIE LOLA FLASH • ZANELE MUHOLI • MICKALENE THOMAS

The experience and importance of 'being seen' and acknowledged on your own terms is a recurring theme throughout this book. Feeling seen or recognizing elements of yourself through the visibility of others can be a powerful point of connection and potential self-realization. This has motivated many to produce expressions of personal experiences – frequently spurred on by recognition of the prevalent vulnerability, persecution or exclusion of LGBTQ+ people within the historic record [see *A Documented History*].

Experience of being confronted by a lack/loss of forebears has inspired the conscious creation of contemporary visual records for future generations. South African Zanele Muholi (1972–) has explained that, 'I have created an archive that never existed in this country before.' In the Netherlands Gon Buurman (1939–2023) was a pioneer of lesbian visibility during the early years of the women's movement. Sunil Gupta (1953–) described his *Exiles* series as 'staged documentary', deriving from an activist motivation to create representational images of a community that 'just didn't seem to exist' within general media and cultural offerings.

Artworks that speak to this theme take many forms. However, frequent adoption of the camera and the presentation or reception of works often prompt wider conversations of relationships and distinctions between art, documentation and archival material. Photographer Joan E. Biren (JEB, 1944–) first considered her work as propaganda, then photojournalism and documentation; it was only on reflection, decades later, that she considered it to also be art.

Jama Masjid, from the series *Exiles*, Sunil Gupta, 1987 (see Works p.121)

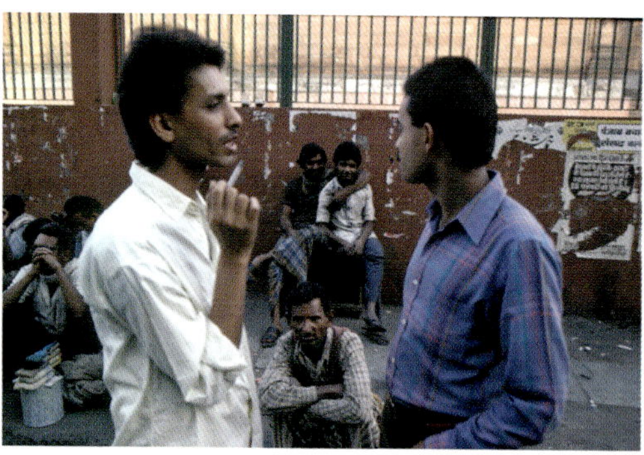

Jama Masjid
I love this part of town. It's got such character
and you can have sex just
walking in the crowd.

KEY DEVELOPMENTS

Capturing and presenting realities of experiences has often been progressively enabled by technological advances and increased access to equipment and materials – most notably with regards to film and photography. The 1970s saw increasing numbers of lesbians in pursuit of personal and political liberation, photographing each other, asserting self-representation. Skill sharing, increased independence of production, expanding networks of exchange, including publications, bookshops and galleries, supported access.

FEMINIST ART **p.30** *JAMA MASJID* **p.120** *NOTES ON THE MARGIN OF THE BLACK BOOK* **p.128** *MEMORIAL TO A MARRIAGE* **p.136** *RESURGENCE OF THE PEOPLE* **p.152**

On Screen

KEY ARTISTS: DEBORAH BRIGHT • BARBARA HAMMER • LAURENCE JAUGEY-PAGET RISK HAZEKAMP

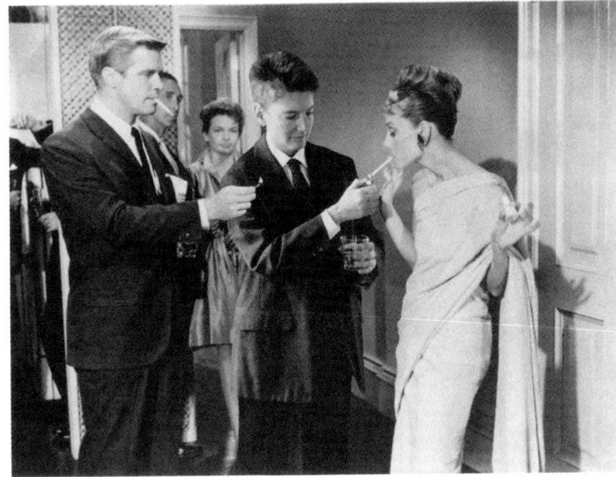

Untitled, from the *Dream Girls* series, 1990, Deborah Bright, photomontage, 28 x 35.5 cm (11 x 14 in), Leslie-Lohman Museum, New York, USA

KEY DEVELOPMENTS

Barbara Hammer (1939–2019) posited 'who makes history and who is left out, is autobiography truth or fiction, and how can a false cultural representation be re-appropriated?'. Her 'History Trilogy' (a trio of films titled *Nitrate Kisses, Tender Fictions* and *History Lessons)* probed the negative and scant representation of lesbians on screen in the twentieth century, reworking archival footage to validate space within a historically narrow and exclusionary frame.

The magic of cinema has drawn audiences into theatrical worlds on the big screen for over a century. The lure of escapism found in the darkness of the movie theatre, opens the door to a world of vicarious living, role models and the projection of our fantasy selves.

A potentially powerful form of propaganda, cinema has also demonstrated clear and covert attempts to shape societal moods and moralities. Hollywood's Hays Code is a stark example. In force between 1930 and 1966, it banned many things including 'any inference of sex perversion' which was understood to include all LGBTQ+ identities. The censorious legislation suppressed the various queer characters seen pre-1930 and led to an increasingly deft use of subtext. Many artists have since tried to tackle this vacuum while also laying bare the structures and manipulations of cinema as cultural production. Filmmaker Barbara Hammer noted, 'As a lesbian artist, I found little existing representation, so I put lesbian life on this blank screen, leaving a cultural record for future generations.'

The *Dream Girls* series by Deborah Bright (1950–) directly tapped into both fantasy projection and exclusion in the so-called Golden Age of Hollywood. The series conveys the simultaneous allure and limitations of archetypal Hollywood roles and suggests a conflicting desire to be recognized by the 'legitimizing' yet artificial and exclusionary lens of Hollywood. The series in turn signals the performativity of gendered roles in the real world.

FEMINIST ART **p.30** *UNTITLED*, FROM *DREAM GIRLS* **p.126**

Dance

KEY ARTISTS: JAMES RICHMOND BARTHÉ • KEITH HARING

Dance is an artform offering multifaceted forms of representation with its own aesthetic and often symbolic language. A subject, theme and symbolic preoccupation of many artists, dance goes beyond providing an opportunity to celebrate and study the human form in motion, and offers a directness of expression whether tender, erotic, escapist, sensuous or challenging. Its rhythm and universality are of underlying importance and can evoke notions of liberatingly primal or spiritual uninhibited expression.

Dance can explore the performative potential of bodies to disrupt or queer gendered and sexual expectations. Les Ballets Trockadero de Monte Carlo has been playfully queering formal ballet since 1974, employing deportment, gesture and pose to express and claim queerness. Queerness and the performativity of gender is directly expressed in Vogueing – a dance form originating in African American and Latino LGBTQ+ cultures of the late 1980s which evolved from the earlier Harlem ballroom scene. For Keith Haring (1958–1990), dance was a metaphor for life itself – his cartoon-style figures radiate energy, celebrating unity, community and freedom of expression.

Dance can prompt or challenge artists to conceive of the core form of the human body – be it geometric shapes or amorphous suggestions of energy. Artists have also sought to convey the experience of being enchanted and transported elsewhere, or drawn into emotional states, via dance, including through Maud Allan's (1873–1956) performances of *The Vision of Salome* [see also *The Ballets Russes*].

KEY DEVELOPMENTS

The figurative expression of François Benga (1906–1957) – muse of modernists, star of Parisian stages and circles of the Harlem Renaissance – captivated many artists who sought to convey his essence. However, he was often fetishized and his one-time lover Geoffrey Gorer (1905–1985) recalled Benga's distress that due to him being Black and a dancer 'everybody considered that they had a right, if not a duty, to make sexual advances to him.'

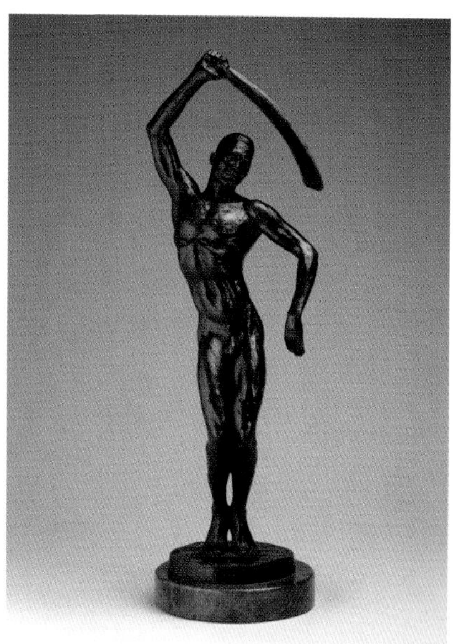

Feral Benga, James Richmond Barthé, 1935, bronze, 48.3 x 17.1 x 11.4 cm (19 x 6¾ x 4½ in), Museum of Fine Arts, Houston, Texas, USA (see Works p.90)

Places to Be

KEY ARTISTS: JEANNE MAMMEN • HÉLIO OITICICA • ROSIE HASTINGS AND HANNAH QUINLAN

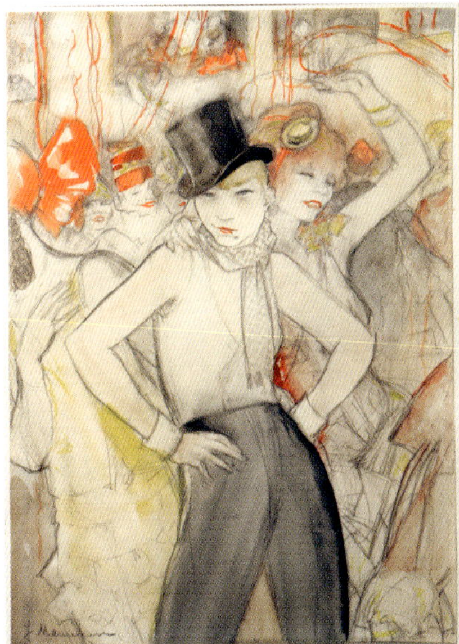

She Represents (Carnival Scene), Jeanne Mammen, c.1928, watercolour and pencil on paper, 42 x 30.4 cm (16½ x 12 in), Private collection

The importance of finding places and spaces 'to be' speaks to issues beyond physical safety, raising questions around how we connect with our surroundings and their influence on how we understand and express ourselves. Queer people have created their own spaces as places of refuge, safety, desire, community and resistance – with aspirations 'to thrive not just survive'.

Photographers Leonard Fink (1930–1992) and Alvin Baltrop (1948–2004) recorded the piers of Manhattan, where gay men sunbathed, cruised and had sex from the years of gay liberation to the AIDS crisis. David Wojnarowicz (1954–1992) created distinctive murals on the dilapidated Pier 34. Artists have explored the 'queering' of public spaces in a multitude of ways. The work of Prem Sahib (1982–) draws on atmospheres of cruising spots including saunas and clubs and Marc Martin (1971–) explores the reappropriation of public toilets as 'tearooms' and 'cottages'.

Hélio Oiticica (1937–1980) foregrounded bodily interactions and ambiences within spatial environments in his *Penetrables* and *Parangolés* or 'habitable paintings'. Prompted by increasing closures, Rosie Hastings and Hannah Quinlan (both 1991–) documented bar interiors in *UK Gay Bar Directory* (2016) noting that, although not all equally welcoming, gay bars can potentially 'offer us glimpses of the queer utopia'. Utopic imaginings were also at the heart of the Ovulars (1979–83), photography workshops at Rootworks, a lesbian community in Oregon, where many participants adopted new names and seminars were dubbed 'ovulars' to distinguish from patriarchal forms of education.

KEY DEVELOPMENTS

Convergences of social and political changes in Weimar Berlin and Paris of the late nineteenth century enabled a powerful (yet still precarious) flourishing of queer expression. Nurtured by these cities boasting reputations of alternative social spaces and legal leniency, Jeanne Mammen (1890–1976) created images of strong, confident women, inspired by nightclubs and public streets. This 'lesbian scene' of the late 1920s and early 1930s attracted the attention of artists, authors, photographers and sexologists.

← *A SUMMER DAY* **p.80** *FREEDOM AND CHANGE* **p.116**

Transforming

KEY ARTISTS: CASSILS • GENESIS BREYER P-ORRIDGE AND LADY JAYE • EVA AND ADELE

In Ovid's *Metamorphoses* humans and heavenly beings morph from plant, to animal, to fantastical creatures, even becoming constellations of stars, evoking concepts of oneness in nature. Multiple iterations of gender and sexualities appear. While some have been taken to conjure sexual revelry others hold more profound connections, raising questions of personal agency and value in potential change.

The first human to undergo a change of gender in *Metamorphoses* is prophet Tiresias. The goddess Hera transformed him into a woman for seven years, making Tiresias sought-after for their wisdom accumulated through living as more than one gender. The legend was taken up by trans non-binary artist Cassils (1975–) in their long-durational performance *Tiresias* (2011), melting an idealized male torso of ice with their body heat to emphasize 'the resolve required to persist at the point of contact between masculine and feminine'. Many of Cassils' ground-breaking performances centre physical endurance to highlight the violence trans bodies are often subjected to in the world.

Pandrogyne Project, by Genesis Breyer P-Orridge (1950–2020) and Lady Jaye (1969–2007), took a radical approach to questioning the malleable and transformable relationship between body and self. Their documented progression of surgical interventions was partly inspired by the 'cut-ups' of William S. Burroughs (1914–1997) and Brion Gysin (1916–1986). They decided, 'we'd do an actual cut-up, and become each other as far as we could. Not just to make a statement, but to demonstrate our absolute commitment.'

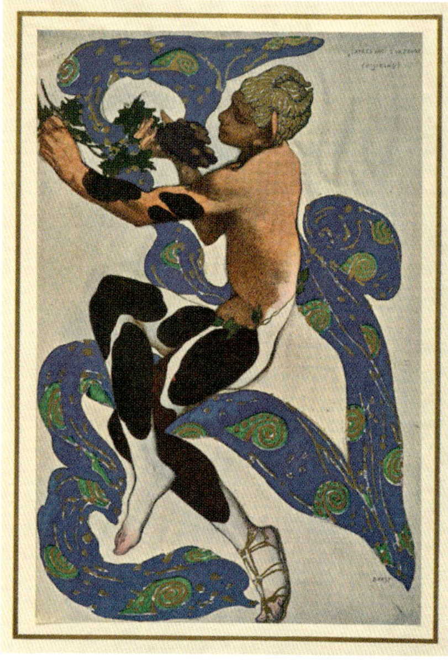

Afternoon of a Faun (L'Après-midi d'un faune), Léon Bakst, 1912, gouache on paper, Bibliotheque de L'Arsenal, Paris, France

KEY DEVELOPMENTS

The epic encyclopaedic poem *Metamorphoses* (8 CE), by Ovid (43 BCE–17/18 CE), charts instances of transformation across Greco-Roman mythology. Its imaginative influence has persisted through the ages, with peaks of interest in the Renaissance, Baroque and fin-de-siècle periods. Extraordinary public reaction to Vaslav Nijinsky (1889–1950) in the form of a faun in 1912 [see *The Ballets Russes*] confirmed public appetite for both imaginative and erotic potential of transmutational and hybrid mythical forms.

PERFORMANCE ART **p.29** DIGITAL ART **p.31** INTERNET ART **p.37** *I.O.U. (SELF-PRIDE)* **p.76** *BECOMING AN IMAGE* **p.140**

Reworking Art History

KEY ARTISTS: MICKALENE THOMAS • JEAN FRASER • KEHINDE WILEY • SALMAN TOOR ATHI-PATRA RUGA

Artists have long been at the vanguard of inclusive progress, refining concepts and visions put forth by forebears. In reworking imagery people have connected with in the past, artists have tapped into a rich visual language to understand our present and formulate visions of the future. Through pastiche, critique, subversion or homage, queering the art historical canon allows for further layering of reappraisal and meaning.

Many have contested dominance of the straight, white male gaze in the history of art by reworking revered familiar scenes. Jean Fraser (1955–) and Mickalene Thomas (1971–) both tackled *Le déjeuner sur l'herbe* (1863) by Édouard Manet (1832–1883). Fraser's features a nude butch woman flanked by nuns and Thomas' depicts three clothed Black women, their gaze turned upon the viewer.

Thomas draws deeply from art history, explaining, 'I was looking at Western figures like Manet and Courbet … Because I was not seeing the black body written about art historically … I wanted to find a way of claiming that space … and entering this discourse.' Her self-portrait *Origin of the Universe I* (2012) is based on *L'Origine du monde* (1866) by Gustave Courbet (1819–1877), which continues to divide opinion with its bold centring of a vulva.

The paintings of Salman Toor (1983–) represent queer people of colour in a melding of the present day with art historical pasts of Western and South Asian references. Toor cites Van Dyck (1599–1641) and Caravaggio (1571–1610) alongside nostalgia for portraiture of Mughal princes as recurring inspirations.

KEY DEVELOPMENTS

Confronting the history of marginalization and consumption of the body from perspectives of gender and race is a positive expansion and reckoning with the history of art as well as its future. Mickalene Thomas is among a generation consciously incorporating references to wider intersections of identity and cultures as they 'queer' conventions of art history, but Thomas keenly encourages expansive connections and readings of her work, emphasizing that many elements speak 'beyond a black aesthetic'.

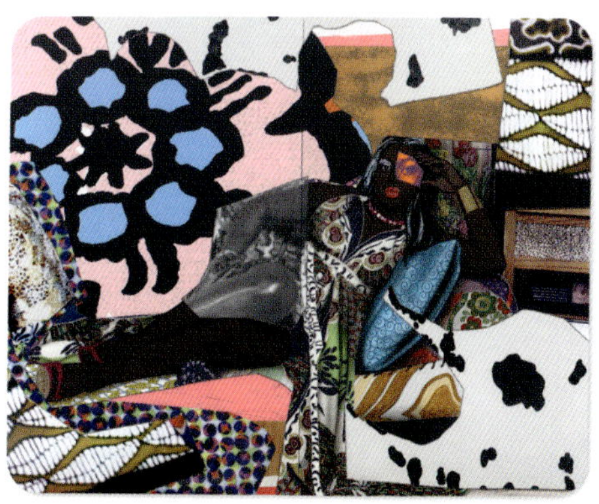

Qusuquzah Lounging with Pink + Black Flower, Mickalene Thomas, 2016, rhinestones, acrylic and oil paint on wood panel, 243.8 x 304.8 cm (96 x 120 in) (see Works p.146)

MEMORIAL TO A MARRIAGE **p.136** *PASSING / POSING FROM CORONATION OF THE VIRGIN* **p.140**
QUSUQUZAH LOUNGING WITH PINK + BLACK FLOWER **p.146** *SOUS LE CIEL DE SHIRAZ (PAYKANARTCAR)* **p.158**

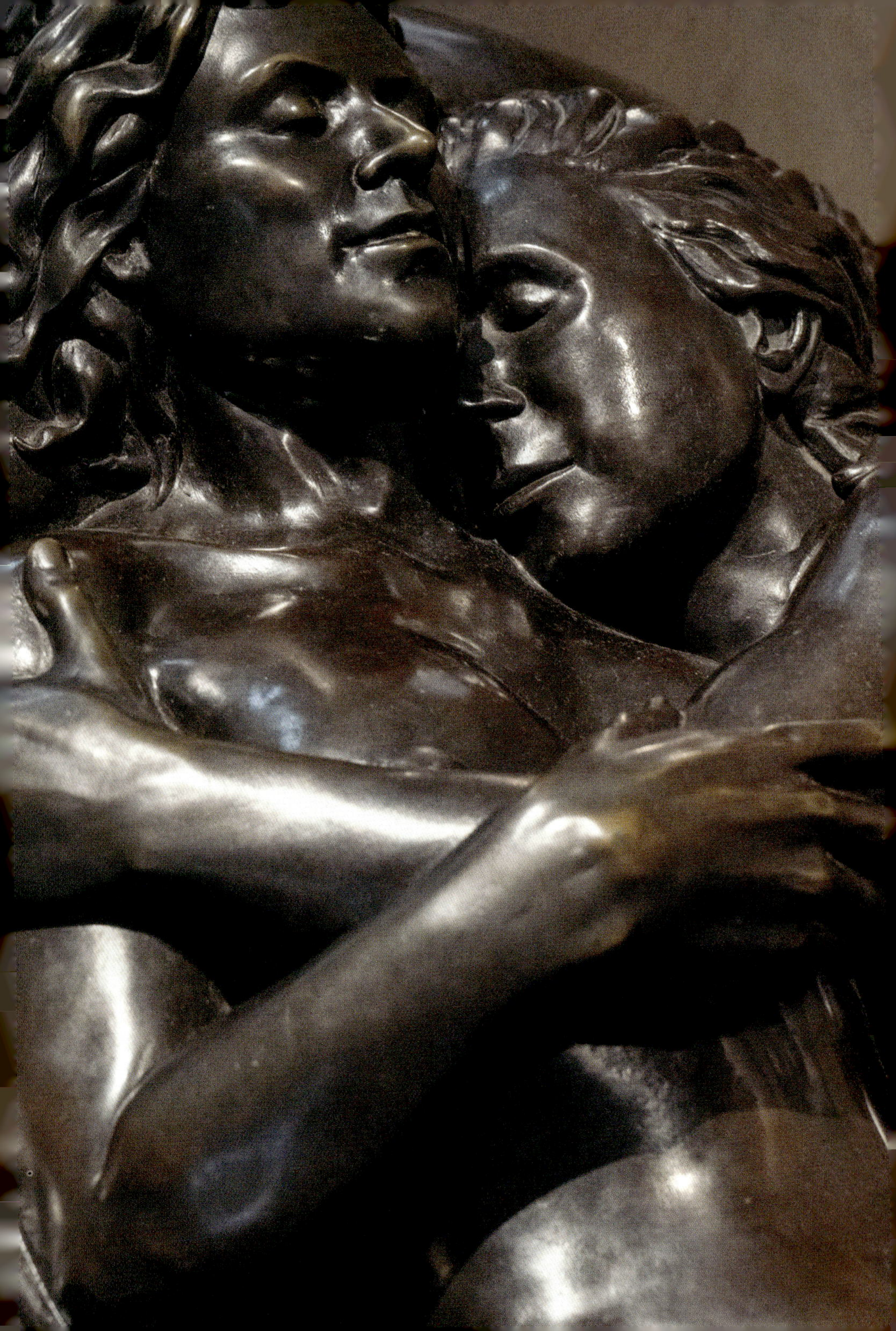

Breakthroughs

DESIRE FOR ANTIQUITY 194 • RULING RELATIONSHIPS 195 • PICTURING A CHEVALIER 196 • PUBLIC PRESENCE 197 • EXPOSING DESIRES 198 • THE BALLETS RUSSES 199 COMMERCIAL ALLURE 200 • WEIMAR BERLIN 201 • BLOOMSBURY SHAPES 202 FIRE!! MAGAZINE 203 • GAY PARIS 204 • MAKING RAINBOWS 205 • FASHIONING STYLE 206 • ON THE COVER 207 • FACING AIDS 208 • COLLECTIVE RESPONSE 209 • QUEER CRIP 210 • OUT IN THE GALLERY 211 • INSTITUTIONAL CRITIQUE 212 • LIFE ONLINE 213 IN MEMORIAL 214 • INDIGENOUS QUEER LOVE 215

Desire for Antiquity

KEY ARTISTS: ANNE SEYMOUR DAMER • MICHELANGELO BUONARROTI • ANTONIO CANOVA JACQUES-LOUIS DAVID • JOHN FLAXMAN • BARON VON GLOEDEN

For centuries Classical Antiquity and its myths provided an acceptable guise under which to depict same-sex couplings and for men to celebrate male physiques. Interpreted by many as possessing an Arcadian attitude towards homosexuality, it provided a screen on which later artists could project their own desires and became a recurring reference point for queer artists across time and art movements.

Johann Joachim Winckelmann (1717–1768) was a key influence on the reception to ancient Greek art that drove Neoclassicism and beyond. His open homoeroticism when discussing beauty enabled others to intellectualize their own similar or associated feelings. His readings fuelled a fashion for homosexual interest, collecting and patronage of Classical Art, which intersected with emerging ideas of a 'homosexual identity' based on shared aesthetic ideals.

His aestheticized homosexual desire also influenced definition of visual ideals in the early development of European art history. Winckelmann exalted the *Apollo Belvedere* as the 'highest ideal of art'. Through circulation of prints and casts, the sculpture received widespread visibility and recognition, and came to set an ideal European aesthetic standard. The lauding of this limited/narrow sculptural representation as a superior example, saw it later being used to bring an 'informed aesthetic dimension' to racial theories and used to endorse aspects of racist pseudoscience.

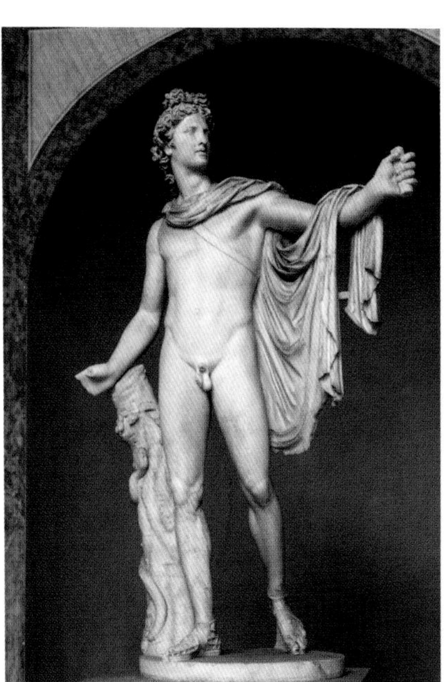

KEY DEVELOPMENTS

An 1867 essay on Winckelmann by art critic Walter Pater (1839–1894) proposed that the scholar's 'affinity with Hellenism was not merely intellectual' but that entwined with it were 'subtler threads of temperament' derived from 'his romantic, fervid friendships with young men'. Pater alluded to the *Apollo Belvedere's* homoerotic appeal as accounting for it being long hailed as epitomizing European ideals of aesthetic perfection/aspiration.

Apollo Belvedere, artist unknown, dated to midway through the 2nd century CE and is considered to be a Roman copy of an original bronze statue created between 330 and 320 BCE by Leochares, marble, 224 cm (88 in), Vatican Museums and Galleries (Musei e Gallerie Pontificie), Vatican City

NEOCLASSICISM **p.15** *DAVID* **p.40** *A PUNCH PARTY* **p.42** *BACCHUS* **p.46**

Ruling Relationships

KEY ARTISTS: MUHAMMAD QASIM • IL SODOMA • MICHELANGELO MERISI DA CARAVAGGIO FRANÇOIS BOUCHER

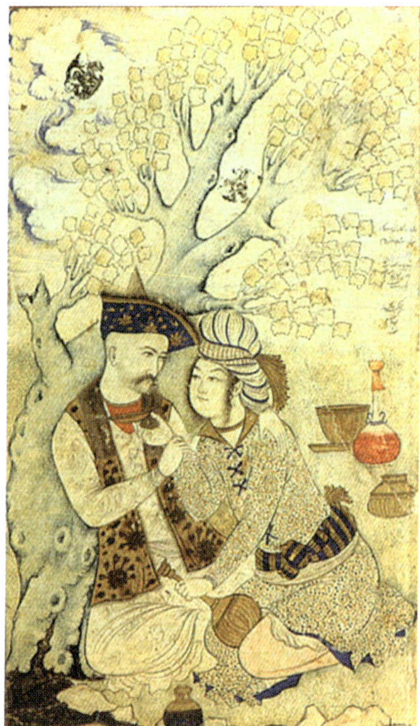

Shah Abbas I with one of his pages, signed Muhammad Qasim, 1627, drawing enhanced with colours, gold and silver on paper, 27.5 x 16.8 cm (10⅝ x 6¾ in), Louvre, Paris, France

KEY DEVELOPMENTS

Representation of homosexual relations is rare in Islamic art, particularly as orthodox Islam disapproves of depicting humans. However, there are moments of visibility, including during the rule of Shah Abbas I (1571–1629) of Safavid Iran. Accomplished miniaturist Mahammad Qasim (c.1575–1659) depicted the formidable ruler in an intimate moment of seduction with his cupbearer who is suggestively gripping a flask.

Across time, place, politics, religion and cultures, individuals in high positions of power have held and exerted levels of influence on social behaviours and expressions, with a considerably higher visual presence in the historic record and the arts, as sitters, patrons and collectors. This has manifested in the relaxing or tightening of rules around behaviours or production of works connected to gender and sexuality.

Lives of royalty and other leaders have been the focus of greater attention and recording than most. With acute recognition of the power of their public image, they often experience a paradox of being constrained by increased public scrutiny while afforded additional protection and freedoms to flout 'the rules'.

The Roman Emperor Hadrian (76–138) commissioned statues celebrating his lover Antinous (c.111–c.130) and on his death pronounced him a deity to be worshipped, prompting a plethora of depictions. Queen Christina of Sweden (1626–1689) had portraits and aspects of her patronage reflect her rejection of feminine standards/ expectations, with features, mannerisms and attire that leant towards the masculine. The art collections by Frederick the Great (1712–1786) overtly reflected homosexual passions. When he visited him in Potsdam, Johann Joachim Winckelmann declared, 'I have enjoyed lusts that I will never enjoy again.' All have become touchstones and symbols alluding to homosexuality or queerness.

BAROQUE **p.13** ROCOCO **p.14** NEOCLASSICISM **p.15** *SOUS LE CIEL DE SHIRAZ (PAYKANARTCAR)* **p.158**

Picturing a Chevalier

KEY ARTISTS: ALEXANDRE-AUGUSTE ROBINEAU • JEAN LAURANT MOSNIER • THOMAS STEWART JOHAN MICHAEL BAADER • RICHARD COSWAY • PIERRE JEAN BAPTISTE BRADEL

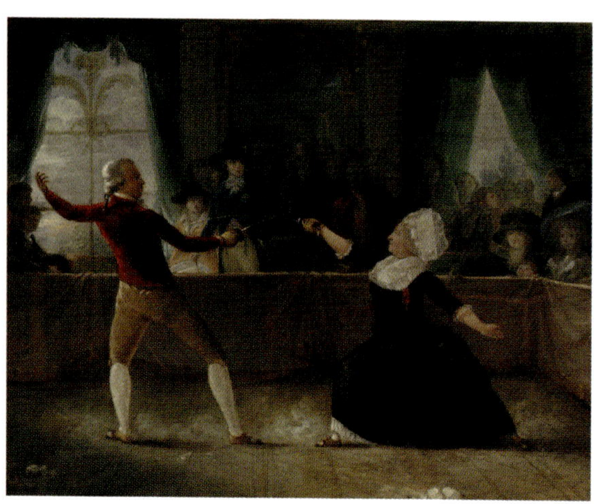

The Fencing-Match between the Chevalier de Saint-George and the Chevalier d'Eon, Alexandre-Auguste Robineau, c.1787–9, oil on canvas, 64.1 x 75.8 cm (25¼ x 29⅝ in), Royal Collection Trust, UK

KEY DEVELOPMENTS

Robineau's respectful painting records a fencing match where D'Eon's opponent was the composer and violinist Joseph Bologne (1745–1799), born in Guadeloupe to a planter and enslaved woman. A newspaper reported that 'a celebrated painter' was to depict 'the hero and heroine, in this very interesting scene.'

Amid a general proliferation of satirical prints and caricature, surviving portraits of the Chevalier d'Éon de Beaumont (1728–1810) offer rare visibility of eighteenth-century 'gender transgression' without condemnation. Now regarded by some as a 'transcestor', their name is the basis for the now defunct term 'eonism', denoting transvestism or transition in people assigned male at birth.

Their life was a rollercoaster of intrigue. After several years of decorated military service, they were stationed in London with ambassadorial status. However, after a quarrel with another ambassador, they were ordered to return to France, but refused to go, instead opting to air French secrets in a scandalous 1764 publication.

After they were forced into exile, speculation mounted around their gender identity, with bookmakers setting odds. In 1775 they signed an agreement with the French King to return official papers and be publicly recognized as a woman. Remaining in London until their death, they were celebrated as a champion female fencer, a celebrity of their day, their image circulating in countless prints.

The 2012 'rediscovery' of a copy of a portrait by Jean Laurent Mosnier (1743–1808), exhibited at the Royal Academy in 1791, revived interest in them. D'Eon's diaries deliberately muddy waters regarding their gender, as do conflicting contemporary and later accounts. Contemporary readings of their autopsy suggest they were intersex.

NEOCLASSICISM **p.15** TO BE SEEN **p.186**

Public Presence

KEY ARTISTS: EMMA STEBBINS • HARRIET GOODHUE HOSMER • EDMONIA LEWIS ANNE SEYMOUR DAMER

Civic sculptures and monuments are the most established forms of 'permanent' public art. Only in recent history and limited places have public sculptures directly representing LGBTQ+ themes been permitted. However, earlier works have become recognized as possessing queer connections or ordained with queer meanings. Sharing this knowledge creates a sense of retrospectively designating or establishing 'queer-connected' art in the public realm.

Angel of the Waters by Emma Stebbins (1815–1882) was the earliest public artwork by a woman in New York City. A biblical reference to healing properties of water, it forms the centrepiece of the Bethesda Fountain in Central Park, New York. Despite its arguably innocuous appearance it has become a convergence point of queer references. Although lacking clear resemblance, there has long been speculation that Stebbins modelled it on her lover, the actress Charlotte Cushman (1816–1876). The angel's connection to healing would have been personal, as Cushman was then fighting breast cancer.

In the early 1970s the fountain was a Sunday afternoon social destination for young gay men and friends. It later formed the backdrop of the final scene of the Perestroika section of the AIDS-themed play *Angels in America* (1993) by Tony Kushner (1956–), making conscious reference to the symbolically suggested curative powers of water.

KEY DEVELOPMENTS

Stebbins was among an early generation of women to forge careers in sculpture and form same-sex relationships. They included Harriet Goodhue Hosmer (1830–1908) and Edmonia Lewis (1844–1907), who she met in Rome when developing her sculpting career. The enthusiasm for civic statuary in the nineteenth century enabled the work of a number of lesbian sculptors to receive public visibility.

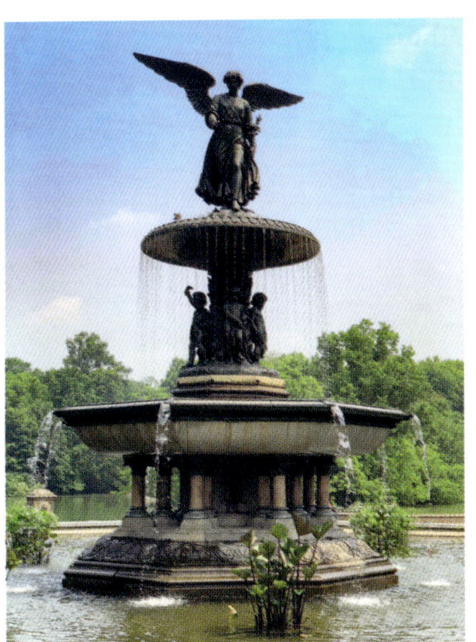

Angel of the Waters, Bethesda Fountain, Emma Stebbins, unveiled 1873, bronze, 240 cm (96 in), Central Park, New York, USA

NEOCLASSICISM **p.15** STREET ART **p.36** *DAVID* **p.40** *MEMORIAL TO A MARRIAGE* **p.136**

Exposing Desires

KEY ARTISTS: BARON WILHELM VON GLOEDEN • GEORGE HOYNINGEN-HUENE • HENRY SCOTT TUKE F. HOLLAND DAY • HORST P. HORST • GEORGE PLATT LYNES

Many wealthy men explored fine art photography to realize their homoerotic fantasies from the nineteenth century onward. In Boston, F. Holland Day (1864–1933) made many amorous platinotypes of the Orpheus and St. Sebastian legends with handsome models he picked up at the city ports. Baron Wilhelm von Gloeden (1856–1931) and his cousin Guglielmo Plüschow (1852–1930) created a hub of homosexual tourism in Taormina, Sicily. Their local philanthropy bought access to the island's best-looking men and boys, smoothing a path towards general tolerance of their homosexuality in the otherwise traditional Catholic community.

By the interwar years, glamour and precision of fashion photography had permeated the scene, thanks to George Hoyningen-Huene (1900–1968) and Horst P. Horst (1906–1999), *Vogue* photographers by day and male physique photographers by night. George Platt Lynes (1907–1955) took the genre to new heights with a surreal yet narrative-based, filmic feel to his magnificent monochrome photographs.

These early artistic pioneers paved the way for more commercial fodder. In Los Angeles, Bob Mizer (1922–1992) created an empire of beefcake, photographing more than 10,000 models for photographs sold through his 'Athletic Model Guild'. His magazine *Physique Pictorial* famously launched Tom of Finland (1920–1991) and spawned many imitators. It is credited with shifting gay male aesthetics and perceptions from the effeminate 'sissy' towards more macho muscle clones.

KEY DEVELOPMENTS

Von Gloeden was one of the earliest gay photographers of the male nude. His images once totalled over 3,000 and were made between 1890 and 1914 in Italy. Depicting young men and teenage boys, pastorally posing with classical overtones, they were shown at illustrious photographic society exhibitions, and widely traded privately, appearing in the collections of Oscar Wilde (1854–1900) and John Singer Sargent (1856–1925).

Study of two male nudes, Baron Wilhelm von Gloeden, albumen print, 1900, Private Collection

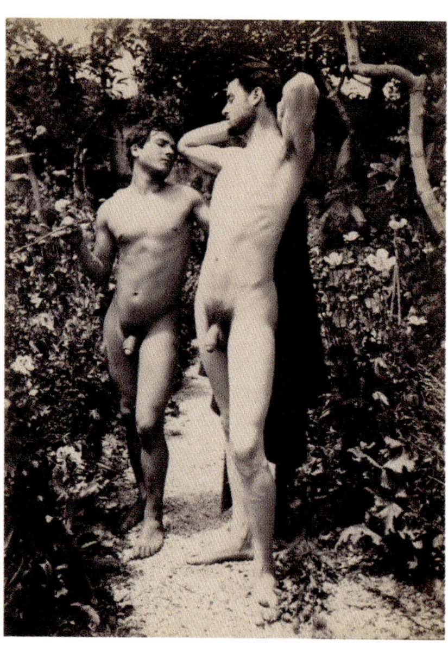

ROCOCO **p.14** NEOCLASSICISM **p.15** *UNTITLED* **p.100** *NOTES ON THE MARGIN OF THE BLACK BOOK* **p.128**

The Ballets Russes

KEY ARTISTS: LÉON BASKT • JEAN COCTEAU • PAVEL TCHELITCHEV • NATALIA GONCHAROVA

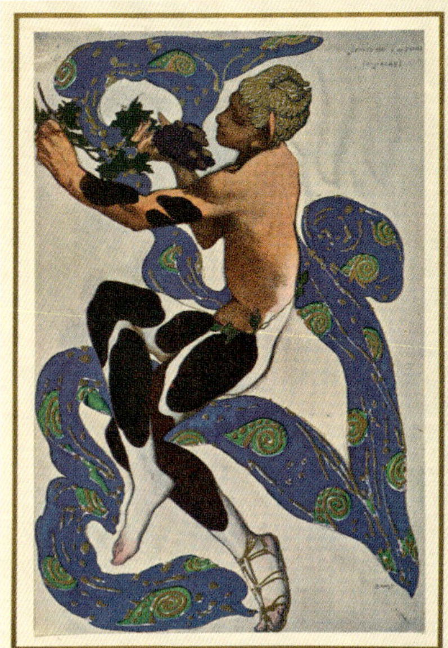

Afternoon of a Faun (L'Après-midi d'un faune), Léon Bakst 1912 (gouache on paper) Bibliotheque de L'Arsenal, Paris, France

The Ballets Russes (1909–29) were pioneering in developing the art of dance. Formed in Paris by Serge Diaghilev (1872–1929), they toured Europe and the Americas extensively. Their spectacular productions were a fusion of the arts, and a constellation of queer-interest artists became associated with them, including Jean Cocteau (1889–1963), Marie Laurencin (1883–1956) and Pavel Tchelitchew (1898–1957). Often controversial, they received both high praise and denouncement.

The troupe's innovative choreographies disrupted gender norms by endowing the male dancer with equal importance as the ballerina. Incorporating motifs from Russian folklore, they were considered 'exotic others', which evoked an element of greater freedom to 'acceptably' explore gender and sexuality. *The Dancer Nijinsky* (1912), a poem by Ludwig Rubiner (1881–1920), vividly evokes the recognized homoeroticism of Vaslav Nijinsky (1889–1950) and his performances.

Léon Bakst (1866–1924) created scenery and costumes for several productions, inspiring fashion designers like Paul Poiret (1879–1944) and Elsa Schiaparelli (1890–1973).

Afternoon of a Faun (1912) is considered one of the first modern ballets. Recounting his five-year affair with Diaghilev, Nijinsky commented 'the Faun is me, and *Jeux* [a controversial 1913 ballet] is the life of which Diaghilev dreamed'. Nijinsky's faun became an iconic image inspiring works by Roberto Montenegro (1885–1968), Malvina Hoffman (1887–1966), Una Troubridge (1887–1963), George Barbier (1882–1932) and Glyn Philpot (1884–1937), who all had 'a queer bent'.

KEY DEVELOPMENTS

The Ballets Russes enticed and cultivated a distinct clientele, including avant-garde creatives and gay men, which a 1928 *Vogue* review considered could 'be distinguished by the beautiful burgeoning boys'. Their cutting-edge performances influenced broader artistic and popular culture, markedly the development of Art Deco.

DADA **p.21** SURREALISM **p.23** ART DECO **p.24** PERFORMANCE ART **p.29**

Commercial Allure

KEY ARTISTS: J. C. LEYENDECKER • PIERRE ET GILLES

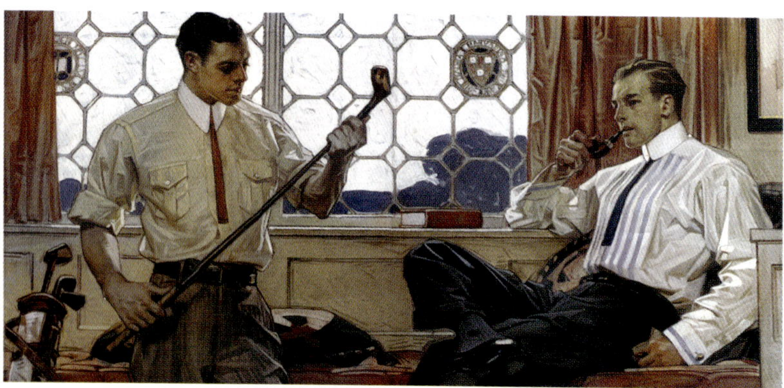

Advertisement for Arrow Shirt Collars, J. C. Leyendecker, 1914, USA

One of the most successful illustrators at the dawn of late nineteenth century mass pictorial advertising, Joseph Christian Leyendecker (1874–1951) carved out a prominent position with his visions of sexy, modern men. Making shirts, socks, shaving products and even thermal underwear sexy, Leyendecker was the man to hire between c.1895 and 1930, to boost sales of products for men.

Projecting health, wealth and affordable sophistication, whether attired for business, or uniformed for warfare, his muscular men blended the decadence of the 1920s with all-American heroic sailor and soldier aesthetics. Hiding homoeroticism in plain sight, his drawings depict men often in a state of dressing, admiring themselves or grouped in cosy, intimate interiors.

'Arrow-collar taste' became 1920s slang for a particular type of attraction to a particular type of man. Even the name Leyendecker itself entered the lexicon. In his story 'The Last of the Belles', F. Scott Fitzgerald describes 'a handsome, earnest face with a Leyendecker forelock'.

Leyendecker's finessing and application of the 'sex sells' doctrine to the masculine form paved the way for later cultural phenomena including the rugged Marlboro Man of the 1950s, fashioning of picture-perfect models in 1980s Giorgio Armani photoshoots and marketing of Calvin Klein underwear in the 1990s.

KEY DEVELOPMENTS

J. C. Leyendecker was the first to elevate male beauty in the early days of advertising. His Arrow Shirt Collar man first appeared in 1905 during the Golden Age of American illustration. His vision of the ideal man in his game-changing commercial illustrations from the 1890s to the 1950s were mainly based on his partner of half a century, Charles Allwood Beach (1881–1954).

HARLEM RENAISSANCE **p.22** ART DECO **p.24** POP ART **p.27** POSTMODERNISM **p.33** QUEER EYE **p.182** 

Weimar Berlin

KEY ARTISTS: JEANNE MAMMEN • FLORENCE HENRI • MARGARATE SCHALL • GERDA WEGENER LOTTE LASERSTEIN • GERTRUDE SANDMANN

Renowned for its thriving entertainment scene, and convergence of spirited art movements including Bauhaus and Dada, the liberal climate of 1920s Berlin made it a magnet for creatives and those in search of 'modern living'. Streets and social spaces provided a sea of inspiration for artists – including clubs and cabarets known for drag, queer performers and patrons.

This gay *joie de vivre* is epitomized in *She Represents*, by Jeanne Mammen (1890–1976), depicting the defiant stance of a top-hatted woman amid a raucous party. Mammen's observational works captured the leers, sneers and sexual come-ons seen in lesbian and queer social spaces. Her unromanticized but often alluring characters avoid undertones of disdain sometimes present in the work of contemporaries Otto Dix (1891–1969) and George Grosz (1893–1959).

Berlin was home to two lesbian magazines which helped establish aesthetic intersections of the emerging 'New Woman' and lesbian identities – one being *Die Freundin* (*The Girlfriend*) which included trans-supportive content.

Police provided 'transvestite certificates' to protect those 'cross-dressing' in public from arrest. However, gender and sexual freedoms were precarious, and homosexuality was still persecuted in accordance with section 175 of the German penal code. Life and art fundamentally changed in 1933 when the Nazi party assumed power in Germany, denouncing such works and LGBTQ+ people as 'degenerate'.

KEY DEVELOPMENTS

Increased understanding and visibility of LGBTQ+ identities in Berlin were significantly buoyed by physician and sexologist Magnus Hirschfeld (1868–1935) whose Institute of Sexual Research provided supportive medical consultations, a library and archives on sexuality and gender, and a 'Museum of Sex'. New terms were developed to describe identities and create a sense of belonging and efforts made to improve scientific and legal recognition.

She Represents (Carnival Scene), Jeanne Mammen, c.1928, watercolour and pencil on paper, 42 x 30.4 cm (16½ x 12 in), Private collection

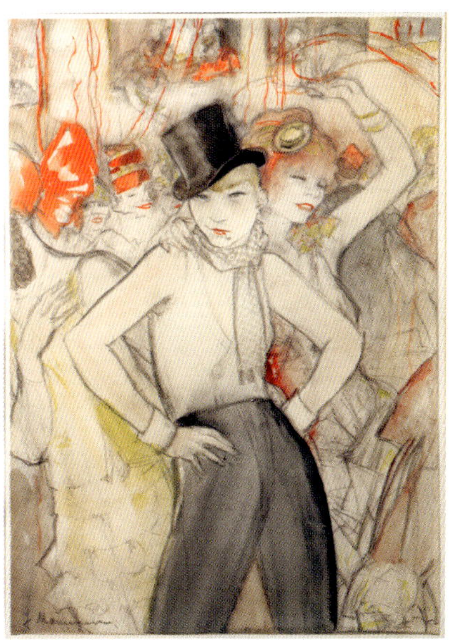

DADA **p.21** *DA-DANDY* **p.62** *A SUMMER DAY* **p.80** PLACES TO BE **p.189**

Bloomsbury Shapes

KEY ARTISTS: STEPHEN TOMLIN • DUNCAN GRANT • VANESSA BELL • NINA HAMNETT
DORA CARRINGTON

The Bloomsbury Group have been summarized as 'living in squares, painting in circles and loving in triangles' in the oft-recycled quip traditionally ascribed to Dorothy Parker (1893–1967). The informal group of intellectuals, artists and writers frequently congregated at the home of artist Vanessa Bell (1879–1961) in Gordon Square, Bloomsbury, London. They included artist Duncan Grant (1885–1978), writer Virginia Woolf (1882–1941) and critic Roger Fry (1866–1934), though an array of artists and creatives came to be associated with them. Engaged with European art movements of the time, they helped introduce Picasso, Matisse and Cézanne to London audiences.

Influential, radical thinkers in each of their fields, they shared a passion for progress, challenging conventions in art, literature and social values. Open-minded and collaborative, they had personal lives that were infamously intertwined. Woolf recalled: 'We were full of experiments and reforms ... Everything was going to be new, everything was going to be different. Everything was on trial.'

Fry established The Omega Workshops (1913), with Bell and Grant as co-directors, which produced a range of furniture, textiles and household items, merging avant-garde ideas with joyful naiveite. Works were marked only with Ω – the Greek Omega symbol – to ensure appreciation for aesthetic appeal rather than the artist's name.

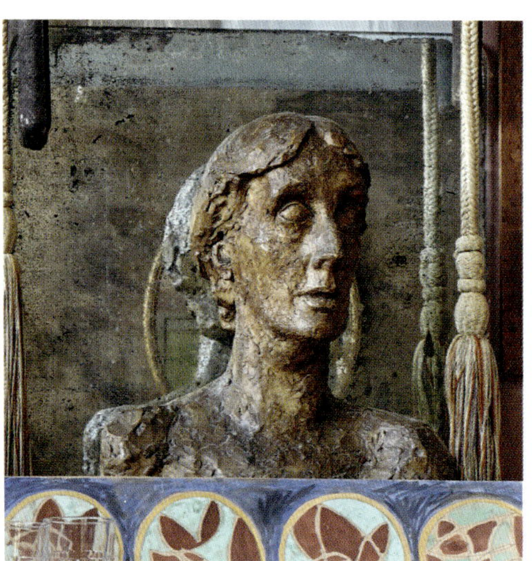

KEY DEVELOPMENTS

Bell rented Charleston House, Sussex, as a country retreat. Her lover Grant and their circle frequently gathered there, and it came to be decorated in their distinct styles. Today it remains an inspiring testament to the group's alternative approaches to art, life and interior décor. Stephen Tomlin (1901–1937) was the group's primary sculptor. A cast of this bust of Woolf is displayed in Bloomsbury.

Bust of Virginia Woolf, Stephen Tomlin, plaster, 1931, displayed at Charleston, Lewes, UK

PRE-RAPHAELITES **p.17** TEXTUAL POWER **p.166** PLACES TO BE **p.189**

FIRE!! Magazine

KEY ARTISTS: RICHARD BRUCE NUGENT • AARON DOUGLAS

Independent publishing played a vital role in the Harlem Renaissance as periodicals shared and developed links between visual artists, writers and audiences. Retrospectively, many gay narratives in the Harlem Renaissance are coming to light through recent issuing of diaries and oral history projects.

Founded by a large group of Black artists and writers including Langston Hughes (1901–1967) and Aaron Douglas (1899–1979), the radical (and controversially received) magazine *FIRE!!* (1926) broke ground and set a precedent for including clear gay and bisexual content among other subjects like sex work, interracial relationships and racism in segregated America.

Author, actor and artist Richard Bruce Nugent (1906–1987) was one of the few who were out and proud at the time. His silhouette artwork and celebrated short story 'Smoke, Lilies, and Jade' were published in *FIRE!!*. Conceived in a modernist stream-of-consciousness style, it is considered the first short story by an African American writer to openly address the author's homosexuality alongside themes of bisexuality and interracial desire. Tragically the first issue was the last because the magazine's headquarters were burned to the ground in an arson attack. The magazine never recovered, making original copies one of the great rarities of the print world.

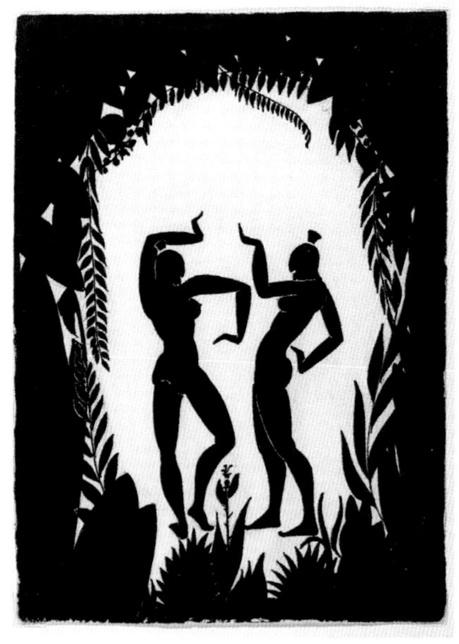

Dancing Figures, Richard Bruce Nugent, c.1935, black ink and graphite on paper, 37.5 x 26.7 cm (14¾ x 10½ in), Brooklyn Museum, New York, USA

KEY DEVELOPMENTS

Nugent managed to save a pristine copy of *FIRE!!* for almost 60 years. When his friend Tom Wirth (1938–2014) discovered this, he used it to produce a replica edition, making it accessible once again. Like a phoenix, its revival in print has forged new community connections and highlighted the importance of archiving to be able to know our histories and inspire future generations.

HARLEM RENAISSANCE **p.22** *FERAL BENGA* **p.90** *DANCING FIGURES* **p.92** TEXTUAL POWER **p.166** DANCE **p.188**

Gay Paris

KEY ARTISTS: HENRI DE TOULOUSE-LAUTREC • FRANCIS ROSE • MARCEL VERTES • DJUNA BARNES ROMAINE BROOKS • BERENICE ABBOTT

Henri de Toulouse-Lautrec (1864–1901) remains synonymous with Paris. His recurring players in posters and paintings were the dancers, performers and sex workers of his beloved Montmartre – frequently lesbian and bisexual women. Those attracted to exploring new ways of living gravitated to Paris and each other. Gertrude Stein (1874–1946) said 'Paris was where the twentieth century was.'

The 'City of Light' gave birth to the Modernist movement, drawing together women who rejected the patriarchy. A renowned salon hostess, publisher and patron of artists, Stein supported a constellation of American émigré artists and writers she dubbed 'The Lost Generation'. In 1910, her partner Alice B. Toklas (1877–1967) moved into the Stein's apartment at 27 rue de Fleurus and their art collection grew along with their avant-garde circle. Refuting threats of homophobia from a society at odds with their lives, they advanced awareness of sexuality, rooted in 'the place that suited those of us that were to create the twentieth-century art and literature'.

Stein was a strikingly original writer of her generation, and in *The Making of Americans* (1925) she addresses her outsider status as one of the 'queer people', which held connotations of non-heteronormativity even then. Her *Miss Furr and Miss Skeene* (1923) is considered the first published work to use 'gay' to describe same-sex relationships.

In bed: The Kiss, Toulouse Lautrec, oil on board, 1892, 70 x 54 cm (27½ x 21⅕ in), Private Collection

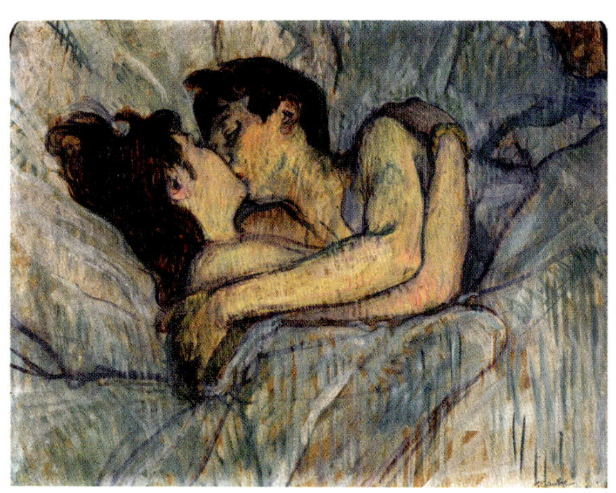

KEY DEVELOPMENTS

Toulouse-Lautrec was among the first modern artists collected by Gertrude Stein and her brother. Tender rather than lascivious, *The Kiss* was forged out of Lautrec's intimacy with bohemia and brothels where he met his models, many of whom preferred the company of women. Also fond of the city's lesbian bars, he documented the owner and patrons of the famous 'La Souris'.

ART NOUVEAU **p.20** SURREALISM **p.23** ART DECO **p.24** *LA VIE PENSIVE* **p.56** *LOGE DE THÉÂTRE* **p.58** *HANDSOME DRINKS* **p.60** *LES AMAZONES* **p.68**

Making Rainbows

KEY ARTISTS: GILBERT BAKER • DEREK JARMAN • ADEJOKE TUGBIYELE • DANIEL QUASAR MOULEE

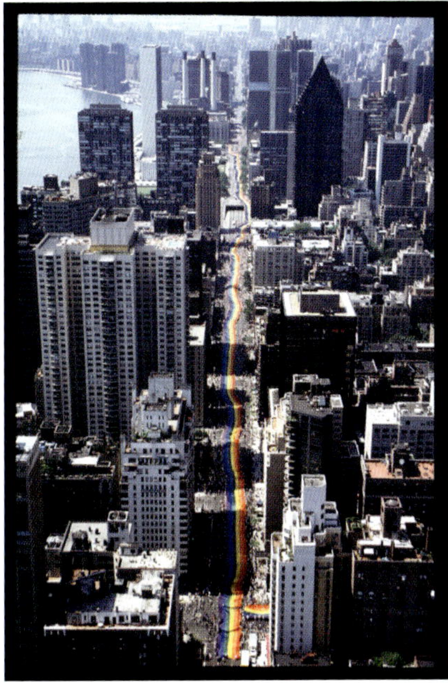

Mile Long Rainbow Flag, photographed by Mick Hicks, 1994, New York City, USA

Rainbows have been imbued with various meanings across time and cultures. Gilbert Baker (1951–2017) described them as a 'natural flag in the sky'. The rainbow flag first flew at the 1978 San Francisco Gay Freedom Day Parade and was created by a group of artists and activists, including Baker, Lynn Segerblom and James McNamara (–1999). Fluttering between art, design, installation and performance, it has become an international symbol now synonymous with LGBTQ+ rights.

Baker reflected 'a flag is different than any other form of art ... it functions in so many different ways'. He valued their transcendent and transformational qualities and 'the emotional connection they hold'. First conceived to represent the diversity of the gay community, the initial design had eight coloured stripes, each representing a value (e.g. orange for healing). A revised six-striped iteration soon followed.

The design wasn't trademarked, in the belief that it belonged to the community. Artists and designers have created iterations representing a range of intersectionalities. Adejoke Tugbiyele (1977–) created *Gele Pride Flag* (2014) from six gele – headscarves worn by Nigerian women. Daniel Quasar's Progress Pride flag (2018) added colours to explicitly represent trans people and people of colour. Considering the latter, Moulee (1947–) noted cultural differences of relevance in India, 'where we are all different shades of brown' and developed a Social Justice Pride flag (2018) incorporating colours representing political ideologies.

KEY DEVELOPMENTS

Today, rainbow colours detached from their flag context are recognized as possessing queer power. In countries, including Saudi Arabia, it is illegal to sell or wear 'rainbow-coloured' items, as they 'promote homosexuality'. Political statements have been made using colours to create 'hidden flags' – at the swearing in of Poland's (anti-LGBTQ+) President Andrzej Duda (1972–) in 2020, opposing politicians each dressed in a colour of the rainbow in protest.

POP ART **p.27** PERFORMANCE ART **p.29**

Fashioning Style

KEY ARTISTS: ERTÉ • GEORGE BARBIER • MÉRET OPPENHEIM • LEIGH BOWERY

Virginia Woolf's groundbreaking gender-shifting fictional-biography *Orlando* (1928) notes the ability of clothing to 'change our view of the world and the world's view of us'.

Sartorial signifiers galore have a powerful resonance across LGBTQ+ history. With long-established and rich relationships between the worlds of art, fashion, theatre, music and performance, mutual references visibly intermingle between clubs, catwalk, canvas and the street. The creative industries have benefitted from the queer eye's perspectives towards gender presentation and flouting the 'rules' around masculinity, femininity and flamboyance.

Recurring resurgences of appreciation for lesbian visual identities include the A/W19 collection by Thom Browne (1965–). Browne directly referenced the portrait by Romaine Brooks (1874–1970) of sculptor Una Troubridge (1887–1963) replete with tailored suit, short hair and monocle as sported by figures in artistic and literary lesbian circles of the 1920s.

The late 1980s onwards has seen designers increasingly embrace gender diversity and incorporate more overt reference to queer signifiers and subculture styles, particularly in terms of drag and occasionally kink. The futuristic fashions of Leigh Bowery (1961–1994) were something thoroughly unique. Inspiring more postmodern takes on drag and interested in pushing bodily boundaries, Bowery is quoted as declaring 'flesh is my most favorite fabric'. Outlandish, conceptual and theatric creations as both performer and designer, Bowery has become the legend to revisit as a pioneer of the queer pantheon.

KEY DEVELOPMENTS

The fast world of fashion magazines has drawn many queer creatives to its helm. In the 1920s, editor Dorothy Todd (1883–1996) and her lover Madge Garland (1898–1990) turned British *Vogue* into a citadel of innovative creativity with frequent allusions to queerness including via the Bright Young Things photographed by Cecil Beaton (1904–1980). The prolific fashion illustrator Erté (1882–1990) designed over 200 covers for rival magazine *Harper's Bazaar*, influencing many couturiers including Yves Saint Laurent (1936–2008).

Loge de Théâtre, Erté, 1912, serigraph print, after original 1912 gouache design, 1980s (see Works p.58)

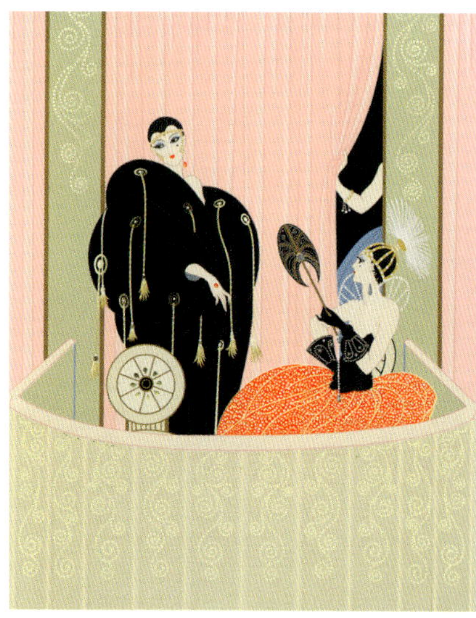

AESTHETICISM **p.19** ART DECO **p.24** *LOGE DE THÉÂTRE* **p.58** LA BAGUE SYMBOLIQUE **p.72**
STEPHEN TENNANT IN COSTUME AS PRINCE CHARMING **p.78** *SELF PORTRAIT WITH CROPPED HAIR* **p.98**

On the Cover

KEY ARTISTS: GLUCK • ROMAINE BROOKS • ESTER HERNÁNDEZ • MICHAEL LEAONARD TEE A. CORINNE

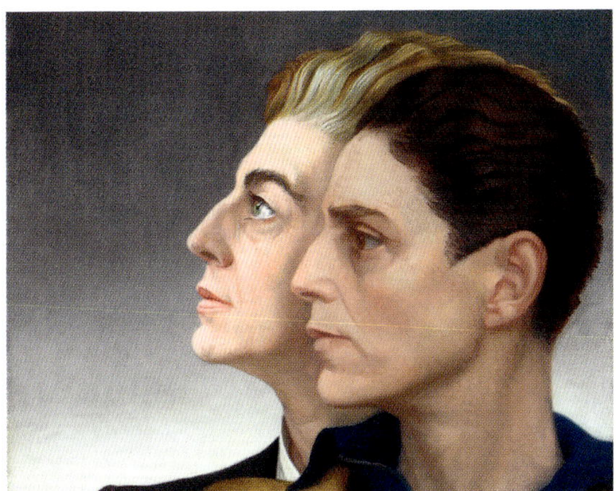

Medallion (YouWe), Gluck, 1936, oil on canvas, 30.5 x 35.6 cm (12 x 14 in), Private Collection (see Works p.94)

KEY DEVELOPMENTS
Republished LGBTQ+ texts with carefully considered cover designs have forged literary links with many queer interest painters. Originally banned in Britain for obscenity, reissues of *The Well of Loneliness* (1928) by Radclyffe Hall (1883–1943) were boosted by covers featuring Gluck's *Medallion* (1936); Romaine Brooks' portrait of Gluck, *Peter (A Young English Girl)* (1923–24); and Tamara de Lempicka's *The Green Turban* (1930).

Content and cover art of LGBTQ+ interest publications have a reciprocal relationship of association, potentially increasing awareness and queer connections of each other. Cover art has provided a variety of visibility and representation, at times evasive, incongruent or meaningfully symbolic.

Changing Head, by Michael Leonard (1933–2023), found wider recognition on a 1986 edition of *Faggots* (1978) by Larry Kramer (1935–2020) and *La Ofrenda* by Ester Hernández (1944–) gained iconic lesbian status when used for *Chicana Lesbians: The Girls Our Mothers Warned Us About* (1991) by Carla Trujillo (1957–). Sensationalist 1950s' and 1960s' pulp fiction often explored illicit lesbian love. For many women, they provided pivotal, if problematic, points of connection, with condemnation as well as recognition of lesbian existence. Several, however, were written by women, for women, including 'lesbian pulp queen' Ann Bannon (1932–). Their distinctive aesthetics were the subject of *Conspiracy of Silence* (1987), a series by Nina Levitt (1955–) exploring negative tropes of lesbian (mis)representation.

The Price of Salt (1952) by Patricia Highsmith (1921–1995) originally circulated as pulp fiction. Naiad Press' 1984 republication replaced pulp aesthetics with a photograph of a saltcellar by Tee A. Corinne (1943–2006) – reflecting increasing (though not universal) moves to feature appropriate LGBTQ+ artists. Gay Men's Press (1979–2000/2006) were also notably considered in selecting suitable cover art.

MEDALLION (YOUWE) **p.94** INTIMACIES **p.165** DIVINE CONNECTION **p.178**

Facing AIDS

KEY ARTISTS: VISUAL AIDS • TESSA BOFFIN • GRAN FURY • KEITH HARING • ROTIMI FANI-KAYODE FELIX GONZALEZ-TORRES

Since the first reported cases in 1981, the HIV/AIDS epidemic continues to be one of the most prevalent and deadliest pandemics worldwide. Its initial presence among gay men prompted homophobic apathy in government responses and an associated stigma continues to surround the virus.

Given limited medical understanding of the virus and escalating homophobic discrimination, communities (predominantly LGBTQ+) fought to share lifesaving information and challenge mainstream media misinformation. The 1980s and 1990s became a period of both great devastation and artistic innovation as the pandemic prompted a range of creative responses. Urgency, fear, anger and loss fuelled striking graphic design to communicate vital information, support and campaign on issues. There was acute awareness that imagery could influence perceptions of those without direct experience of AIDS, shaping their view of the epidemic and (by association) gay and bisexual men. Activist organizations and artist collectives emerged, including ACT UP (AIDS Coalition to Unleash Power) and Gran Fury. Demanding improved funding for healthcare, they consciously crafted visuals of direct action and protest for impact. Many artists looked to expand conversations around AIDS beyond relaying information – to reflect and express complex personal realities. Works frequently challenged pervasive negative images associating gay and queer bodies with threat and death rather than pleasure.

Unfolding Ceremony '96 Quilt Display, 1996 AIDS Memorial Quilt Display on the mall in Washington D.C., USA

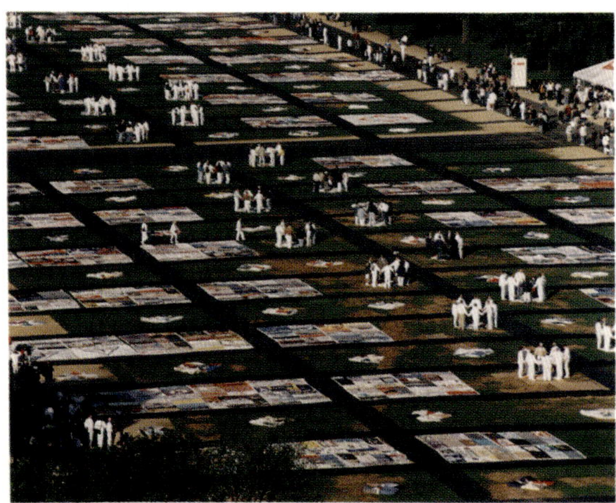

KEY DEVELOPMENTS

Described as 'the largest ongoing community arts project in the world', the AIDS Quilt is composed of thousands of panels, each commemorating the life of someone who died from AIDS-related illness. Conceived in 1985, it became an expanding public manifestation of grief and memorial, visualizing and humanizing the overwhelming numbers of lives lost to the HIV/AIDS pandemic.

CONCEPTUAL ART **p.32** STREET ART **p.36** *EVERY MOMENT COUNTS (ECSTATIC ANTIBODIES)* **p.122**
ONCE UPON A TIME **p.124**

Collective Response

KEY ARTISTS: VISUAL AIDS ARTISTS' CAUCUS

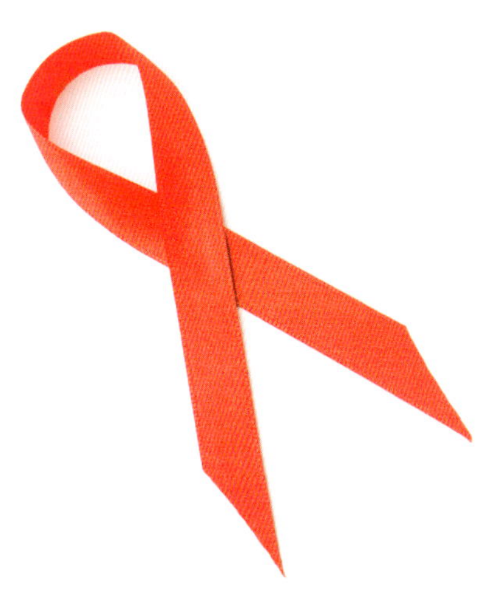

A red ribbon – as prompted by The Ribbon Project, Visual AIDS Artists' Caucus, 1991

The Red Ribbon is one of the most recognized symbols of the late twentieth century. Introduced in 1991, it continues to be used worldwide as visual shorthand for supporting those living with HIV and AIDS.

The Ribbon Project was created by the Visual AIDS Artists' Caucus, a group of artists supporting the New York arts organization to raise awareness. They demonstrated the power of collective queer creativity in connecting art and design with social justice to galvanize support. The Ribbon was not a tool to communicate information *at* individuals, but an expression *by* individuals of awareness and support.

The shape was chosen because it was simple to replicate. The artists wanted to convey that HIV went beyond the gay community, so avoided associated pink and rainbow colours, selecting red for its boldness and connection to blood, passion and love.

Intended as a consciousness-raising symbol (not for fundraising or profit), it has never been copyrighted. The caucus chose to remain anonymous as individuals, emphasizing, 'The Ribbon Project is a grass-roots effort. There is no official ribbon. Do it yourself.'

An open-source artwork of group expression, the ribbons have a visual impact that could be considered akin to a large-scale Art Happening. The Ribbon has become a visual prompt for innumerable artworks and designs.

KEY DEVELOPMENTS

Important moments of visibility were red ribbons being worn by guests and presenters at the 45th Tony Awards in June 1991 and in November of the same year 100,000 ribbons being given out at the widely televised Freddie Mercury Memorial concert at Wembley Stadium. Ribbons were originally distributed with an explanatory text which was abandoned as their meaning quickly became well-known.

CONCEPTUAL ART **p.32** *EVERY MOMENT COUNTS (ECSTATIC ANTIBODIES)* **p.122** ONCE UPON A TIME **p.124**

Queer Crip

KEY ARTISTS: LORENZA BÖTTNER • STEVEN SOLBRIG • FRANK MOORE • RIVA LEHRER • PEREL

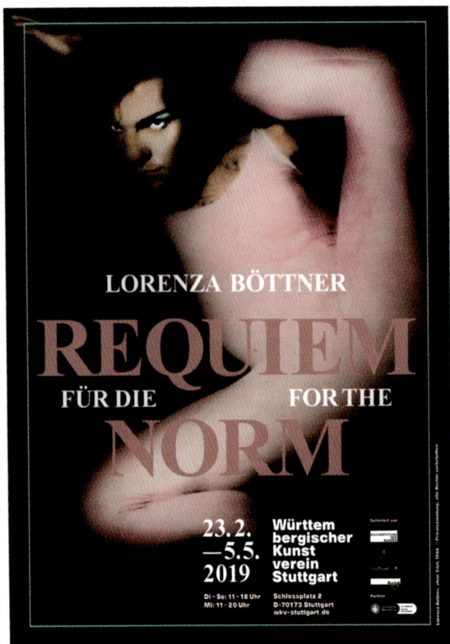

Exhibition poster for 'Lorenza Böttner: Requiem for the Norm', Württembergischer Kunstverein Stuttgart, 2019, design: Till Gathmann

KEY DEVELOPMENTS

A revival of interest in Böttner was sparked after trans writer and curator Paul B. Preciado accessed an archive of their work and featured it in *Documenta 14* (2017) and *Requiem for the Norm* (2018–2020). Böttner also featured in 'Queering the Crip, Cripping the Queer' at the Schwules Museum, Berlin (2022–23), the first international exhibition to explore intersectionalities of queerness and disability.

Similar to 'queer', 'crip(ple)' is an outdated term widely considered offensive but increasingly reclaimed by physically disabled people, who often also identify as LGBTQ+. Sexual and gender minorities and those with disabilities share histories of discrimination and fighting for self-determination in the face of stereotyping, pathologizing and demonizing. In *Crip Theory: Cultural Signs of Queerness and Disability* (2006) Robert McRuer (1966-) theorizes a dominant system of 'compulsory able-bodiedness' that produces disability as intersecting with a system of 'compulsory heterosexuality' that produces queerness.

Chilean-German performance artist and painter Lorenza Böttner (1959–1994) credited her disability as prompting her to become an 'exhibitionist'. After a childhood accident resulted in her arms being amputated, she rejected prosthetics and 'disability education'. Attending art school in Kassel, she began identifying as female but maintained a fluid gender identity. Her thesis *Behindert? [Disabled?]* challenged typical representations of non-conforming bodies, a subject continued throughout her artwork. Using an array of methods, including painting and drawing with her feet and mouth, street performance, dance, sculpture and photography, she celebrated complexities of gender expression presenting herself as having joyful agency and sexuality. Referencing the *Venus de Milo*, she emphasized: 'A sculpture is always admired even if limbs are missing, whereas a handicapped human being arouses feelings of uncertainness and shame.'

PERFORMANCE ART **p.29** PRESENTING THE ARTIST **p.167** SPACE OF THE BODY **p.172** TO BE SEEN **p.186**

Out in the Gallery

KEY ARTISTS: TESSA BOFFIN • SUNIL GUPTA • HARMONY HAMMOND • GUERRILLA GIRLS

Long-running discrimination against LGBTQ+ people is reflected in a history of artists, institutions and critics excluding, ignoring or denying public acknowledgement of LGBTQ+ aspects of artworks and biographies. For artists, this is often motivated by a need for survival. Many kept more obviously queer creations separate from their public work, instead circulating it among trusted circles. Some institutions have given contradictory stances on whether personal information is relevant to include in interpretation texts – frequently only to the exclusion of LGBTQ+ aspects.

AA Bronson (1946–) of artist group General Idea noted that their work spoke to queer identities but that critics didn't address this until the mid-1980s, adding 'to call yourself a gay artist would be, of course, the death knell of your career'.

Globally, acknowledgement of 'queer art' has developed in various manners and speeds, reflecting legal and cultural differences (including language around 'queerness'). This has provided a range of 'breakthrough' moments – particularly exhibitions directly addressing subjects that are non-heterosexual, usually cultivated by artists at grassroots level before featuring within larger institutions.

Examples include 'Great American Lesbian Art Show' (1980), the Woman's Building, Los Angeles; 'Extended Sensibilities', The New Museum, New York (1982); 'Queer British Art 1861–1967', Tate Britain, London (2017); and 'Spectrosynthesis-Asian LGBTQ Issues and Art Now', Taipei Museum of Contemporary Art (2017).

KEY DEVELOPMENTS

Tessa Boffin (1960–1993) was influential as an artist and organizer. She co-curated *Ecstatic Antibodies: Resisting the AIDS mythology* (1990–1991) with Sunil Gupta (1953–) and with Jean Fraser (1955–) the touring *Stolen Glances: Lesbians Take Photographs* (1991). Her series *Angelic Rebels* (1989) addressed the lack of lesbian safe-sex campaigns during the AIDS crisis. Her advocacy for creating and exhibiting sex-positive lesbian and BDSM imagery prompted conflict within the lesbian-feminist movement.

Untitled #6, from the series *Angelic Rebels*, Tessa Boffin, 1989/2023, photograph

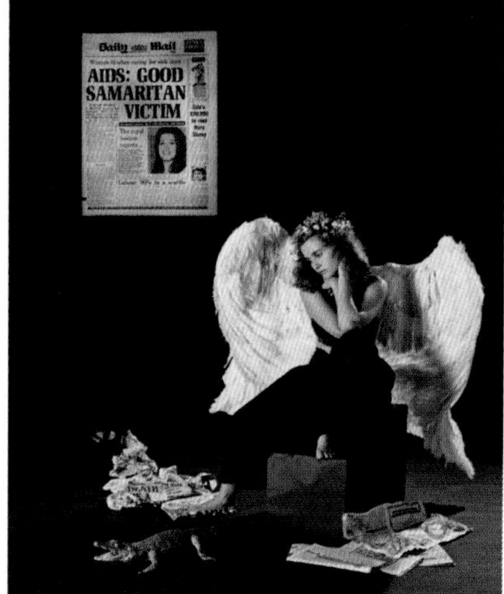

FEMINIST ART **p.30** DIGITAL ART **p.31** *JAMA MASJID* **p.120** *EVERY MOMENT COUNTS (ECSTATIC ANTIBODIES)* **p.122**

Institutional Critique

KEY ARTISTS: GLENN LIGON • MATT SMITH • BIRD LA BIRD • WOLFGANG TILMANS MARTINE GUTIERREZ

Queer artists have taken a critical eye to challenge restrictions and failings of social and legal systems. Many have similarly directed this gaze to the world of galleries, museums and archives – highlighting biases, errors and erasure. Recent decades have seen increasing works that question institutional operations and their role in privileging particular perspectives.

Glenn Ligon's *Notes on the Margin of the Black Book* (1991–93) focuses on another artist's work to raise wider questions of white privilege, stereotyping and obscuring of Black identities. Artists increasingly use interventions within spaces to disrupt and introduce new narratives and intersections, approaching curation as creative activism – often at the invitation of institutions. A key cited influence is Fred Wilson (1954–), whose 'Mining the Museum' (1992) at the Maryland Historical Society juxtaposed collection objects to unsettle predominant white, upper-class narratives and draw attention to histories of Black and Native Americans. Matt Smith (1971–) has developed several works in this vein in museums and historic houses, creating and inserting his own works with a decidedly queer intersectional stance. Straddling comedy and performance art, Bird la Bird (1971–) has developed irreverent yet hard-hitting gallery tours and spoof lectures that take a queer DIY punk approach to interlocking histories of 'British Empire, class exploitation, racism and homophobia'.

KEY DEVELOPMENTS

Notes on the Margin of the Black Book (1991–93) famously interrogates Robert Mapplethorpe's *The Black Book* (1986), a photography collection of homoerotic Black nudes. Combining pages from the book with a range of responses from different cultural voices, Ligon restages the debates sparked by the controversial book in a gallery space, considering construction of racial and sexual identities, and privileged gazes.

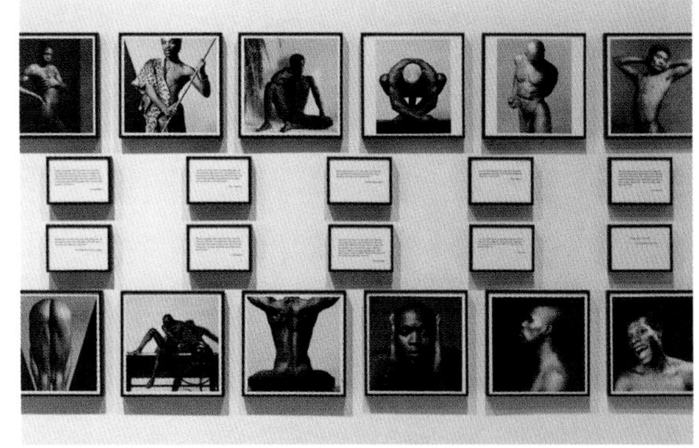

Notes on the Margin of the Black Book (1991–93), Glenn Ligon, detail from installation of offset prints and text, 91 offset prints, framed: 29.2 x 29.2 cm (11½ x 11½ in) each; 78 text pages, framed: 13.3 x 18.4 cm (5¼ x 7¼ in) each, Solomon R. Guggenheim Museum, New York, USA (see Works p.128)

FILM AND VIDEO ART **p.28** PERFORMANCE ART **p.29** CONCEPTUAL ART **p.32** INTERNET ART **p.37**
NOTES ON THE MARGIN OF THE BLACK BOOK **p.128** POWERFUL PROTEST **p.169** TO BE SEEN **p.186**

Life Online

KEY ARTISTS: SHU LEA CHEANG

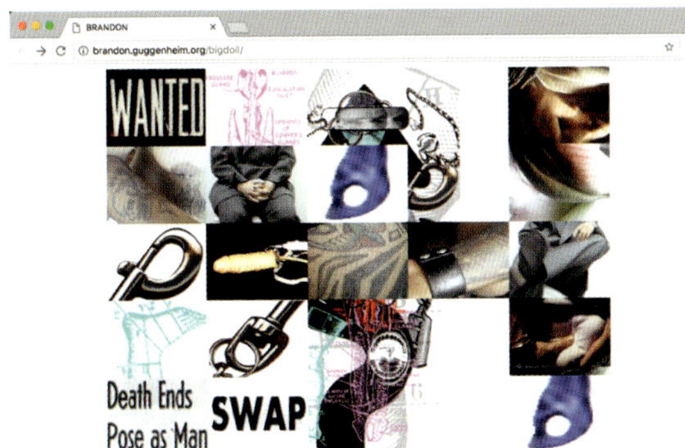

Brandon, part of Big Doll interface, Shu Lea Cheang, 1998–1999, web interface screen grab, Solomon R. Guggenheim Museum, New York, USA

Expansion of the internet in the 1990s increased access to information and ways to connect with others with shared interests. Virtual spaces enabled gender and sexual identities to be explored (via characters and avatars) in ways that could potentially inform real-world experiences. Video and new-media artist Shu Lea Cheang (1954–) noted, 'If virtual worlds are used as laboratories, it's easier to recognize the possibilities for change.'

Cheang's multifaceted project *Brandon* (1998–99) was the first digital web-based work commissioned and acquired by the Guggenheim Museum. Inspired by the life of Brandon Teena (1972–1993), a trans man murdered in Nebraska in 1993, Cheang used the nonlinear nature of the internet to create a 'multi-artist/multi-author/multi-institutional collaboration'.

Users are introduced to historic figures with varied gender identities and ideas of structural control and restriction. Its aesthetics and interfaces (including hyperlinked images and chat rooms) reflect the early 1990s internet as it evolved from being text-based to a more audiovisual experience. The five web interfaces (*bigdoll*, *roadtrip*, *mooplay*, *panopticon* and *theatrum anatomicum*) are intentionally frustrating to navigate through. Live events formed other components.

Futures of gender and sexual identities are recurrent themes in Cheang's work including films *I.K.U.* (2000) and *Fluidø* (2017); location-based mobi-web-serial *Wonders Wanders* (2017) and the panoptic installation *3x3x6* (2019).

KEY DEVELOPMENTS

Brandon's collaborative creation reflects a recurring core trait of early web-based artwork. Its multifaceted nature required the Guggenheim to develop ways of combining virtual and physical spaces. As technology progressed, the artwork became inaccessible as features were no longer supported by browsers and in 2017 it became one of the first large-scale digital art restoration projects.

DIGITAL ART **p.31** INTERNET ART **p.37** ASSEMBLING **p.171** SPACE OF THE BODY **p.172** TO BE SEEN **p.186** TRANSFORMING **p.190**

In Memorial

KEY ARTISTS: PATRICIA CRONIN • GEORGE SEGAL • ELMGREEN & DRAGSET
PAUL HARFLEET'S PANSY PROJECT

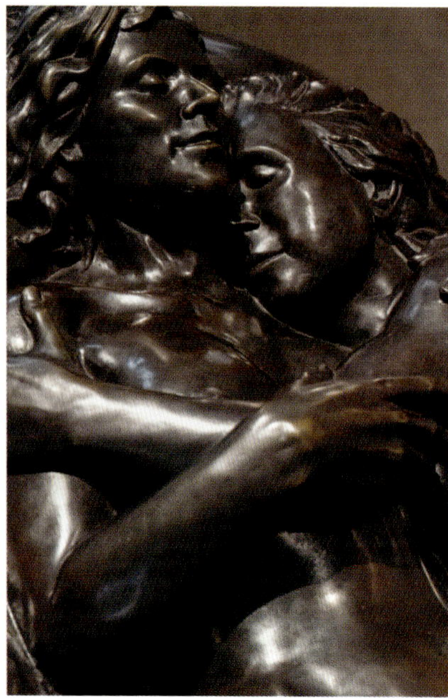

Memorial to a Marriage, Patricia Cronin, 2002, bronze, 68.5 x 107 x 213 cm (27 x 42 x 84 in)

As sites of memory and connection to the past, monuments play an important role in bringing communities together in remembrance and celebration. Public monuments are political signifiers reflecting ideas of civic values and what a society deems worthy of celebration or memorial.

Some areas of the world have indicated advances with increasing numbers of LGBTQ+-focused public sculpture and monuments, of varying intentions. *Gay Liberation Monument* (1980) by George Segal (1924–2000) forms part of the Stonewall National Monument commemorating the 1969 Stonewall uprising and has been considered the first official public art dedicated to gay rights and solidarity for LGBT individuals.

Other notable works predominantly memorialize LGBTQ+ victims of persecution, including Berlin's *Memorial to the Homosexuals Persecuted Under Nazism* (2008) designed by Elmgreen & Dragset; and Amsterdam's *Homomonument* (1987), designed by Karin Daan (1944–) to commemorate all gay men and lesbians persecuted for their sexual orientation.

Memorial To A Marriage (2002) by Patricia Cronin (1963–) was the world's first Marriage Equality monument, created when same-sex marriage was still illegal across the United States. Cronin reflected on differences in visibility and recognition in life and death. Sometimes calling it an 'anti-monument', she commented: 'If all I'm legally afforded is death, I'm going to make the most elegant protest piece I can muster.'

KEY DEVELOPMENTS

Cronin created the large mortuary statue of herself and partner, artist Deborah Kass (1952–), originally in marble for their burial plot, but editions have featured in numerous exhibitions and collections. It addresses lesbian invisibility, gay marriage, love, loss, power and status. Cronin reflected, 'The history of sculpture is dominated by death, burials, and memorials. In fact, the history of sculpture IS the history of death.'

FEMINIST ART **p.30** STREET ART **p.36** PUBLIC PRESENCE **p.197** 

Indigenous Queer Love

KEY ARTISTS: KENT MONKMAN • JEFFREY GIBSON • R E A • KARLA DICKENS • NICHOLAS HLOBO
LUKAS AVENDAÑO

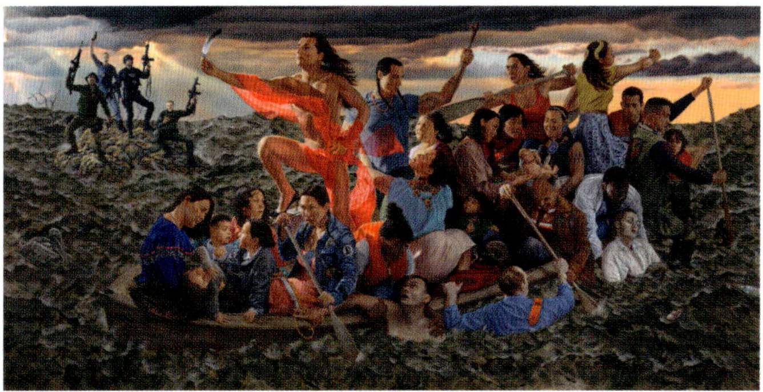

Resurgence of the People, Kent Monkman, 2019, acrylic on canvas, 335.28 x 670.6 cm (132 x 264 in), Collection of the Metropolitan Museum of Art, New York, USA (see Works p.152)

LGBTQ+ identities and terminologies have predominantly formed around European and North American cultural contexts and language, which don't always translate universally. Multifarious forms of gender and sexuality have existed within many cultures and Indigenous communities who were largely excluded by the traditional European construction of 'art history', and whose exploration within art has developed in varying ways.

Indigenous and global-majority artists have increasingly explored these subjects through distinct cultural lenses to navigate intersections, amplify voices and bring a conscious 'decolonizing' approach to portrayals.

FAFSWAG, a Queer Indigenous, interdisciplinary arts collective from Moana, New Zealand, work collaboratively across a multitude of art forms. Harry Fonseca (1946–2006) expressed experiences as a gay Native American living off-reservation, including dressing the trickster coyote of Maidu ancestral stories in fashions of San Francisco's gay scene. Tejal Shah (1979–) considers queer lives within Indian contexts in *Hijra fantasy series* (2006), and worked with hijra communities in Bombay and Bangalore to 'breathe life into' some of their fantasies. Cree artist Kent Monkman adopted European-style painting 'to bring Indigenous experience into this canon of art history'. Monkman's reinterpretations of European and American art history often include his gender-fluid Two-Spirit persona, Miss Chief Eagle Testickle, bringing an empowered Indigenous perspective into periods colonial policies were taking root.

KEY DEVELOPMENTS

Resurgence of the People (2019) is one of two monumental paintings that Kent Monkman (1965–) was commissioned to create for the Metropolitan Museum of Art's Great Hall in 2019. It is a reinterpretation of *Washington Crossing the Delaware* (1851) by Emanuel Leutze (1816–1868). Monkman's Two-Spirit persona Miss Eagle Testickle stands at the helm in place of George Washington.

HARLEM RENAISSANCE **p.22** FEMINIST ART **p.30** AFROFUTURISM **p.34** *POLYCHROME BOWL* **p.48**
RESURGENCE OF THE PEOPLE **p.152**

Index

Illustrations are indicated in *italic*
Main entries are indicated in **bold**

A

Abbas I, Shah 195, *195*
Abstract Art 21
Abstract Expressionism **26**
ACT UP (AIDS Coalition to Unleash Power) 165, 169, 208
Action Painting 26
Adonis *153*
Aestheticism 17, **19**, 168
Afrofuturism **34**
Agostino 12
Aguiler, Laura 177
AIDS 165, **208**, 209, 211
AIDS Quilt 208, *208*
Alien 114
Allan, Maud 50, 188
Alma-Tadema, Lawrence 176
Amerika, Mark, *'Do Ya Wanna Funk'* 34, *34*
Anselmino, Luciano 102
Antinous 195
antiquity, desire for **194**
Apollinaire, Guillaume 23, 68
Apollo Belvedere 194, *194*
Aristotle 56
Armani, Giorgio 200
Art Deco **24**, 58, 72, 80, 81, 84, 92, 156, 199
Art et Industrie 58
Art Nouveau **20**
Artificial Intelligence (A.I.) 37
the artist, presenting **167**
Arts and Crafts 17, 20, 52
Ashbee, Charles Robert, *Twin-handled Cup* 20, *20*
Asia Now (2021) 158
assembling objects and imagery **171**
Athey, Ron 29, 184
Atwood, Clare (Tony) 170
Auden, W. H. 179
Austen, Alice 167
The Darned Club 162, 162
Autograph 122

B

Bacchus 42, **46**, *47*
Bacon, Francis 173
The Wrestlers after Muybridge 114, 115
Baker, Gilbert 205
Baker, Josephine 58
Bakst, Léon, *Afternoon of a Faun 190*, 199, *199*
Baldwin, James 129
The Ballets Russes 24, 64, **199**
Baltrop, Alvin 189
Bannon, Ann 207
Barbier, George 24, 80, 176, 181, 199, 206
La Bague Symbolique **72**, *73*
Barney, Natalie 84, 176, *176*
Baroque **13**, 14, 15
Barthé, James Richmond 22
Feral Benga **90**, *91, 188*
Bas, Edward le 183
Baskt, Léon 199
Basquiat, Jean-Michel 34, 36, 124
Bass, Math 35
Battleship Potemkin 114
Bauhaus 52, 201
Beach, Charles Allwood 200
Beardsley, Aubrey 181
The Peacock Skirt 19, 19, **50**, *51*
Beat Generation 27
Beaton, Cecil 64, 180, 182, 206
Stephen Tennant in Costume as Prince Charming **78**, *79*
Bell, Vanessa 202
Benga, François 90, 188, *188*
Benglis, Lynda 140
Bennett, Gwendolyn 22
Benning, Sadie 28
If Every Girl Had a Diary 164, 164
Bentley, Gladys 22
Bernhardt, Sarah 58, 181
Berry, Mary 15, *15*
the Bible 40
Bilitis 72
Billing, Noel Pemberton 50
Bird la Bird 212
Biren, Joan E. (JEB) 162, 170, 186
Blacklips Performance Cult 29
Blank, Joani 105
the Blatant Image, A Magazine of Feminist Photography 105
BLK Art Group 117
Bloolips 29
Bloomsbury Group 170, **202**
the body, the space of **172**
Boffin, Tessa 181, 208
Angelic Rebels 211, 211
Bologne, Joseph 196, *196*
Bonheur, Rosa 16, 167
Anna Klumpke 167
Botticelli, Sandro 12, 17
Böttner, Lorenza 172
'Lorenza Böttner: Requiem for the Norm' (2019) 210, 210
Boucher, François 195
Jupiter and Callisto 14, 14
Boudry, Pauline 162
Bowery, Leigh 206
Bowie, David 76
Boyland, Jarvis 165
Brackens, Diedrick 165, 175
Bradley, Katherine 52, 53, *53*
Breakfast at Tiffany's 126
Breslau, Louise Catherine, *La vie pensive* **56**, *57*
Breton, André 23, 96
Bright, Deborah, *Dream Girls* **126**, *127*, 187, *187*
Bright Young Things 78, 206
Brodell, Ria 162, 184
Bronson, AA 211
Brooks, Romaine 64, 167, 204, 206
Peter, a Young English Girl 94, 207
Browne, Thom 206
Brugman, Mathilda 52
Buonarroti, Michelangelo, *David* **40**, *41*
Burne-Jones, Edward 19
Burra, Edward 182
Three Sailors at the Bar 179, 179
Burroughs, William S. 190
Burton, Scott, *Two-Part Chair* 35, *35*
Butler, Lady Eleanor 170
Butler, Judith 129
Butler, Octavia 34
Buurman, Gon 186

C

Cadmus, Paul 168, 179
The Fleet's In! 86, **86–7**, *87, 88–9*
Cahun, Claude 167

I.O.U. (Self-Pride) **76**, *77*, *174*, *174*
Caillebotte, Gustave 18
Les raboteurs de parquet 16, *16*
Callisto 14, *14*
camp, rise of **180**
Campbell, Anna 170
Vanishing Point 32, **144**, *145*
Campuzano, Giuseppe 162
Cañedo, Alexander 23
Canova, Antonio 15, 194
Capote, Truman 78, 94, 167
Caravaggio, Michelangelo Merisi da 182, 191, 195
The Martyrdom of Saint Matthew 13, *13*
Carpenter, Edward 20, 22
Cartier 72
Cassatt, Mary 18
Cassils 172, 190
Becoming an Image **140**, *141*
Catholic Church 13, 178
Cave, Nick 34
Soundsuit 171, *171*
Centurión, Feliciano 175
Cézanne, Paul 60, 202
Chaclacayo, Grupo 178
Chaich, John 175
Cheang, Shu Lea 31, 37
Brandon 213, *213*
chevaliers, picturing **196**
Christ 178
Christ, Peaches 184
Christina, Queen of Sweden 195
cinema **187**
Classical Antiquity 194
Classicism 90
The Cockettes 29, 34
Cocteau, Jean 23, 24, 68, 182, 199
coding, queer **168**
collective response **209**
Colour Field Painting 26
commercial allure **200**
Conceptual Art **32**, 33
Constructivism **25**
Cooper, Edith 52, 53
Cooper, Emmanuel 162
Corinne, Tee A. 165, 207
Cunt Coloring Book **104**, *105*, *106–7*
Cottrell, Honey Lee 105
Courbet, Gustave 16, 136, 191
cover art **207**
crafting threads **175**
Craig, Edith (Edy) 170
Crawford, Joan 58
crazinisT artisT 172
crip, queer **210**
Cronin, Patricia, *Memorial to a Marriage* **136**, *137*, 214, *214*
Cruz, Salustiano García 178
Cubism 24, 60, 68
Curtis, Jackie 102
Cushman, Charlotte 197
Cyber Feminism 31
Czech Surrealist Group 23

D

Daan, Karin 214
Dada **21**, 23, 29, 32, 33, 52, 171, 201
Damer, Anne Seymour 15, 194, 197
Mary Berry 15
Damon, Betsy 29, 30
dance **188**
Dancing Faun 42, *42*
Danger, Dayna 174
Darling, Candy 102, 173
Daughters of Bilitis 72
David, Jacques-Louis 15, 138, 194
David, Suzun 50
Davis, Alex Rosborough 25
Dawe, Philip, *The Macaroni. A Real Character at the Late Masquerade* *180*
De Carlo, Tony 178
De Morgan, Evelyn, *Flora* 17, *17*
De Morgan, William 17
Dement, Linda, *Cyberflesh Girlmonster* 31, *31*
Demuth, Charles 64, 179, 182
Deren, Maya 28
Dery, Mark 34
desires, exposing **198**
Diaghilev, Serge 199
Diana 14
Dickens, Karla 164, 215
Die Dame 24, 84
Dietrich, Marlene 175, 180
digital art **31**, 37
DinéYazhi, Demian 48
Dionysus 46
divine connection **178**
Dix, Otto 201
Donatello 12, 40
Douglas, Aaron 203
Study for Aspects of Negro Life: The Negro in an African Setting 22, *22*
Douglas, Lord Alfred 20, 166
Duchamp, Marcel 21, 64, 65, *65*
Duda, Andrzej 205
Dulac, Edmund 52
Duncan, Isadora 180
Dyck, Anthony van 191
Dyer, George 114, 173
Dyke Action Machine! (DAM!) 36

E

Eakins, Thomas 16, 126
ecologies, queer **177**
Elbe, Lile 80, 81
Ellis, Havelock 52
Elmgreen & Dragset 214
Elwes, Jake 31, 37
Zizi in Motion: A Deepfake Drag Utopia (Movement by Wet Mess) 37
Éon de Beaumont, Chevalier d' 196, *196*
erotic exchanges **183**
Erté 24, 72, 80, 206
Loge de Théâtre **58**, *59*, *206*
Etienne 100
exhibitions **211**
Expressionism 24

F

FAFSWAG 215
Falbalas et Fanfreluches 72
family, chosen **170**
Fani-Kayode, Rotimi 208
Every Moment Counts (Ecstatic Antibodies) **122**, *123*
Fassbinder, Rainer Werner 179
Feminist Art **30**, 185
Feminist Photography Ovulars 105
Field, Michael 52, 53
Fierce Pussy 166, 169
film art **28**, **187**
Fini, Leonor 23, 185
Fink, Leonard 189
FIRE!! 92, **203**
Fischer, Hal 168
Fitzgerald, F. Scott 200
Flash, Lola 169, 186
Flaxman, John 15, 194
Folies-Bergère 58, 90
Fonseca, Harry 215
Fraser, Jean 191, 211
Frederick the Great 195
French, Jared 87
French, Margaret 87
French Romanticism 50
Freyburg, Karl von 60

Friedan, Betty 166
Fry, Roger 202
Furies Collective 170
Futurism 24, 29, 84

G

Gainsborough, Thomas 138
Garbo, Greta 78
Garland, Madge 206
Gaultier, Jean Paul 179
Gautier, Théophile 166
Gay Men's Press 207
Gebhardt, Amos 170
General Idea 27, 211
Genet, Jean 129
Querelle de Brest 78, 179
Gentileschi, Artemisia 13
German Expressionism 60
Getsy, David J. 35
Ghirlandaio, Domenico 40
Gibson, Jeffrey 171, 215
Ginsberg, Allen 27, *27*
Giulpin, Edward 181
Gloeden, Baron Wilhelm von 183, 194, 198
Study of two male nudes 198
Gluck 167, 181
Medallion (YouWe) **94**, *95, 207, 207*
Goldendean (Dean Hutton), *Soft Vxnxs 172*
Gonzalez-Torres, Felix 35, 144, 208
"Untitled" (Portrait of Ross in L.A.) 32
Gorer, Geoffrey 188
graffiti 36
Gran Fury 208
Kissing Doesn't Kill: Greed and Indifference Do 169, 169
The Grand Tour 15, 42, 43
Grant, Duncan 183, 202
Greene, Ruby Mae 65
Grey, Lord, 5th Earl of Stamford 42
Groeneboer, Jonah 35
Grosser, Maurice 64
Grosz, George 201
Guerrilla Girls 36, 169, 211
Gupta, Sunil 170, 211
Exiles 186, 186
Jama Masjid **120**, *121*
Gutenberg, Johannes 12
Guyot, Madame 81
Gysin, Brion 190

H

Hadfield, Charles 42
Hadrian, Roman Emperor 195
Hales, Jane 17
Hall, Radclyffe 207
Halls, Roxana 168
Hamburg Art Group 70
Hammer, Barbara 187
Dyketactics 28, 28
Hammond, Harmony 30, 211
Hunkertime 110, **110–11**, *112–13*
Haraway, Donna 31
Harflett, Paul, Pansy Project 214
Hari, Mata 58
Haring, Keith 36, 188, 208
Once Upon A Time 36, **124**, *125*
Harlem Renaissance **22**, 90, 92, 188, 203
Harris, Lyle Ashton 34, 174
Hartley, Marsden 168
Handsome Drinks **60**, *61, 168, 168*
Hasegawa, Sadao 100
Hastings, Rosie 189
Hazekamp, Risk 126, 187
Headlam, James 20
Hemphill, Essex *129*
Henri, Florence 23, 201
Hepburn, Audrey 126
Hera 190
Hernández, Ester, *La Ofrenda* 178, *178*, 207
Hernandez, Joel 174
Hicks, Mick, *Mile Long Rainbow Flag 205*
Highsmith, Patricia 207
Himid, Lubaina, *Freedom and Change 116,* **116–17**, *117, 118–19*
Hippocrene 53, *53*
Hirschfeld, Magnus 80, 201
Hirst, Alex 122
history: documented history **162**
reworking art history **191**
Hlobo, Nicholas 171, 215
Höch, Hannah 21, 31, 52
Da-Dandy 21, **62**, *63*
Hockney, David 78, 164, 166
Hoffman, Malvina 199
Hokusai, Katsushika 183
Lesbian Lovers 183
Holland Day, F. 198
Hollyer, Frederick 46
Horst, Horst P. 198
Hosmer, Harriet Goodhue 136, 197
Hot Peaches 29
House, Rachael, *Welcome Lavender Menace* 166, *166*
Hughes, Langston 22, 203
Hunt, William Holman 17
Huxtable, Juliana 34

I

icons, queer **184**
Il Sodoma (Giovanni Antonio Bazzi) 195
Saint Sebastian 12, 12
Impressionism 16, **18**, 74
Indiana, Robert 27
Indigenous queer love **215**
institutional critique **212**
internet art **37**, **213**
intimacies **165**
Isherwood, Christopher 180
Itō, Miwako 29
Ives, George Cecil 20

J

James, George Wharton 48
Jarman, Derek 13, 162, 170, 184, 205
Blue **134**, *135*
Jaugey-Paget, Laurence 126, 187
Jaye, Lady 172, 190
The Jazz Age 22
Jeckyll, Thomas 19
Johnson, Charles S. 92
Johnson, Marsha P. 102, *103*, 184, *184*
Jonathan 40
Jones, G. B. 100, 183
Jones, Grace 34, 124
Judd, Donald 128
Julien, Isaac 22, 28
Julius II, Pope 12
Jung, Krzysztof 175
Jupiter 14

K

Kahlo, Frida 177
Self Portrait with Cropped Hair **98**, *99*
Kandinsky, Wassily 26
Kass, Deborah 102, 136, 214
Keir, Sophie 30
Kelly, Ellsworth 26, 27
Khakhar, Bhupen, *Ranchodbhai Relaxing in the Winter* **108**, *109*
King, Rodney 171

Klein, Calvin 200
Klein, Yves 134
Klint, Hilma af 26
The Ten Largest, No. 7, Adulthood, Group IV 26
Klumpke, Anna 167, *167*
Kolhamana 48
Kramer, Larry 165, 207
Kruger, Barbara 33, 172
Kruglikova, Elizaveta Sergeevna, *Self-portrait in Studio* 173, *173*
Kupffer, Elisàr von 163, 178
Kushner, Tony 197

L

Laaksonen, Touko, Untitled 100, 101
The Ladder 110
Lane, John 50
Las Yeguas del Apocalipsis 29, 90, 169
Laserstein, Lotte 16, 167, 201
Laurencin, Marie 199
Les Amazones **68**, *69*
Laycock, Ross 128
Leighton, Frederic 17, 19
Lempicka, Tamara de 156, 207
Autoportrait (Tamara in a Green Bugatti) 24, 24, **84**, *85*
Lentz, Robert 48, 184
Leonard, Michael, *Changing Head* 165, *165*, 207
Leonardo da Vinci 12
Lepape, Georges 72
Leroy, Louis 18
Les Ballets Trockadero de Monte Carlo 188
Les Chansons de Bilitis 72
Leutze, Emanuel 152, 215
Levitt, Nina 207
Lewis, Edmonia 197
Leyendecker, J. C. 24
Advertisement for Arrow Shirt Collars 200, 200
Leyland, Frederick 19
Lhote, André 84
Liberty 20
Ligon, Glenn 166
Notes on the Margin of the Black Book 128, **128–9**, *129, 130–1, 212, 212*
Lister, Anne 170
Locke, Alain Leroy 22, 90
Lorenz, Renate 162
Louis XIV *81*
Louys, Pierre 72
Lynes, George Platt 87, 167, 198

M

Maar, Dora 96
Machine Age 84
McNamara, James 205
McRuer, Robert 210
Madonna 124
Makos, Chris 102
Mammen, Jeanne 189
She Represents 189, 201, 201
Mamyshev-Monroe, Vladislav 167
Mandela, Nelson 142
Manet, Édouard 16
Le Déjeuner sur l'herbe 96, 147, 191
Olympia 146, 147
Mao, Chairman 102
Mapplethorpe, Robert 102
'The Black Book' 128, 129, *129, 212, 212*
Marinoff, Fania *65*
Martin, Agnes 26
Martin, Marc 189
Marty, André 72
masks **174**
Matisse, Henri 70, 202
Maupin, Armistead 184
Maya 24
Medievalism 52
memorials **214**
Meurent, Victorine 147
Meyer, Baron Adolph de 64
Micas, Nathalie 167
Michelangelo Buonarroti 12, 182, 194
Milk, Harvey 184
Millais, John Everett 17
Millett, Kate 185
Love Seat 30, 30, 185
Mingming 177
Minimalism 32, 35
Mishima, Go (Tsuyoshi Yoshida) 100, 183
Mishima, Yukio 184
Mizer, Bob 100, 198
Modernism 33, 60, 204
Moleski, Amaryllis DeJesus 34, 163
Molière 180
Monáe, Janelle 34
Mondrian, Piet 26
Monea, Alexander 37
Monfared, Ali Fazeli 158
Monkman, Kent, *Resurgence of the People 152,* **152–3**, *153, 154–5,* 215, *215*
Monnier, Adrienne 68
Monroe, Marilyn 184
Montenegro, Roberto 199
Montesquiou, Robert de 20
Moore, Marcel 76
More, Sir Thomas 163
Moreau, Suzanne 68
Morimura, Yasumasa 90
Morisot, Berthe 18
Morris, William 17, 20
Mosnier, Jean Laurent 196
Moss, Marlow 25
Spatial Construction in Steel 25
Motta, Carlos 162
Moulee 205
Mucha, Alphonse 181
Muholi, Zanele 165, 167, 186
Phila I, Parktown **150**, *151*
Muñoz, Esteban 144, 163
Muses 53
Mussolini, Benito 84
Muybridge, Eadweard 114

N

Naiad Press 207
Naturalism 18
Nazimova, Alla 175
Neoclassicism **15**, 136, 138, 194
Neo-Cubism 24
Newsome, Rashaad 31, 37, 171
Nicholls, Tom 100
Nijinsky, Vaslav 190, 199
Nochlin, Linda 30, 64
Nomi, Klaus 21, 33
"Untitled" Klaus Nomi 33
Nugent, Richard Bruce 22, 203
Dancing Figures **92**, *93*

O

Obama, Barack 138
Obermer, Nesta 94
Oiticica, Hélio 189
The Omega Workshops 202
Onassis, Jackie 102
online life **213**
Opie, Catherine 170, 184, 186
Oppenheim, Méret 206
Object (Le Déjeuner en Fourrure) 23, 23, **96**, *97*
Order of Chaeronea 20
Orpheus 198
Osborne, John 181

Ottinger, Ulrike, *Allen Ginsberg* 27, *27*
Ouroussoff, Prince Nicolas 58
Ovid 14, 190
Ovulars 189

P

Paik, Nam June 28
PaJaMa collective 87
Pan 42
Paris **204**
Parker, Dorothy 202
Parker, Mary, after, *Ladies of Llangollen 170*
Parsons, Betty 26
Patch, Thomas, *A Punch Party 42*, **42–3**, *43*, *44–5*
Pater, Walter 19, 194
Patoun, William 43
Pavlova, Anna 58
Pegasus 53, *53*
Perel 210
Performance Art 21, **29**
Perry, Cory 171
personal realization **164**
PESTS 169
Philpot, Glyn 199
Glen Byam Shaw as 'Laertes' 181, 181
Physique Pictorial 100, 183, 198
Picasso, Pablo 25, 70, 96, 117, 168, 202
Pierre et Gilles 179, 180, 184, 200
Pissarro, Camille 18
places to be **189**
Plato 176
Plüschow, Guglielmo 198
Pointon, Marcia 74
Poiret, Paul 199
Pompadour, Madame de 14
Ponsonby, Sarah 170
Pop Art 21, **27**, 33
P-Orridge, Genesis Breyer 172, 190
Posener, Jill 36
Postminimalism **35**
Postmodernism 21, **33**
Pougy, Liane de 176
Poulenc, Francis 68
Pre-Raphaelites **17**, 19, 46
Preciado, Paul B. 210
Prinner, Anton 25
protest, powerful **169**
public presence **197**

Q

Qasim, Muhammad, Shah Abbas I with one of his pages 195, *195*
Qollar-Aghasi, Hossein 158
Quaintance, George 100, 179
Quasar, Daniel 205
queer eye **182**
Quinlan, Hannah 189
Quirk, Cai 178
Qusuquzah *146*, **146–7**, *147*, *148–9*

R

r e a 31, 172, 215
Radziszewski, Karol 162
Raffalovich, André 50
rainbow colours **205**
Rainey, Ma 22
Raphael 12, 17
Raqeeb 165
Rauschenberg, Robert 26, 27
Ray, Man 21, 72, 96
realization, personal **164**
Realism **16**, 18
Red Rose Collective 170
Rée, Anita, *Semi-Nude in Front of Prickly Pear Cactus* **70**, *71*
Renaissance **12**, 17, 40, 138
Reni, Guido 184
The Ribbon Project 209, *209*
Ricketts, Charles de Sousy, *Pegasus Drinking from the Fountain of Hippocrene* **52–3**, *53*, *54–5*
Riggs, Marlon 128
riot grrrl 164
Rivera, Diego 90, 177
Roberts, LJ, *VanDykesTrans* 175, *175*
Robineau, Alexandre-Auguste, *The Fencing-Match between the Chevalier de Saint-George and the Chevalier d'Eon* 196, *196*
Rococo **14**, 15, 138
Rodchenko, Alexander 25
Rodman, Hugh 86
Rootworks 189
Rosoman, Leonard 181
Rossetti, Dante Gabriel 17, 46
Rubens, Peter Paul 14
Rubiner, Ludwig 199
Ruga, Athi-Patra 191
Future White Women of Azania 142, 163, *163*
Night of the Long Knives I **142**, *143*

S

Sacher-Masoch, Leopold von 96
Sahib, Prem 189
St John, Christopher (Christabel Marshall) 170
Saint Laurent, Yves 206
Salome 50
Samat, Anne 171
Sappho 72, 76, 170, **176**, *176*
Sargent, John Singer 78, 198
Satie, Erik 68
Scharf, Kenny 33
Schiaparelli, Elsa 96, 199
Schneemann, Carolee 140
Schneider-Kainer, Lene 80
Scott of London 100
the sea, call of the **179**
Sebastian, Saint 12, *12*, 178, 184, 198
Segal, George 214
Segerblom, Lynn 205
Seiko, Okuhara 167
Sekula, Sonja 26
Sélavy, Rrose *65*
Shah, Tejal 215
Shannon, Charles Haslewood 52, 53
Shaw, Glen Byam 181, *181*
Sherman, Cindy 33, 76
Shitou 177
Shojaian, Alireza 169
Sous le ciel de Shiraz (PaykanArtCar) **158**, *159*
Sickert, Walter 181
Silenus 42
The Sisters of Perpetual Indulgence 29, *29*, 184
Smith, Jack 28
Smith, Matt 212
Smithers, Leonard 50
Sodoma, Uýra 177
Mud 177
Solidor, Suzy 84
Solomon, Simeon 17, 176
Bacchus **46**, *47*
Somov, Konstantin 19, 174
Sontag, Susan 180
Souhami, Diana 94
Sperber, Klaus 33
Stebbins, Emma, *Angel of the Waters* 197, *197*
Steers, Hugh 165
Stein, Gertrude 60, 65, 68, 102, 129, 168, 204

Stella, Frank 128
Stettheimer, Florine: *Asbury Park South* **64**, *64*, *65*, *66–7*
La Fete a Duchamp 65
Stieglitz, Alfred 60
straight expectations **185**
Street Art **36**
Streisand, Barbra 102
studios **173**
style, fashioning **206**
Sulter, Maud 30, 116
Sun-Ra 34
Surrealism **23**, 30, 96, 174
Swan, Paul 180
Swinburne, Algernon Charles 46
Sylvester, *'Do Ya Wanna Funk'* 34, *34*
Symonds, John Addington 12, 40, 46

T

Takano, Masahiro 68
Tan, Truong 185
Tāri 29
Tate, Gertrude 162
Tatlin, Vladimir 25
Tchelitchew, Pavel 199
Teena, Brandon 213
Tegner, Elna 81
Tennant, Stephen 78, *79*
Testickle, Miss Chief Eagle 152, *152*, *153*, *154–5*, 215
textual power **166**
Thalia 29
Thatcher, Margaret 120
theatrical types **181**
Thomas, Mickalene 138, 186, 191
Qusuquzah Lounging with Pink + Black Flower 146, **146–7**, *147*, *148–9*
Thomson, Virgil 64, 65
Tiresias 190
Titian 43, 153
Todd, Dorothy 206
Toklas, Alice B. 204
Tom of Finland 179, 183, 198
Untitled **100**, *101*
Tomlin, Stephen, bust of Virginia Woolf 202, *202*
Toor, Salman 191
The Latecomer **156**, *157*
Toulouse-Lautrec, Henri de 20, 156
In bed: The Kiss 204, *204*
Toyen 23
transformation **190**
Troubridge, Una 199, 206
Trujillo, Carla 207
Tseng Kwong Chi 124
Tugbiyele, Adejoke 205
Tuke, Henry Scott 18, 198
The Critics 18, **74**, *75*
Two-Spirit movement 48
Tzara, Tristan 21

U

Underhill, Linn 167
Unfolding Ceremony '96 Quilt Display 208
utopia, glimpses of **163**
Uýra, Emerson 177

V

Van Vechten, Carl 65, *65*, 90
Vasari, Giorgio 12
Vendryes, Margaret Rose 174
Venus *116*, 117, *153*
Venus de Milo 210
video art 28
Virgin Mary 138, 178, 178, 184
visibility 186
Visual AIDS Artists' Caucus 208, 209, *209*
Vogue 72, 198, 199, 206
Vogueing 188
Vorticism 24

W

Walker, Kara 92
Walpole, Horace 15
Warhol, Andy 27, 28, 124, 144, 173, 180
Ladies and Gentlemen (Marsha P. Johnson) **102**, *103*, *184*, *184*
Washington, George 152
Watteau, Jean-Antoine 14
Wearing, Gillian 76
Wegener, Gerda 20, 183, 201
A Summer Day 80, **80–1**, *81*, *82–3*
Weimar Berlin 189, **201**
Werefkin, Marianne 167
We'wha, polychrome bowl **48**, *49*
Whistler, James McNeill 19, 52
Whitman, Walt 60
Wilde, Oscar 19, 20, 46, 50, 52, 166, 184, 198
Wilding, Faith 37
Wiley, Kehinde 184, 191
Passing / Posing from Coronation of the Virgin **138**, *139*
Wilgefortis, Saint 178
Wilson, Fred 212
Wilson, Millie 35
Winckelmann, Johann Joachim 15, 194, 195
Wirth, Tom 203
Wojnarowicz, David 28, 36, 169, 171, 178, 189
Wood, Christopher, *'Dogs at Play'* 182, *182*
Woodlawn, Holly 102, 173
Woolf, Virginia 202, *202*, 206
The Wrestlers 43
Wyndham, Pamela 78

X

Xiyadie 164, 185
Gate **132**, *133*

Z

Zenil, Nahum B. 90, 178
Zillhardt, Madeleine 56, *57*
Zoffany, Johan 43
Zuni culture 48

Museums

Works from the following museums and institutions are featured in this book.

FRANCE

Bibliothèque de l'Arsenal, Paris
Louvre Museum, Paris
Musée d'Orsay, Paris

GERMANY

Hamburger Kunsthalle, Hamburg
Kunsthalle zu Kiel, Kiel

ITALY

Galleria dell'Accademia di Firenze, Florence
San Luigi dei Francesi, Rome
Palazzo Pitti, Florence

RUSSIA

Pushkin Museum, Moscow
The State Tretyakov Gallery, Moscow

SOUTH AFRICA

Zeitz Museum of Contemporary Art Africa, Cape Town

SWEDEN

Hilma af Klint Foundation, Stockholm

SWITZERLAND

Musée cantonal des Beaux-Arts, Lausanne

UK

De Morgan Collection, Barnsley
The Fitzwilliam Museum, Cambridge
Leamington Spa Art Gallery & Museum, Leamington Spa
Leeds Art Gallery, Leeds
National Portrait Gallery, London
Tate, London

USA

Alice Austen House, New York
Art Institute of Chicago, Chicago
Brooklyn Museum, New York
Elizabeth A. Sackler Center for Feminist Art, Brooklyn Museum, New York
Leslie-Lohman Museum of Art, New York
Los Angeles County Museum of Art, Los Angeles
Metropolitan Museum of Art, New York
Museum of Fine Arts, Houston, Texas
Museum of Modern Art, New York
Navy Art Collection, Washington D.C.
The Lesbian, Gay, Bisexual & Transgender Community Center, New York
San Francisco Museum of Modern Art, San Francisco
Smithsonian American Art Museum, Washington D.C.
Solomon R. Guggenheim Museum, New York

VATICAN CITY

Vatican Museums and Galleries (Musei e Gallerie Pontificie), The Vatican

Picture Credits

Akg Images: p162, pp160, 189, 201 © Jeanne Mammen/ADAGP/© DACS 2024; **Alamy Stock Photo:** p12 Chronicle/ Alamy Stock Photo, p13 ICP/Alamy Stock Photo, p14 Artefact/Alamy Stock Photo, p15 Tolo Balaguer/Alamy Stock Photo p17 History and Art Collection/Alamy Stock Photo, pp19, 51 Lordprice Collection/Alamy Stock Photo, p16 IanDagnall Computing/Alamy Stock Photo, pp24, 85 Artepics/Alamy Stock Photo/© Tamara de Lempicka Estate, LCC/DACS 2024, p29 Associated Press/Alamy Stock Photo, p40 Granger, NYC./Alamy Stock Photo, pp42, 43, 44, 45, Thomas Patch, The Picture Art Collection/Alamy Stock Photo, p47 Painters/Alamy Stock Photo, pp61, 168 ARTGEN / Alamy Stock Photo,p57 ARTGEN/Alamy Stock Photo, pp80, 81, 82, 83 VTR / Alamy Stock Photo, pp93, 203, Bruce Nugent, BBM/Alamy Stock Photo/Gift of Dr. Thomas H. Wirth, gift of Frederick J. Adler, by exchange, bequest of Richard J. Kempe, by exchange, and gift of Abraham Walkowitz, by exchange, p99 Artepics/Alamy Stock Photo/© Banco de México Diego Rivera Frida Kahlo Museums Trust, Mexico, D.F./DACS 2024, p116 Andrew Lalchan/Alamy Stock Photo/© Lubaina Himid Courtesy the artist and Hollybush Gardens, London, pp137, 192, 214 Gina Rodgers/ Alamy Stock Photo/© ARS, NY and DACS, London 2024, p167 Granger, NYC./Alamy Stock Photo, p170 Science History Images/Alamy Stock Photo, p176 ARCHIVIO GBB/Alamy Stock Photo, pp190, 199 BG/OLOU/Alamy Stock Photo, p194 B.O'Kane / Alamy Stock Photo, p195 Historic Collection/Alamy Stock Photo, p196 Zoom Historical/ Alamy Stock Photo, p197 Woodward/Woody/Alamy Stock Photo, p204 classicpaintings/Alamy Stock Photo, p209 Wavebreakmedia Ltd PH15/Alamy Stock Photo; **Art Institute of Chicago:** p49 We'wha, Gift of Charles and Marjorie Benton; **Autograph:** p123 © Rotimi Fani-Kayode, Courtesy of Autograph, London; **Charles Robert Ashbee:** p20 Clare Borg/Courtesy of Mallams, Oxford; **Sadie Benning:** p164 Image copyright of the artist, courtesy of Video Data Bank, School of the Art Institute of Chicago; **Blind Spot Gallery:** p133 Xiyadie, Image courtesy of artist and Blindspot Gallery. Photographer: South Ho; **Tessa Boffin:** p221 © Tessa Boffin. Courtesy of the Estate of Tessa Boffin and the Gupta+Singh Archive; **Bridgeman Images:** pp18, 75 Leamington Spa Art Gallery & Museum/Bridgeman Images, p22, Photo © Art Institute of Chicago/Solomon Byron Smith and Margaret Fisher funds/Bridgeman Images/© Heirs of Aaron Douglas/VAGA at ARS, NY and DACS, London 2024, pp21, 63, Hannah Hoch, Bridgeman Images/© DACS 2024, p24, Marlow Moss, Photo, © Peter Nahum at The Leicester Galleries, London/Bridgeman Images, p26 Photo © Fine Art Images/Bridgeman Images, pp53, 54, 55 Charles Ricketts, Photo © Fitzwilliam Museum/Bridgeman Images, p59 Erte Erte Romain de Tirtoff, Bridgeman Images/© ARS, NY and DACS, London 2024, p69 Marie Laurencin, Bridgeman Images/© Fondation Foujita/ADAGP, Paris and DACS, London 2024, p95 Christie's Images/Bridgeman Images/© The Gluck Estate. All rights reserved, DACS 2024, p73 The Stapleton Collection/Bridgeman Images, p91, 188, James Richmond Barthé, Photo: Museum of Fine Arts, Houston/Museum purchase funded by the African American Art Advisory Association/Bridgeman Images/Stella Jones Gallery, p101 San Francisco Museum of Modern Art/Bridgeman Images/© Tom of Finland Foundation/Artists Rights Society (ARS), New York/DACS, London 2024, p103, 184 © 2024 The Andy Warhol Foundation for the Visual Arts, Inc./ Licensed by DACS, London/Christie's Images/Bridgeman Images, p115 Bridgeman Images/© The Estate of Francis Bacon. All rights reserved. DACS 2024, p109 Christie's Images/Bridgeman Images/Dhaval Khakhar/Vivek Khakhar, p139 Christie's Images/Bridgeman Images/Kehinde Wiley, From the Coronation of the Virgin, 2005. © Kehinde Wiley, p181 Glyn Philpot, Christie's Images/Bridgeman Images, p171 Photo: San Francisco Museum of Modern Art/ Bridgeman Images/© Nick Cave. Photo by James Prinz Photography. Courtesy of the artist and Jack Shainman Gallery, New York, p182 Christie's Images/Bridgeman Images, p183 Bridgeman Images, p198 Prismatic Pictures/ Bridgeman Images, p200 Granger/Bridgeman Images; **Deborah Bright:** p127, 187 Photograph courtesy of the artist; **Anna Campbell:** pp 32, 145 Courtesy of Anna Campbell; **Cassils:** p141 Courtesy of the artist; **Shu Lea Cheang:** p213 Courtesy of the artist, Shu Lea Cheang/Commissioned by the Solomon R. Guggenheim Museum, and produced in association with the Waag Society for Old and New Media, The Institute on the Arts and Civic Dialogue at Harvard University, and The Banff Centre, with additional funding from The Bohen Foundation, The Rockefeller Foundation, the New York Foundation for the Arts, and the Mondriaan Foundation. © Solomon R. Guggenheim Museum; **Condé Nast:** p79 Cecil Beaton Archive, ©Condé Nast; **DACS:** pp121, 186 © Sunil Gupta. All rights reserved, DACS 2024; **Linda Dement:** p31 Courtesy of Linda Dement; **Edward Burra:** p179, Copyright: Estate of the Artist, c/o Lefevre Fine Art Ltd, London/Lefevre Fine Art Ltd., London/Bridgeman Images; **Jake Elwes:** p37 c:o the artist Jake Elwes; **Flickr creative commons:** p180 2.0 peacay https://www.flickr.com/photos/ bibliodyssey/3939818894/in/photolist-719vaG-719ATY-719PWT; **Getty Images:** ppp110, 111, 112, 111 Getty Images/Wally Skalij/Contributor/© Harmony Hammond/VAGA at ARS, NY and DACS, London 2024/GIFT OF ELIZABETH A. SACKLER IN HONOR OF CATHERINE MORRIS, SENIOR SACKLER CURATOR OF THE

ELIZABETH A. SACKLER CENTER FOR FEMINIST ART; **Goldendean:** p172 Dillon Marsh/ Zeitz MOCCA/ courtesy of the artist; **Hales Gallery:** p175 L J Roberts, Courtesy the artist and Hales, London and New York/Photo by Madhouse Creative; **Estate of Barbara Hammer:** p28 Courtesy of the Estate of Barbara Hammer, New York; Electronic Arts Intermix (EAI), New York; KOW, Berlin, Germany; and Company Gallery, New York; **Ester Hernandez:** p178 Courtesy of the artist, © 1988 Ester Hernandez; **Mick Hicks:** p205 Photo by Mick Hicks; **Rachael House:** p166 the work is copyright Rachael House, made in 2022. The photograph is also copyright Rachael House; **Gavin Kingcome:** p202 Stephen Tomlin bust of Virginia Woolf; **Last Gasp Publishing:** pp 105, 106, 107 Images from *Cunt Coloring Book* copyright Tee Corinne, reprinted by permission of the publisher, Last Gasp; **Michael Leonard:** p165 Courtesy of the estate of Michael Leonard; **Glenn Ligon:** pp128, 129, 130, 131, 212 © Glenn Ligon; Courtesy of the artist, Hauser & Wirth and Thomas Dane Gallery; **Luhring Augustine:** p157 © Salman Toor; Courtesy of the artist and Luhring Augustine, New York. Photo: Farzad Owrang; **Kate Millett:** pp 10, 30, 185 Image courtesy of The Kate Millett Trust and Salon 94 Design. © The Kate Millett Trust. Photo: Dan Bradica; **Kent Monkman:** pp152, 153, 154, 155, 215 Courtesy of the artist; **N.A. Nekrasov Library:** p173, Elizaveta Sergeyevna Kruglikova, Image courtesy of N.A. Nekrasov Library; **National AIDS Memorial:** p208 NAMES Project, Courtesy of National AIDS Memorial; **Navy Art Collection:** pp 86-89 Courtesy of Navy Art Collection, Naval History and Heritage Command "Use of released U.S. Navy imagery does not constitute product or organizational endorsement of any kind by the U.S. Navy"; **Ulrike Ottinger:** p27 © Ulrike Ottinger; **Scala Archives:** p23, 97, Méret Oppenheim, Digital image, The Museum of Modern Art, New York/Scala, Florence/© DACS 2024, p35, Scott Burton, Digital image Whitney Museum of American Art / Licensed by Scala/© ARS, NY and DACS, London 2024, Claude Cahun pp77, 174 Digital Image Museum Associates/LACMA/Art Resource NY/Scala, Florence; **Scharf Studio:** p33 Kenny Scharf, Courtesy of Scharf Studio; **Alireza Shojaian:** p159 Alireza Shojaian - PaykanArtCar; **Uýra Sodoma:** p177 Courtesy of the artist, Atmos Uýra Sodoma; **Tate Images:** p135, Derek Jarman Courtesy Basilisk Communications/ Photo: Tate; **The NYC LGBT Community Center:** pp36, 124 Keith Haring artwork © Keith Haring Foundation/Liz Lignon, Courtesy of The NYC LGBT Community Center; **Mickalene Thomas:** pp146, 147, 148, 149, 191 © Mickalene Thomas/© ARS, NY and DACS, London 2024; **Victoria and Albert Museum:** p169 Gran Fury, © [As specified by the work's rightsholders] / Victoria and Albert Museum, London; **WHAT IF THE WORLD:** p143, 163 Image courtesy of Athi-Patra Ruga and WHATIFTHEWORLD; **Württembergischer Kunstverein Stuttgart:** p210 Lorenza Böttner, Courtesy of Württembergischer Kunstverein Stuttgart; **Yancey Richardson Gallery:** pp38, 151 © Zanele Muholi. Courtesy of the artist and Yancey Richardson, New York; **YouTube:** p34 Mark Amerika/YOUTUBE.

Picture Research by Penny Bowden: Proudfoot Pictures.